NEGIMA!

4

Ken Akamatsu

TRANSLATED BY

Douglas Varenas

ADAPTED BY

Peter David and Kathleen O'Shea David

LETTERED BY

Steve Palmer

LONDON

Published in the United Kingdom by Tanoshimi in 2006

1 3 5 7 9 10 8 6 4 2

First published in serial form by Shonen Magazine Comics and subsequently published in book form by
Kodansha Ltd, Tokyo in 2004. Copyright © 2004 by Ken Akamatsu.

Published by arrangement with Kodansha Ltd., Tokyo and with Del Rey,
an imprint of Random House Inc., New York

Tanoshimi
The Random House Group Limited
20 Vauxhall Bridge Road, London, SW1V 2SA

Random House Australia (Pty) Limited
20 Alfred Street, Milsons Point, Sydney
New South Wales 2061, Australia

Random House New Zealand Limited
18 Poland Road, Glenfield
Auckland 10, New Zealand

Random House (Pty) Limited
Isle of Houghton, Corner of Boundary Road & Carse O'Gowrie
Houghton 2198, South Africa

Random House Publishers India Private Limited
301 World Trade Tower, Hotel Intercontinental Grand Complex,
Barakharnba Lane, New Delhi 110 001, India

Random House Group Limited Reg. No. 954009

www.tanoshimi.tv
www.randomhouse.co.uk

A CIP catalogue record for this book is available from the British Library

Papers used by Random House
are natural, recyclable products made from wood grown in sustainable forests.
The manufacturing processes conform to the environmental regulations of the country of origin

ISBN 9780099505006 (from Jan 2007)
ISBN 0 09 950504 2

Printed and bound in Germany by GGP Media GmbH, Pößneck

Translator — Douglas Varenas
Adapters — Peter David and Kathleen O'Shea David
Lettering — Steve Palmer
Cover Design — David Stevenson

A Word from the Author

Finally, here's Volume 4 of *Negima!* Between trying to guide his tumultuous group of students through a wild field trip in Kyoto and Nara and dealing with a new menace, Negi-sensei has his hands full! (The field trip will continue into the next book.)

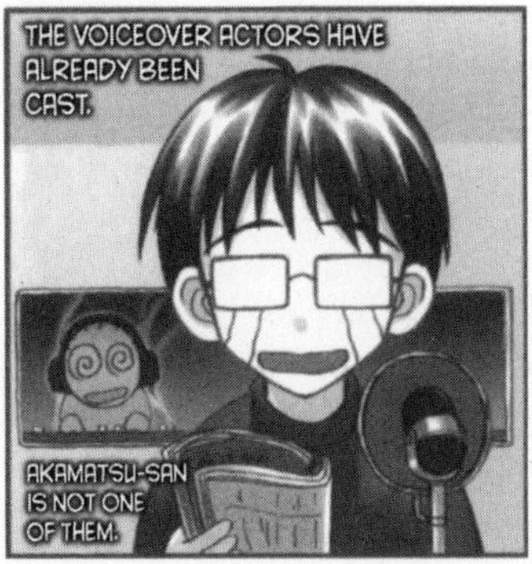
THE VOICEOVER ACTORS HAVE ALREADY BEEN CAST.
AKAMATSU-SAN IS NOT ONE OF THEM.

By the way, the "Character CD" of the digitized classmates of *Negima!* is now on sale. We've got thirty-one talented voice actors helping create a maxi CD single packed with imaging, mini-dramas, and more of each character. As a bonus, we included a Pactio Card (Probationary Contract). Don't miss it! For more information, check out my website.

Ken Akamatsu
http://www.ailove.net

Honorifics

Throughout the Tanoshimi Manga books, you will find Japanese honorifics left intact in the translations. For those not familiar with how the Japanese use honorifics, and more important, how they differ from English honorifics, we present this brief overview.

Politeness has always been a critical facet of Japanese culture. Ever since the feudal era, when Japan was a highly stratified society, use of honorifics — which can be defined as polite speech that indicates relationship or status — has played an essential role in the Japanese language. When addressing someone in Japanese, an honorific usually takes the form of a suffix attached to one's name (example: "Asuna-san"), or as a title at the end of one's name or in place of the name itself (example: "Negi-sensei," or simply "Sensei!").

Honorifics can be expressions of respect or endearment. In the context of manga and anime, honorifics give insight into the nature of the relationship between characters. Many translations into English leave out these important honorifics, and therefore distort the "feel" of the original Japanese. Because Japanese honorifics contain nuances that English honorifics lack, it is our policy at Tanoshimi not to translate them. Here, instead, is a guide to some of the honorifics you may encounter in Tanoshimi Manga.

-*san:* This is the most common honorific, and is equivalent to Mr., Miss, Ms., Mrs., etc. It is the all-purpose honorific and can be used in any situation where politeness is required.

-*sama:* This is one level higher than -*san.* It is used to confer great respect.

-*dono:* This comes from the word *tono,* which means *lord.* It is an even higher level than -*sama,* and confers utmost respect.

-kun: This suffix is used at the end of boys' names to express familiarity or endearment. It is also sometimes used by men among friends, or when addressing someone younger or of a lower station.

-chan: This is used to express endearment, mostly toward girls. It is also used for little boys, pets, and even among lovers. It gives a sense of childish cuteness.

Bozu: This is an informal way to refer to a boy, similar to the English term "kid".

Sempai: This title suggests that the addressee is one's "senior" in a group or organization. It is most often used in a school setting, where underclassmen refer to their upperclassmen as *sempai*. It can also be used in the workplace, such as when a newer employee addresses an employee who has seniority in the company.

Kohai: This is the opposite of *sempai*, and is used toward underclassmen in school or newcomers in the workplace. It connotes that the addressee is of lower station.

Sensei: Literally meaning "one who has come before," this title is used for teachers, doctors, or masters of any profession or art.

-[blank]: Usually forgotten in these lists, but perhaps the most significant difference between Japanese and English. The lack of honorific means that the speaker has permission to address the person in a very intimate way. Usually, only family, spouses, or very close friends have this kind of permission. Known as *yobisute*, it can be gratifying when someone who has earned the intimacy starts to call one by one's name without an honorific. But when that intimacy hasn't been earned, it can also be very insulting.

魔法先生ネギま!

4

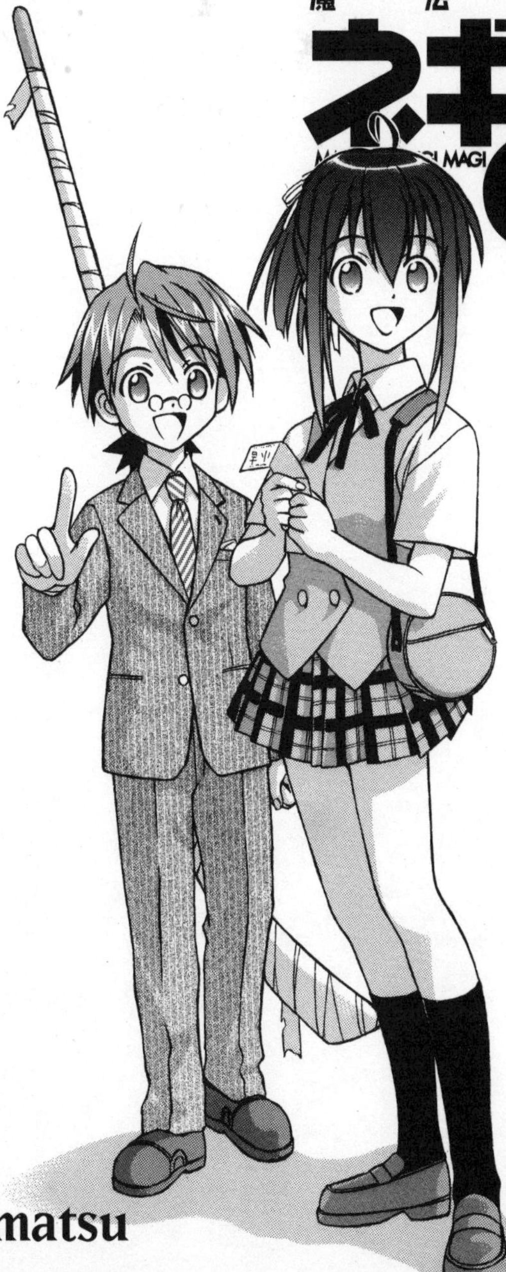

赤松 健

Ken Akamatsu

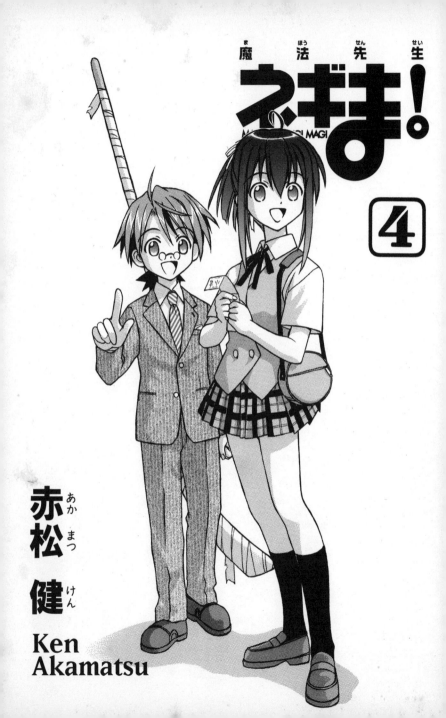

CONTENTS

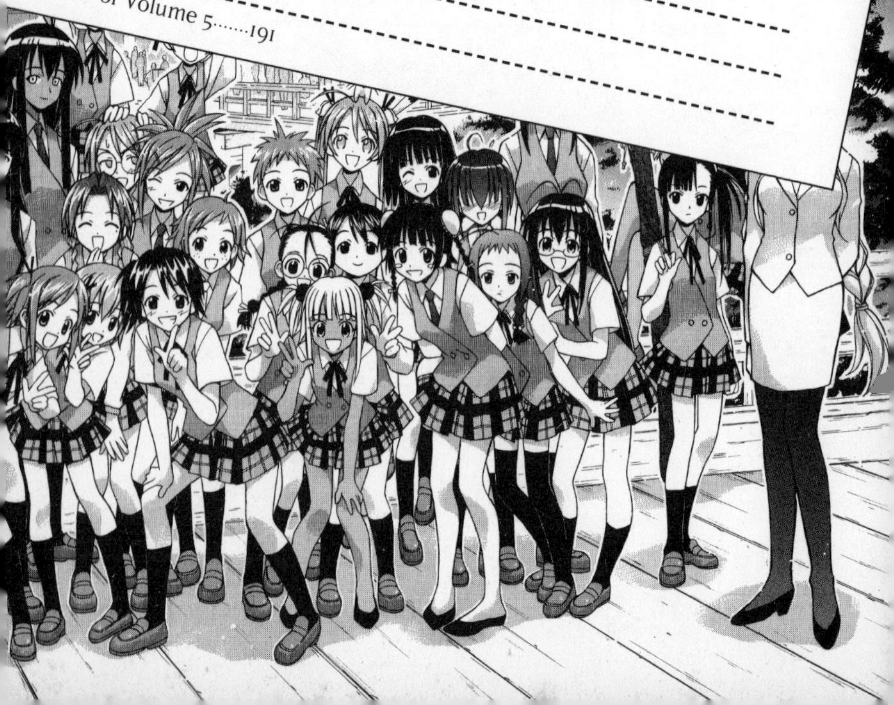

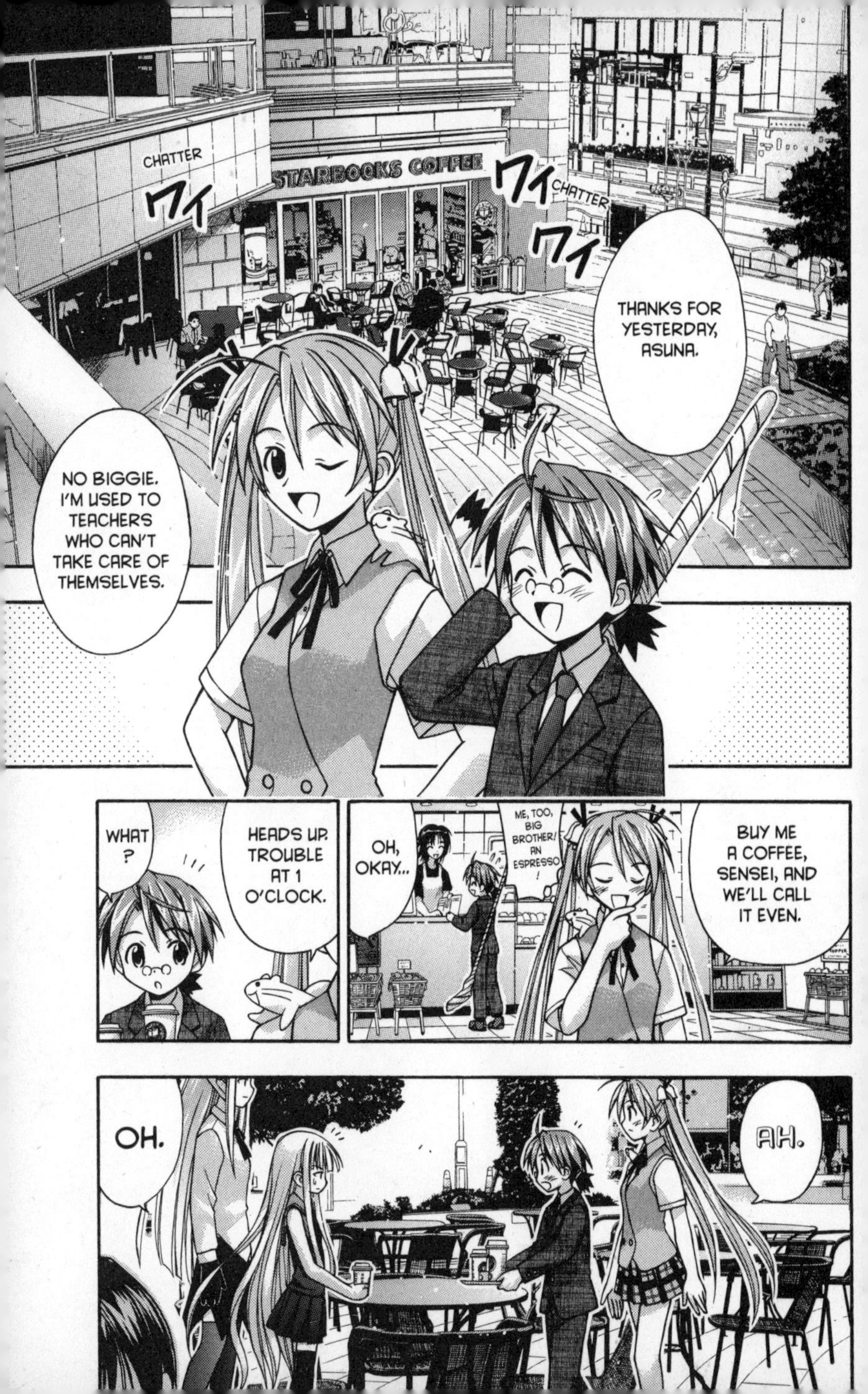
STARBOOKS COFFEE
ワイ
CHATTER
ワイ
CHATTER
ワイ
THANKS FOR YESTERDAY, ASUNA.
NO BIGGIE. I'M USED TO TEACHERS WHO CAN'T TAKE CARE OF THEMSELVES.
BUY ME A COFFEE, SENSEI, AND WE'LL CALL IT EVEN.
ME, TOO, BIG BROTHER! AN ESPRESSO!
OH, OKAY...
HEADS UP. TROUBLE AT 1 O'CLOCK.
WHAT?
AH.
OH.

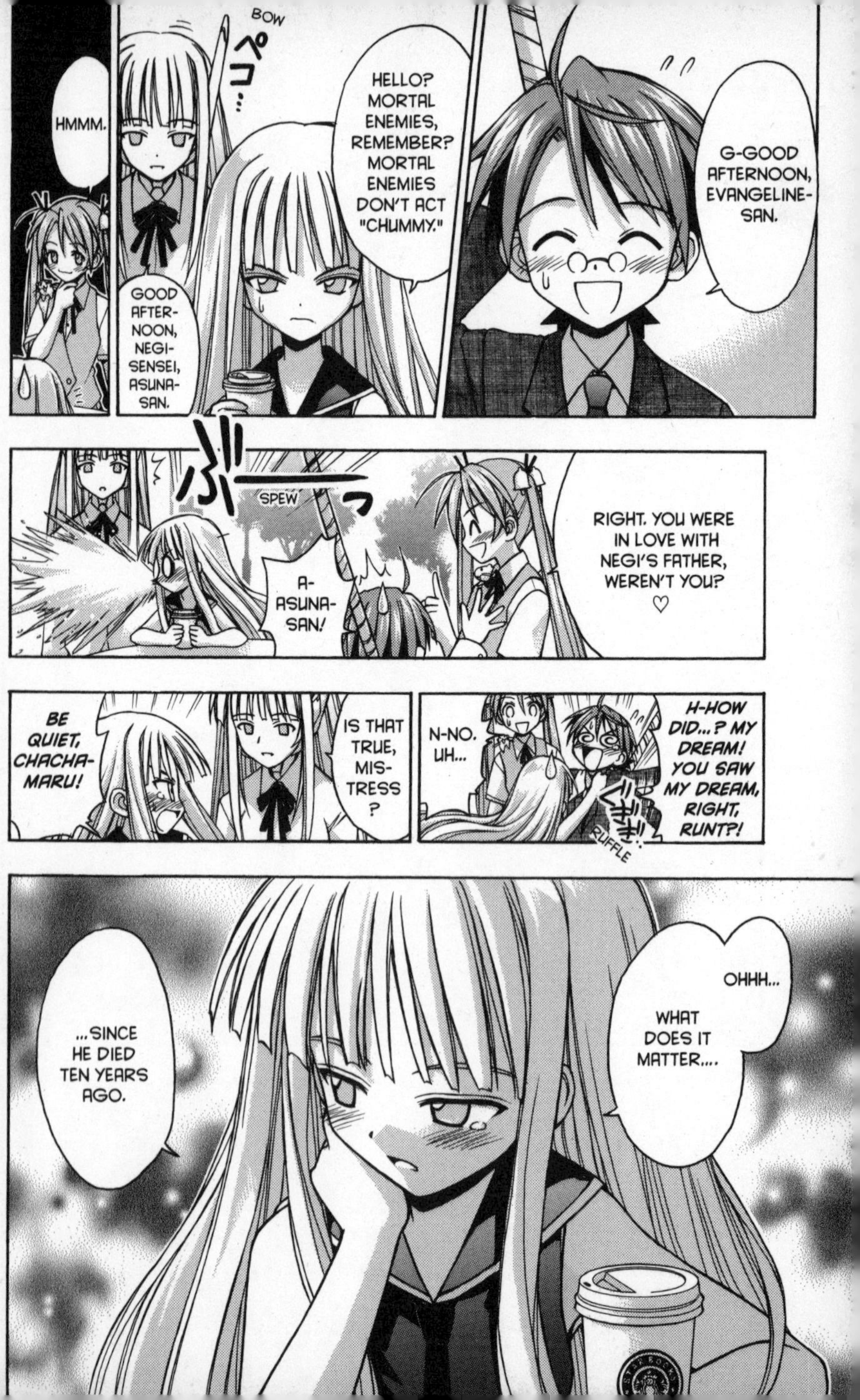
G-GOOD AFTERNOON, EVANGELINE-SAN.
HELLO? MORTAL ENEMIES, REMEMBER? MORTAL ENEMIES DON'T ACT "CHUMMY."
BOW
ペコ…
GOOD AFTERNOON, NEGI-SENSEI, ASUNA-SAN.
HMMM.
RIGHT. YOU WERE IN LOVE WITH NEGI'S FATHER, WEREN'T YOU? ♡
SPEW
A-ASUNA-SAN!
H-HOW DID...? MY DREAM! YOU SAW MY DREAM, RIGHT, RUNT?!
RUFFLE
N-NO. UH...
IS THAT TRUE, MISTRESS?
BE QUIET, CHACHAMARU!
OHHH...
WHAT DOES IT MATTER....
...SINCE HE DIED TEN YEARS AGO.

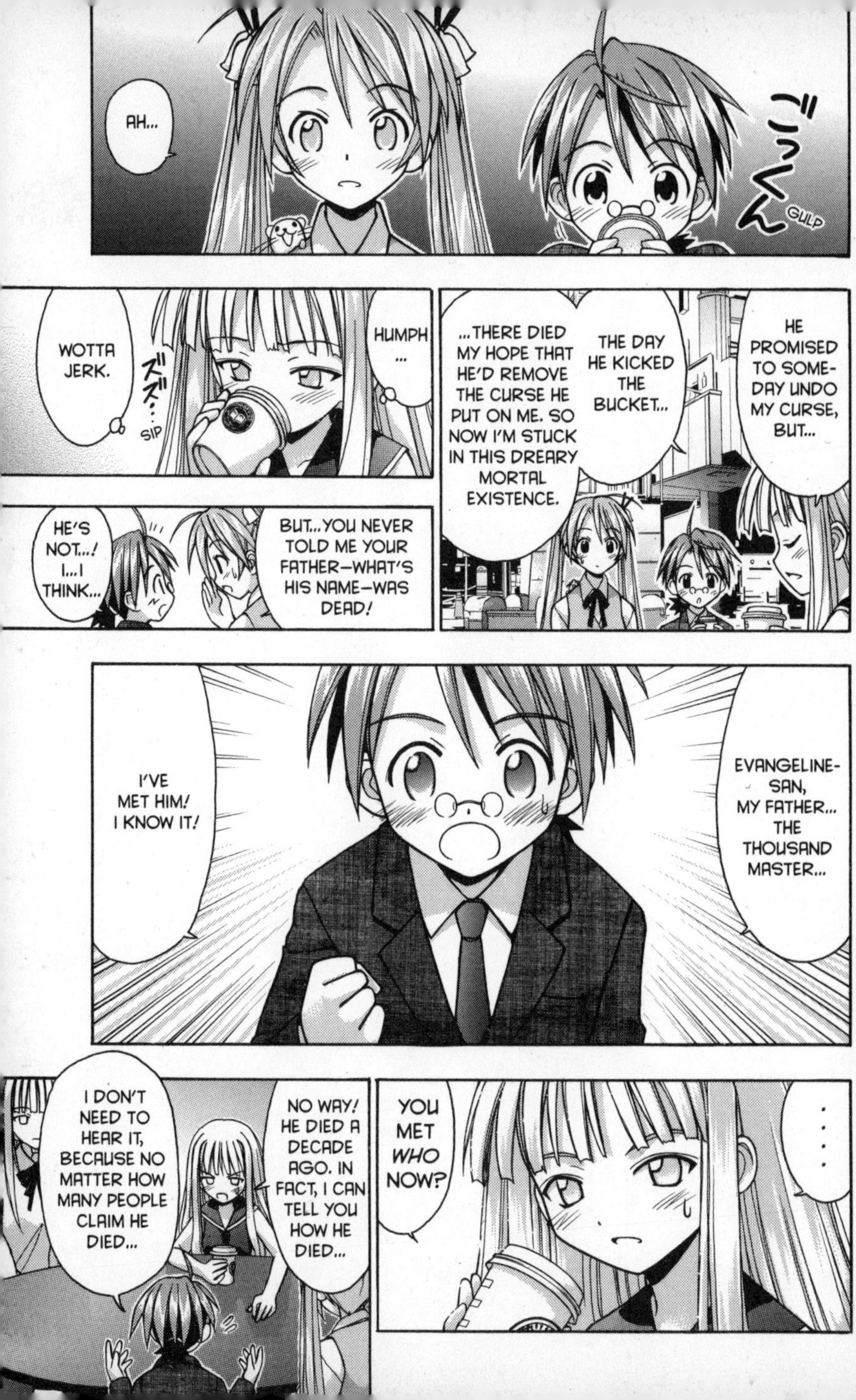
ごっくん
GULP
AH...
HE PROMISED TO SOME-DAY UNDO MY CURSE, BUT...
THE DAY HE KICKED THE BUCKET...
...THERE DIED MY HOPE THAT HE'D REMOVE THE CURSE HE PUT ON ME. SO NOW I'M STUCK IN THIS DREARY MORTAL EXISTENCE.
HUMPH ...
ズズ...
SIP
WOTTA JERK.
BUT...YOU NEVER TOLD ME YOUR FATHER—WHAT'S HIS NAME—WAS DEAD!
HE'S NOT...! I...I THINK...
EVANGELINE-SAN, MY FATHER... THE THOUSAND MASTER...
I'VE MET HIM! I KNOW IT!
....
YOU MET WHO NOW?
NO WAY! HE DIED A DECADE AGO. IN FACT, I CAN TELL YOU HOW HE DIED...
I DON'T NEED TO HEAR IT, BECAUSE NO MATTER HOW MANY PEOPLE CLAIM HE DIED...

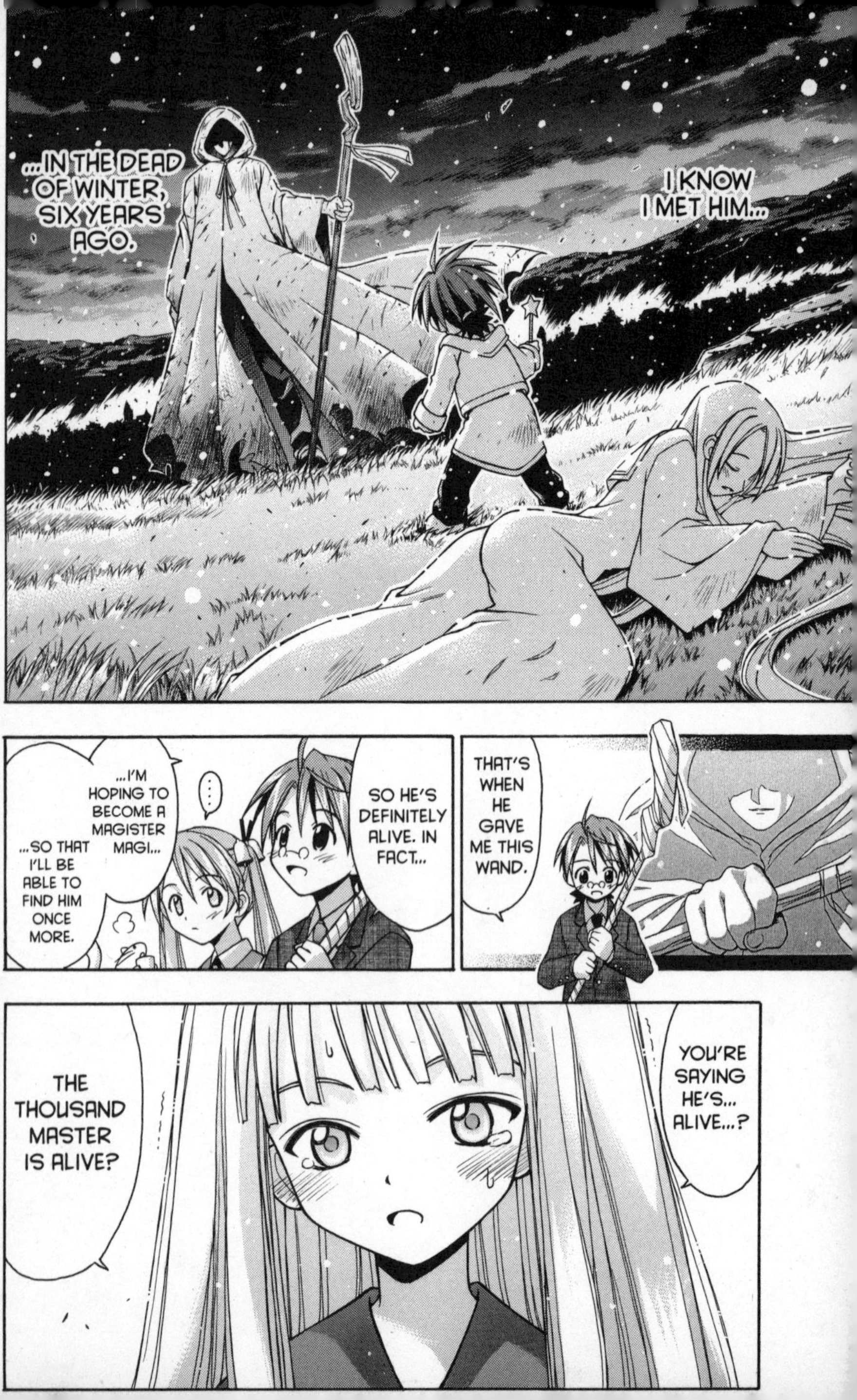

I KNOW I MET HIM...
...IN THE DEAD OF WINTER, SIX YEARS AGO.
THAT'S WHEN HE GAVE ME THIS WAND.
SO HE'S DEFINITELY ALIVE. IN FACT...
...
...I'M HOPING TO BECOME A MAGISTER MAGI...
...SO THAT I'LL BE ABLE TO FIND HIM ONCE MORE.
YOU'RE SAYING HE'S... ALIVE...?
THE THOUSAND MASTER IS ALIVE?

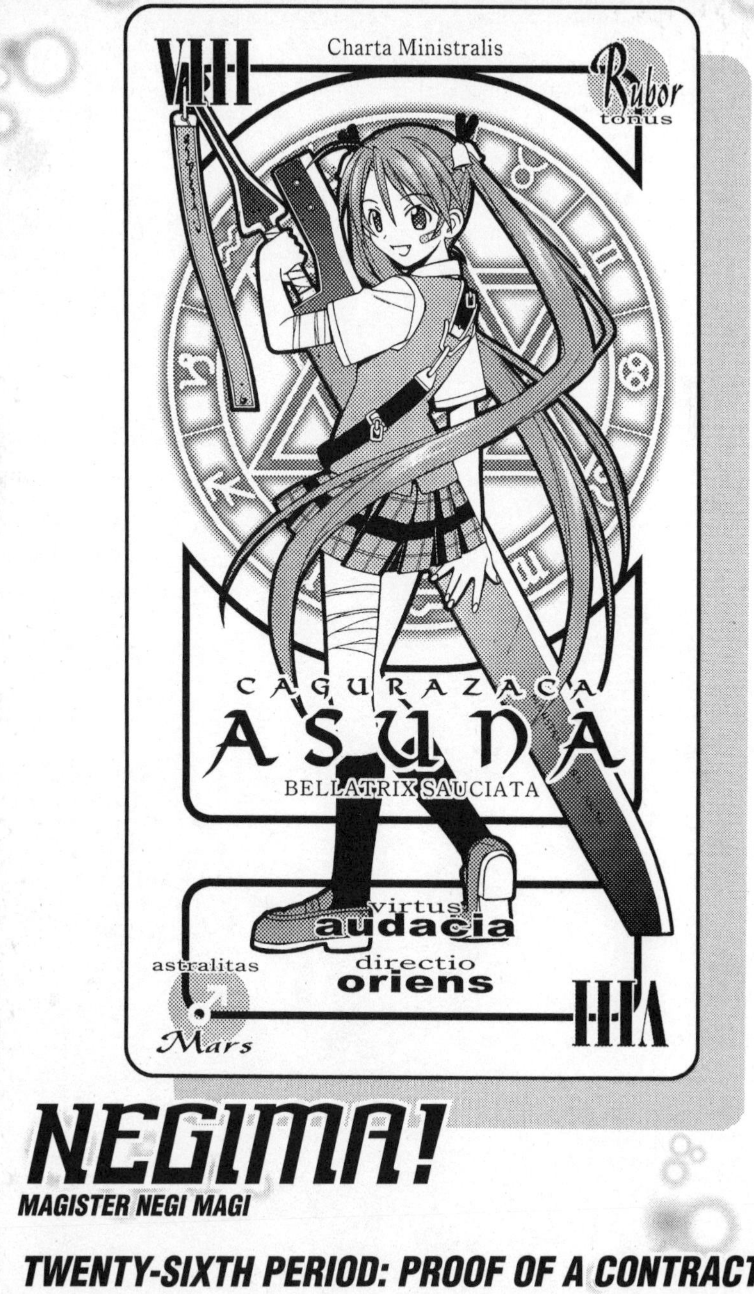
Charta Ministralis
VIII
Rubor
tonus
CAGURAZACA
ASUNA
BELLATRIX SAUCIATA
virtus
audacia
astralitas
directio
oriens
Mars

NEGIMA!

MAGISTER NEGI MAGI

TWENTY-SIXTH PERIOD: PROOF OF A CONTRACT!?

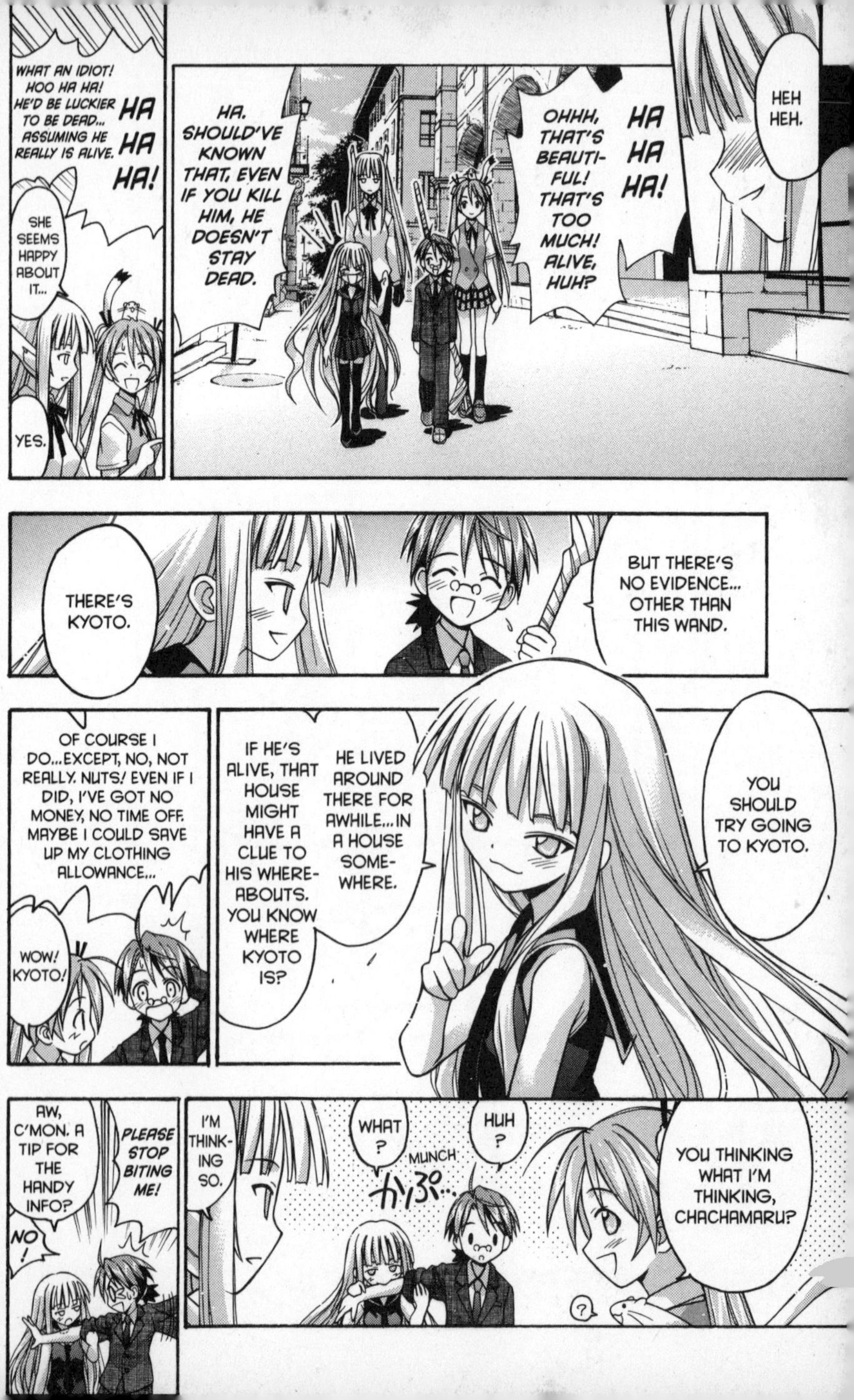
HEH HEH.
OHHH, THAT'S BEAUTI-FUL! THAT'S TOO MUCH! ALIVE, HUH?
HA HA HA!
HA. SHOULD'VE KNOWN THAT, EVEN IF YOU KILL HIM, HE DOESN'T STAY DEAD.
WHAT AN IDIOT! HOO HA HA! HE'D BE LUCKIER TO BE DEAD... ASSUMING HE REALLY IS ALIVE.
HA HA HA!
SHE SEEMS HAPPY ABOUT IT...
YES.
BUT THERE'S NO EVIDENCE... OTHER THAN THIS WAND.
THERE'S KYOTO.
YOU SHOULD TRY GOING TO KYOTO.
HE LIVED AROUND THERE FOR AWHILE... IN A HOUSE SOME-WHERE.
IF HE'S ALIVE, THAT HOUSE MIGHT HAVE A CLUE TO HIS WHERE-ABOUTS. YOU KNOW WHERE KYOTO IS?
OF COURSE I DO...EXCEPT, NO, NOT REALLY. NUTS! EVEN IF I DID, I'VE GOT NO MONEY, NO TIME OFF. MAYBE I COULD SAVE UP MY CLOTHING ALLOWANCE...
WOW! KYOTO!
YOU THINKING WHAT I'M THINKING, CHACHAMARU?
HUH?
WHAT?
MUNCH
かぷ...
?
I'M THINK-ING SO.
PLEASE STOP BITING ME!
AW, C'MON. A TIP FOR THE HANDY INFO?
NO!

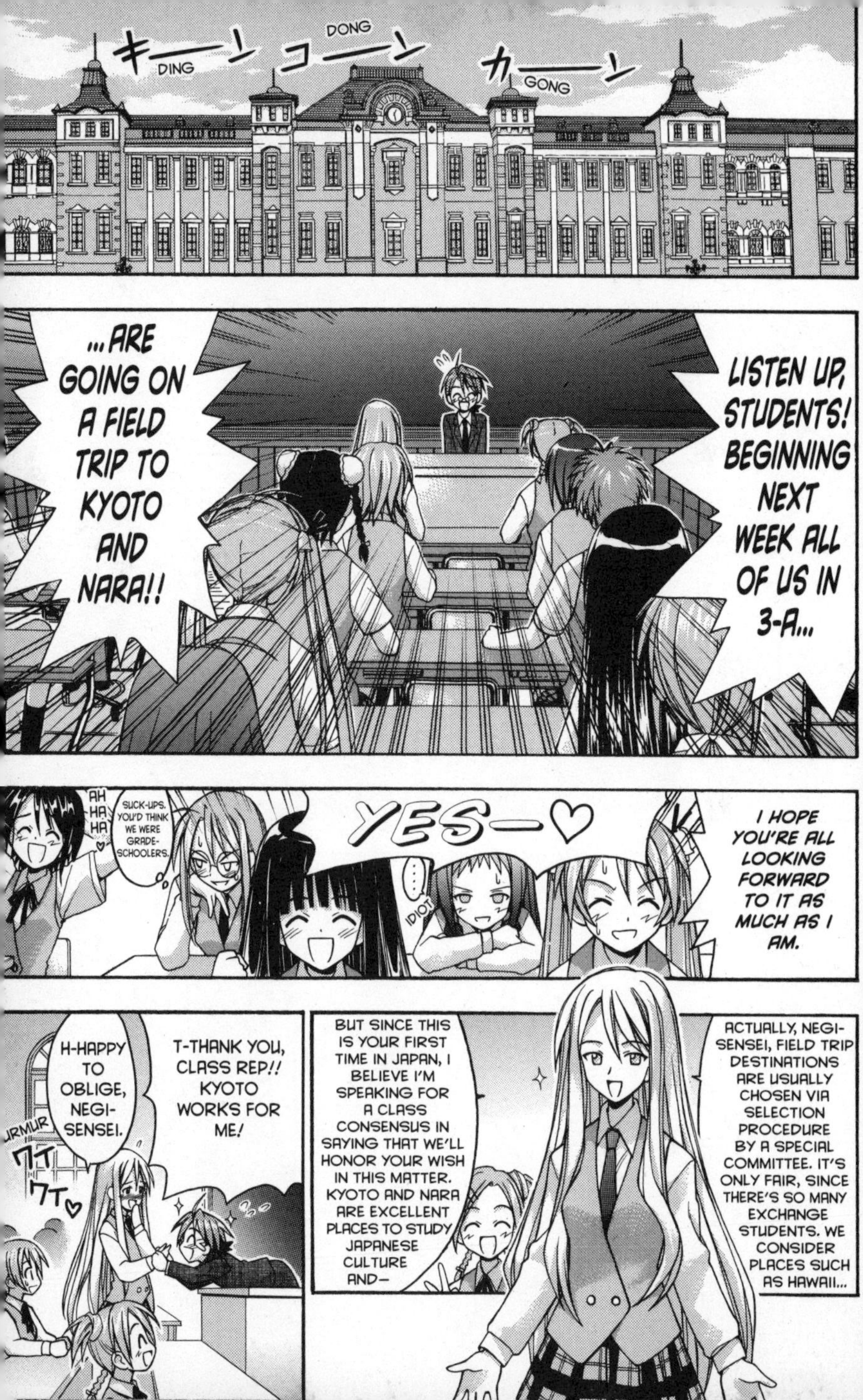
キーン DING
コーン DONG
カーン GONG
LISTEN UP, STUDENTS! BEGINNING NEXT WEEK ALL OF US IN 3-A...
...ARE GOING ON A FIELD TRIP TO KYOTO AND NARA!!
I HOPE YOU'RE ALL LOOKING FORWARD TO IT AS MUCH AS I AM.
YES—♡
......
IDIOT
SUCK-UPS. YOU'D THINK WE WERE GRADE-SCHOOLERS.
AH HA HA ♡
ACTUALLY, NEGI-SENSEI, FIELD TRIP DESTINATIONS ARE USUALLY CHOSEN VIA SELECTION PROCEDURE BY A SPECIAL COMMITTEE. IT'S ONLY FAIR, SINCE THERE'S SO MANY EXCHANGE STUDENTS. WE CONSIDER PLACES SUCH AS HAWAII...
BUT SINCE THIS IS YOUR FIRST TIME IN JAPAN, I BELIEVE I'M SPEAKING FOR A CLASS CONSENSUS IN SAYING THAT WE'LL HONOR YOUR WISH IN THIS MATTER. KYOTO AND NARA ARE EXCELLENT PLACES TO STUDY JAPANESE CULTURE AND—
T-THANK YOU, CLASS REP!! KYOTO WORKS FOR ME!
H-HAPPY TO OBLIGE, NEGI-SENSEI.

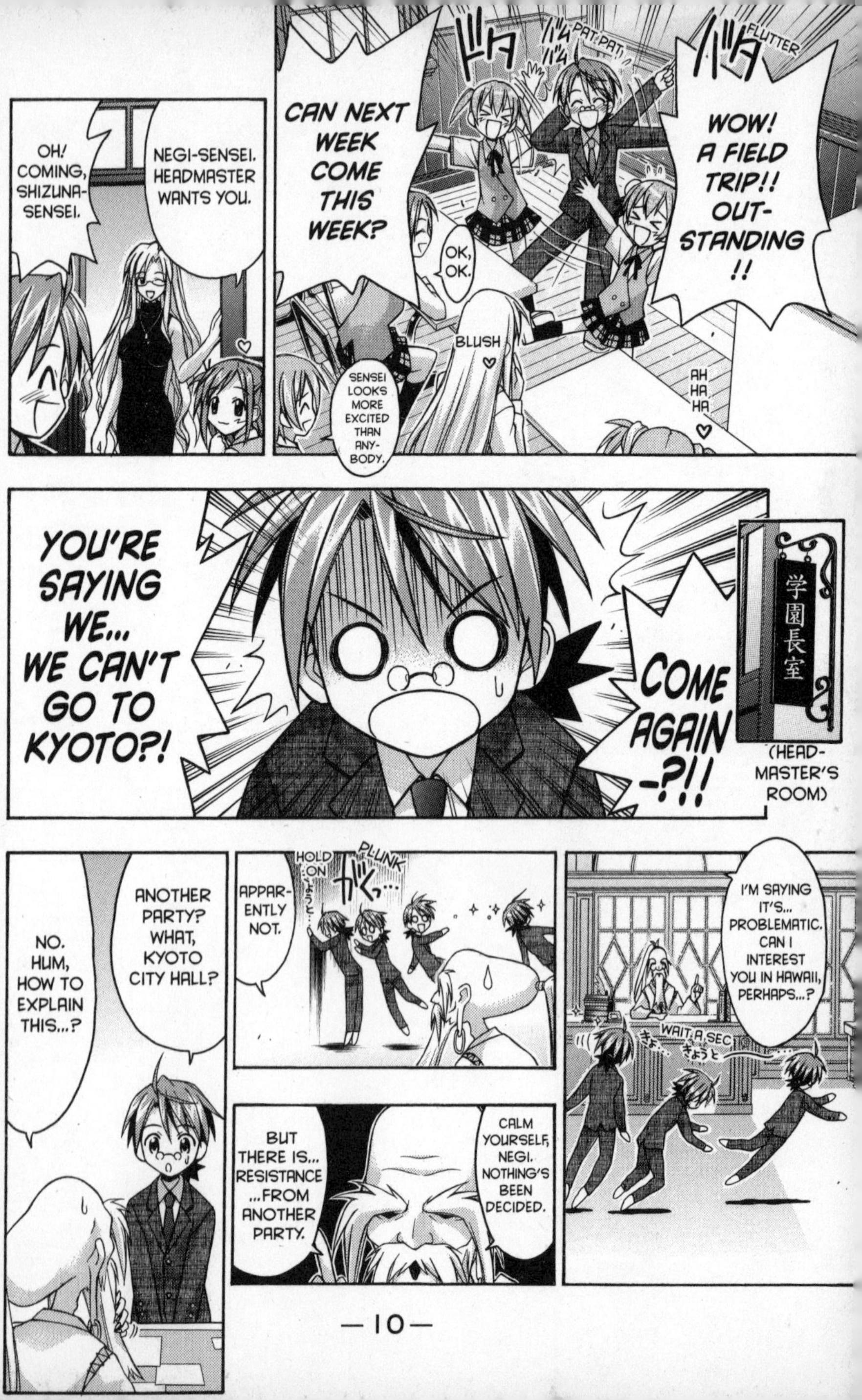
バタ
FLUTTER
WOW! A FIELD TRIP!! OUT-STANDING!!
PAT PAT
ドタ
CAN NEXT WEEK COME THIS WEEK?
OK, OK.
BLUSH
AH HA HA
SENSEI LOOKS MORE EXCITED THAN ANYBODY.
NEGI-SENSEI. HEADMASTER WANTS YOU.
OH! COMING, SHIZUNA-SENSEI.
学園長室
(HEADMASTER'S ROOM)
COME AGAIN-?!!
YOU'RE SAYING WE... WE CAN'T GO TO KYOTO?!
I'M SAYING IT'S... PROBLEMATIC. CAN I INTEREST YOU IN HAWAII, PERHAPS...?
WAIT A SEC
PLUNK
HOLD ON
APPARENTLY NOT.
CALM YOURSELF, NEGI. NOTHING'S BEEN DECIDED.
BUT THERE IS... RESISTANCE ...FROM ANOTHER PARTY.
ANOTHER PARTY? WHAT, KYOTO CITY HALL?
NO. HUM, HOW TO EXPLAIN THIS...?

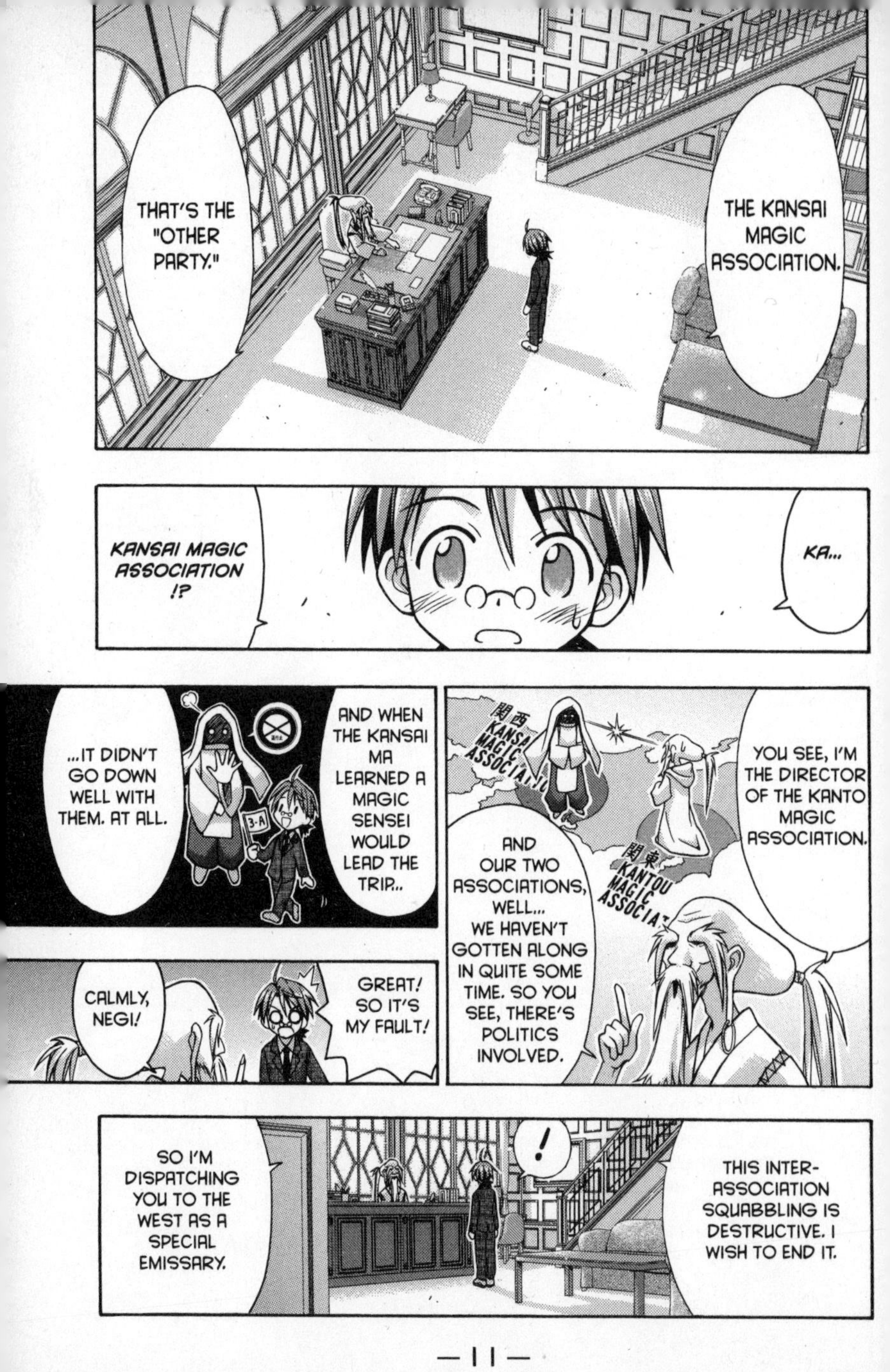
THE KANSAI MAGIC ASSOCIATION.
THAT'S THE "OTHER PARTY."
KA...
KANSAI MAGIC ASSOCIATION !?
YOU SEE, I'M THE DIRECTOR OF THE KANTO MAGIC ASSOCIATION.
関西
関東
KANTOU
AND OUR TWO ASSOCIATIONS, WELL... WE HAVEN'T GOTTEN ALONG IN QUITE SOME TIME. SO YOU SEE, THERE'S POLITICS INVOLVED.
AND WHEN THE KANSAI MA LEARNED A MAGIC SENSEI WOULD LEAD THE TRIP...
3-A
...IT DIDN'T GO DOWN WELL WITH THEM. AT ALL.
GREAT! SO IT'S MY FAULT!
CALMLY, NEGI!
THIS INTER-ASSOCIATION SQUABBLING IS DESTRUCTIVE. I WISH TO END IT.
!
SO I'M DISPATCHING YOU TO THE WEST AS A SPECIAL EMISSARY.

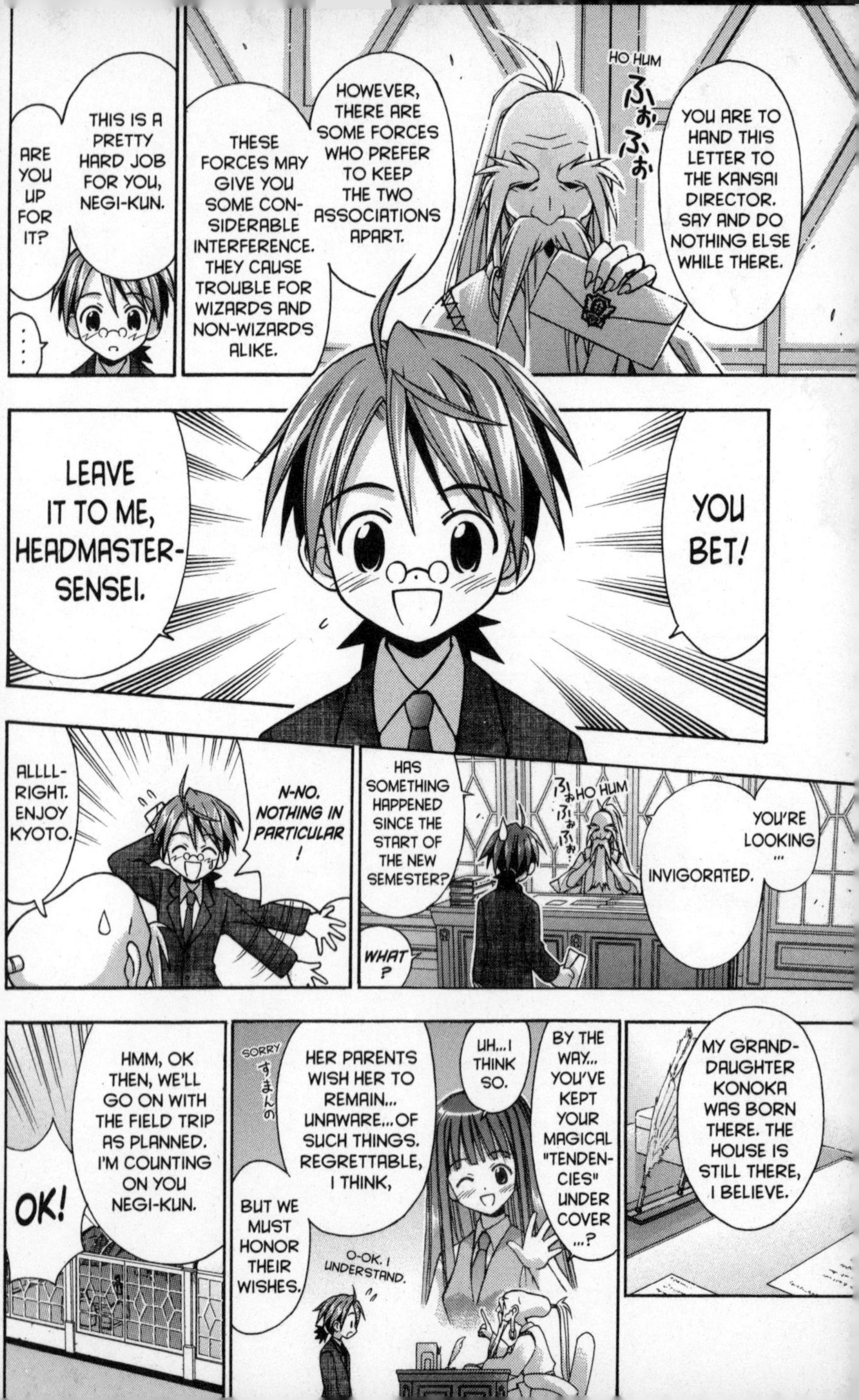
HO HUM
ふぉふぉ
YOU ARE TO HAND THIS LETTER TO THE KANSAI DIRECTOR. SAY AND DO NOTHING ELSE WHILE THERE.
HOWEVER, THERE ARE SOME FORCES WHO PREFER TO KEEP THE TWO ASSOCIATIONS APART.
THESE FORCES MAY GIVE YOU SOME CON-SIDERABLE INTERFERENCE. THEY CAUSE TROUBLE FOR WIZARDS AND NON-WIZARDS ALIKE.
THIS IS A PRETTY HARD JOB FOR YOU, NEGI-KUN.
ARE YOU UP FOR IT?
...
YOU BET!
LEAVE IT TO ME, HEADMASTER-SENSEI.
YOU'RE LOOKING... INVIGORATED.
HO HUM
ふぉふぉふぉ...
HAS SOMETHING HAPPENED SINCE THE START OF THE NEW SEMESTER?
WHAT?
N-NO. NOTHING IN PARTICULAR!
ALLLL-RIGHT. ENJOY KYOTO.
MY GRAND-DAUGHTER KONOKA WAS BORN THERE. THE HOUSE IS STILL THERE, I BELIEVE.
BY THE WAY... YOU'VE KEPT YOUR MAGICAL "TENDEN-CIES" UNDER COVER ...?
UH...I THINK SO.
HER PARENTS WISH HER TO REMAIN... UNAWARE...OF SUCH THINGS. REGRETTABLE, I THINK,
SORRY
すまんの
BUT WE MUST HONOR THEIR WISHES.
O-OK. I UNDERSTAND.
HMM, OK THEN, WE'LL GO ON WITH THE FIELD TRIP AS PLANNED. I'M COUNTING ON YOU NEGI-KUN.
OK!

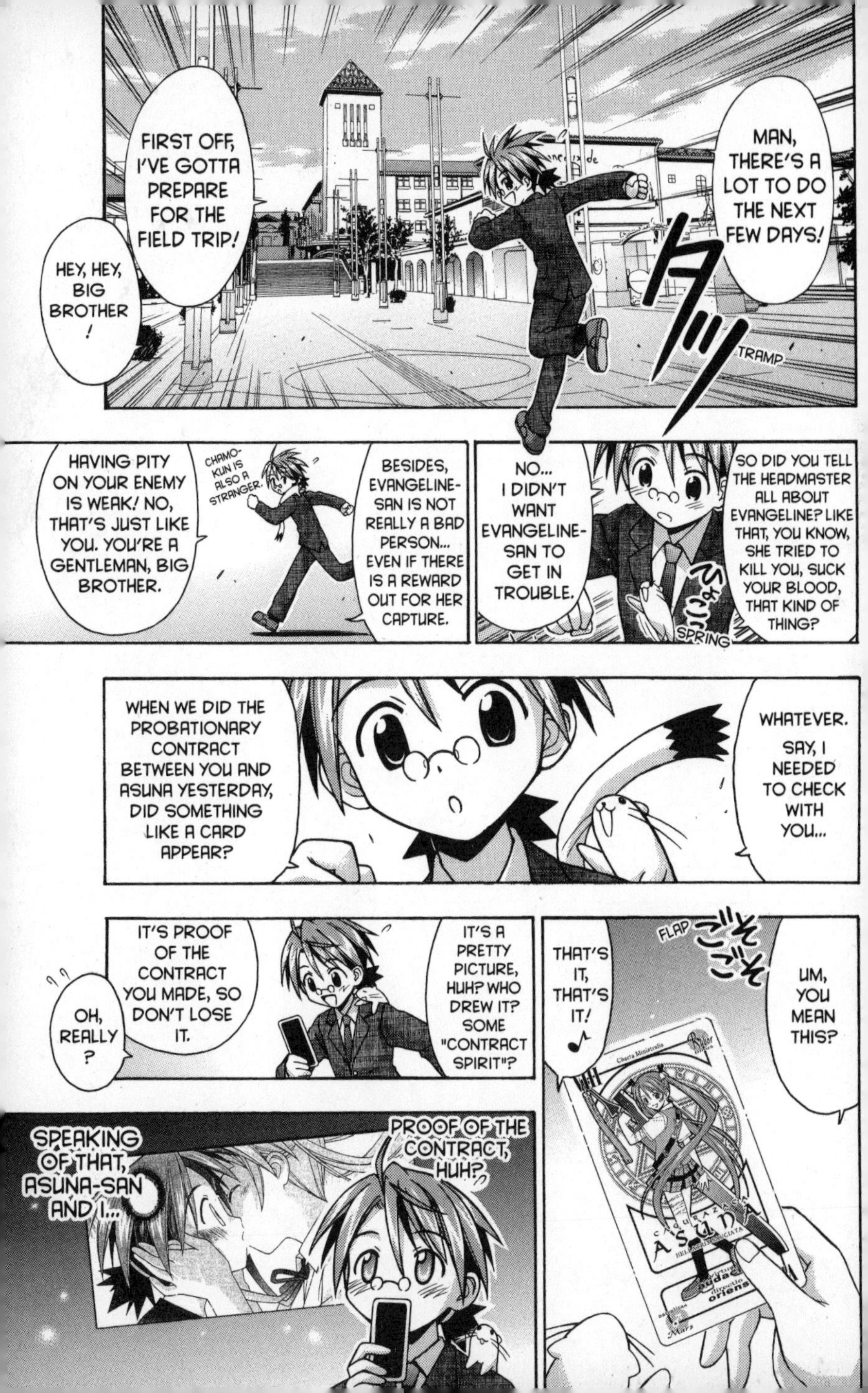
MAN, THERE'S A LOT TO DO THE NEXT FEW DAYS!
TRAMP
FIRST OFF, I'VE GOTTA PREPARE FOR THE FIELD TRIP!
HEY, HEY, BIG BROTHER!
SO DID YOU TELL THE HEADMASTER ALL ABOUT EVANGELINE? LIKE THAT, YOU KNOW, SHE TRIED TO KILL YOU, SUCK YOUR BLOOD, THAT KIND OF THING?
SPRING
NO... I DIDN'T WANT EVANGELINE-SAN TO GET IN TROUBLE.
BESIDES, EVANGELINE-SAN IS NOT REALLY A BAD PERSON... EVEN IF THERE IS A REWARD OUT FOR HER CAPTURE.
CHAMO-KUN IS ALSO A STRANGER.
HAVING PITY ON YOUR ENEMY IS WEAK! NO, THAT'S JUST LIKE YOU. YOU'RE A GENTLEMAN, BIG BROTHER.
WHATEVER.
SAY, I NEEDED TO CHECK WITH YOU...
WHEN WE DID THE PROBATIONARY CONTRACT BETWEEN YOU AND ASUNA YESTERDAY, DID SOMETHING LIKE A CARD APPEAR?
FLAP
UM, YOU MEAN THIS?
THAT'S IT, THAT'S IT! ♪
IT'S A PRETTY PICTURE, HUH? WHO DREW IT? SOME "CONTRACT SPIRIT"?
IT'S PROOF OF THE CONTRACT YOU MADE, SO DON'T LOSE IT.
OH, REALLY?
PROOF OF THE CONTRACT, HUH?
SPEAKING OF THAT, ASUNA-SAN AND I...

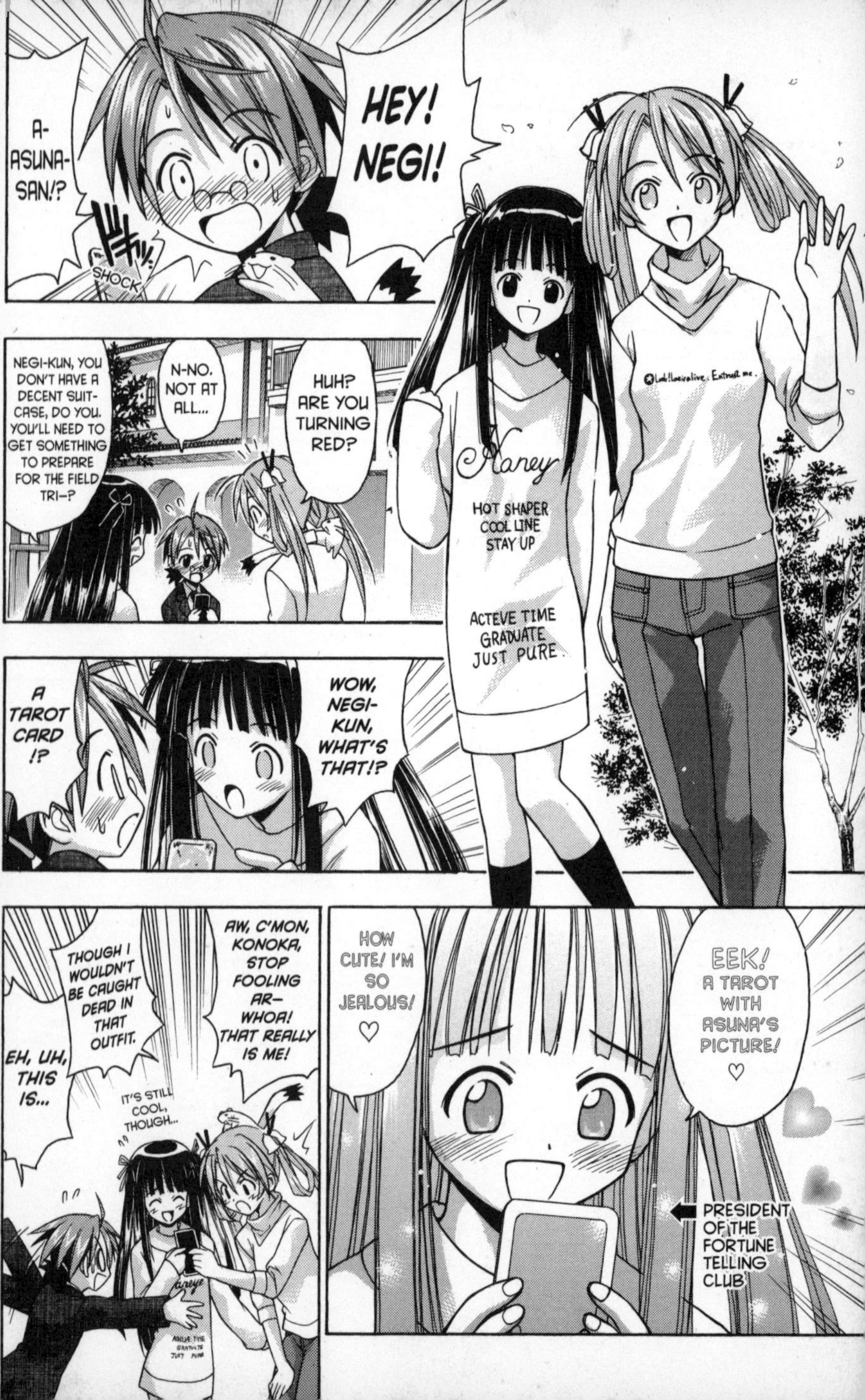
HEY! NEGI!
A-ASUNA-SAN!?
SHOCK
HUH? ARE YOU TURNING RED?
N-NO. NOT AT ALL...
NEGI-KUN, YOU DON'T HAVE A DECENT SUIT-CASE, DO YOU. YOU'LL NEED TO GET SOMETHING TO PREPARE FOR THE FIELD TRI–?
HOT SHAPER COOL LINE STAY UP
ACTEVE TIME GRADUATE JUST PURE
WOW, NEGI-KUN, WHAT'S THAT!?
A TAROT CARD !?
EEK! A TAROT WITH ASUNA'S PICTURE! ♡
HOW CUTE! I'M SO JEALOUS! ♡
PRESIDENT OF THE FORTUNE TELLING CLUB
AW, C'MON, KONOKA, STOP FOOLING AR— WHOA! THAT REALLY IS ME!
THOUGH I WOULDN'T BE CAUGHT DEAD IN THAT OUTFIT.
IT'S STILL COOL, THOUGH...
EH, UH, THIS IS...

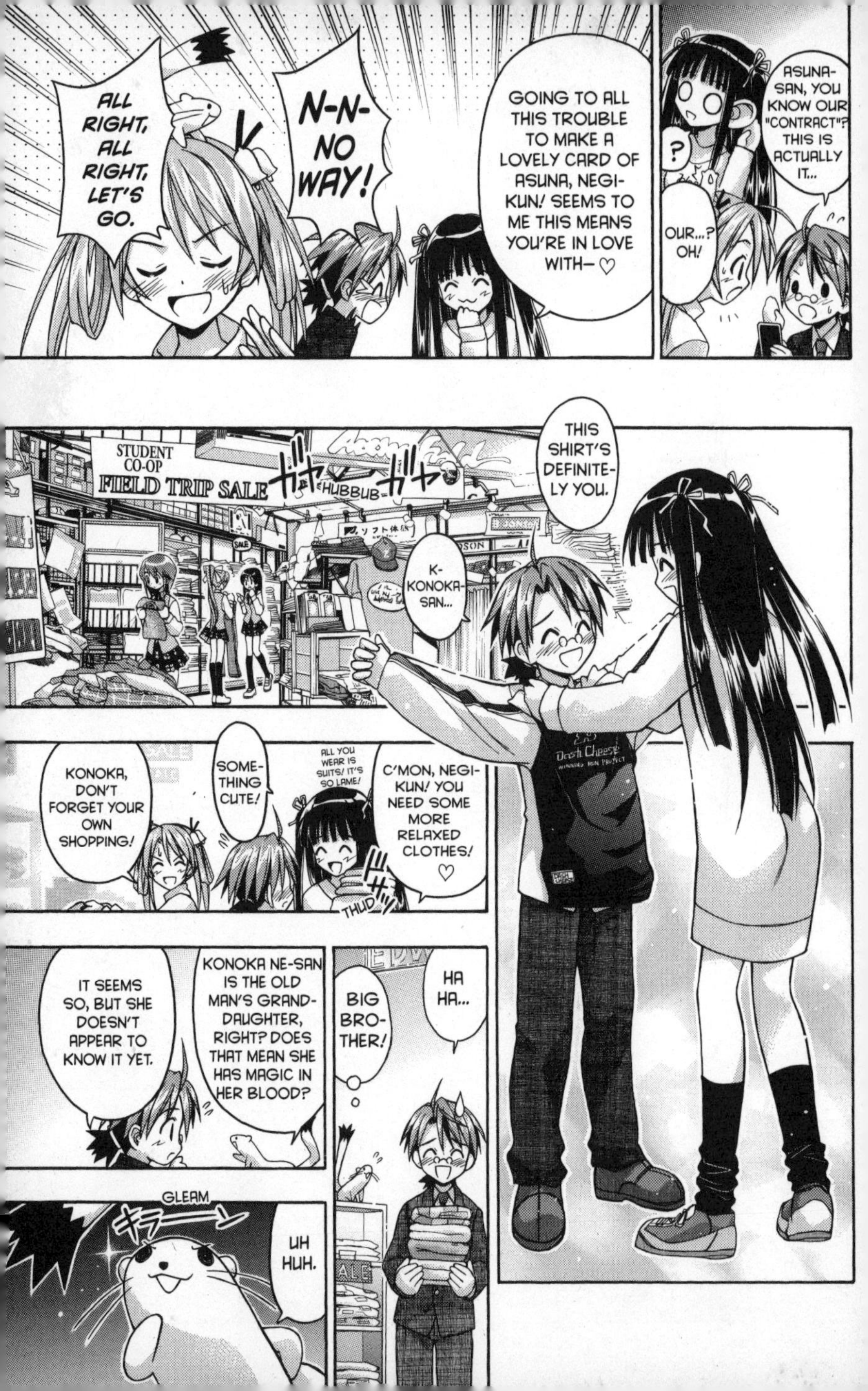
ASUNA-SAN, YOU KNOW OUR "CONTRACT"? THIS IS ACTUALLY IT...
?
OUR...? OH!
GOING TO ALL THIS TROUBLE TO MAKE A LOVELY CARD OF ASUNA, NEGI-KUN! SEEMS TO ME THIS MEANS YOU'RE IN LOVE WITH— ♡
N-N-NO WAY!
ALL RIGHT, ALL RIGHT, LET'S GO.
THIS SHIRT'S DEFINITE-LY YOU.
K-KONOKA-SAN...
STUDENT CO-OP
FIELD TRIP SALE
HUBBUB
C'MON, NEGI-KUN! YOU NEED SOME MORE RELAXED CLOTHES! ♡
THUD
ALL YOU WEAR IS SUITS! IT'S SO LAME!
SOME-THING CUTE!
KONOKA, DON'T FORGET YOUR OWN SHOPPING!
HA HA...
BIG BRO-THER!
KONOKA NE-SAN IS THE OLD MAN'S GRAND-DAUGHTER, RIGHT? DOES THAT MEAN SHE HAS MAGIC IN HER BLOOD?
IT SEEMS SO, BUT SHE DOESN'T APPEAR TO KNOW IT YET.
UH HUH.
GLEAM

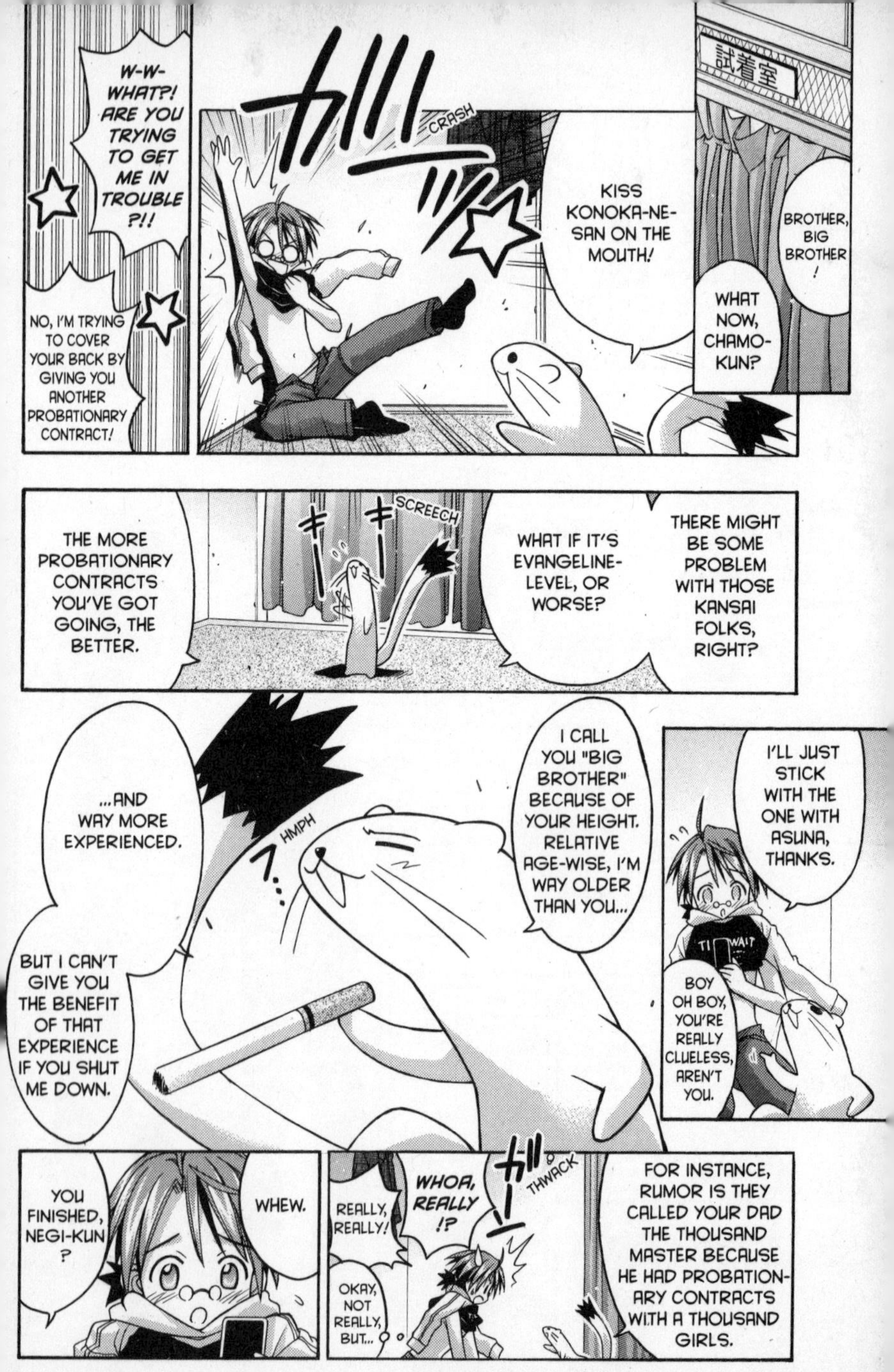
試着室
BROTHER, BIG BROTHER!
WHAT NOW, CHAMO-KUN?
KISS KONOKA-NE-SAN ON THE MOUTH!
CRASH
W-W-WHAT?! ARE YOU TRYING TO GET ME IN TROUBLE?!!
NO, I'M TRYING TO COVER YOUR BACK BY GIVING YOU ANOTHER PROBATIONARY CONTRACT!
THERE MIGHT BE SOME PROBLEM WITH THOSE KANSAI FOLKS, RIGHT?
WHAT IF IT'S EVANGELINE-LEVEL, OR WORSE?
SCREECH
THE MORE PROBATIONARY CONTRACTS YOU'VE GOT GOING, THE BETTER.
I'LL JUST STICK WITH THE ONE WITH ASUNA, THANKS.
BOY OH BOY, YOU'RE REALLY CLUELESS, AREN'T YOU.
I CALL YOU "BIG BROTHER" BECAUSE OF YOUR HEIGHT. RELATIVE AGE-WISE, I'M WAY OLDER THAN YOU...
HMPH
...AND WAY MORE EXPERIENCED.
BUT I CAN'T GIVE YOU THE BENEFIT OF THAT EXPERIENCE IF YOU SHUT ME DOWN.
FOR INSTANCE, RUMOR IS THEY CALLED YOUR DAD THE THOUSAND MASTER BECAUSE HE HAD PROBATIONARY CONTRACTS WITH A THOUSAND GIRLS.
THWACK
WHOA, REALLY!?
REALLY, REALLY!
OKAY, NOT REALLY, BUT...
WHEW.
YOU FINISHED, NEGI-KUN?

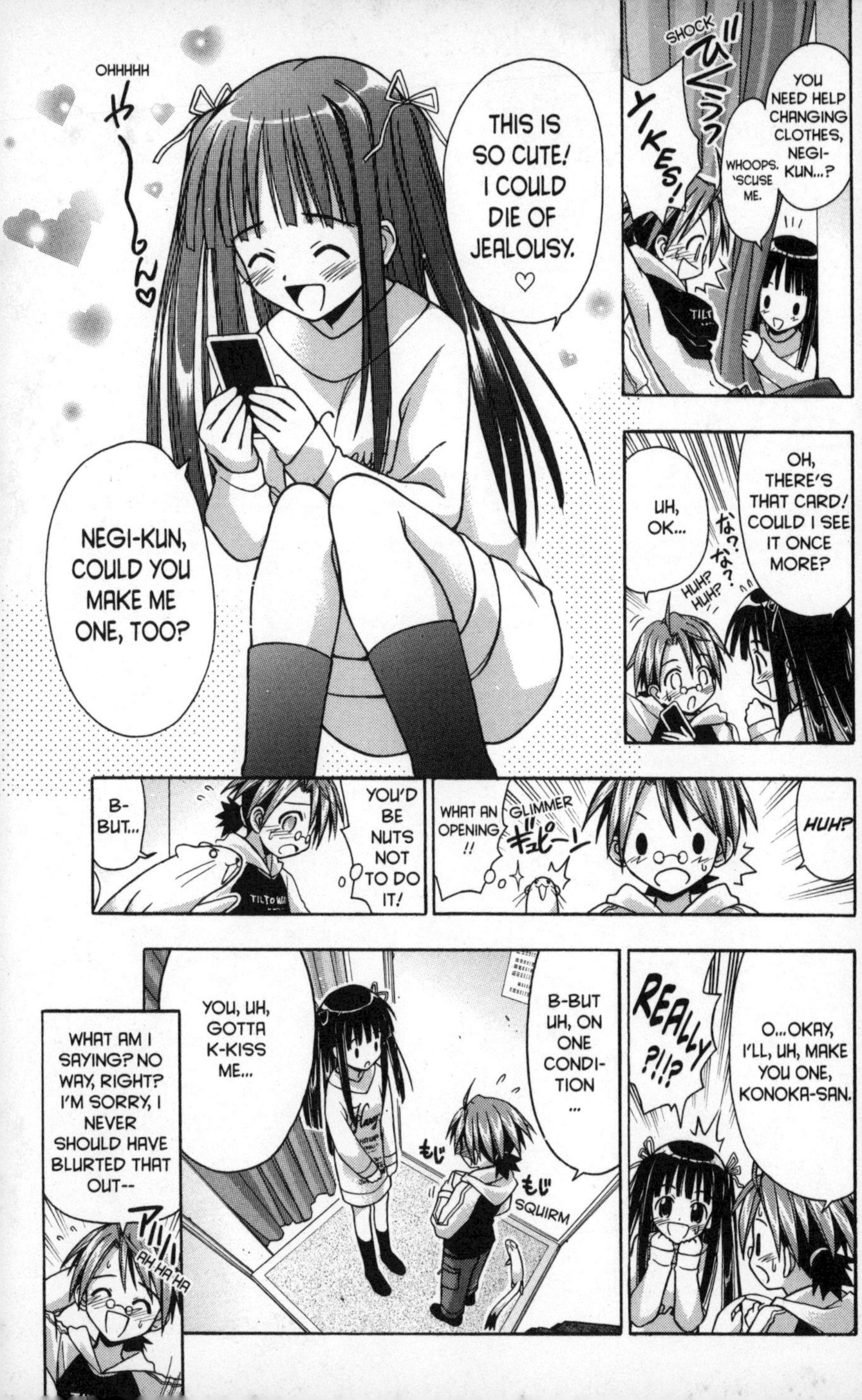

SHOCK
YIKES!
YOU NEED HELP CHANGING CLOTHES, NEGI-KUN...?
WHOOPS. 'SCUSE ME.
THIS IS SO CUTE! I COULD DIE OF JEALOUSY. ♡
OHHHHH
NEGI-KUN, COULD YOU MAKE ME ONE, TOO?
OH, THERE'S THAT CARD! COULD I SEE IT ONCE MORE?
UH, OK...
HUH? HUH?
HUH?
GLIMMER
WHAT AN OPENING!!
YOU'D BE NUTS NOT TO DO IT!
B-BUT...
REALLY?!!?
O...OKAY, I'LL, UH, MAKE YOU ONE, KONOKA-SAN.
B-BUT UH, ON ONE CONDITION...
YOU, UH, GOTTA K-KISS ME...
SQUIRM
WHAT AM I SAYING? NO WAY, RIGHT? I'M SORRY, I NEVER SHOULD HAVE BLURTED THAT OUT--
AH HA HA

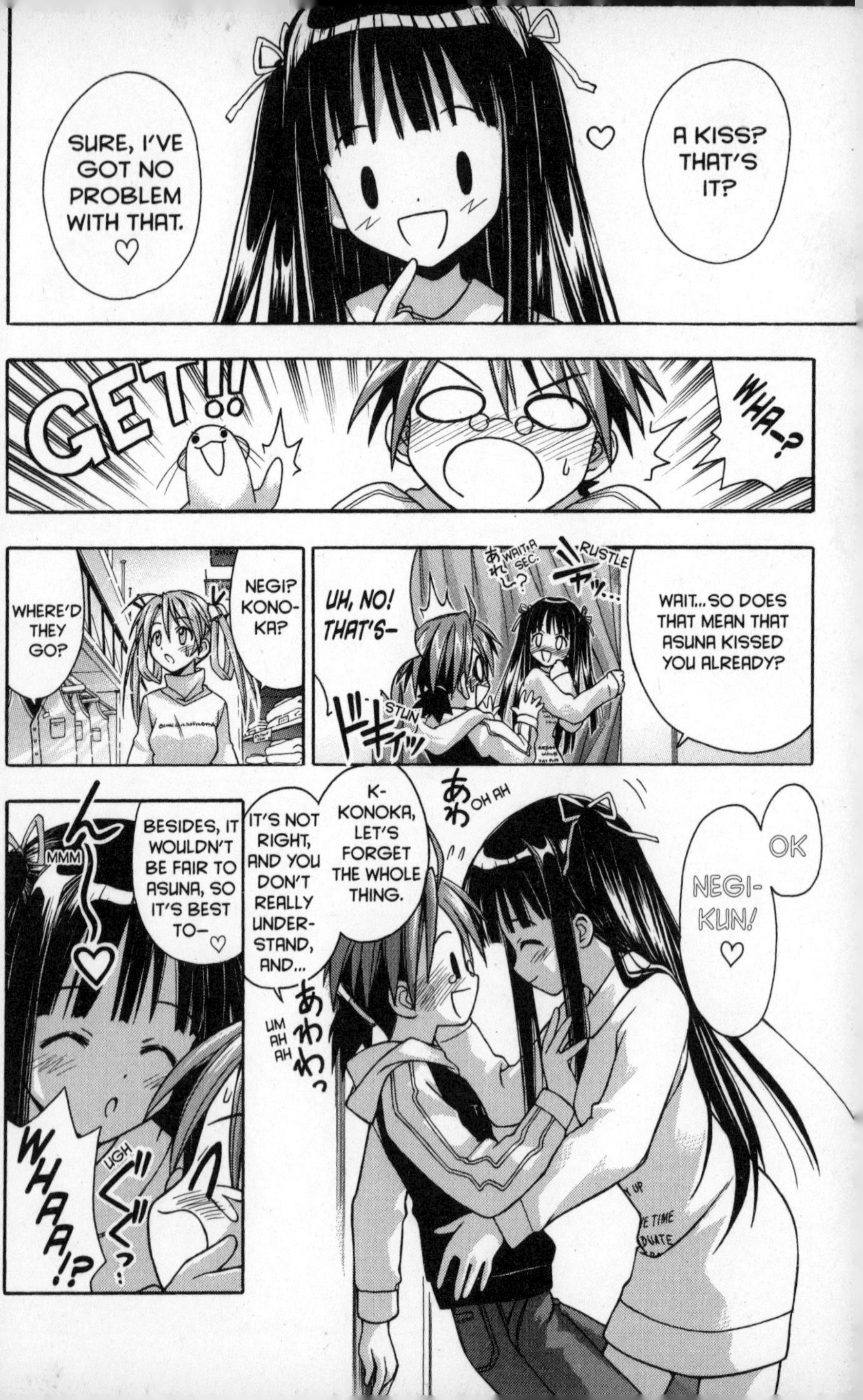
A KISS? THAT'S IT?
SURE, I'VE GOT NO PROBLEM WITH THAT. ♡
WHA-?
GET!!
WAIT...SO DOES THAT MEAN THAT ASUNA KISSED YOU ALREADY?
RUSTLE
WAIT A SEC.
UH, NO! THAT'S—
STUN
NEGI? KONOKA?
WHERE'D THEY GO?
OK NEGI-KUN! ♡
OH AH
K-KONOKA, LET'S FORGET THE WHOLE THING.
IT'S NOT RIGHT, AND YOU DON'T REALLY UNDERSTAND, AND...
UM AH AH
BESIDES, IT WOULDN'T BE FAIR TO ASUNA, SO IT'S BEST TO— ♡
MMM
UGH
WHAAA!?

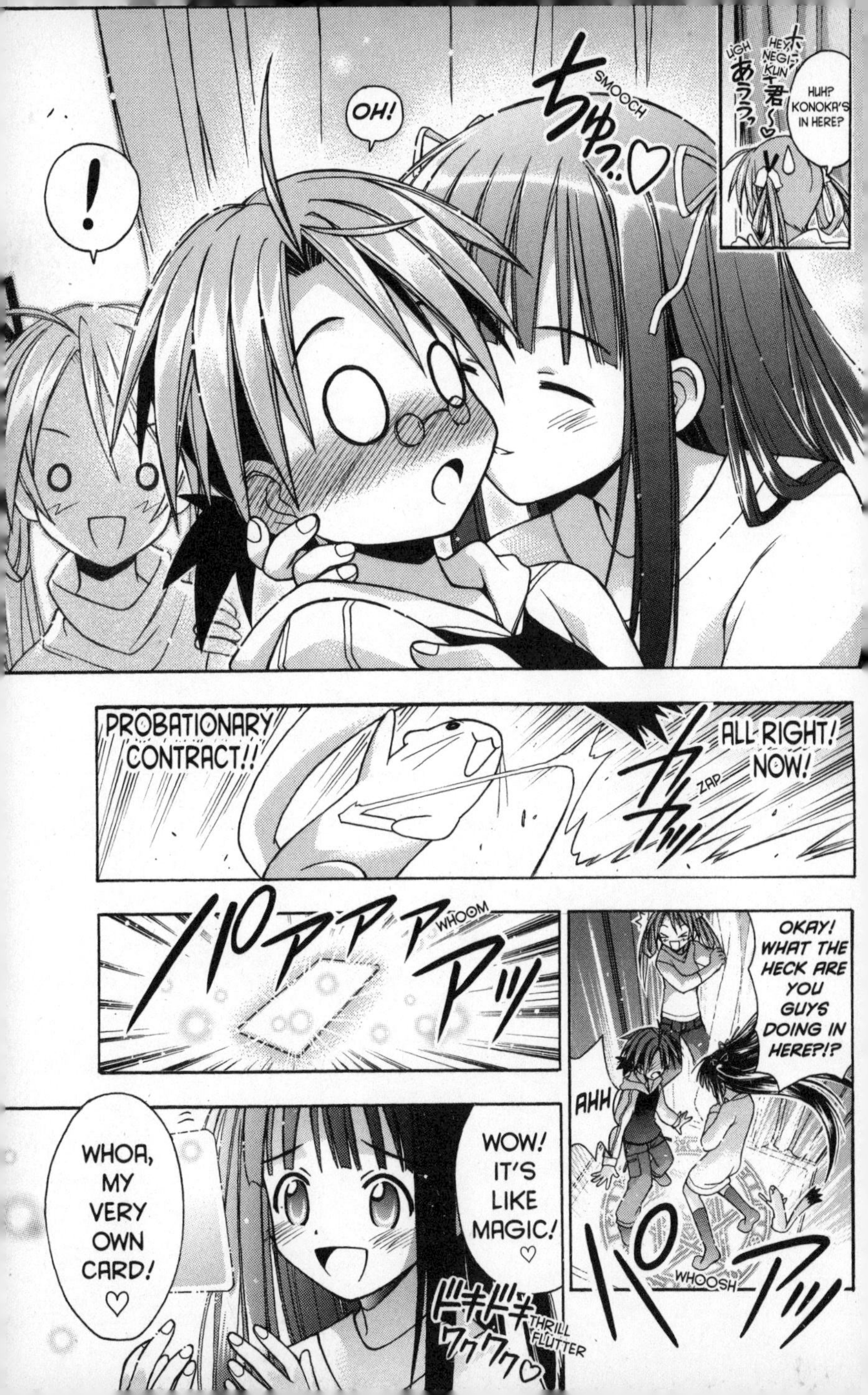
HEY NEGI-KUN
UGH
HUH? KONOKA'S IN HERE?
SMOOCH
OH!
!
ALL RIGHT! NOW!
ZAP
PROBATIONARY CONTRACT!!
OKAY! WHAT THE HECK ARE YOU GUYS DOING IN HERE?!?
AHH
WHOOM
WHOOSH
WOW! IT'S LIKE MAGIC! ♡
WHOA, MY VERY OWN CARD! ♡
THRILL FLUTTER

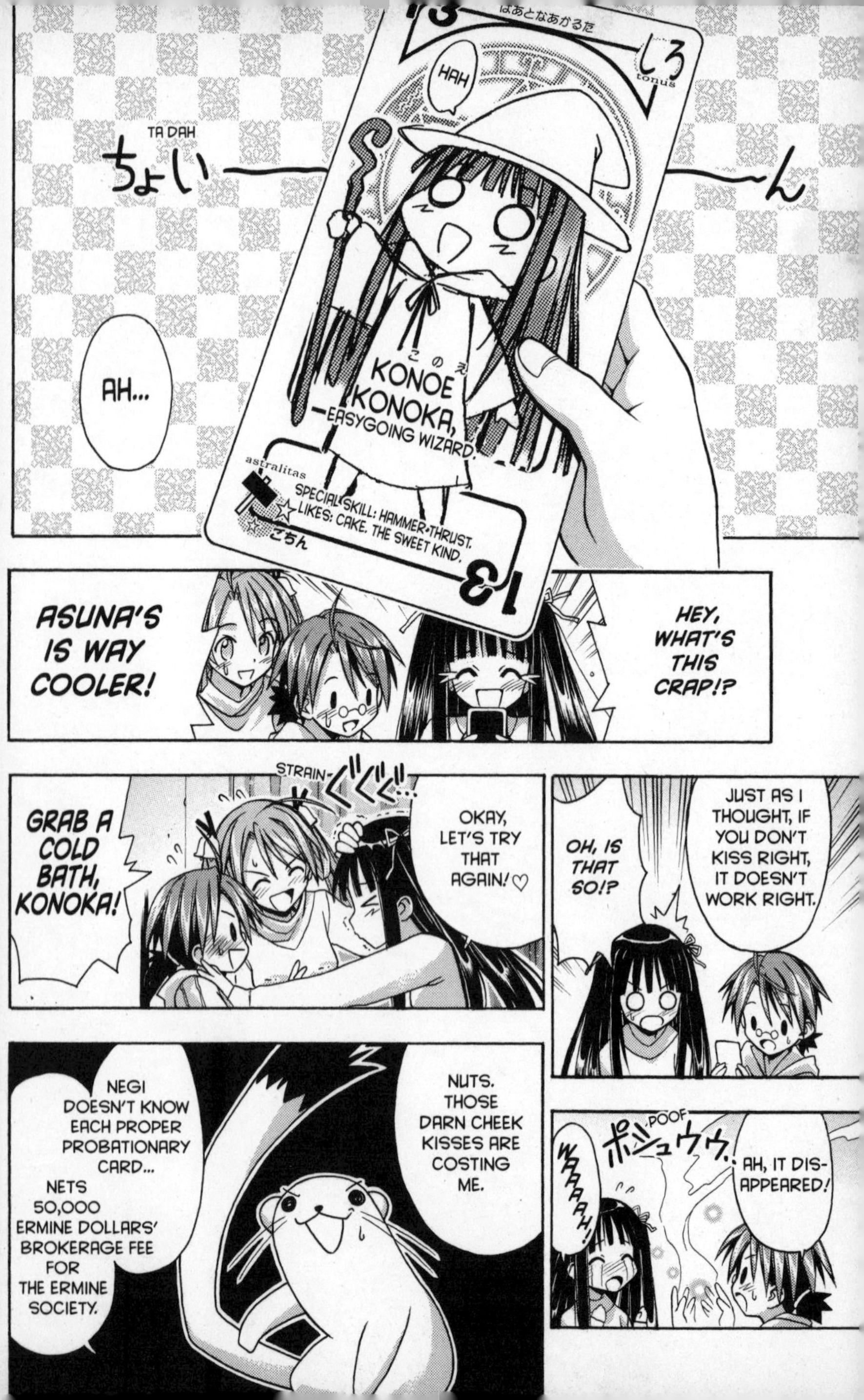
TA DAH
ちょい〜〜ん
13
はあとなあかるた
しろ
tonus
HAH
このえ
KONOE KONOKA,
—EASYGOING WIZARD.
astralitas
SPECIAL SKILL: HAMMER-THRUST.
LIKES: CAKE. THE SWEET KIND.
こちん
13
AH...
HEY, WHAT'S THIS CRAP!?
ASUNA'S IS WAY COOLER!
JUST AS I THOUGHT, IF YOU DON'T KISS RIGHT, IT DOESN'T WORK RIGHT.
OH, IS THAT SO!?
STRAIN- ぐぐぐ...
OKAY, LET'S TRY THAT AGAIN! ♡
GRAB A COLD BATH, KONOKA!
POOF ポシュウウ..
AH, IT DISAPPEARED!
WAAAAAH!
NUTS. THOSE DARN CHEEK KISSES ARE COSTING ME.
NEGI DOESN'T KNOW EACH PROPER PROBATIONARY CARD...
NETS 50,000 ERMINE DOLLARS' BROKERAGE FEE FOR THE ERMINE SOCIETY.

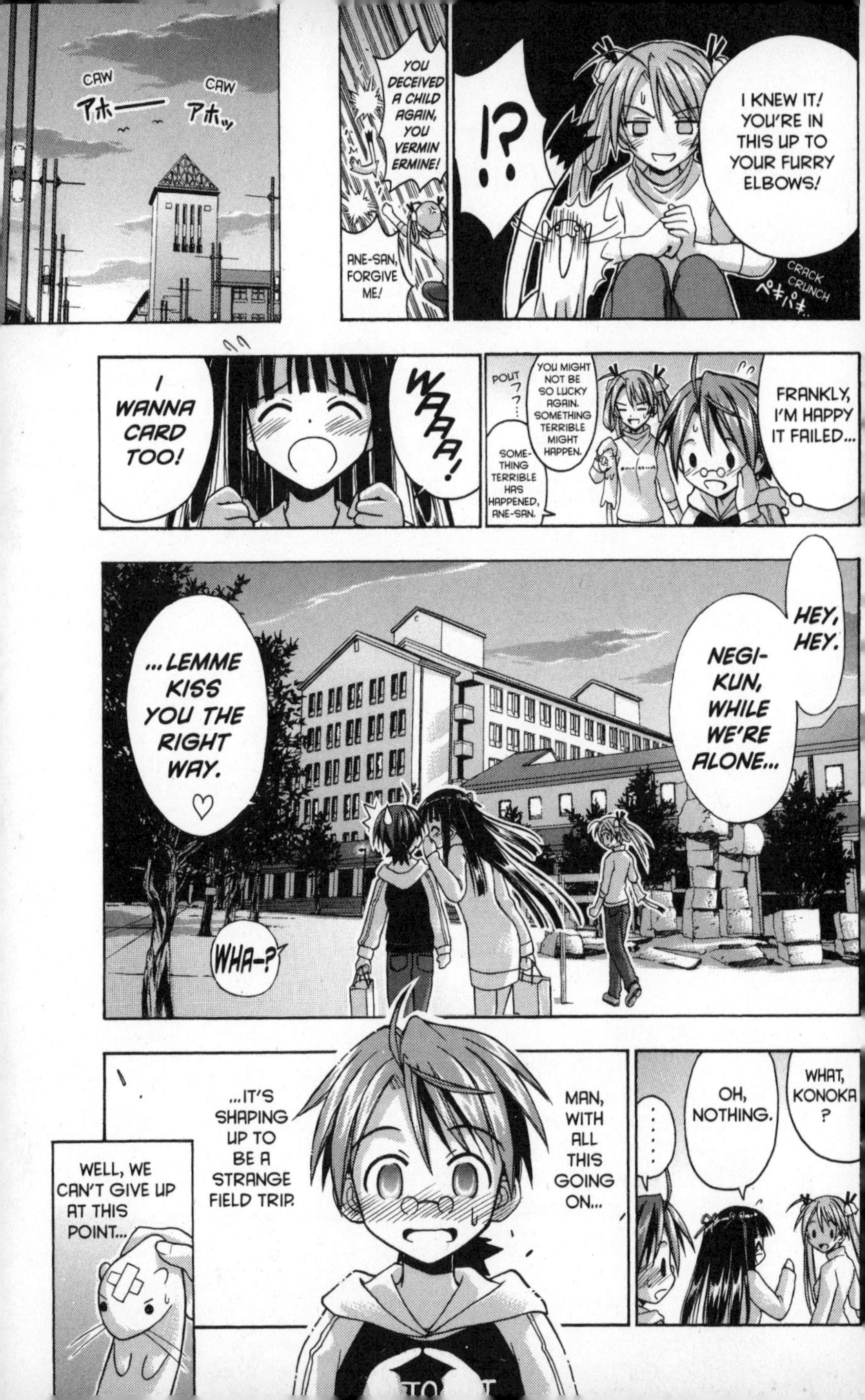
I KNEW IT! YOU'RE IN THIS UP TO YOUR FURRY ELBOWS!
CRACK CRUNCH ペキパキ..
!?
YOU DECEIVED A CHILD AGAIN, YOU VERMIN ERMINE!
ANE-SAN, FORGIVE ME!
CAW アホッ
CAW アホー
FRANKLY, I'M HAPPY IT FAILED...
YOU MIGHT NOT BE SO LUCKY AGAIN. SOMETHING TERRIBLE MIGHT HAPPEN.
POUT
SOMETHING TERRIBLE HAS HAPPENED, ANE-SAN.
WAAA!
I WANNA CARD TOO!
HEY, HEY.
NEGI-KUN, WHILE WE'RE ALONE...
...LEMME KISS YOU THE RIGHT WAY. ♡
WHA-?
WHAT, KONOKA?
OH, NOTHING.
......
MAN, WITH ALL THIS GOING ON...
...IT'S SHAPING UP TO BE A STRANGE FIELD TRIP.
WELL, WE CAN'T GIVE UP AT THIS POINT...

3-A STUDENT PROFILE

STUDENT NUMBER 7
MISA KAKIZAKI (MIDDLE)

BORN: MAY 15, 1988
BLOOD TYPE: O
ASTROLOGICAL SIGN: TAURUS
LIKES: PRUNES, SHOPPING
      (EVERY WEEKEND DOWNTOWN)
DISLIKES: CARBONATED DRINKS
AFFILIATIONS: MAHORA CHEERLEADING,
      CHORUS CLUB

STUDENT NUMBER 11
MADOKA KUGIMIYA (RIGHT)

BORN: MARCH 3, 1989
BLOOD TYPE: AB
ASTROLOGICAL SIGN: PISCES
LIKES: MATSUYA BEEF BOWL, SILVER
      ACCESSORIES, WESTERN MUSIC
      (LATELY, IT'S AVRIL LAVIGNE)
DISLIKES: SHOWY GUYS THAT COME AND
      HIT ON HER, HAS A COMPLEX ABOUT
      HER OWN HUSKY VOICE
AFFILIATIONS: MAHORA CHEERLEADING

STUDENT NUMBER 17
SAKURAKO SHIINA (LEFT)

BORN: JUNE 9, 1988
BLOOD TYPE: B
ASTROLOGICAL SIGN: GEMINI
LIKES: KARAOKE, COOKIE AND BIKKE (HER CATS)
DISLIKES: BLACK FURRY THINGS STARTLING
      HER IN PLACES LIKE THE KITCHEN
      (SPECIFICALLY, HER CATS)
AFFILIATIONS: MAHORA CHEERLEADING,
      LACROSSE CLUB

NEGIMA!

MAGISTER NEGI MAGI

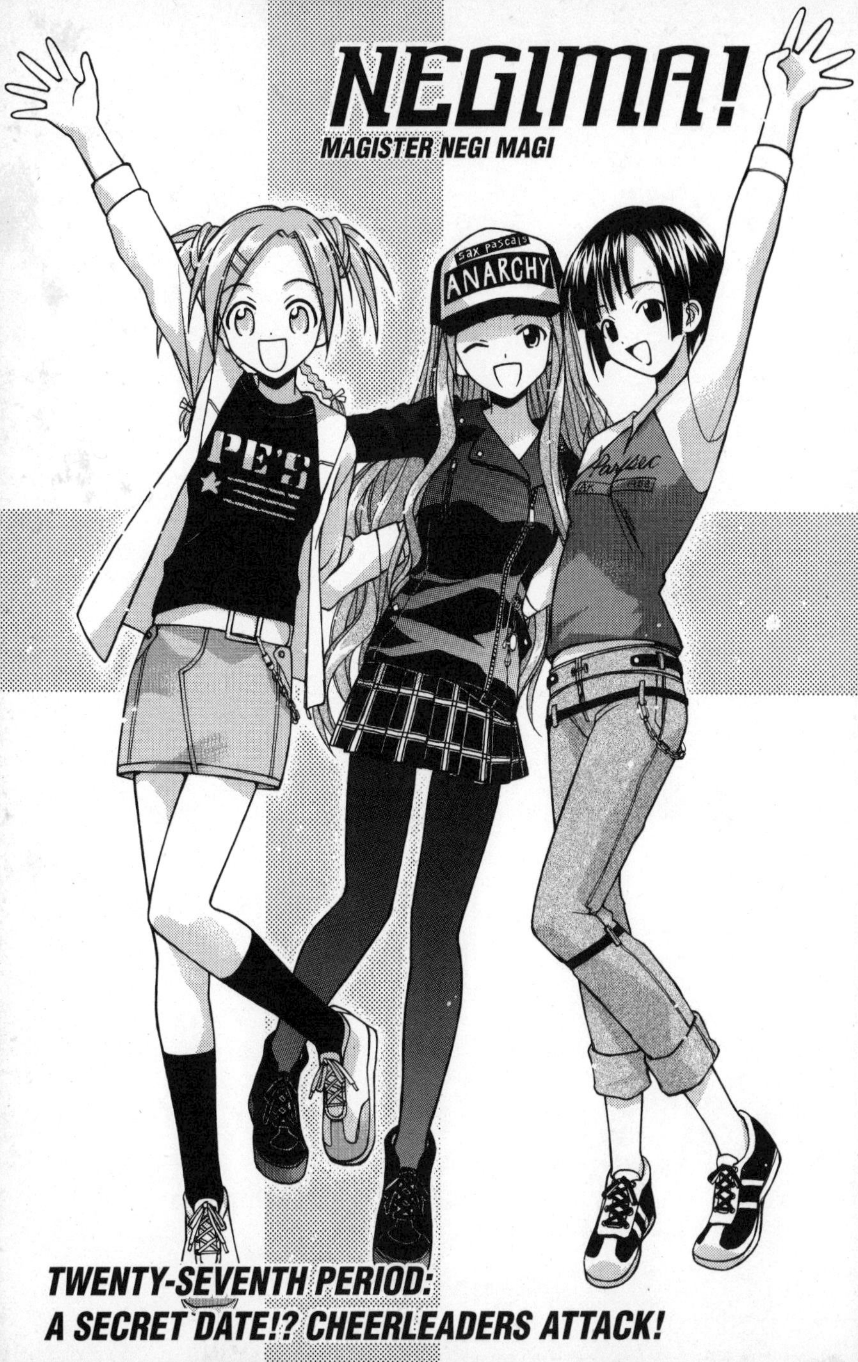
sax pascals
ANARCHY
PE'S

TWENTY-SEVENTH PERIOD: A SECRET DATE!? CHEERLEADERS ATTACK!

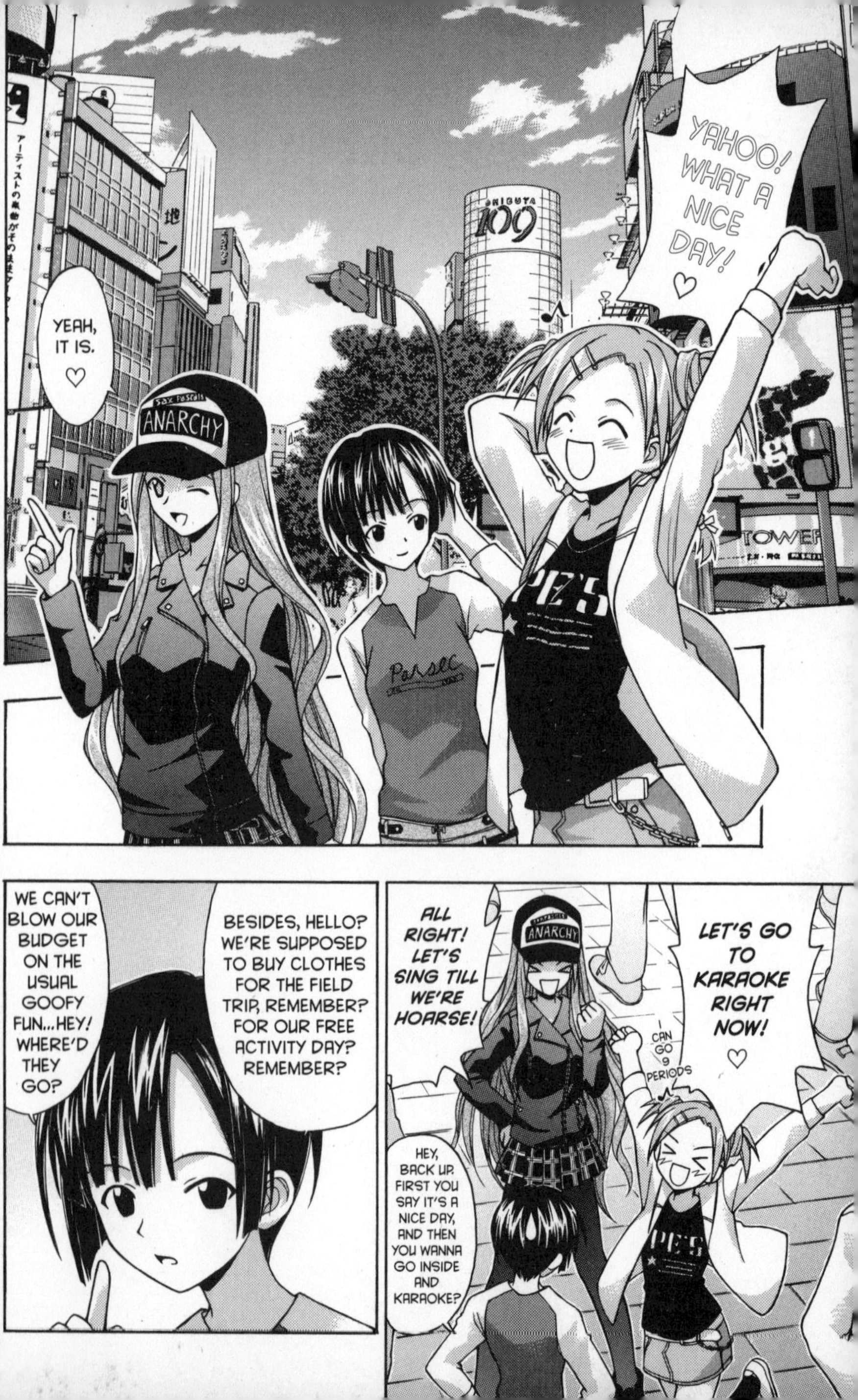
YAHOO! WHAT A NICE DAY! ♡
YEAH, IT IS. ♡
SHIBUYA 109
ANARCHY
TOWER
LET'S GO TO KARAOKE RIGHT NOW! ♡
I CAN GO 9 PERIODS
ALL RIGHT! LET'S SING TILL WE'RE HOARSE!
HEY, BACK UP. FIRST YOU SAY IT'S A NICE DAY, AND THEN YOU WANNA GO INSIDE AND KARAOKE?
BESIDES, HELLO? WE'RE SUPPOSED TO BUY CLOTHES FOR THE FIELD TRIP, REMEMBER? FOR OUR FREE ACTIVITY DAY? REMEMBER?
WE CAN'T BLOW OUR BUDGET ON THE USUAL GOOFY FUN...HEY! WHERE'D THEY GO?

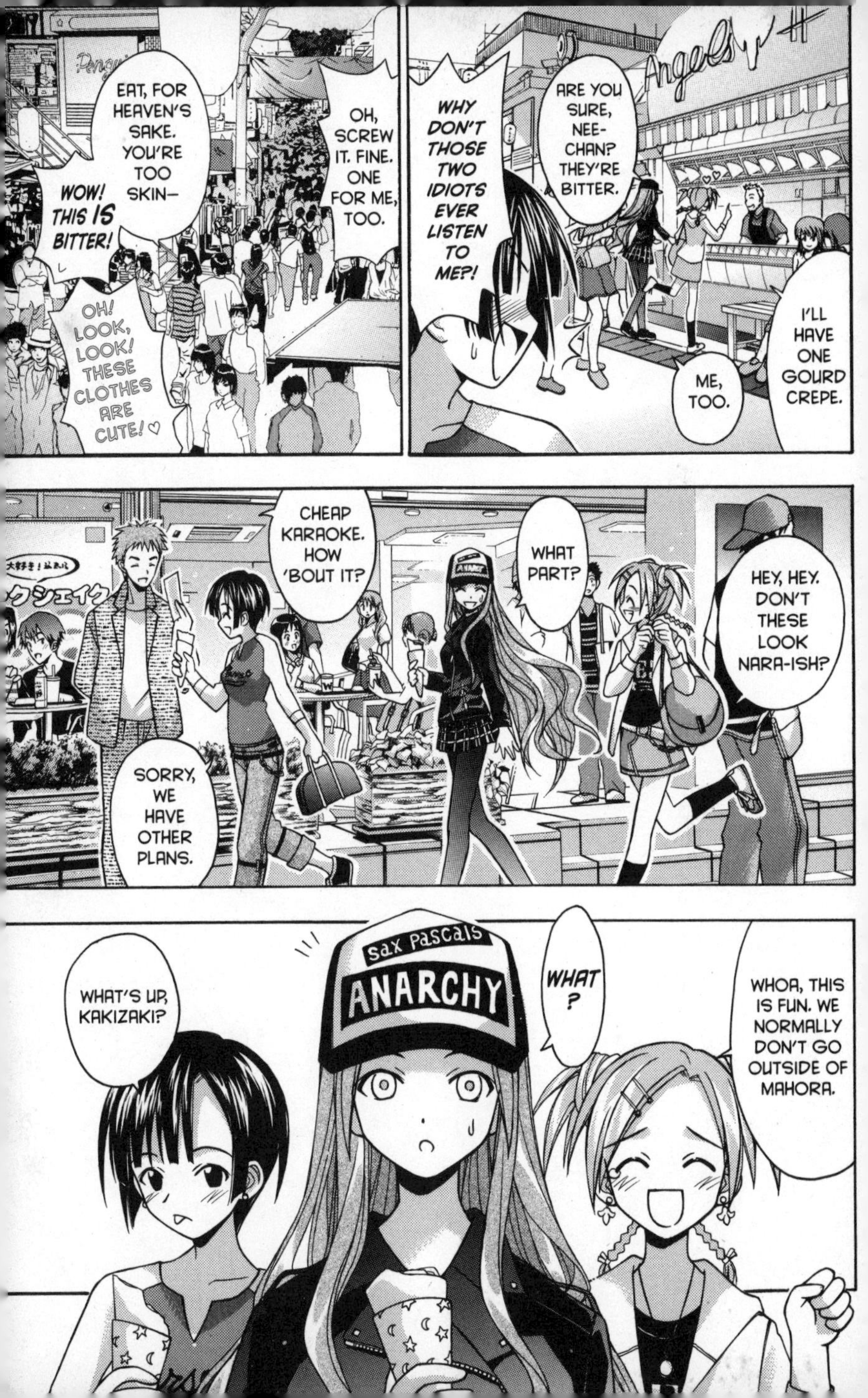
Angels
I'LL HAVE ONE GOURD CREPE.
ME, TOO.
ARE YOU SURE, NEE-CHAN? THEY'RE BITTER.
WHY DON'T THOSE TWO IDIOTS EVER LISTEN TO ME?!
OH, SCREW IT. FINE. ONE FOR ME, TOO.
EAT, FOR HEAVEN'S SAKE. YOU'RE TOO SKIN–
WOW! THIS IS BITTER!
OH! LOOK, LOOK! THESE CLOTHES ARE CUTE! ♡
HEY, HEY. DON'T THESE LOOK NARA-ISH?
WHAT PART?
CHEAP KARAOKE. HOW 'BOUT IT?
SORRY, WE HAVE OTHER PLANS.
WHOA, THIS IS FUN. WE NORMALLY DON'T GO OUTSIDE OF MAHORA.
WHAT?
sax pascals
ANARCHY
WHAT'S UP, KAKIZAKI?

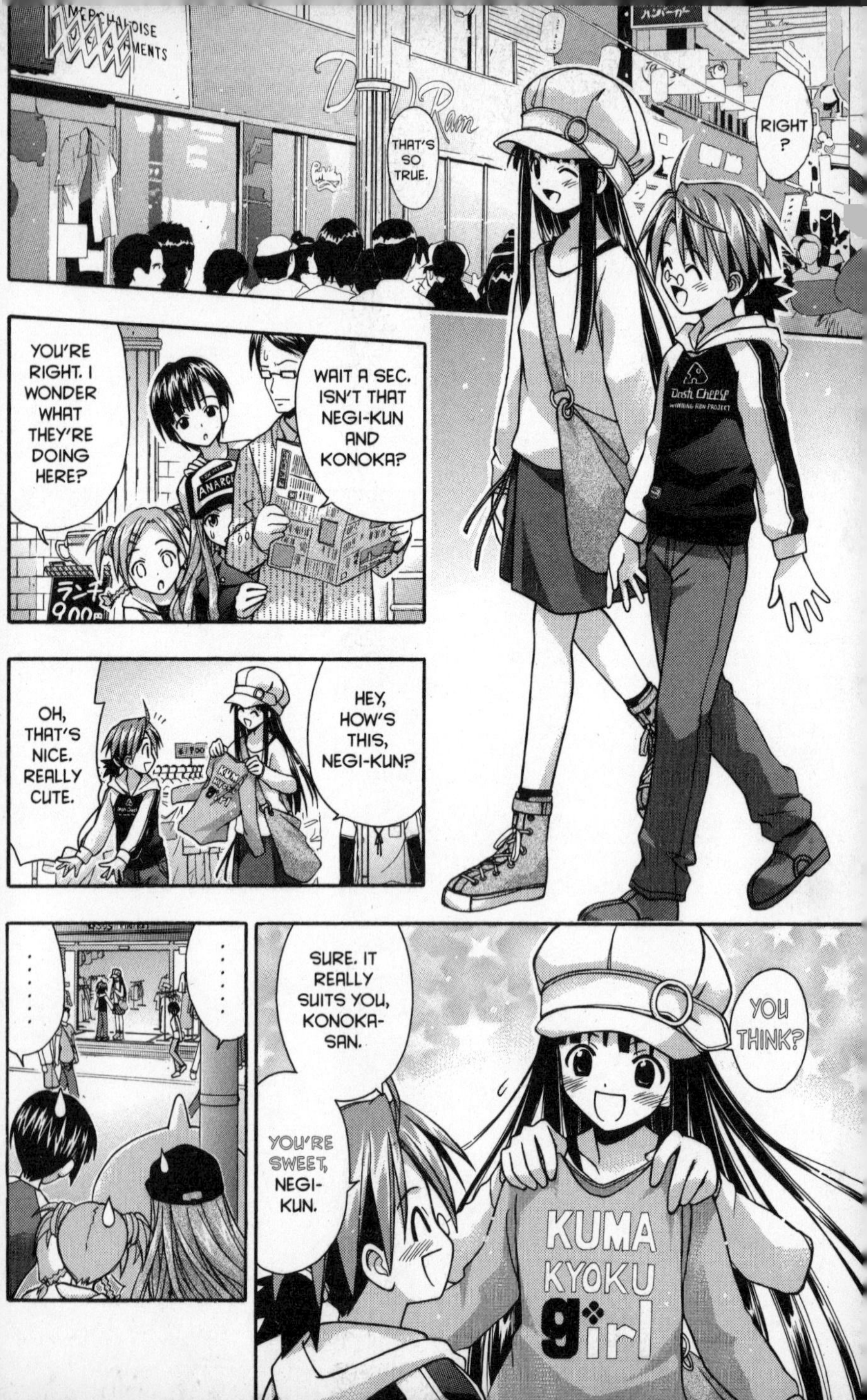
RIGHT?
THAT'S SO TRUE.
WAIT A SEC. ISN'T THAT NEGI-KUN AND KONOKA?
YOU'RE RIGHT. I WONDER WHAT THEY'RE DOING HERE?
HEY, HOW'S THIS, NEGI-KUN?
OH, THAT'S NICE. REALLY CUTE.
SURE. IT REALLY SUITS YOU, KONOKA-SAN.
YOU THINK?
YOU'RE SWEET, NEGI-KUN.
KUMA KYOKU girl
......
......

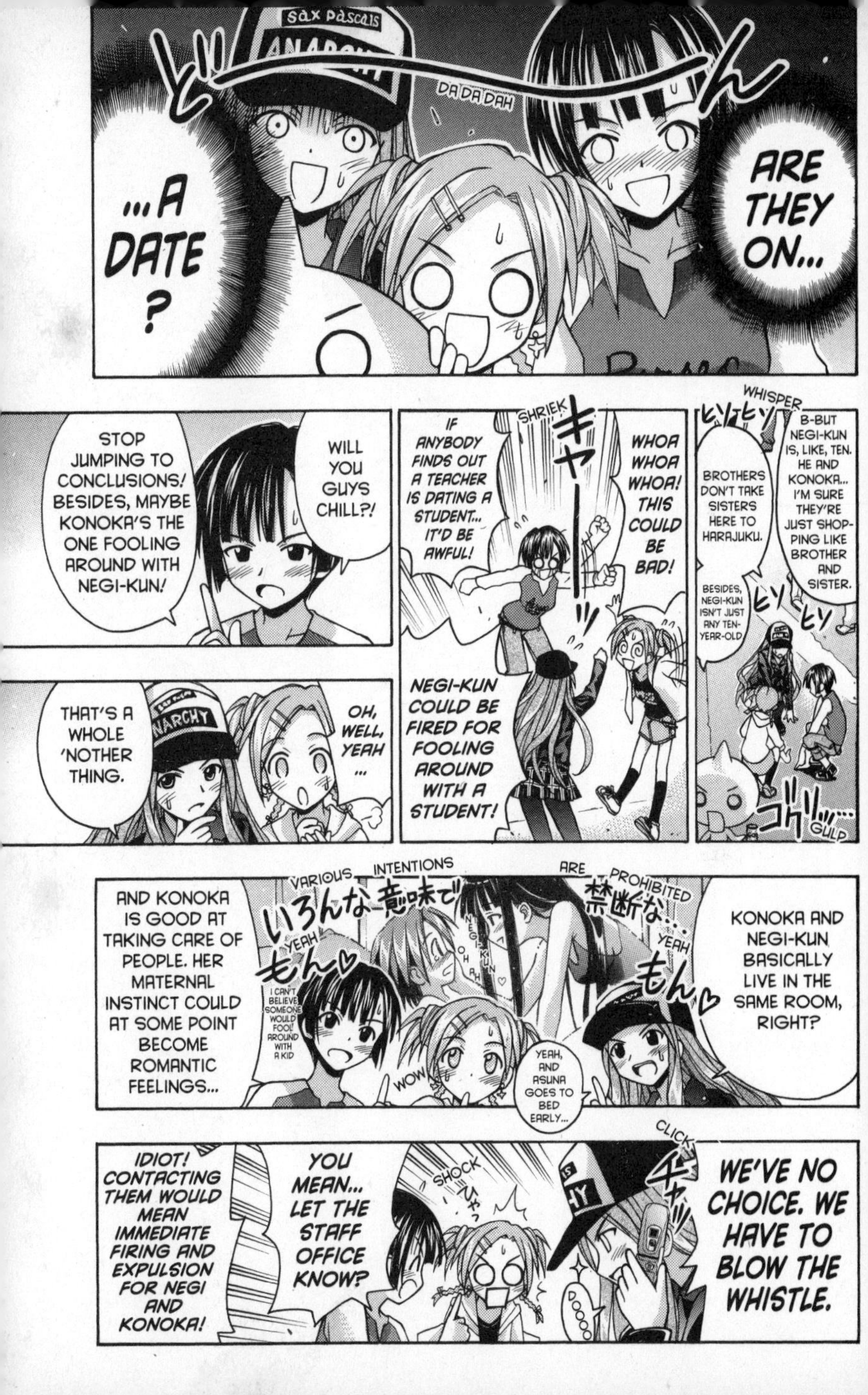

sax pascals
DA DA DAH
ARE THEY ON...
...A DATE?
WHISPER
B-BUT NEGI-KUN IS, LIKE, TEN. HE AND KONOKA... I'M SURE THEY'RE JUST SHOPPING LIKE BROTHER AND SISTER.
BROTHERS DON'T TAKE SISTERS HERE TO HARAJUKU.
BESIDES, NEGI-KUN ISN'T JUST ANY TEN-YEAR-OLD
GULP
SHRIEK
WHOA WHOA WHOA! THIS COULD BE BAD!
IF ANYBODY FINDS OUT A TEACHER IS DATING A STUDENT... IT'D BE AWFUL!
NEGI-KUN COULD BE FIRED FOR FOOLING AROUND WITH A STUDENT!
WILL YOU GUYS CHILL?!
STOP JUMPING TO CONCLUSIONS! BESIDES, MAYBE KONOKA'S THE ONE FOOLING AROUND WITH NEGI-KUN!
OH, WELL, YEAH...
THAT'S A WHOLE 'NOTHER THING.
KONOKA AND NEGI-KUN BASICALLY LIVE IN THE SAME ROOM, RIGHT?
PROHIBITED
禁断な…
ARE
YEAH
もん♥
YEAH, AND ASUNA GOES TO BED EARLY...
INTENTIONS
VARIOUS
いろんな意味で
NEGI-KUN
OH AH
WOW
YEAH
もん♥
I CAN'T BELIEVE SOMEONE WOULD FOOL AROUND WITH A KID
AND KONOKA IS GOOD AT TAKING CARE OF PEOPLE. HER MATERNAL INSTINCT COULD AT SOME POINT BECOME ROMANTIC FEELINGS...
CLICK
WE'VE NO CHOICE. WE HAVE TO BLOW THE WHISTLE.
DOOOO
SHOCK
YOU MEAN... LET THE STAFF OFFICE KNOW?
IDIOT! CONTACTING THEM WOULD MEAN IMMEDIATE FIRING AND EXPULSION FOR NEGI AND KONOKA!

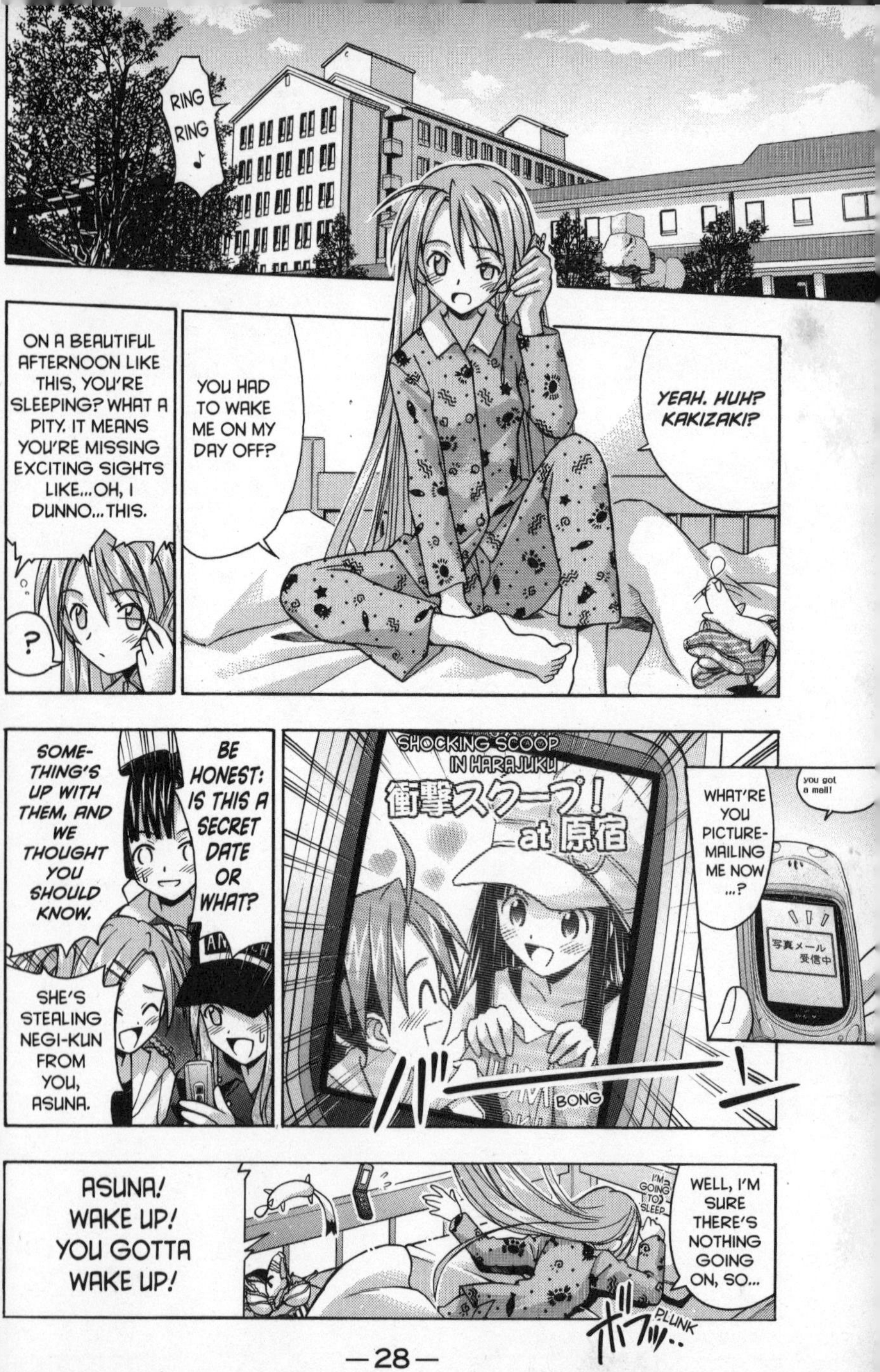
RING RING ♪
YEAH. HUH? KAKIZAKI?
YOU HAD TO WAKE ME ON MY DAY OFF?
ON A BEAUTIFUL AFTERNOON LIKE THIS, YOU'RE SLEEPING? WHAT A PITY. IT MEANS YOU'RE MISSING EXCITING SIGHTS LIKE...OH, I DUNNO...THIS.
?
you got a mail!
WHAT'RE YOU PICTURE-MAILING ME NOW ...?
写真メール受信中
SHOCKING SCOOP IN HARAJUKU
衝撃スクープ！ at 原宿
BONG
BE HONEST: IS THIS A SECRET DATE OR WHAT?
SOME-THING'S UP WITH THEM, AND WE THOUGHT YOU SHOULD KNOW.
SHE'S STEALING NEGI-KUN FROM YOU, ASUNA.
WELL, I'M SURE THERE'S NOTHING GOING ON, SO...
I'M GOING TO SLEEP
PLUNK
ASUNA! WAKE UP! YOU GOTTA WAKE UP!

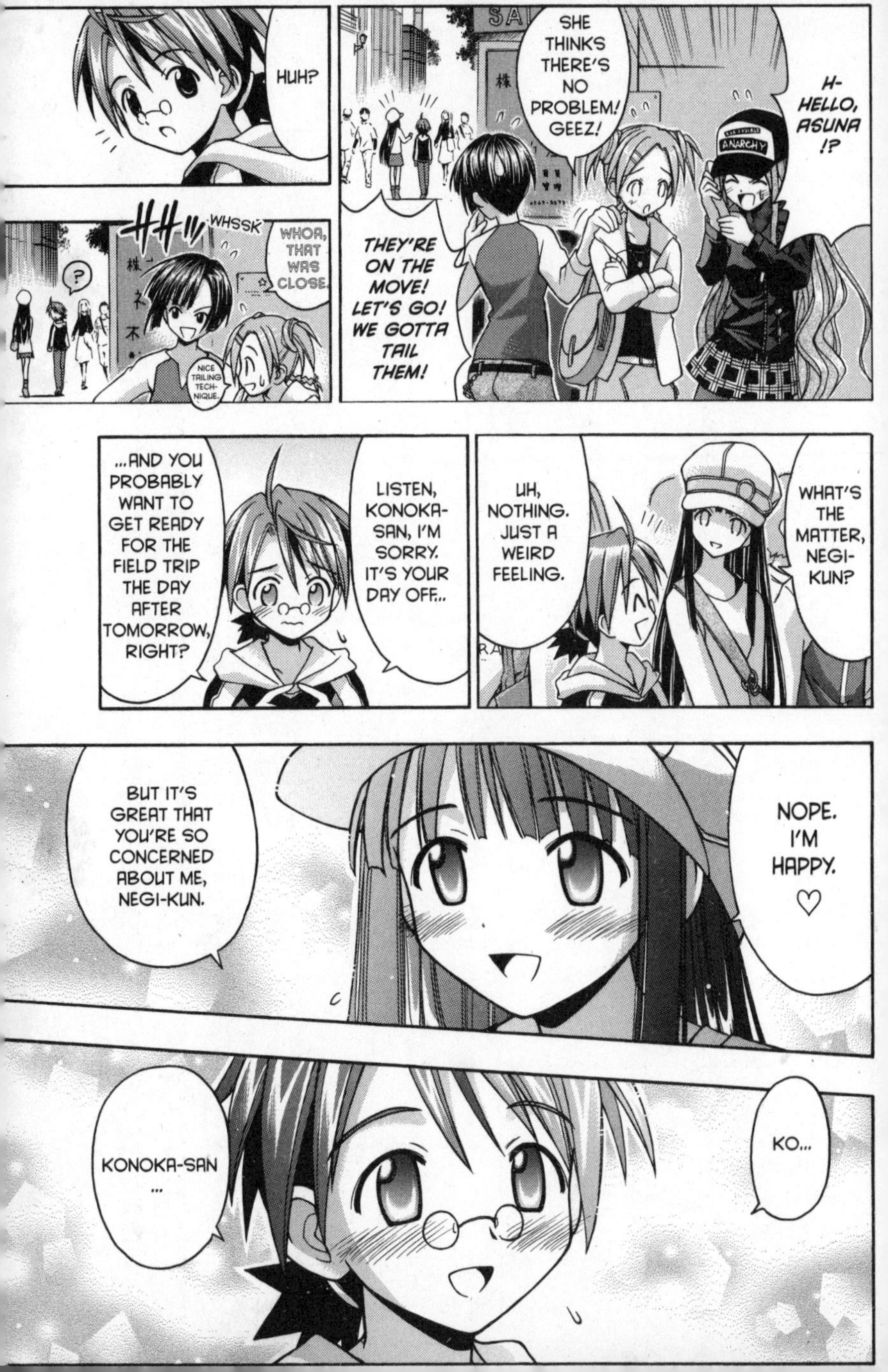
H-HELLO, ASUNA!?
SHE THINKS THERE'S NO PROBLEM! GEEZ!
THEY'RE ON THE MOVE! LET'S GO! WE GOTTA TAIL THEM!
HUH?
WHSSK
WHOA, THAT WAS CLOSE.
NICE TAILING TECHNIQUE.
WHAT'S THE MATTER, NEGI-KUN?
UH, NOTHING. JUST A WEIRD FEELING.
LISTEN, KONOKA-SAN, I'M SORRY. IT'S YOUR DAY OFF...
...AND YOU PROBABLY WANT TO GET READY FOR THE FIELD TRIP THE DAY AFTER TOMORROW, RIGHT?
NOPE. I'M HAPPY. ♡
BUT IT'S GREAT THAT YOU'RE SO CONCERNED ABOUT ME, NEGI-KUN.
KO...
KONOKA-SAN...

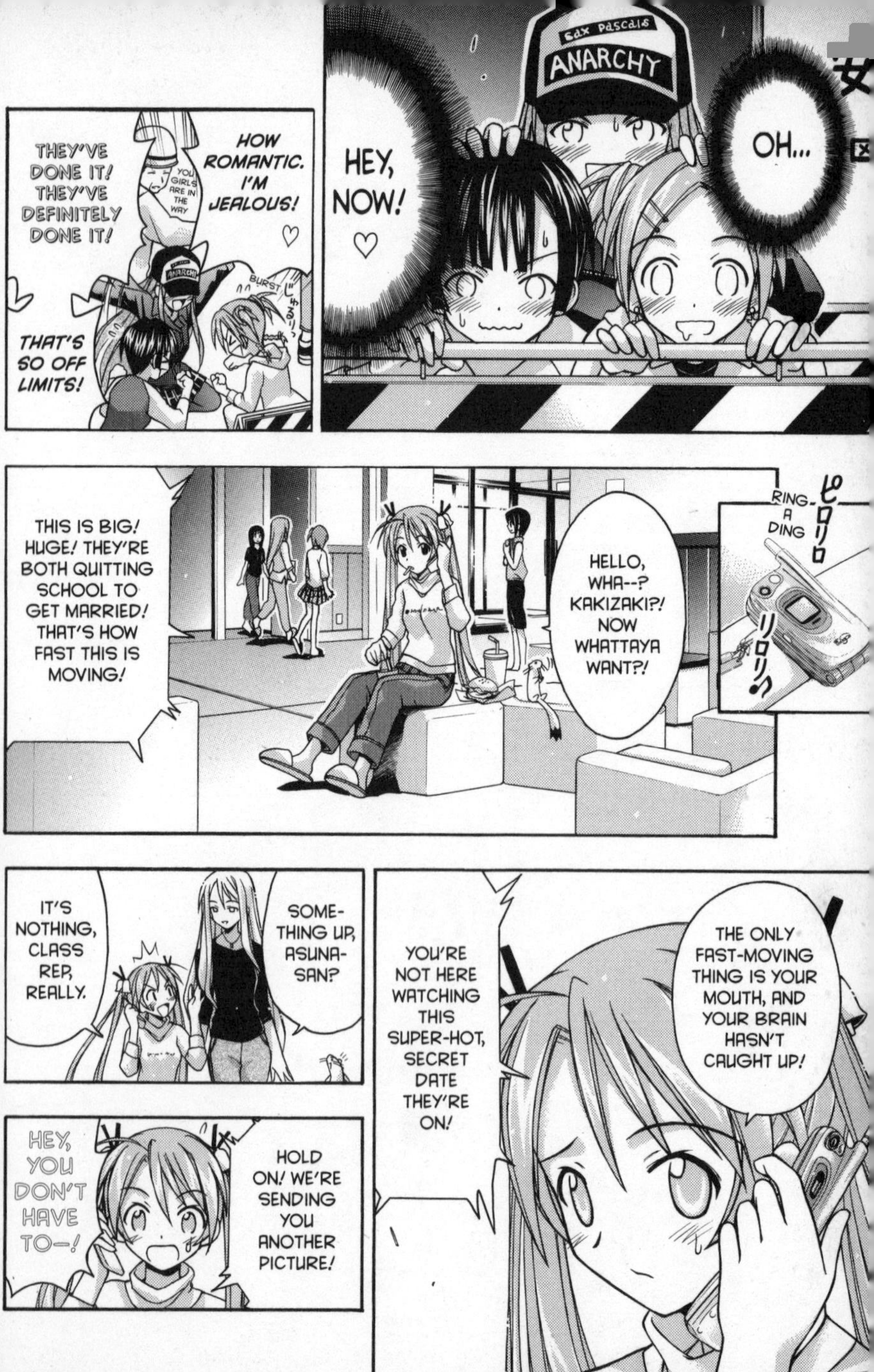
sax pascals
ANARCHY
OH...
HEY, NOW!
HOW ROMANTIC. I'M JEALOUS!
THEY'VE DONE IT! THEY'VE DEFINITELY DONE IT!
YOU GIRLS ARE IN THE WAY
BURST
THAT'S SO OFF LIMITS!
RING-A DING
HELLO, WHA--? KAKIZAKI?! NOW WHATTAYA WANT?!
THIS IS BIG! HUGE! THEY'RE BOTH QUITTING SCHOOL TO GET MARRIED! THAT'S HOW FAST THIS IS MOVING!
THE ONLY FAST-MOVING THING IS YOUR MOUTH, AND YOUR BRAIN HASN'T CAUGHT UP!
YOU'RE NOT HERE WATCHING THIS SUPER-HOT, SECRET DATE THEY'RE ON!
SOME-THING UP, ASUNA-SAN?
IT'S NOTHING, CLASS REP, REALLY.
HOLD ON! WE'RE SENDING YOU ANOTHER PICTURE!
HEY, YOU DON'T HAVE TO—!

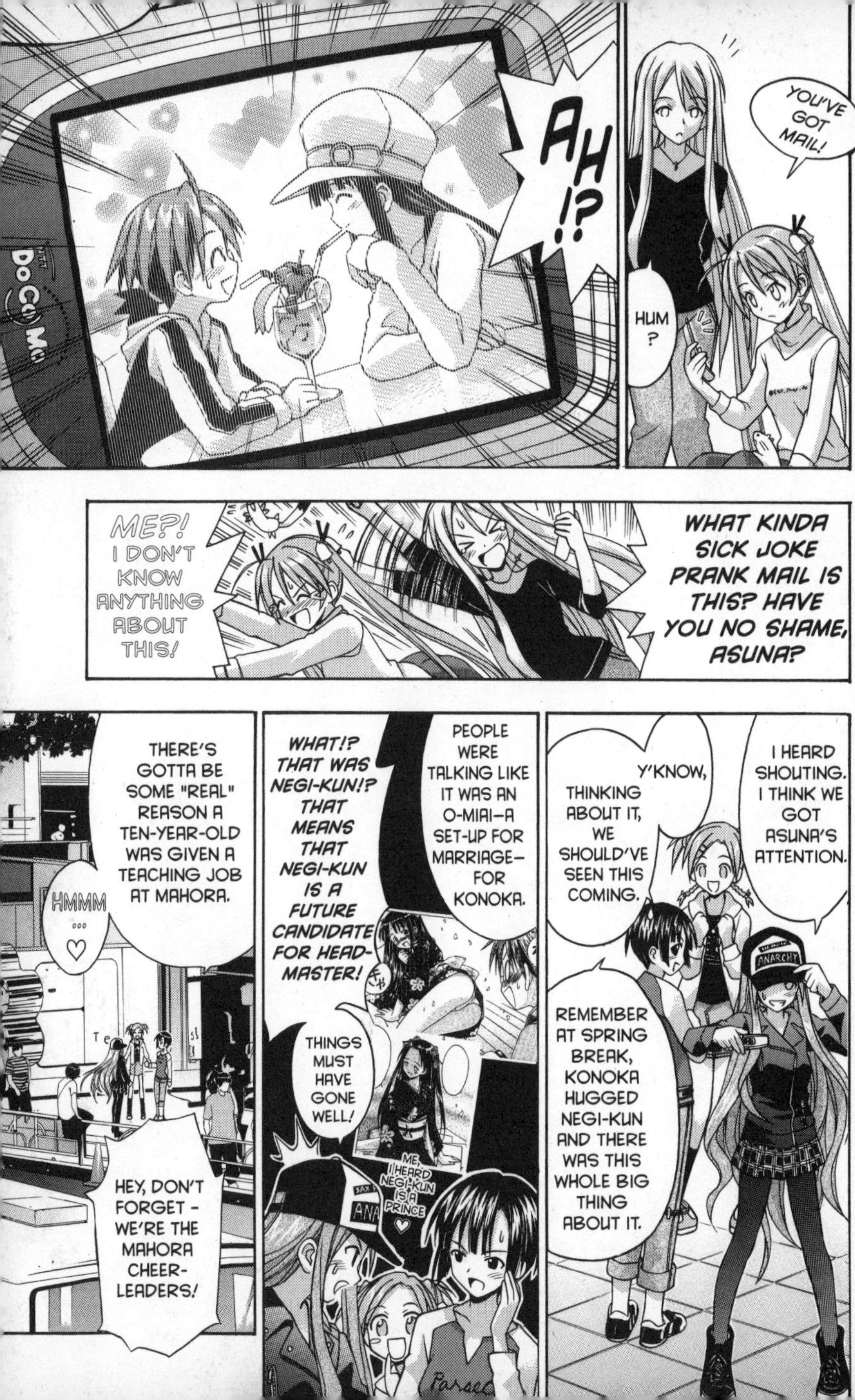
YOU'VE GOT MAIL!
HUM ?
NTT DoCoMo
AH !?
WHAT KINDA SICK JOKE PRANK MAIL IS THIS? HAVE YOU NO SHAME, ASUNA?
ME?! I DON'T KNOW ANYTHING ABOUT THIS!
I HEARD SHOUTING. I THINK WE GOT ASUNA'S ATTENTION.
Y'KNOW,
THINKING ABOUT IT, WE SHOULD'VE SEEN THIS COMING.
ANARCHY
REMEMBER AT SPRING BREAK, KONOKA HUGGED NEGI-KUN AND THERE WAS THIS WHOLE BIG THING ABOUT IT.
PEOPLE WERE TALKING LIKE IT WAS AN O-MIAI—A SET-UP FOR MARRIAGE—FOR KONOKA.
WHAT!? THAT WAS NEGI-KUN!? THAT MEANS THAT NEGI-KUN IS A FUTURE CANDIDATE FOR HEAD-MASTER!
THINGS MUST HAVE GONE WELL!
ME, I HEARD NEGI-KUN IS A PRINCE ♥
THERE'S GOTTA BE SOME "REAL" REASON A TEN-YEAR-OLD WAS GIVEN A TEACHING JOB AT MAHORA.
HMMM ... ♥
HEY, DON'T FORGET - WE'RE THE MAHORA CHEER-LEADERS!

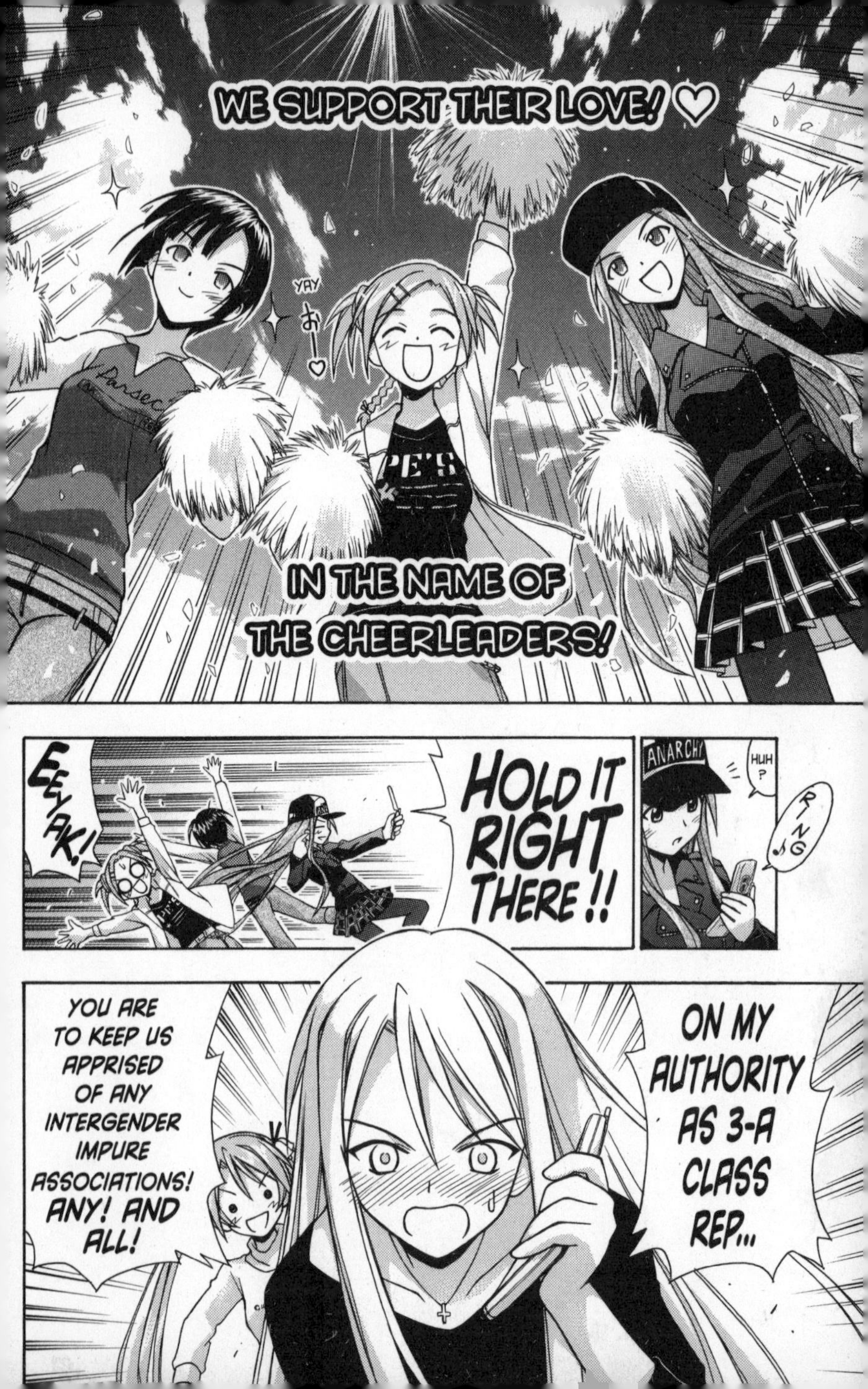
WE SUPPORT THEIR LOVE! ♡
YAY
お―♡
IN THE NAME OF THE CHEERLEADERS!
ANARCHY
HUH?
RING
HOLD IT RIGHT THERE!!
EEYAK!
ON MY AUTHORITY AS 3-A CLASS REP...
YOU ARE TO KEEP US APPRISED OF ANY INTERGENDER IMPURE ASSOCIATIONS! ANY! AND ALL!

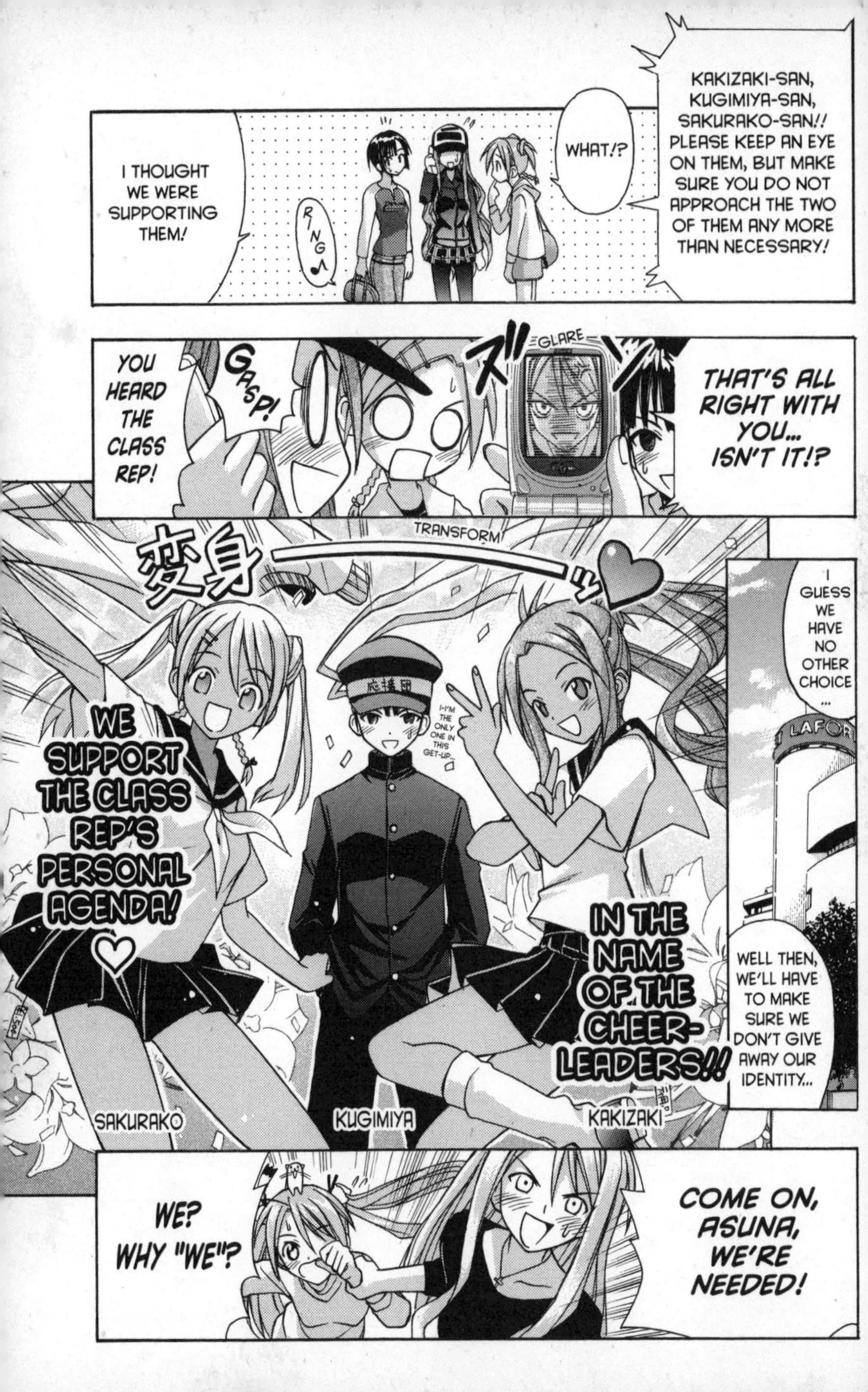
KAKIZAKI-SAN, KUGIMIYA-SAN, SAKURAKO-SAN!! PLEASE KEEP AN EYE ON THEM, BUT MAKE SURE YOU DO NOT APPROACH THE TWO OF THEM ANY MORE THAN NECESSARY!
WHAT!?
RING♪
I THOUGHT WE WERE SUPPORTING THEM!
THAT'S ALL RIGHT WITH YOU... ISN'T IT!?
GLARE
GASP!
YOU HEARD THE CLASS REP!
I GUESS WE HAVE NO OTHER CHOICE ...
WELL THEN, WE'LL HAVE TO MAKE SURE WE DON'T GIVE AWAY OUR IDENTITY...
変身
TRANSFORM
IN THE NAME OF THE CHEER-LEADERS!!
I-I'M THE ONLY ONE IN THIS GET-UP...
WE SUPPORT THE CLASS REP'S PERSONAL AGENDA! ♡
KAKIZAKI
KUGIMIYA
SAKURAKO
COME ON, ASUNA, WE'RE NEEDED!
WE? WHY "WE"?

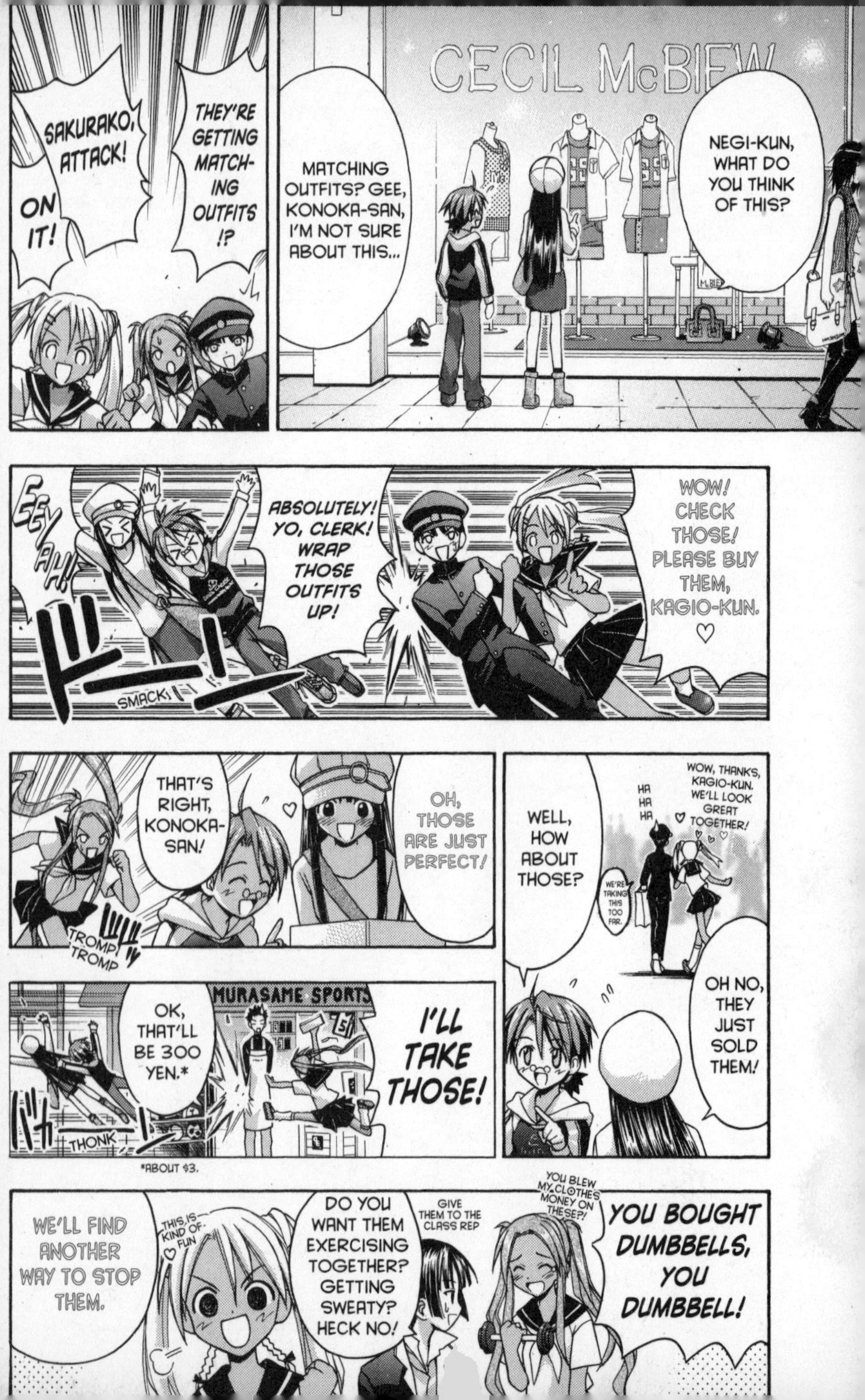
CECIL McBIEW
NEGI-KUN, WHAT DO YOU THINK OF THIS?
MATCHING OUTFITS? GEE, KONOKA-SAN, I'M NOT SURE ABOUT THIS...
THEY'RE GETTING MATCHING OUTFITS!?
SAKURAKO, ATTACK!
ON IT!
WOW! CHECK THOSE! PLEASE BUY THEM, KAGIO-KUN. ♡
ABSOLUTELY! YO, CLERK! WRAP THOSE OUTFITS UP!
EEYAAH!!
SMACK!
WOW, THANKS, KAGIO-KUN. WE'LL LOOK GREAT TOGETHER! ♡
HA HA HA
WE'RE TAKING THIS TOO FAR.
WELL, HOW ABOUT THOSE?
OH, THOSE ARE JUST PERFECT!
THAT'S RIGHT, KONOKA-SAN!
TROMP TROMP
I'LL TAKE THOSE!
MURASAME SPORTS
OK, THAT'LL BE 300 YEN.*
THONK
OH NO, THEY JUST SOLD THEM!
YOU BOUGHT DUMBBELLS, YOU DUMBBELL!
YOU BLEW MY CLOTHES MONEY ON THESE?!
GIVE THEM TO THE CLASS REP
DO YOU WANT THEM EXERCISING TOGETHER? GETTING SWEATY? HECK NO!
THIS IS KIND OF FUN ♡
WE'LL FIND ANOTHER WAY TO STOP THEM.

*ABOUT $3.

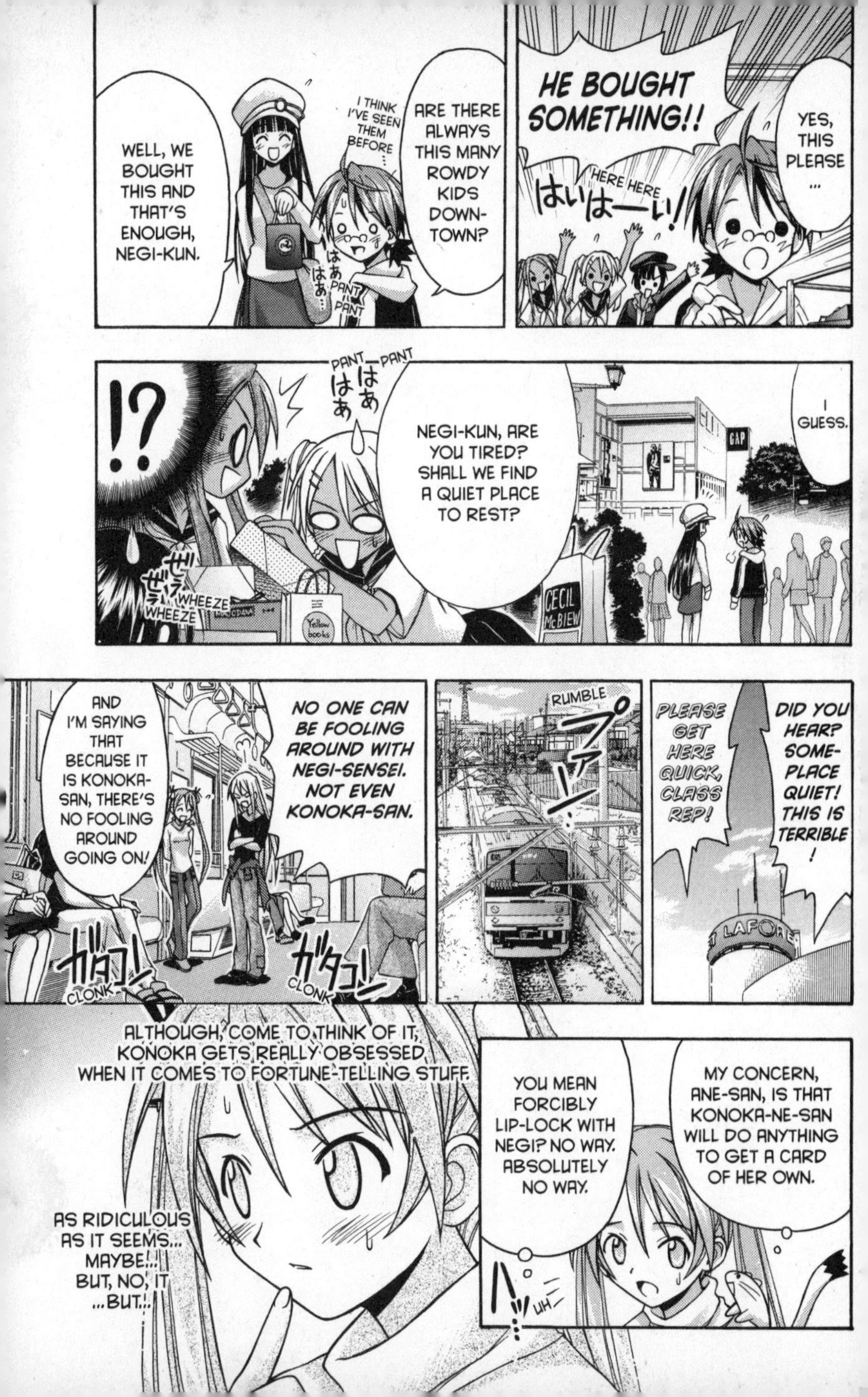
YES, THIS PLEASE ...
HERE HERE
はいはーい!
HE BOUGHT SOMETHING!!
ARE THERE ALWAYS THIS MANY ROWDY KIDS DOWN-TOWN?
I THINK I'VE SEEN THEM BEFORE ...
はぁはぁ...
PANT PANT
WELL, WE BOUGHT THIS AND THAT'S ENOUGH, NEGI-KUN.
I GUESS.
NEGI-KUN, ARE YOU TIRED? SHALL WE FIND A QUIET PLACE TO REST?
はぁはぁ
PANT PANT
!?
ぜぇぜぇ
WHEEZE WHEEZE
DID YOU HEAR? SOME-PLACE QUIET! THIS IS TERRIBLE!
PLEASE GET HERE QUICK, CLASS REP!
RUMBLE
プアン
NO ONE CAN BE FOOLING AROUND WITH NEGI-SENSEI. NOT EVEN KONOKA-SAN.
AND I'M SAYING THAT BECAUSE IT IS KONOKA-SAN, THERE'S NO FOOLING AROUND GOING ON!
ガタコン
CLONK
ガタコン
CLONK
MY CONCERN, ANE-SAN, IS THAT KONOKA-NE-SAN WILL DO ANYTHING TO GET A CARD OF HER OWN.
YOU MEAN FORCIBLY LIP-LOCK WITH NEGI? NO WAY. ABSOLUTELY NO WAY.
ハッ
UH
ALTHOUGH, COME TO THINK OF IT, KONOKA GETS REALLY OBSESSED WHEN IT COMES TO FORTUNE-TELLING STUFF.
AS RIDICULOUS AS IT SEEMS... MAYBE... BUT, NO, IT ...BUT...

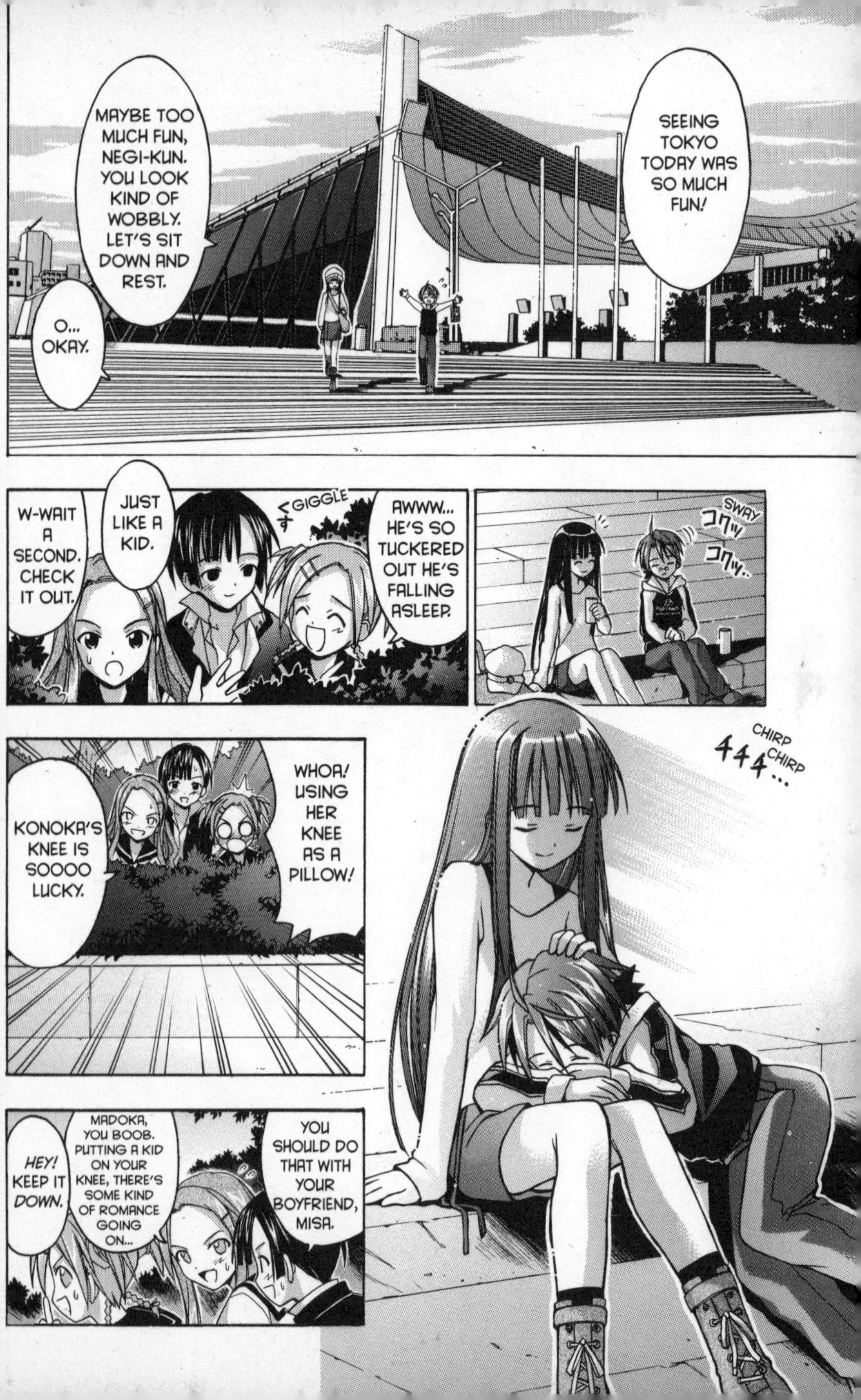
SEEING TOKYO TODAY WAS SO MUCH FUN!
MAYBE TOO MUCH FUN, NEGI-KUN. YOU LOOK KIND OF WOBBLY. LET'S SIT DOWN AND REST.
O... OKAY.
SWAY
コクッ コクッ..
AWWW... HE'S SO TUCKERED OUT HE'S FALLING ASLEEP.
GIGGLE
JUST LIKE A KID.
W-WAIT A SECOND. CHECK IT OUT.
CHIRP CHIRP
WHOA! USING HER KNEE AS A PILLOW!
KONOKA'S KNEE IS SOOOO LUCKY.
YOU SHOULD DO THAT WITH YOUR BOYFRIEND, MISA.
MADOKA, YOU BOOB. PUTTING A KID ON YOUR KNEE, THERE'S SOME KIND OF ROMANCE GOING ON...
HEY! KEEP IT DOWN.

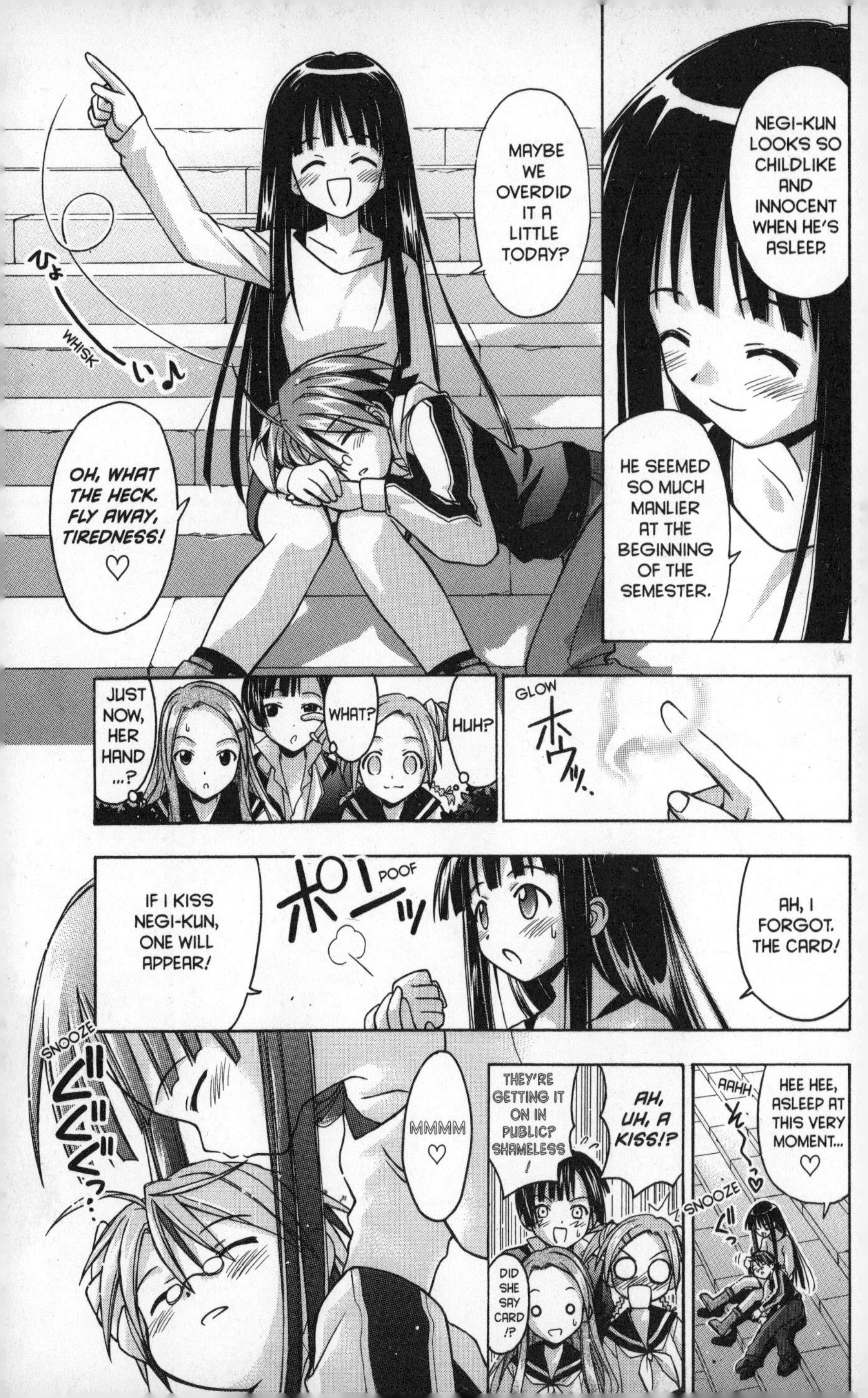
NEGI-KUN LOOKS SO CHILDLIKE AND INNOCENT WHEN HE'S ASLEEP.
HE SEEMED SO MUCH MANLIER AT THE BEGINNING OF THE SEMESTER.
MAYBE WE OVERDID IT A LITTLE TODAY?
ひょーーい♪
WHISK
OH, WHAT THE HECK. FLY AWAY, TIREDNESS! ♡
GLOW
ホウッ..
HUH?
WHAT?
JUST NOW, HER HAND ...?
AH, I FORGOT. THE CARD!
POOF
ポーッ
IF I KISS NEGI-KUN, ONE WILL APPEAR!
HEE HEE, ASLEEP AT THIS VERY MOMENT... ♡
AAHH
SNOOZE
AH, UH, A KISS!?
THEY'RE GETTING IT ON IN PUBLIC? SHAMELESS!
DID SHE SAY CARD!?
MMMM ♡
SNOOZE

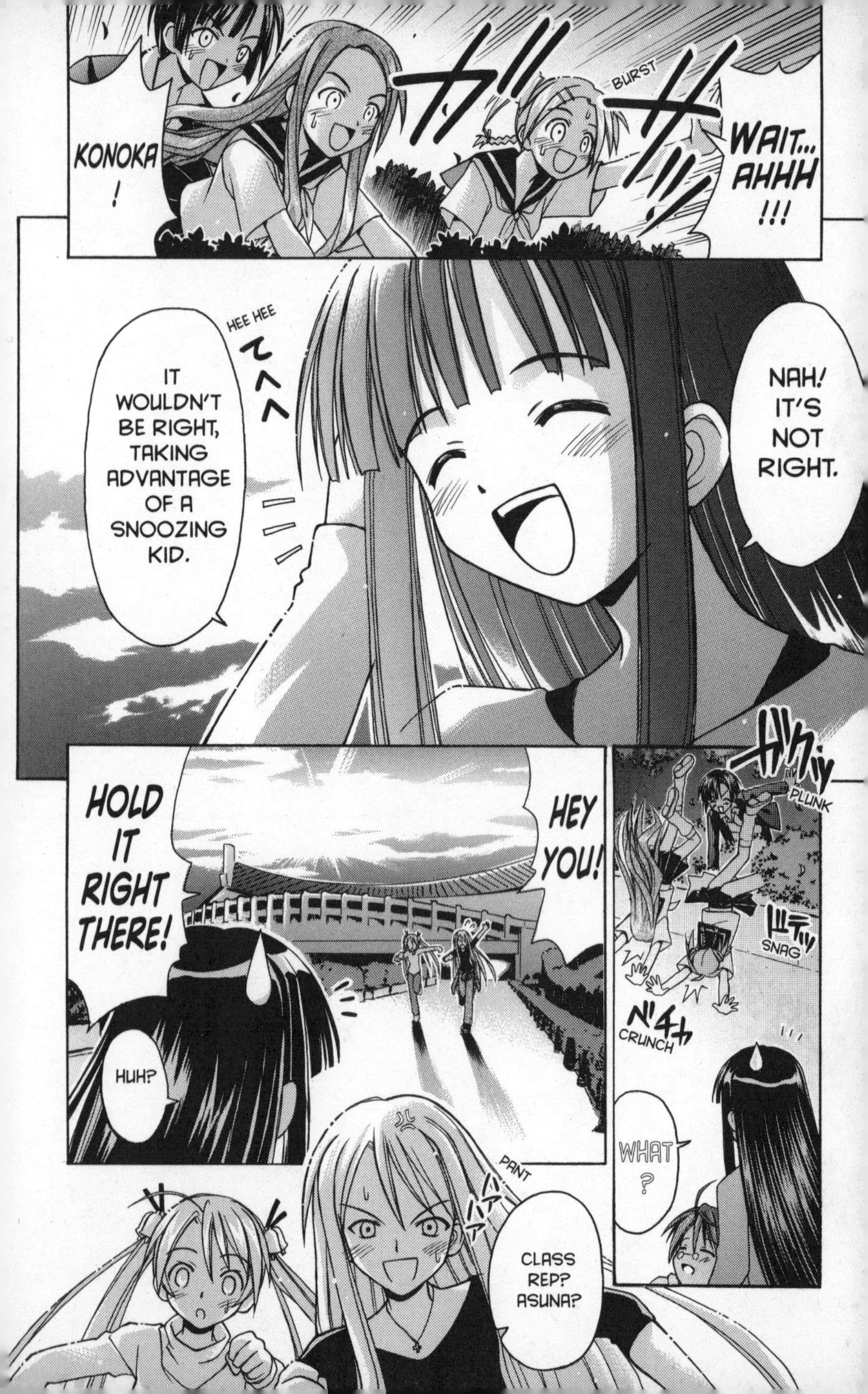

WAIT... AHHH !!!
BURST
KONOKA !
NAH! IT'S NOT RIGHT.
HEE HEE
IT WOULDN'T BE RIGHT, TAKING ADVANTAGE OF A SNOOZING KID.
PLUNK
SNAG
CRUNCH
WHAT ?
HEY YOU!
HOLD IT RIGHT THERE!
HUH?
PANT
CLASS REP? ASUNA?

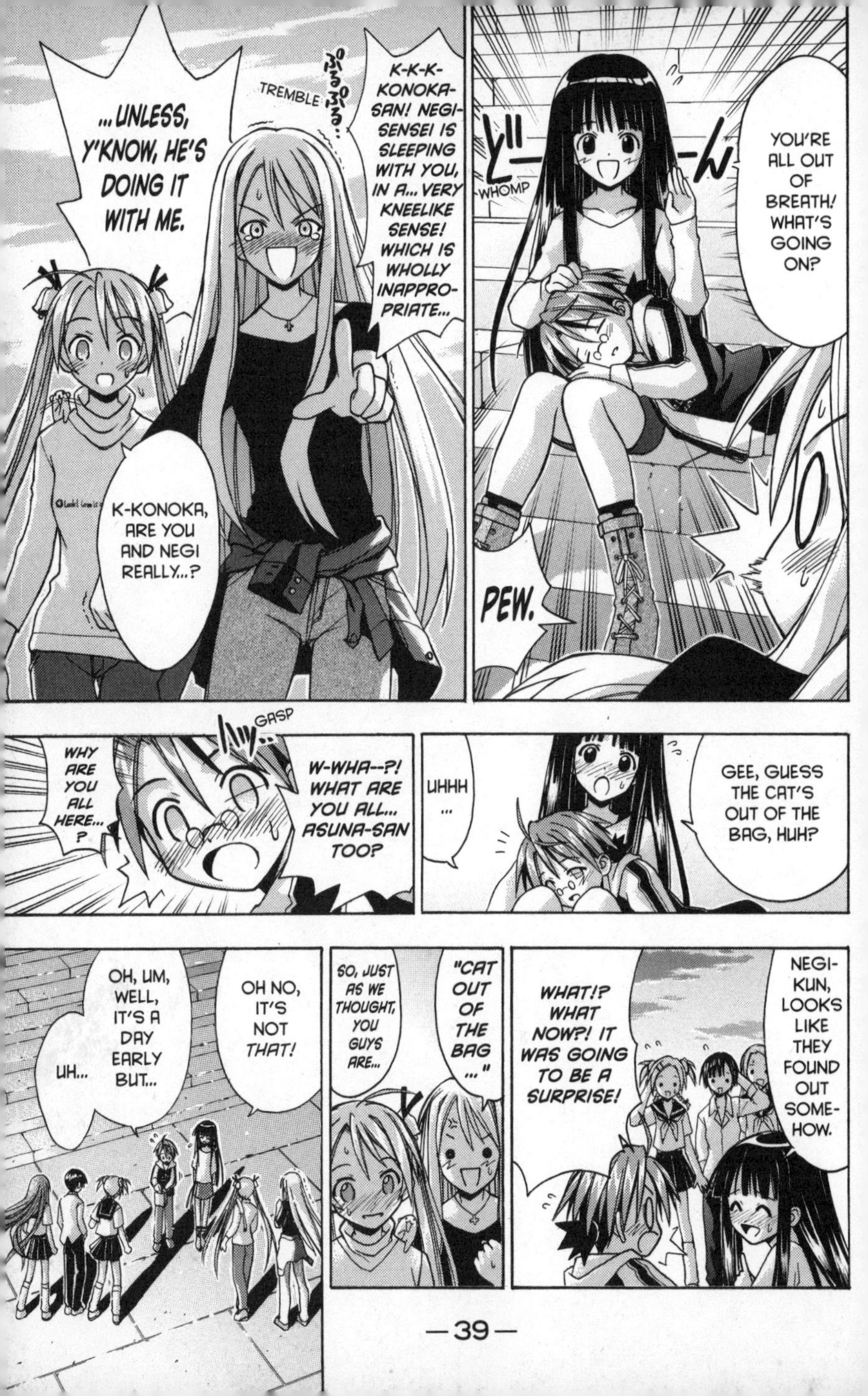
YOU'RE ALL OUT OF BREATH! WHAT'S GOING ON?
WHOMP
PEW.
K-K-K-KONOKA-SAN! NEGI-SENSEI IS SLEEPING WITH YOU, IN A... VERY KNEELIKE SENSE! WHICH IS WHOLLY INAPPROPRIATE...
TREMBLE
...UNLESS, Y'KNOW, HE'S DOING IT WITH ME.
K-KONOKA, ARE YOU AND NEGI REALLY...?
GEE, GUESS THE CAT'S OUT OF THE BAG, HUH?
UHHH ...
GASP
W-WHA--?! WHAT ARE YOU ALL... ASUNA-SAN TOO?
WHY ARE YOU ALL HERE... ?
NEGI-KUN, LOOKS LIKE THEY FOUND OUT SOMEHOW.
WHAT!? WHAT NOW?! IT WAS GOING TO BE A SURPRISE!
"CAT OUT OF THE BAG ..."
SO, JUST AS WE THOUGHT, YOU GUYS ARE...
OH NO, IT'S NOT THAT!
OH, UM, WELL, IT'S A DAY EARLY BUT...
UH...

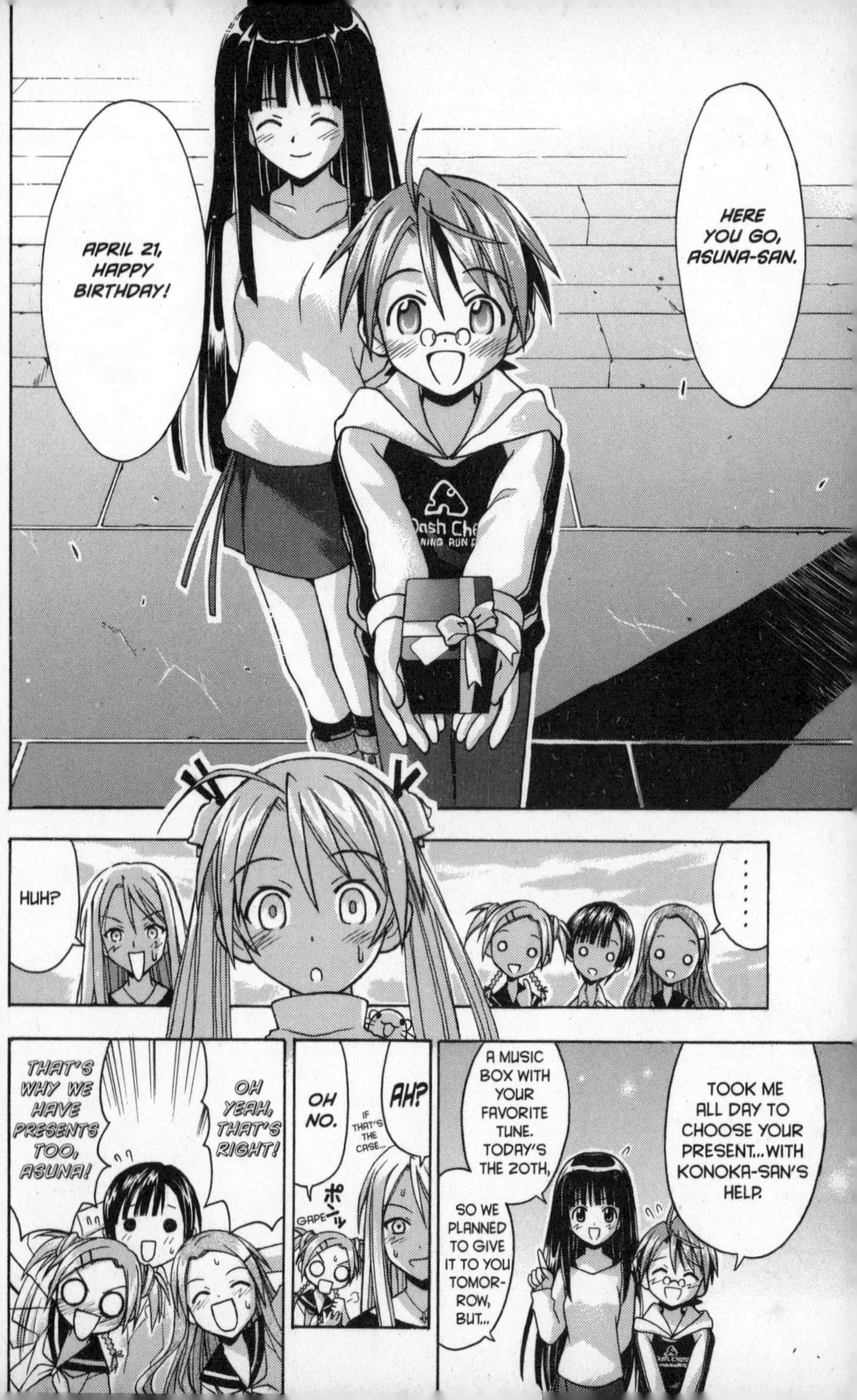
HERE YOU GO, ASUNA-SAN.
APRIL 21, HAPPY BIRTHDAY!
......
HUH?
TOOK ME ALL DAY TO CHOOSE YOUR PRESENT...WITH KONOKA-SAN'S HELP.
A MUSIC BOX WITH YOUR FAVORITE TUNE. TODAY'S THE 20TH,
SO WE PLANNED TO GIVE IT TO YOU TOMOR-ROW, BUT...
AH?
IF THAT'S THE CASE...
OH NO.
GAPE
OH YEAH, THAT'S RIGHT!
THAT'S WHY WE HAVE PRESENTS TOO, ASUNA!

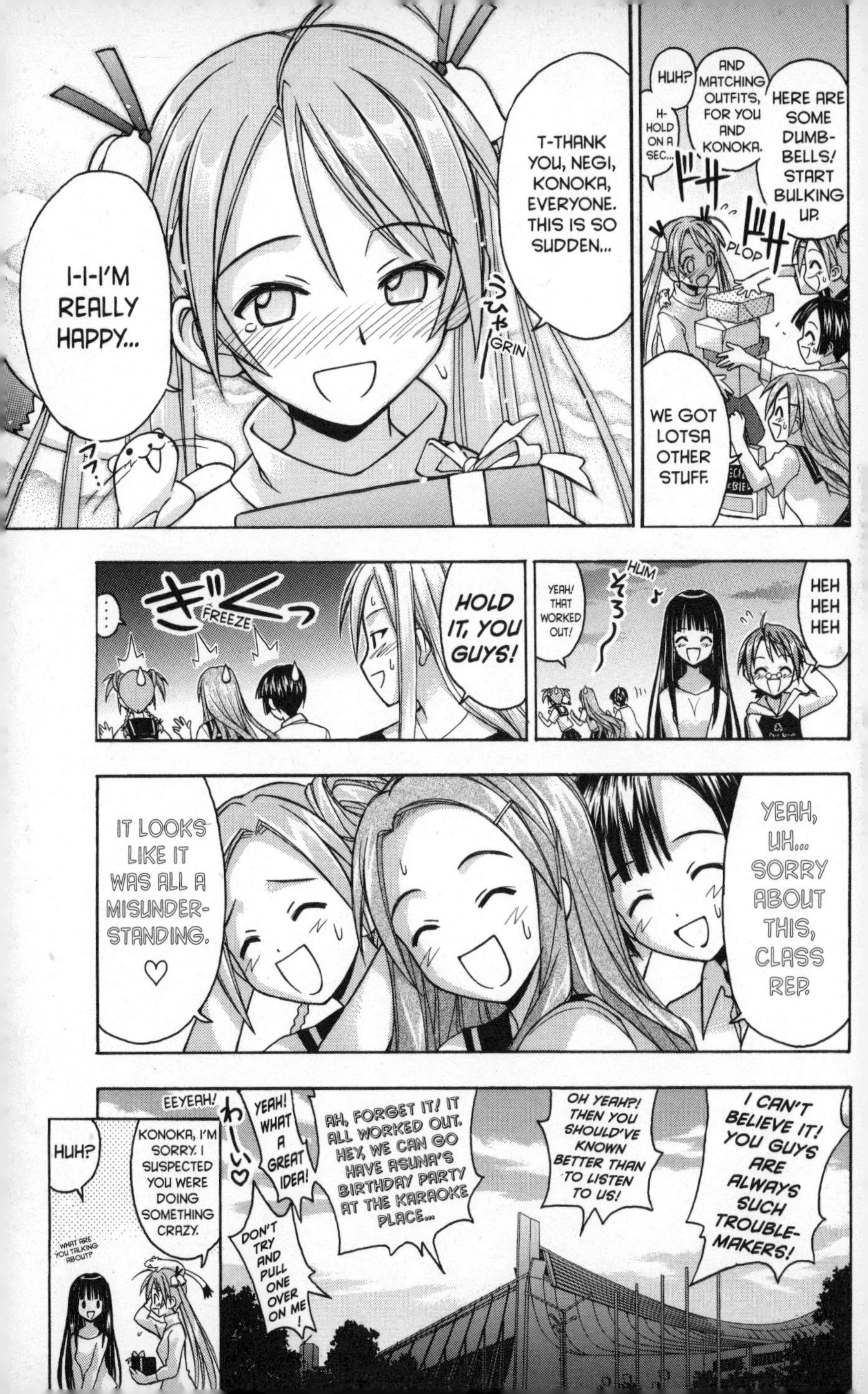
HERE ARE SOME DUMB-BELLS! START BULKING UP.
AND MATCHING OUTFITS, FOR YOU AND KONOKA.
HUH?
H-HOLD ON A SEC...
PLOP
WE GOT LOTSA OTHER STUFF.
T-THANK YOU, NEGI, KONOKA, EVERYONE. THIS IS SO SUDDEN...
GRIN
I-I-I'M REALLY HAPPY...
HEH HEH HEH
HUM
YEAH! THAT WORKED OUT!
HOLD IT, YOU GUYS!
FREEZE
...
YEAH, UH... SORRY ABOUT THIS, CLASS REP.
IT LOOKS LIKE IT WAS ALL A MISUNDER-STANDING. ♡
I CAN'T BELIEVE IT! YOU GUYS ARE ALWAYS SUCH TROUBLE-MAKERS!
OH YEAH?! THEN YOU SHOULD'VE KNOWN BETTER THAN TO LISTEN TO US!
AH, FORGET IT! IT ALL WORKED OUT. HEY, WE CAN GO HAVE ASUNA'S BIRTHDAY PARTY AT THE KARAOKE PLACE...
DON'T TRY AND PULL ONE OVER ON ME!
YEAH! WHAT A GREAT IDEA!
EEYEAH!
KONOKA, I'M SORRY. I SUSPECTED YOU WERE DOING SOMETHING CRAZY.
HUH?
WHAT ARE YOU TALKING ABOUT?

STUDENT NUMBER 15
SETSUNA SAKURAZAKI

BORN: JANUARY 17, 1989
BLOOD TYPE: A
ASTROLOGICAL SIGN: CAPRICORN
LIKES: SWORD TRAINING, KONOKA
DISLIKES: INJUSTICE, CHATTING
AFFILIATIONS: KENDO CLUB
NOTES: BECAME A FOLLOWER OF SHINMEI RYU
    SCHOOL OF KYOTO AND IS A
    SWORDSMAN WISE IN THE WAY
    OF ONMYOU

NEGIMA!

MAGISTER NEGI MAGI

TWENTY-EIGHTH PERIOD: RIBBIT RIBBIT — PANIC ON THE BULLET TRAIN!?

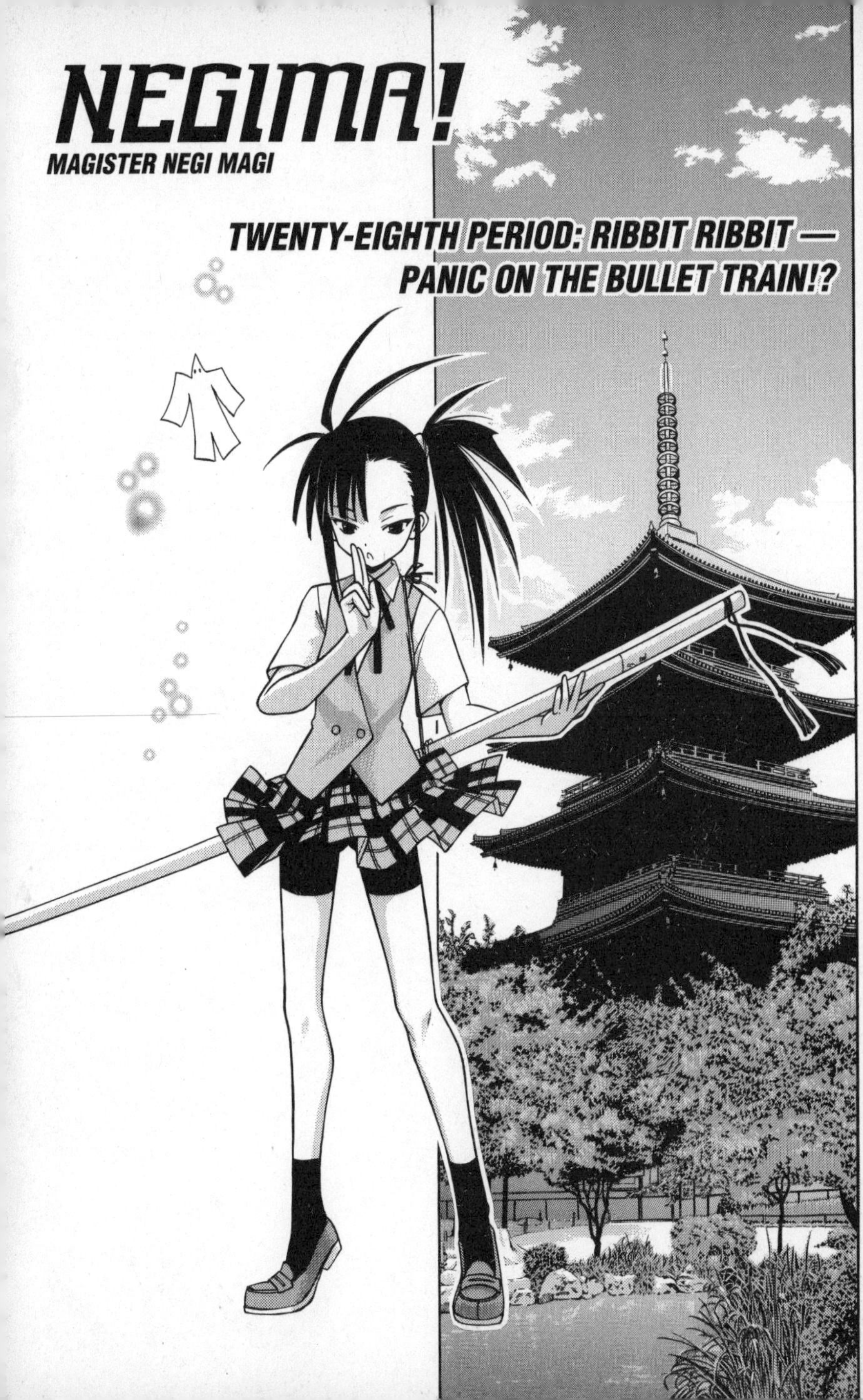

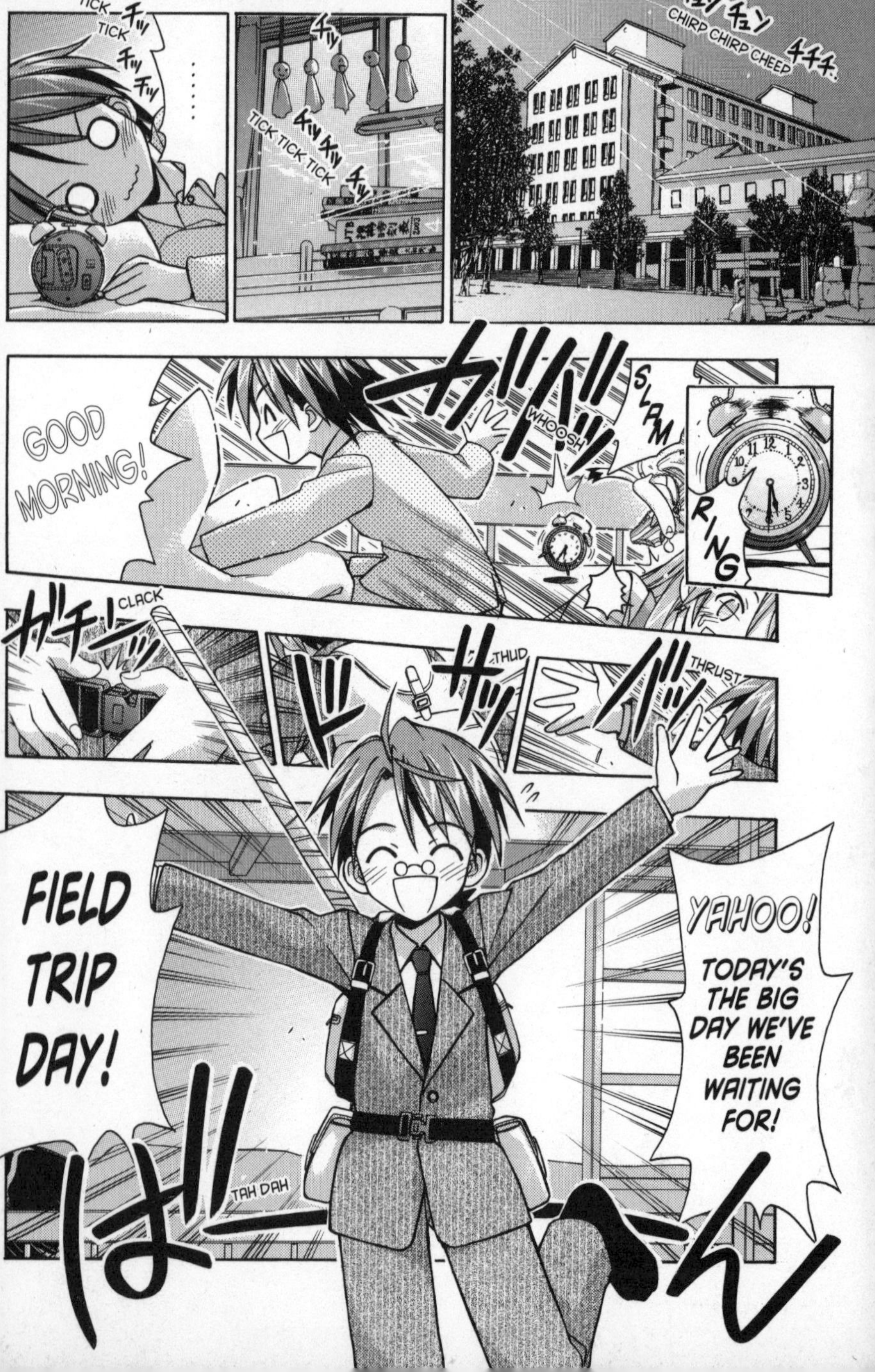

チュン チュン
CHIRP CHIRP CHEEP
チチチ.
チッ
TICK TICK TICK
TICK
TICK
チッ
......
SLAM
WHOOSH
GOOD MORNING!
RING
CLACK
THUD
THRUST
YAHOO!
TODAY'S THE BIG DAY WE'VE BEEN WAITING FOR!
FIELD TRIP DAY!
TAH DAH

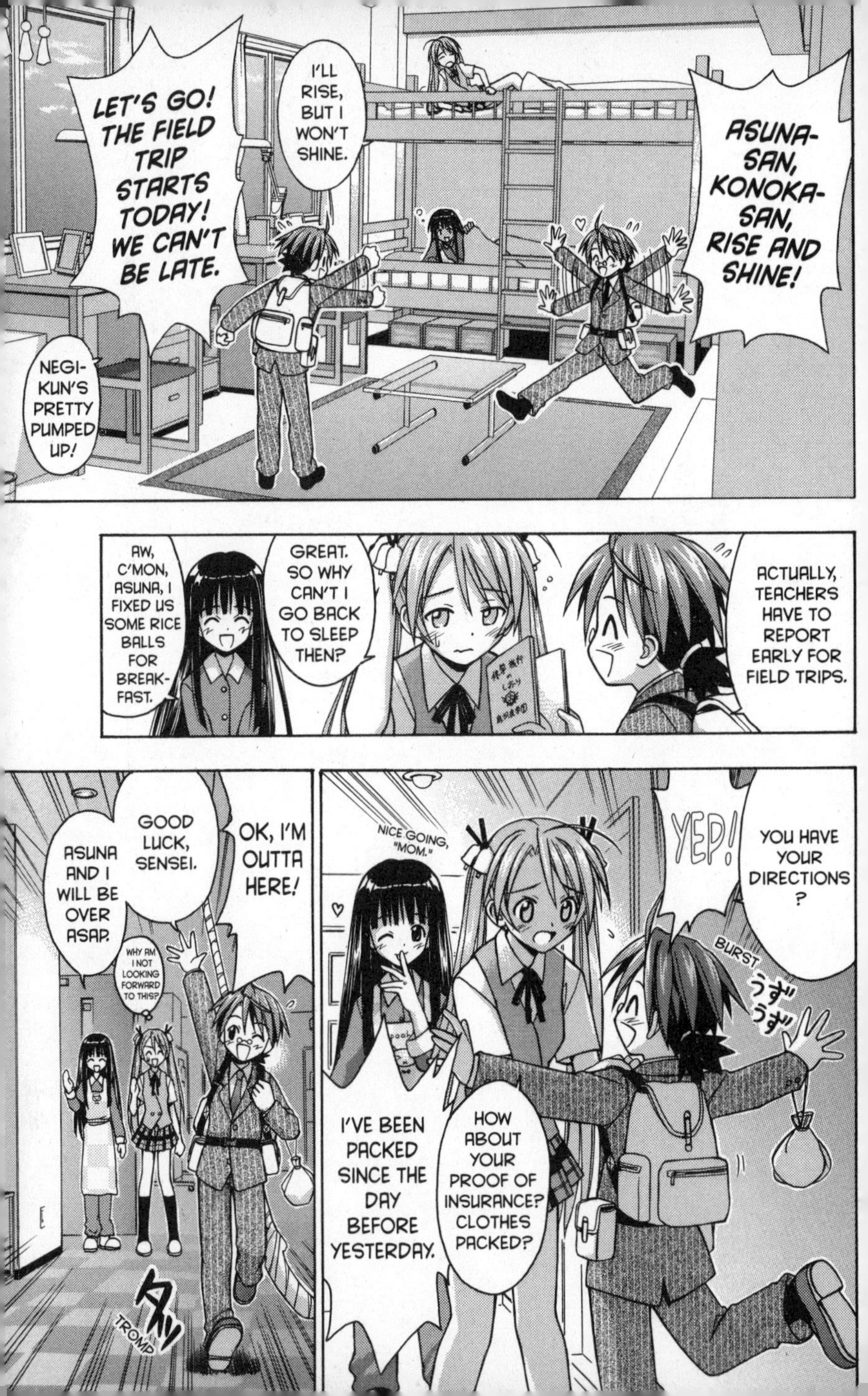
ASUNA-SAN, KONOKA-SAN, RISE AND SHINE!
I'LL RISE, BUT I WON'T SHINE.
LET'S GO! THE FIELD TRIP STARTS TODAY! WE CAN'T BE LATE.
NEGI-KUN'S PRETTY PUMPED UP!
ACTUALLY, TEACHERS HAVE TO REPORT EARLY FOR FIELD TRIPS.
GREAT. SO WHY CAN'T I GO BACK TO SLEEP THEN?
AW, C'MON, ASUNA, I FIXED US SOME RICE BALLS FOR BREAKFAST.
YOU HAVE YOUR DIRECTIONS?
YEP!
うずうず
BURST
HOW ABOUT YOUR PROOF OF INSURANCE? CLOTHES PACKED?
I'VE BEEN PACKED SINCE THE DAY BEFORE YESTERDAY.
NICE GOING, "MOM."
OK, I'M OUTTA HERE!
GOOD LUCK, SENSEI.
ASUNA AND I WILL BE OVER ASAP.
WHY AM I NOT LOOKING FORWARD TO THIS?
タッ
TROMP

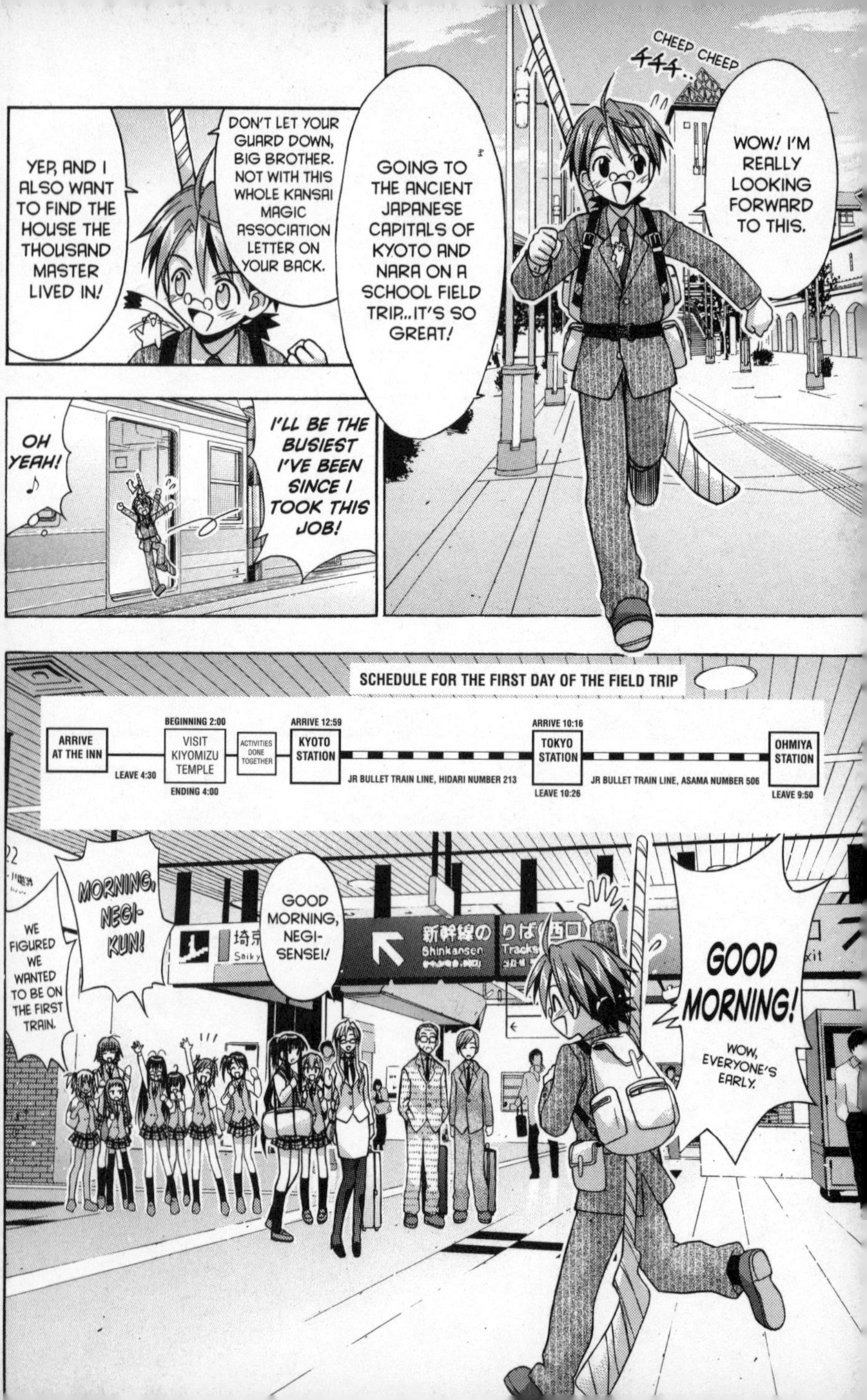
CHEEP CHEEP
WOW! I'M REALLY LOOKING FORWARD TO THIS.
GOING TO THE ANCIENT JAPANESE CAPITALS OF KYOTO AND NARA ON A SCHOOL FIELD TRIP...IT'S SO GREAT!
DON'T LET YOUR GUARD DOWN, BIG BROTHER. NOT WITH THIS WHOLE KANSAI MAGIC ASSOCIATION LETTER ON YOUR BACK.
YEP, AND I ALSO WANT TO FIND THE HOUSE THE THOUSAND MASTER LIVED IN!
I'LL BE THE BUSIEST I'VE BEEN SINCE I TOOK THIS JOB!
OH YEAH! ♪
SCHEDULE FOR THE FIRST DAY OF THE FIELD TRIP
OHMIYA STATION
LEAVE 9:50
JR BULLET TRAIN LINE, ASAMA NUMBER 506
ARRIVE 10:16
TOKYO STATION
LEAVE 10:26
JR BULLET TRAIN LINE, HIDARI NUMBER 213
ARRIVE 12:59
KYOTO STATION
ACTIVITIES DONE TOGETHER
BEGINNING 2:00
VISIT KIYOMIZU TEMPLE
ENDING 4:00
LEAVE 4:30
ARRIVE AT THE INN
新幹線のりば西口
Shinkansen Tracks
GOOD MORNING!
WOW, EVERYONE'S EARLY.
GOOD MORNING, NEGI-SENSEI!
MORNING, NEGI-KUN!
WE FIGURED WE WANTED TO BE ON THE FIRST TRAIN.

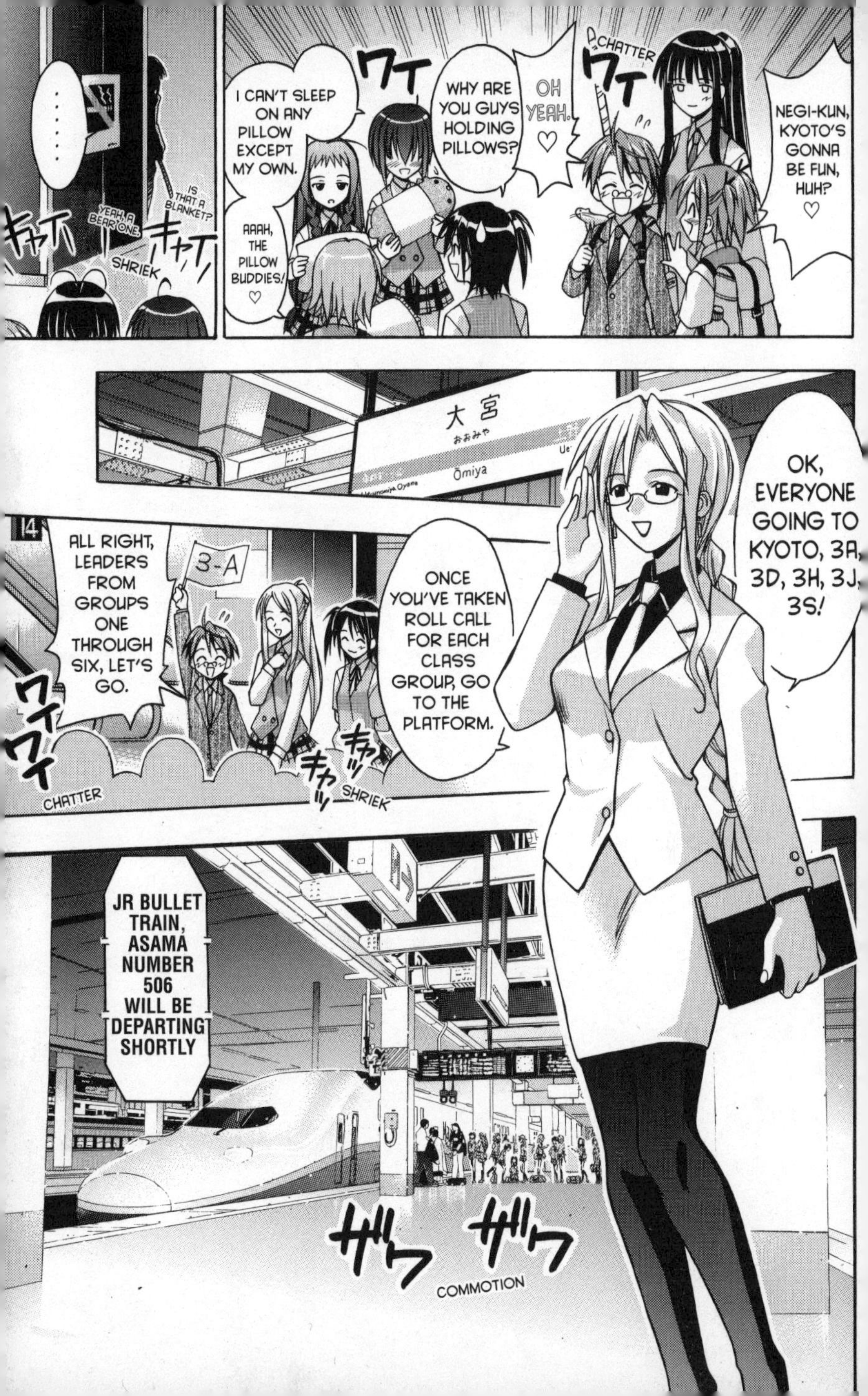
NEGI-KUN, KYOTO'S GONNA BE FUN, HUH? ♡
CHATTER
ワイ
OH YEAH. ♡
WHY ARE YOU GUYS HOLDING PILLOWS?
ワイ
I CAN'T SLEEP ON ANY PILLOW EXCEPT MY OWN.
AAAH, THE PILLOW BUDDIES! ♡
IS THAT A BLANKET?
YEAH, A BEAR ONE.
キャア キャア
SHRIEK
......
大宮
おおみや
Ōmiya
OK, EVERYONE GOING TO KYOTO, 3A, 3D, 3H, 3J, 3S!
ONCE YOU'VE TAKEN ROLL CALL FOR EACH CLASS GROUP, GO TO THE PLATFORM.
3-A
ALL RIGHT, LEADERS FROM GROUPS ONE THROUGH SIX, LET'S GO.
キャッ キャッ
SHRIEK
ワイワイ
CHATTER
14
JR BULLET TRAIN, ASAMA NUMBER 506 WILL BE DEPARTING SHORTLY
ザワ ザワ
COMMOTION

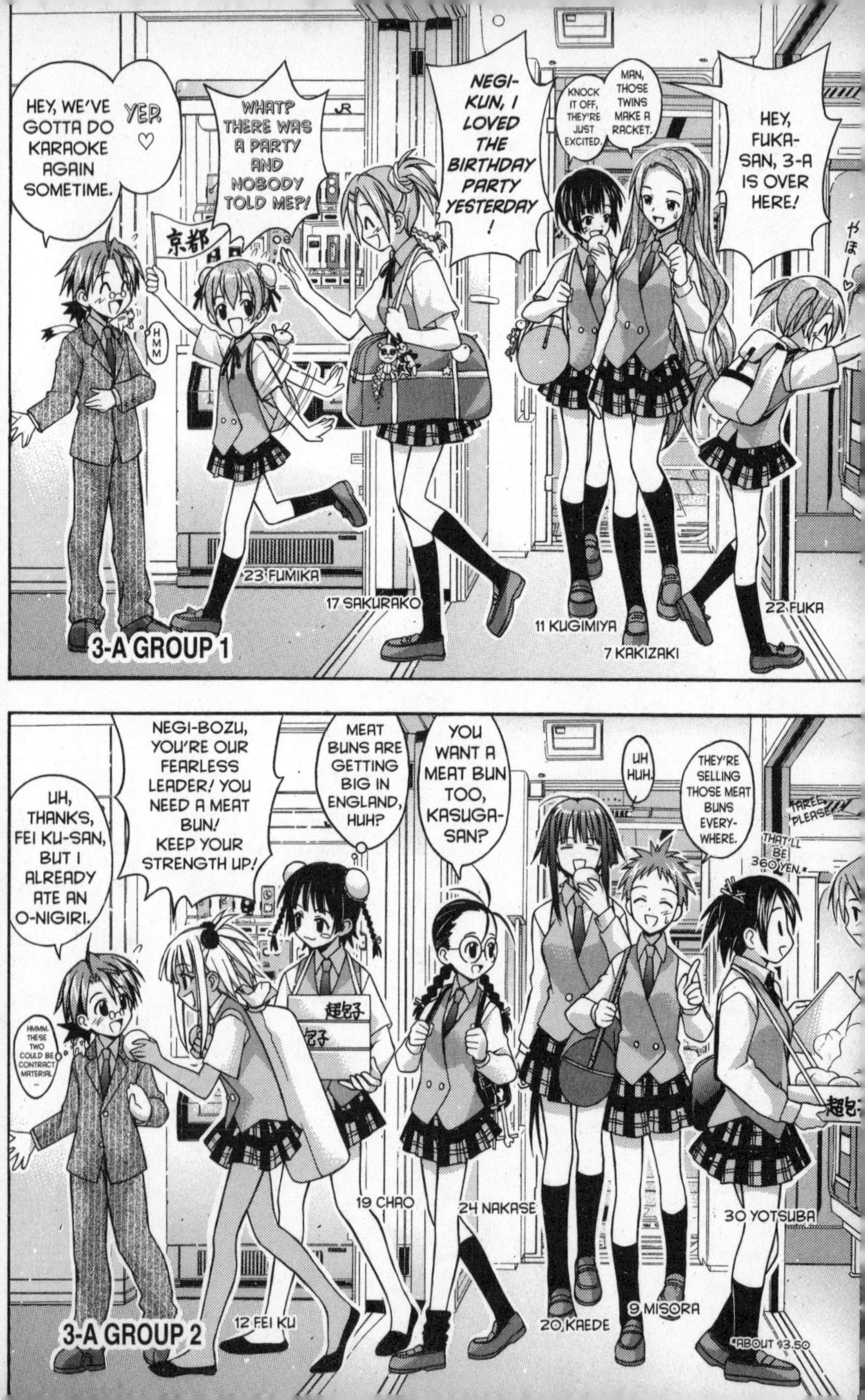
HEY, WE'VE GOTTA DO KARAOKE AGAIN SOMETIME.
YEP. ♡
HMM
WHAT? THERE WAS A PARTY AND NOBODY TOLD ME?!
京都
NEGI-KUN, I LOVED THE BIRTHDAY PARTY YESTERDAY!
KNOCK IT OFF, THEY'RE JUST EXCITED.
MAN, THOSE TWINS MAKE A RACKET.
HEY, FUKA-SAN, 3-A IS OVER HERE!
やほー♡
23 FUMIKA
17 SAKURAKO
11 KUGIMIYA
7 KAKIZAKI
22 FUKA
3-A GROUP 1
UH, THANKS, FEI KU-SAN, BUT I ALREADY ATE AN O-NIGIRI.
HMMM. THESE TWO COULD BE CONTRACT MATERIAL...
NEGI-BOZU, YOU'RE OUR FEARLESS LEADER! YOU NEED A MEAT BUN! KEEP YOUR STRENGTH UP!
MEAT BUNS ARE GETTING BIG IN ENGLAND, HUH?
YOU WANT A MEAT BUN TOO, KASUGA-SAN?
UH HUH.
THEY'RE SELLING THOSE MEAT BUNS EVERY-WHERE.
THREE, PLEASE!
THAT'LL BE 360 YEN.*
19 CHAO
24 NAKASE
30 YOTSUBA
12 FEI KU
20 KAEDE
9 MISORA
3-A GROUP 2
*ABOUT $3.50

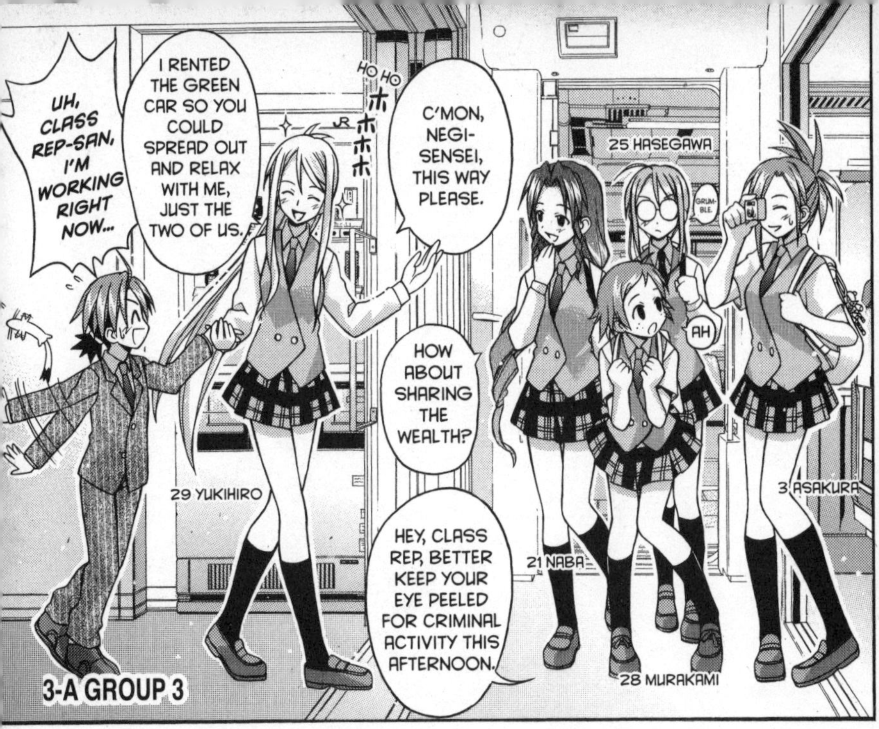
UH, CLASS REP-SAN, I'M WORKING RIGHT NOW...
I RENTED THE GREEN CAR SO YOU COULD SPREAD OUT AND RELAX WITH ME, JUST THE TWO OF US.
HO HO
ホホホホ
C'MON, NEGI-SENSEI, THIS WAY PLEASE.
HOW ABOUT SHARING THE WEALTH?
HEY, CLASS REP, BETTER KEEP YOUR EYE PEELED FOR CRIMINAL ACTIVITY THIS AFTERNOON.
GRUMBLE.
AH
25 HASEGAWA
29 YUKIHIRO
3 ASAKURA
21 NABA
28 MURAKAMI
3-A GROUP 3

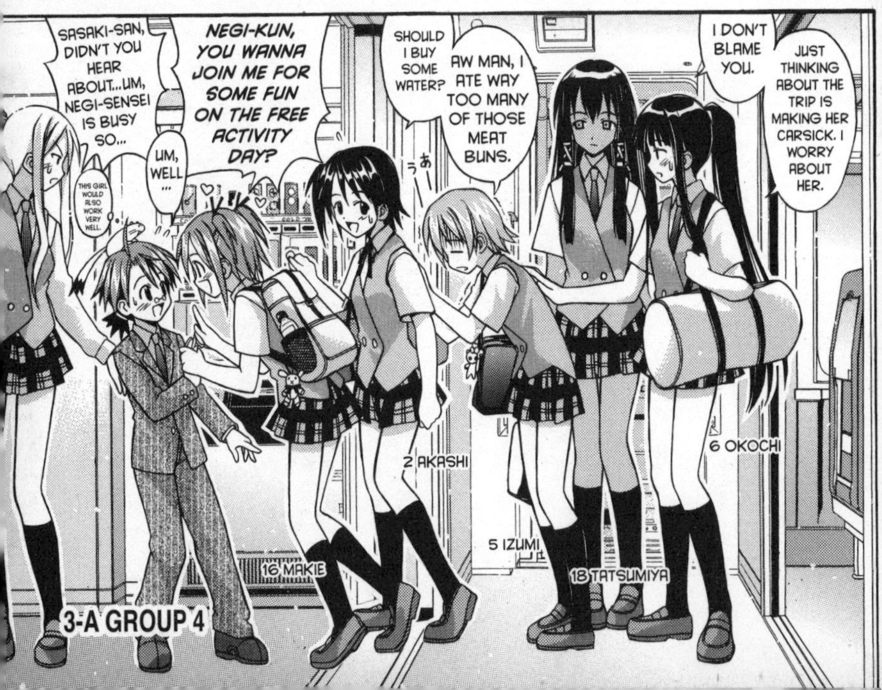
SASAKI-SAN, DIDN'T YOU HEAR ABOUT...UM, NEGI-SENSEI IS BUSY SO...
THIS GIRL WOULD ALSO WORK VERY WELL.
NEGI-KUN, YOU WANNA JOIN ME FOR SOME FUN ON THE FREE ACTIVITY DAY?
UM, WELL ...
SHOULD I BUY SOME WATER?
AW MAN, I ATE WAY TOO MANY OF THOSE MEAT BUNS.
I DON'T BLAME YOU.
JUST THINKING ABOUT THE TRIP IS MAKING HER CARSICK. I WORRY ABOUT HER.
2 AKASHI
6 OKOCHI
5 IZUMI
16 MAKIE
18 TATSUMIYA
3-A GROUP 4

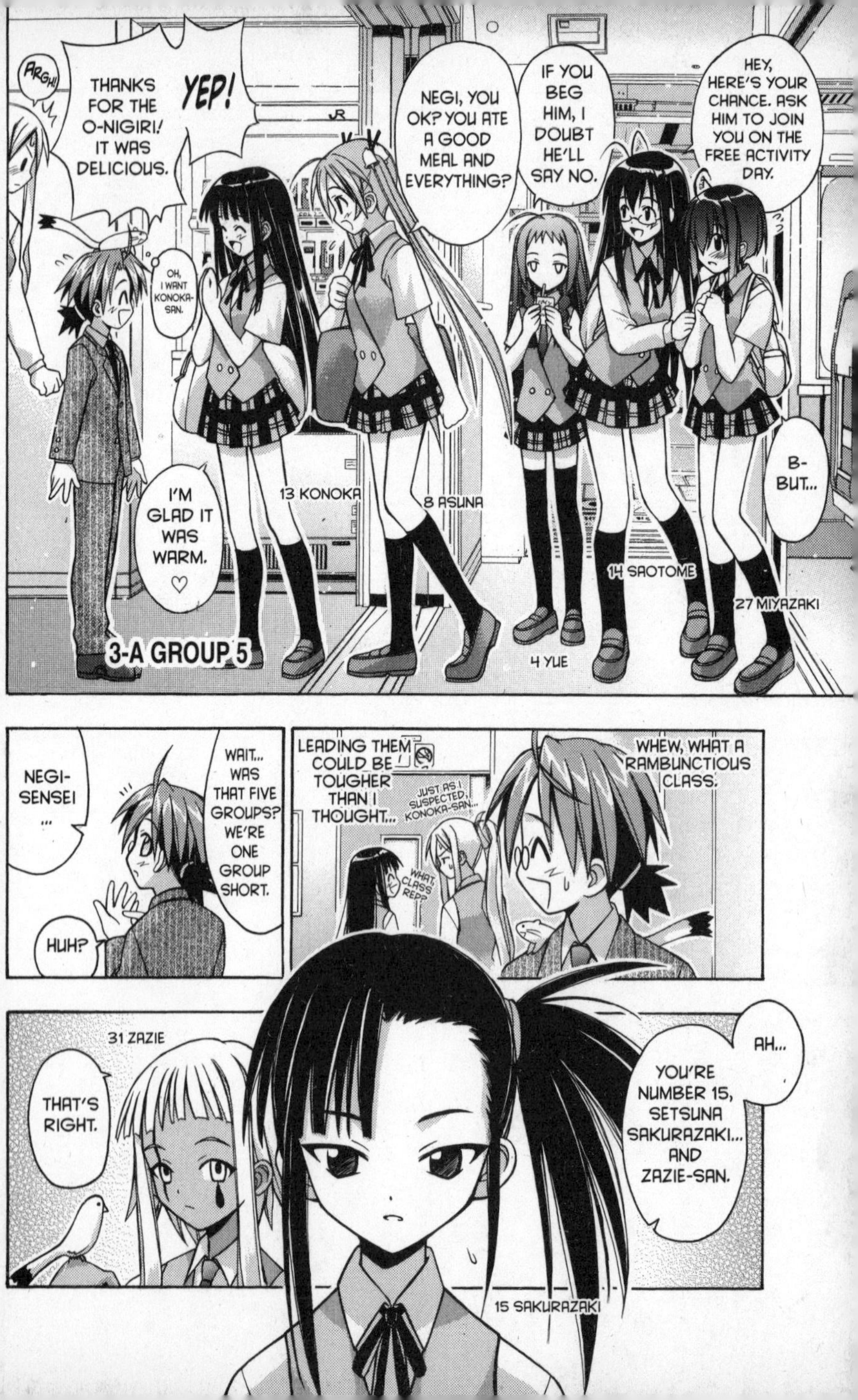
HEY, HERE'S YOUR CHANCE. ASK HIM TO JOIN YOU ON THE FREE ACTIVITY DAY.
IF YOU BEG HIM, I DOUBT HE'LL SAY NO.
NEGI, YOU OK? YOU ATE A GOOD MEAL AND EVERYTHING?
YEP!
THANKS FOR THE O-NIGIRI! IT WAS DELICIOUS.
ARGH!
OH, I WANT KONOKA-SAN.
I'M GLAD IT WAS WARM. ♡
B-BUT...
13 KONOKA
8 ASUNA
14 SAOTOME
27 MIYAZAKI
4 YUE
3-A GROUP 5
WHEW, WHAT A RAMBUNCTIOUS CLASS.
LEADING THEM COULD BE TOUGHER THAN I THOUGHT...
JUST AS I SUSPECTED, KONOKA-SAN...
WHAT, CLASS REP?
WAIT... WAS THAT FIVE GROUPS? WE'RE ONE GROUP SHORT.
NEGI-SENSEI ...
HUH?
AH...
YOU'RE NUMBER 15, SETSUNA SAKURAZAKI... AND ZAZIE-SAN.
31 ZAZIE
THAT'S RIGHT.
15 SAKURAZAKI

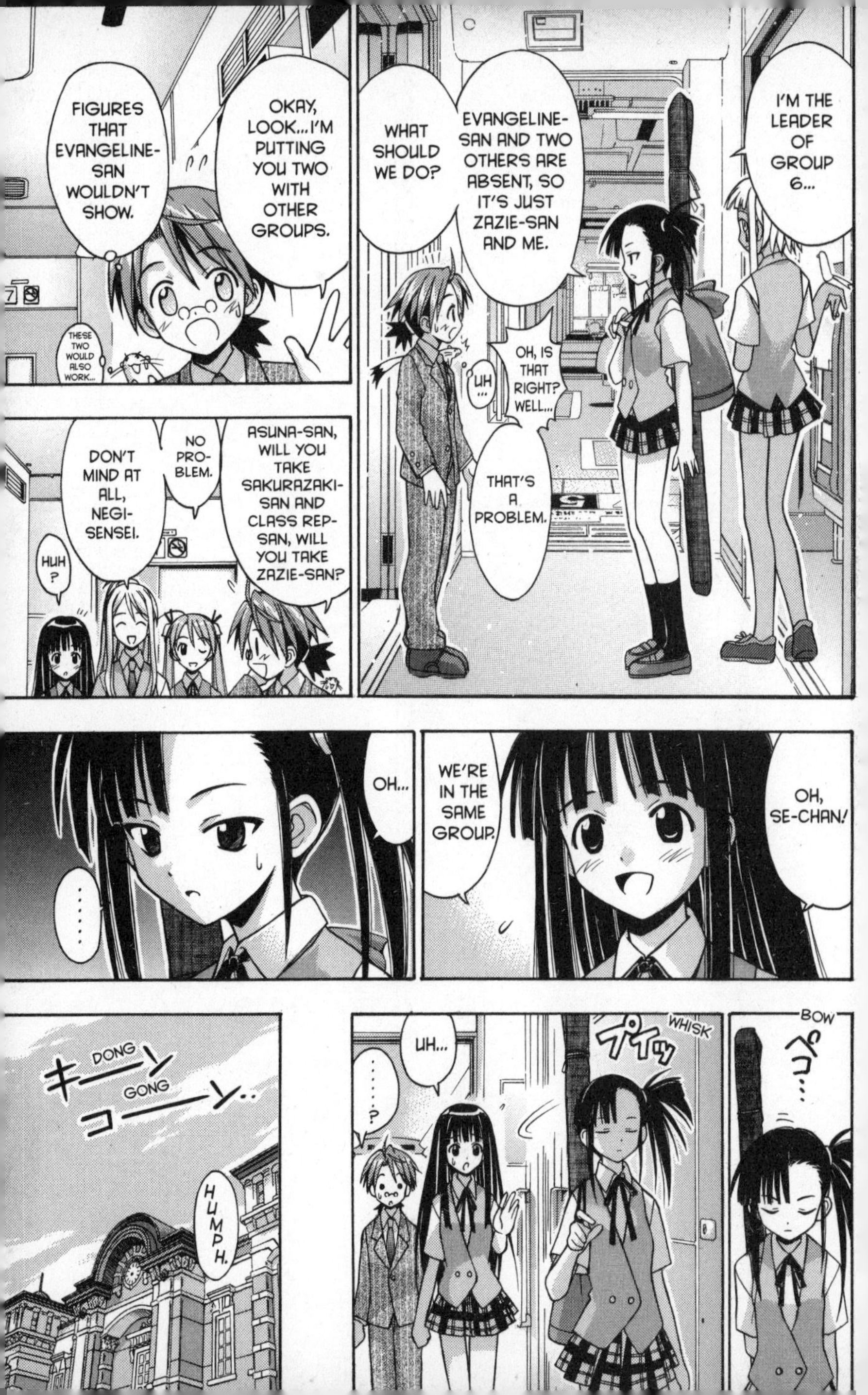
I'M THE LEADER OF GROUP 6...
EVANGELINE-SAN AND TWO OTHERS ARE ABSENT, SO IT'S JUST ZAZIE-SAN AND ME.
WHAT SHOULD WE DO?
UH...
OH, IS THAT RIGHT? WELL...
THAT'S A PROBLEM.
OKAY, LOOK...I'M PUTTING YOU TWO WITH OTHER GROUPS.
FIGURES THAT EVANGELINE-SAN WOULDN'T SHOW.
THESE TWO WOULD ALSO WORK...
ASUNA-SAN, WILL YOU TAKE SAKURAZAKI-SAN AND CLASS REP-SAN, WILL YOU TAKE ZAZIE-SAN?
NO PROBLEM.
DON'T MIND AT ALL, NEGI-SENSEI.
HUH?
OH, SE-CHAN!
WE'RE IN THE SAME GROUP.
OH...
......
ペコ...
BOW
ピイッ
WHISK
UH...
......?
キーンコーン..
DONG GONG
HUMPH.

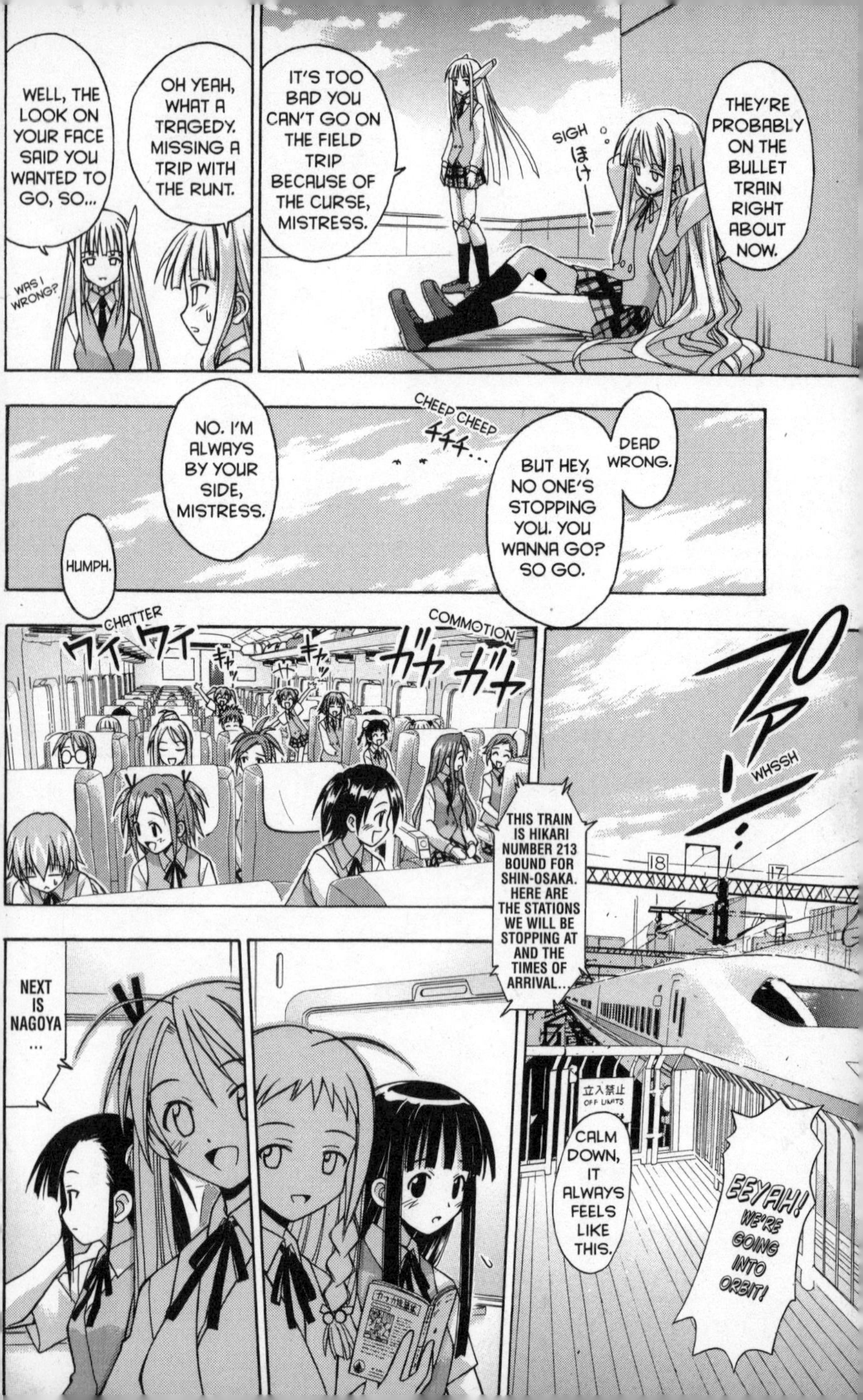
THEY'RE PROBABLY ON THE BULLET TRAIN RIGHT ABOUT NOW.
SIGH
ほけ〜〜
IT'S TOO BAD YOU CAN'T GO ON THE FIELD TRIP BECAUSE OF THE CURSE, MISTRESS.
OH YEAH, WHAT A TRAGEDY. MISSING A TRIP WITH THE RUNT.
WELL, THE LOOK ON YOUR FACE SAID YOU WANTED TO GO, SO...
WAS I WRONG?
DEAD WRONG.
BUT HEY, NO ONE'S STOPPING YOU. YOU WANNA GO? SO GO.
CHEEP CHEEP
チチチ...
NO. I'M ALWAYS BY YOUR SIDE, MISTRESS.
HUMPH.
WHSSH
THIS TRAIN IS HIKARI NUMBER 213 BOUND FOR SHIN-OSAKA. HERE ARE THE STATIONS WE WILL BE STOPPING AT AND THE TIMES OF ARRIVAL...
COMMOTION
ガヤガヤ
キャッ キャッ
CHATTER
ワイワイー
EEYAH! WE'RE GOING INTO ORBIT!
CALM DOWN, IT ALWAYS FEELS LIKE THIS.
立入禁止
OFF LIMITS
NEXT IS NAGOYA ...

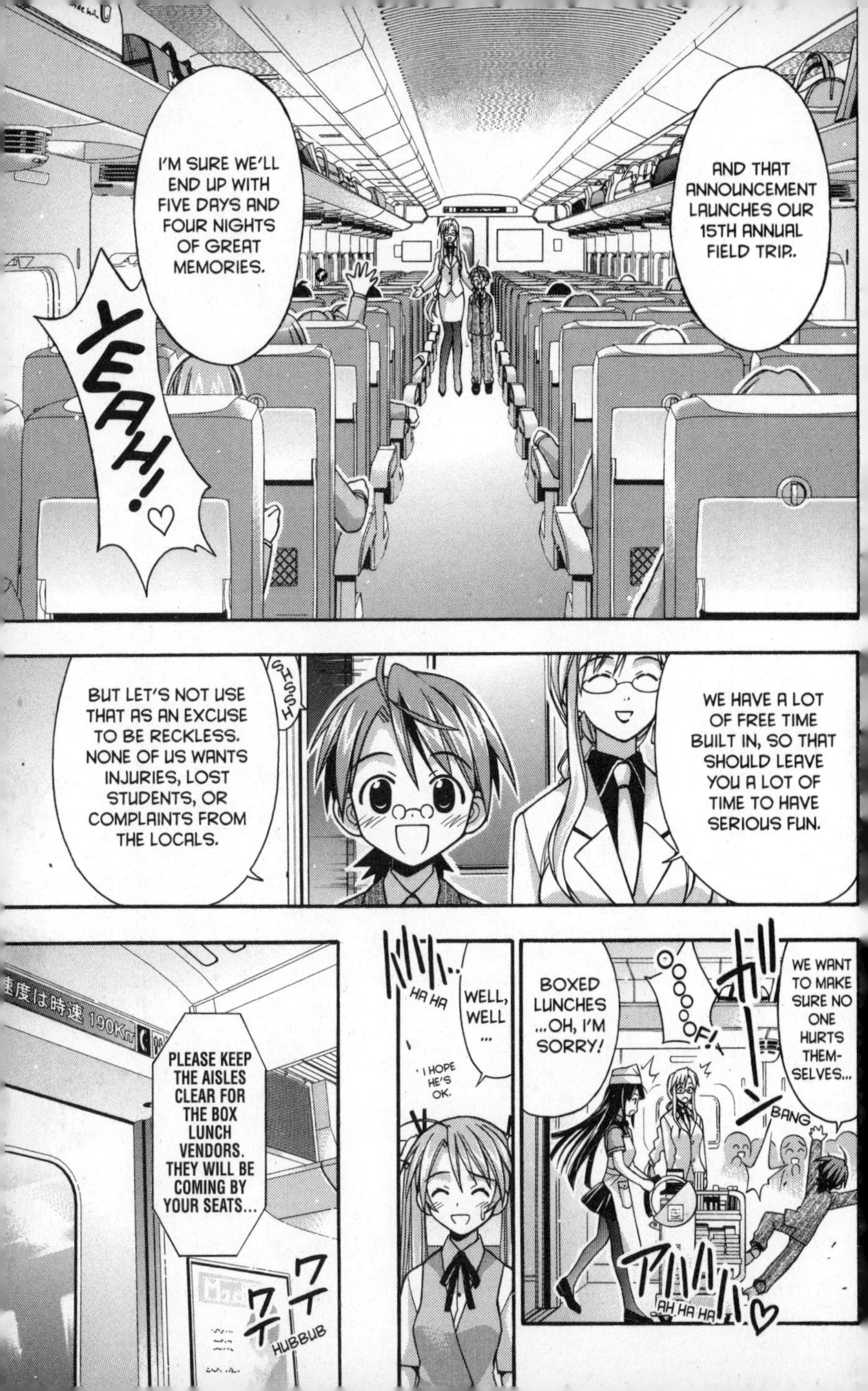
AND THAT ANNOUNCEMENT LAUNCHES OUR 15TH ANNUAL FIELD TRIP..
I'M SURE WE'LL END UP WITH FIVE DAYS AND FOUR NIGHTS OF GREAT MEMORIES.
YEAH! ♡
WE HAVE A LOT OF FREE TIME BUILT IN, SO THAT SHOULD LEAVE YOU A LOT OF TIME TO HAVE SERIOUS FUN.
SHSSH
BUT LET'S NOT USE THAT AS AN EXCUSE TO BE RECKLESS. NONE OF US WANTS INJURIES, LOST STUDENTS, OR COMPLAINTS FROM THE LOCALS.
WE WANT TO MAKE SURE NO ONE HURTS THEM-SELVES...
OOOOOF!
BANG
BOXED LUNCHES ...OH, I'M SORRY!
AH HA HA
WELL, WELL ...
HA HA
I HOPE HE'S OK.
速度は時速 190Km
PLEASE KEEP THE AISLES CLEAR FOR THE BOX LUNCH VENDORS. THEY WILL BE COMING BY YOUR SEATS...
HUBBUB

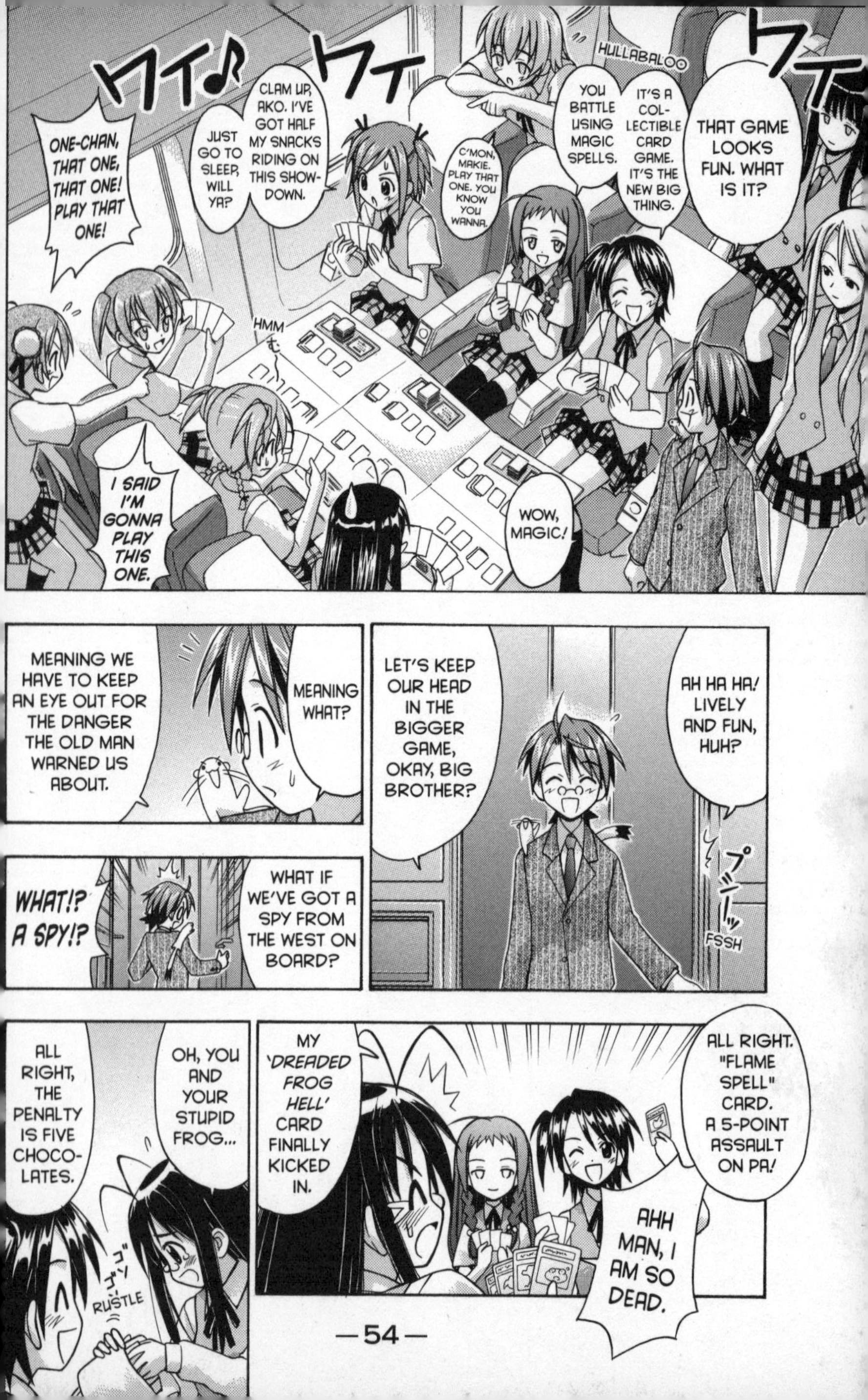
HULLABALOO
THAT GAME LOOKS FUN. WHAT IS IT?
IT'S A COLLECTIBLE CARD GAME. IT'S THE NEW BIG THING.
YOU BATTLE USING MAGIC SPELLS.
C'MON, MAKIE. PLAY THAT ONE. YOU KNOW YOU WANNA.
CLAM UP, AKO. I'VE GOT HALF MY SNACKS RIDING ON THIS SHOWDOWN.
JUST GO TO SLEEP, WILL YA?
ONE-CHAN, THAT ONE, THAT ONE! PLAY THAT ONE!
HMM
WOW, MAGIC!
I SAID I'M GONNA PLAY THIS ONE.
AH HA HA! LIVELY AND FUN, HUH?
FSSH
LET'S KEEP OUR HEAD IN THE BIGGER GAME, OKAY, BIG BROTHER?
MEANING WHAT?
MEANING WE HAVE TO KEEP AN EYE OUT FOR THE DANGER THE OLD MAN WARNED US ABOUT.
WHAT IF WE'VE GOT A SPY FROM THE WEST ON BOARD?
WHAT!? A SPY!?
ALL RIGHT. "FLAME SPELL" CARD. A 5-POINT ASSAULT ON PA!
AHH MAN, I AM SO DEAD.
MY 'DREADED FROG HELL' CARD FINALLY KICKED IN.
OH, YOU AND YOUR STUPID FROG...
ALL RIGHT, THE PENALTY IS FIVE CHOCOLATES.
RUSTLE

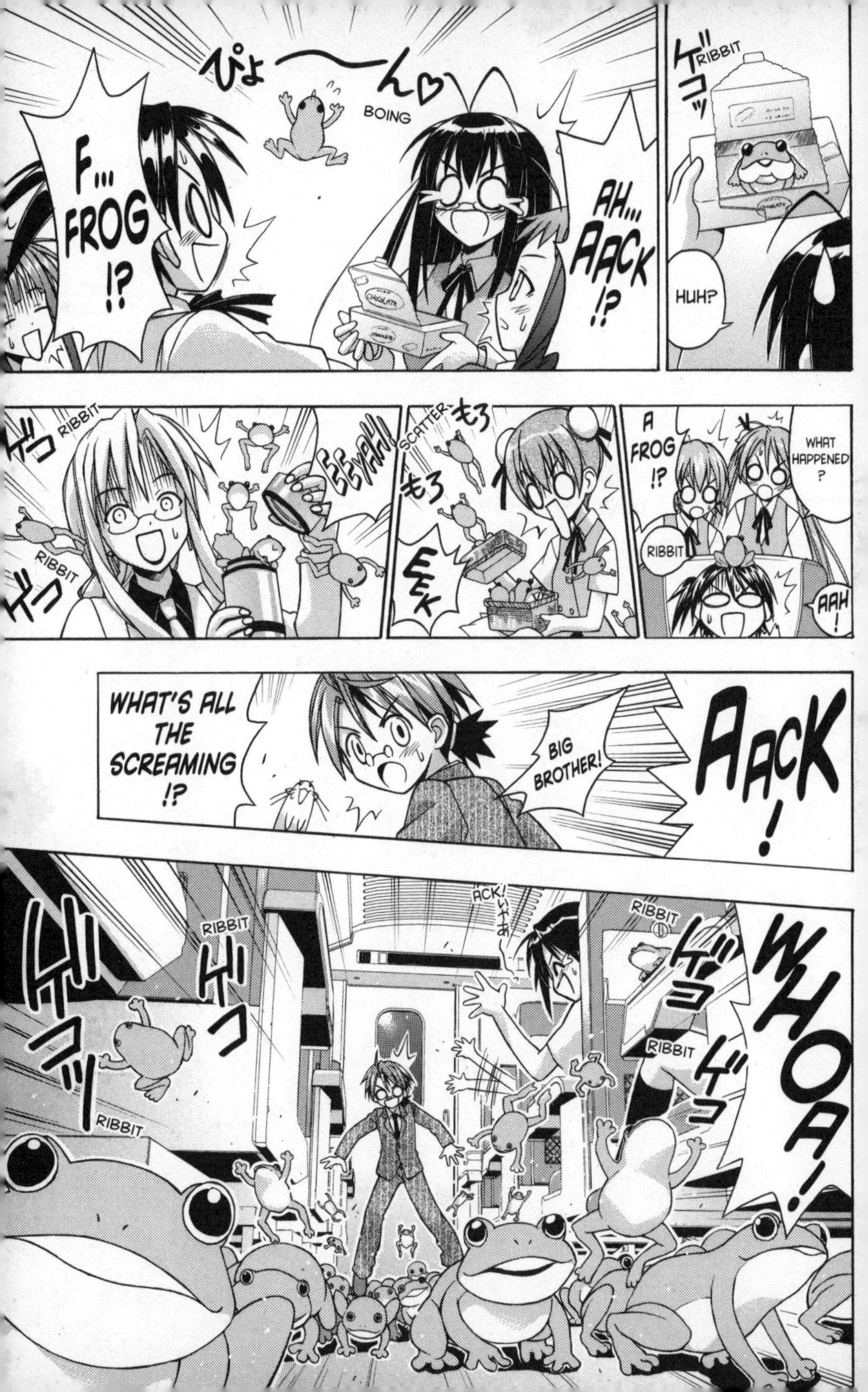
RIBBIT
ゲコッ
HUH?
AH... AACK !?
ぴょ〜ん♡
BOING
F... FROG !?
WHAT HAPPENED ?
A FROG !?
RIBBIT
AAH !
SCATTER
もろ
もろ
EEK
ゲコ
RIBBIT
RIBBIT
ゲコ
AACK !
BIG BROTHER!
WHAT'S ALL THE SCREAMING !?
WHOA!!
RIBBIT
ゲコ
RIBBIT
ゲコ
ACK!
いやあ
RIBBIT
ゲコ
RIBBIT
ゲコッ

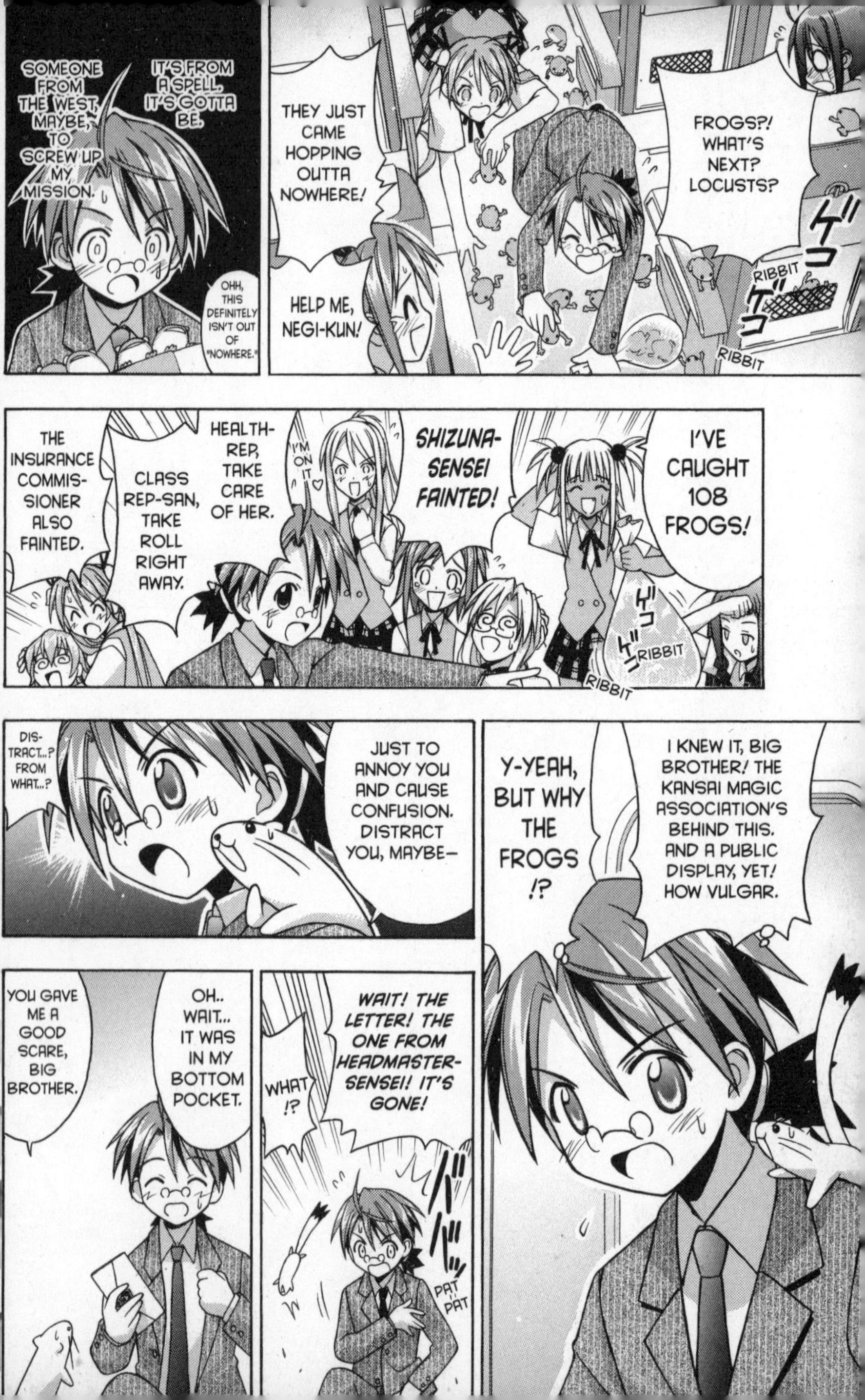
FROGS?! WHAT'S NEXT? LOCUSTS?
THEY JUST CAME HOPPING OUTTA NOWHERE!
HELP ME, NEGI-KUN!
RIBBIT
RIBBIT
IT'S FROM A SPELL. IT'S GOTTA BE.
SOMEONE FROM THE WEST, MAYBE, TO SCREW UP MY MISSION.
OHH, THIS DEFINITELY ISN'T OUT OF "NOWHERE."
I'VE CAUGHT 108 FROGS!
RIBBIT
RIBBIT
SHIZUNA-SENSEI FAINTED!
I'M ON IT ♡
HEALTH-REP, TAKE CARE OF HER.
CLASS REP-SAN, TAKE ROLL RIGHT AWAY.
THE INSURANCE COMMISSIONER ALSO FAINTED.
I KNEW IT, BIG BROTHER! THE KANSAI MAGIC ASSOCIATION'S BEHIND THIS. AND A PUBLIC DISPLAY, YET! HOW VULGAR.
Y-YEAH, BUT WHY THE FROGS!?
JUST TO ANNOY YOU AND CAUSE CONFUSION. DISTRACT YOU, MAYBE—
DISTRACT...? FROM WHAT...?
WAIT! THE LETTER! THE ONE FROM HEADMASTER-SENSEI! IT'S GONE!
WHAT!?
PAT PAT
OH.. WAIT... IT WAS IN MY BOTTOM POCKET.
YOU GAVE ME A GOOD SCARE, BIG BROTHER.

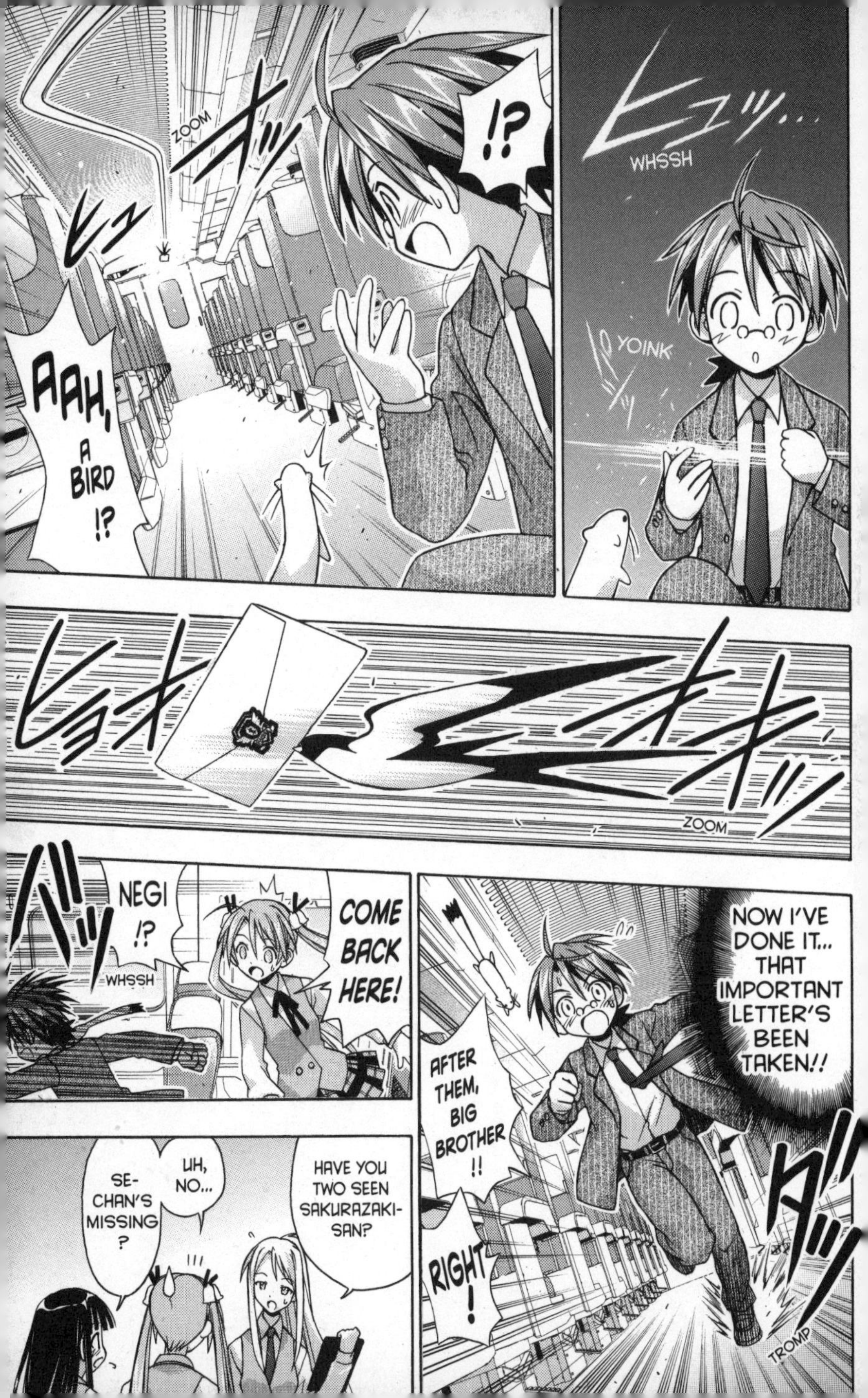
WHSSH
YOINK
!?
ZOOM
AAH, A BIRD!?
ZOOM
NOW I'VE DONE IT... THAT IMPORTANT LETTER'S BEEN TAKEN!!
AFTER THEM, BIG BROTHER!!
RIGHT!
TROMP
COME BACK HERE!
NEGI!?
WHSSH
HAVE YOU TWO SEEN SAKURAZAKI-SAN?
UH, NO...
SE-CHAN'S MISSING?

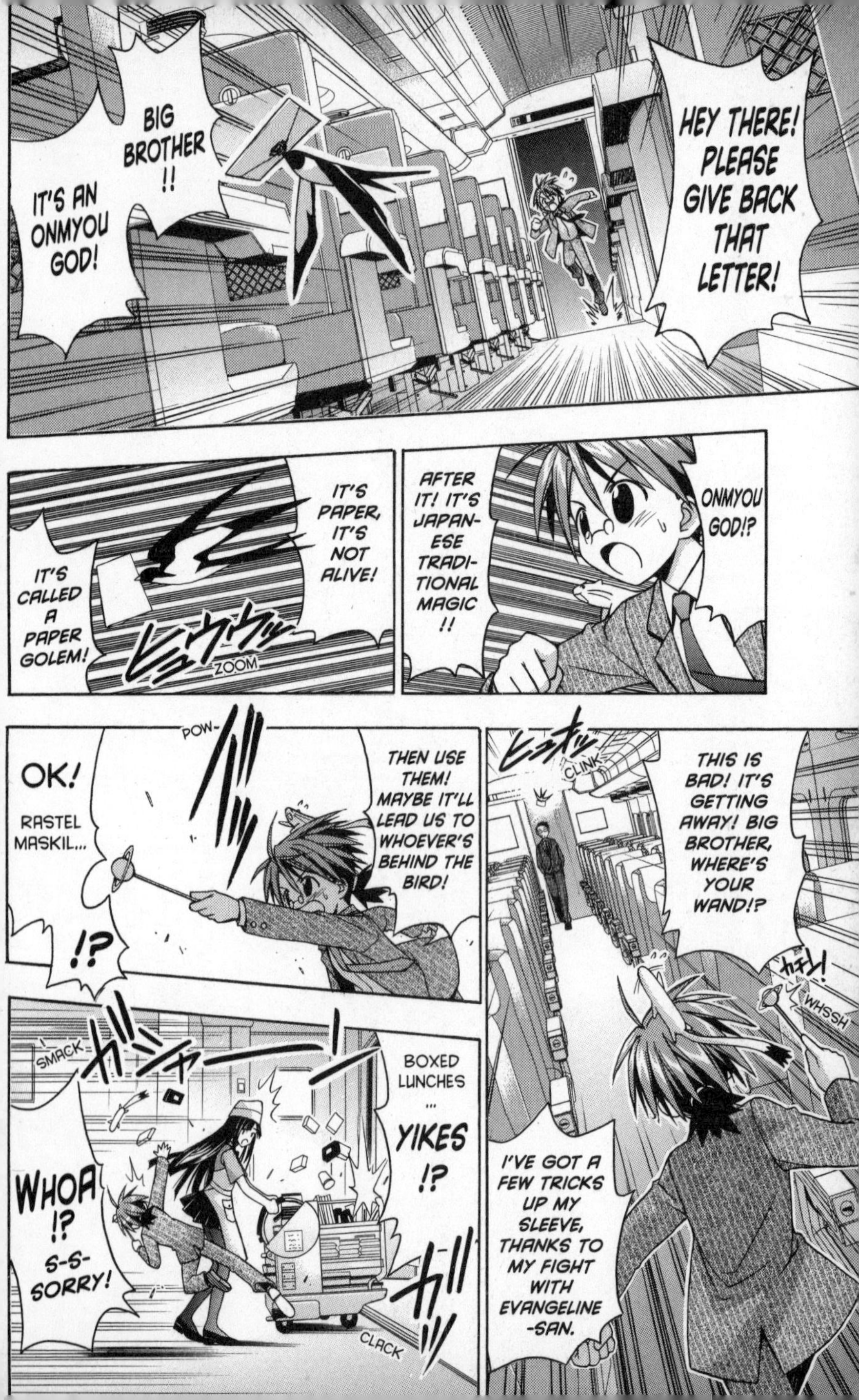

HEY THERE! PLEASE GIVE BACK THAT LETTER!
BIG BROTHER !!
IT'S AN ONMYOU GOD!
ONMYOU GOD!?
AFTER IT! IT'S JAPANESE TRADITIONAL MAGIC !!
IT'S PAPER, IT'S NOT ALIVE!
IT'S CALLED A PAPER GOLEM!
ZOOM
THIS IS BAD! IT'S GETTING AWAY! BIG BROTHER, WHERE'S YOUR WAND!?
CLINK
WHSSH
I'VE GOT A FEW TRICKS UP MY SLEEVE, THANKS TO MY FIGHT WITH EVANGELINE -SAN.
THEN USE THEM! MAYBE IT'LL LEAD US TO WHOEVER'S BEHIND THE BIRD!
POW-
OK!
RASTEL MASKIL...
!?
SMACK
BOXED LUNCHES ...
YIKES !?
WHOA !?
S-S-SORRY!
CLACK

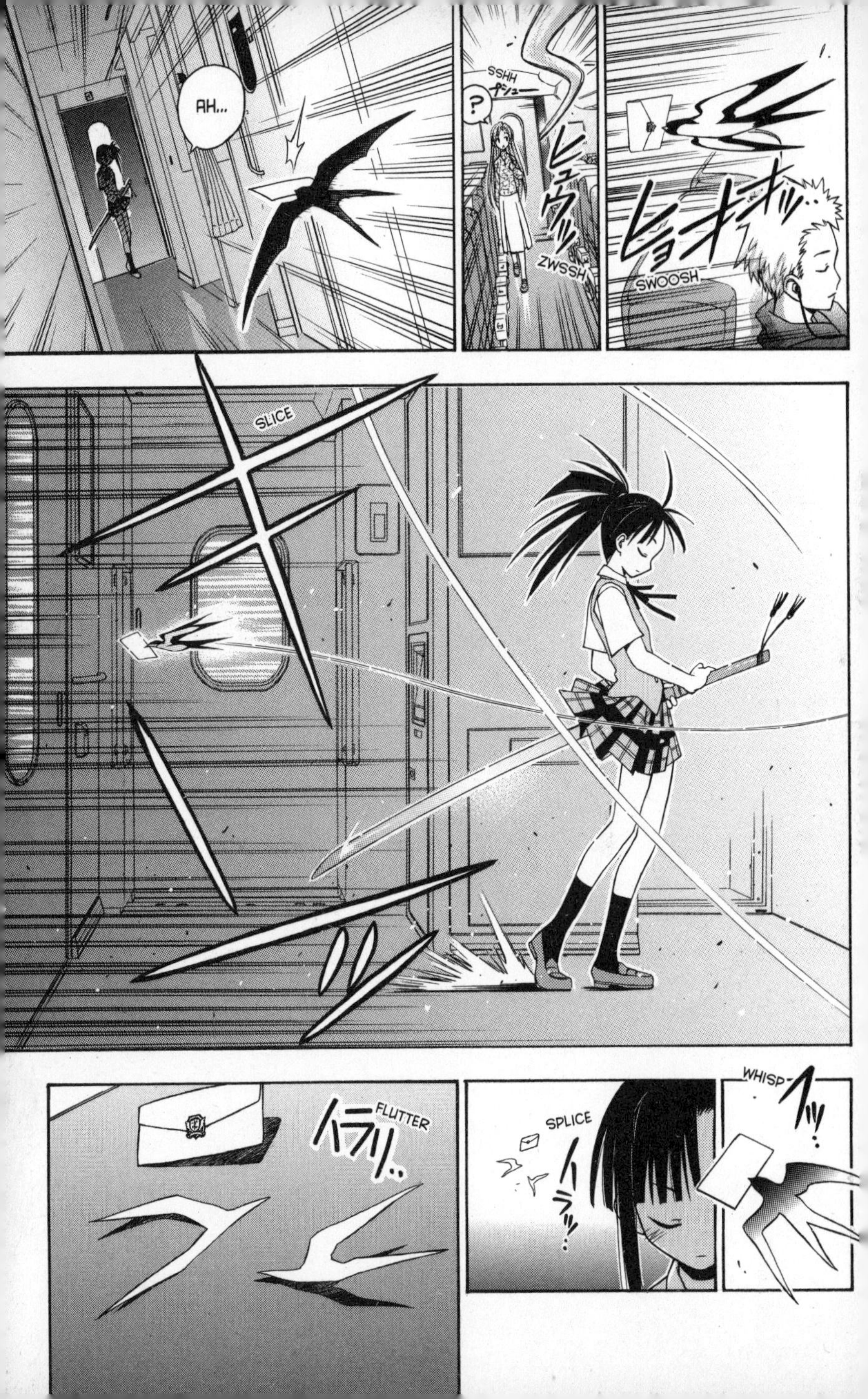

SWOOSH
SSHH
?
ZWSSH
AH...
SLICE
WHISP-
SPLICE
FLUTTER

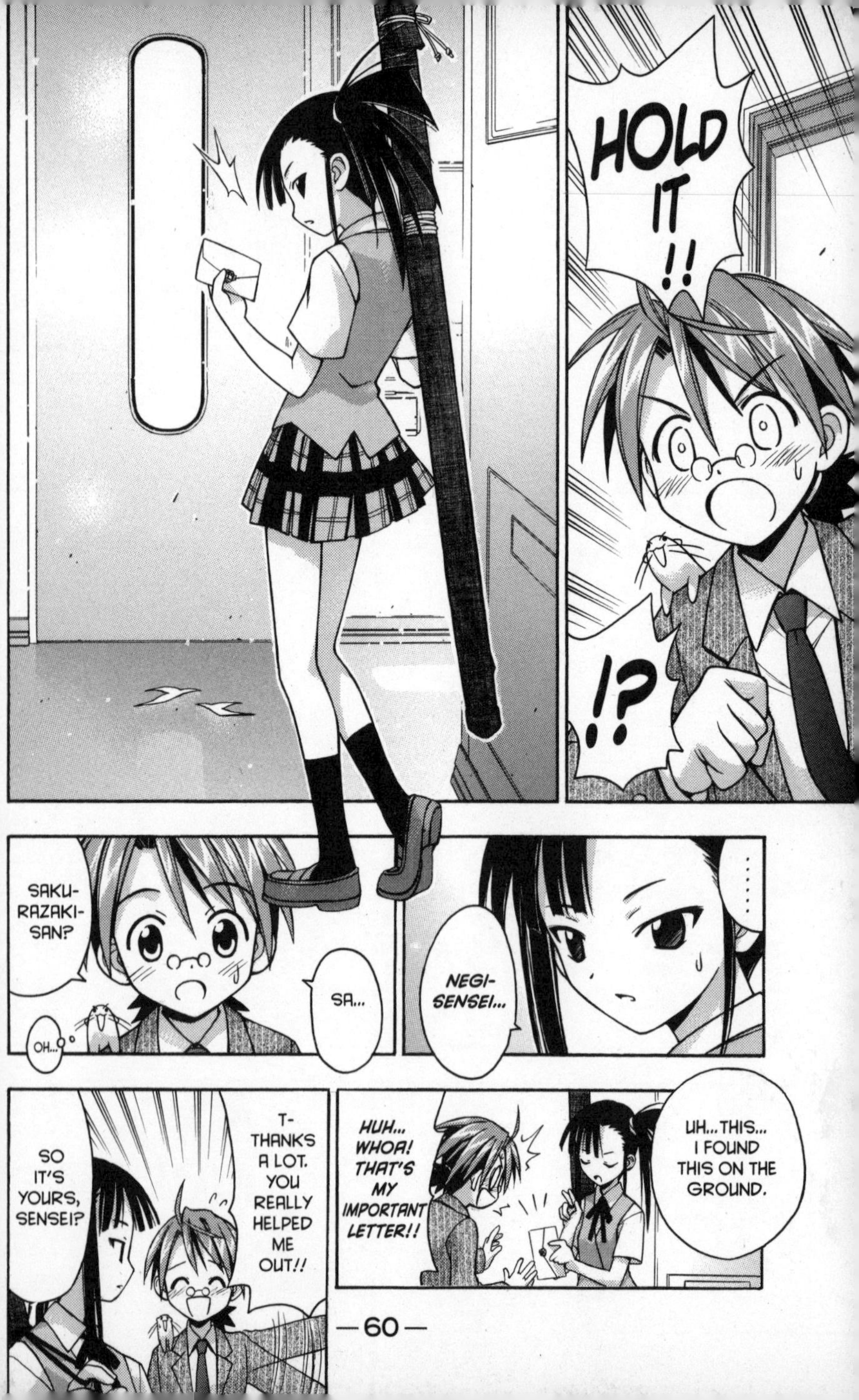
HOLD IT!!
!?
SAKU-RAZAKI-SAN?
OH...
SA...
NEGI-SENSEI...
......
UH...THIS... I FOUND THIS ON THE GROUND.
HUH... WHOA! THAT'S MY IMPORTANT LETTER!!
T-THANKS A LOT. YOU REALLY HELPED ME OUT!!
SO IT'S YOURS, SENSEI?

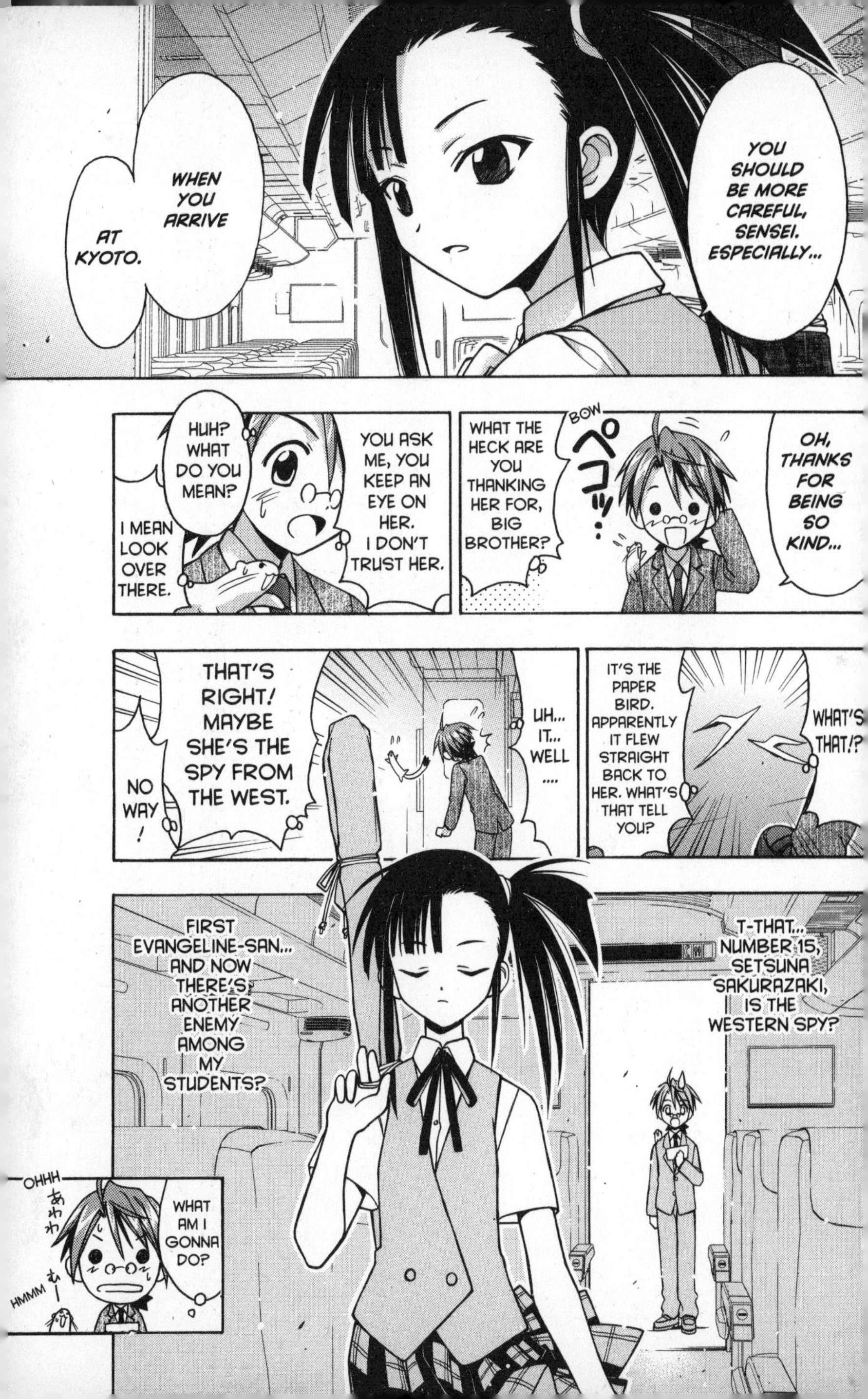
YOU SHOULD BE MORE CAREFUL, SENSEI. ESPECIALLY...
WHEN YOU ARRIVE AT KYOTO.
OH, THANKS FOR BEING SO KIND...
BOW
ペコッ
WHAT THE HECK ARE YOU THANKING HER FOR, BIG BROTHER?
YOU ASK ME, YOU KEEP AN EYE ON HER. I DON'T TRUST HER.
HUH? WHAT DO YOU MEAN?
I MEAN LOOK OVER THERE.
WHAT'S THAT!?
IT'S THE PAPER BIRD. APPARENTLY IT FLEW STRAIGHT BACK TO HER. WHAT'S THAT TELL YOU?
UH... IT... WELL ....
THAT'S RIGHT! MAYBE SHE'S THE SPY FROM THE WEST.
NO WAY!
T-THAT... NUMBER 15, SETSUNA SAKURAZAKI, IS THE WESTERN SPY?
FIRST EVANGELINE-SAN... AND NOW THERE'S ANOTHER ENEMY AMONG MY STUDENTS?
OHHH
あわわ
WHAT AM I GONNA DO?
HMMM
むー

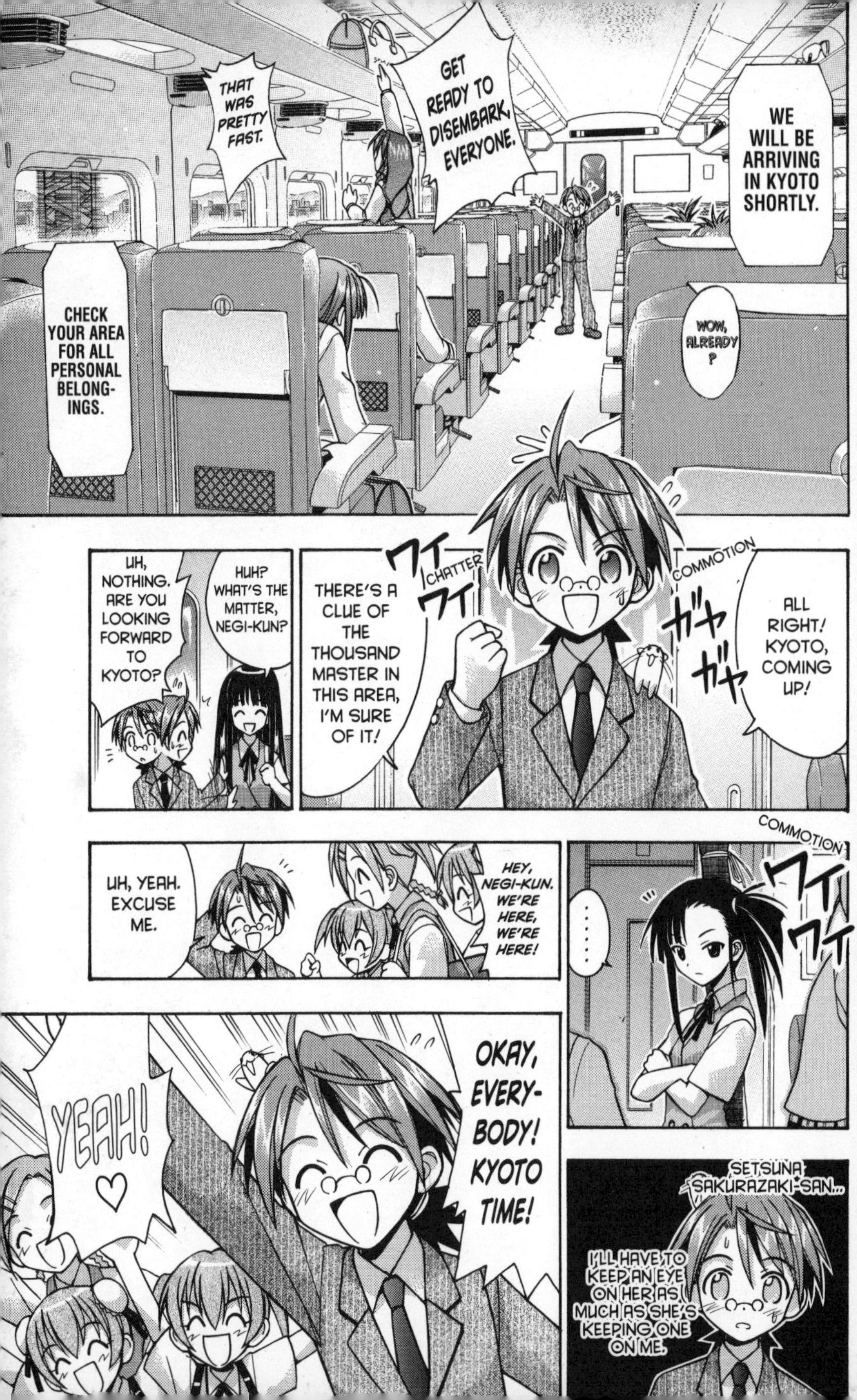

WE WILL BE ARRIVING IN KYOTO SHORTLY.
GET READY TO DISEMBARK, EVERYONE.
THAT WAS PRETTY FAST.
CHECK YOUR AREA FOR ALL PERSONAL BELONGINGS.
WOW, ALREADY?
ガヤ ガヤ COMMOTION
ALL RIGHT! KYOTO, COMING UP!
ワイ ワイ CHATTER
THERE'S A CLUE OF THE THOUSAND MASTER IN THIS AREA, I'M SURE OF IT!
HUH? WHAT'S THE MATTER, NEGI-KUN?
UH, NOTHING. ARE YOU LOOKING FORWARD TO KYOTO?
ワイ ワイ COMMOTION
......
HEY, NEGI-KUN. WE'RE HERE, WE'RE HERE!
UH, YEAH. EXCUSE ME.
SETSUNA SAKURAZAKI-SAN...
I'LL HAVE TO KEEP AN EYE ON HER AS MUCH AS SHE'S KEEPING ONE ON ME.
OKAY, EVERYBODY! KYOTO TIME!
YEAH! ♥

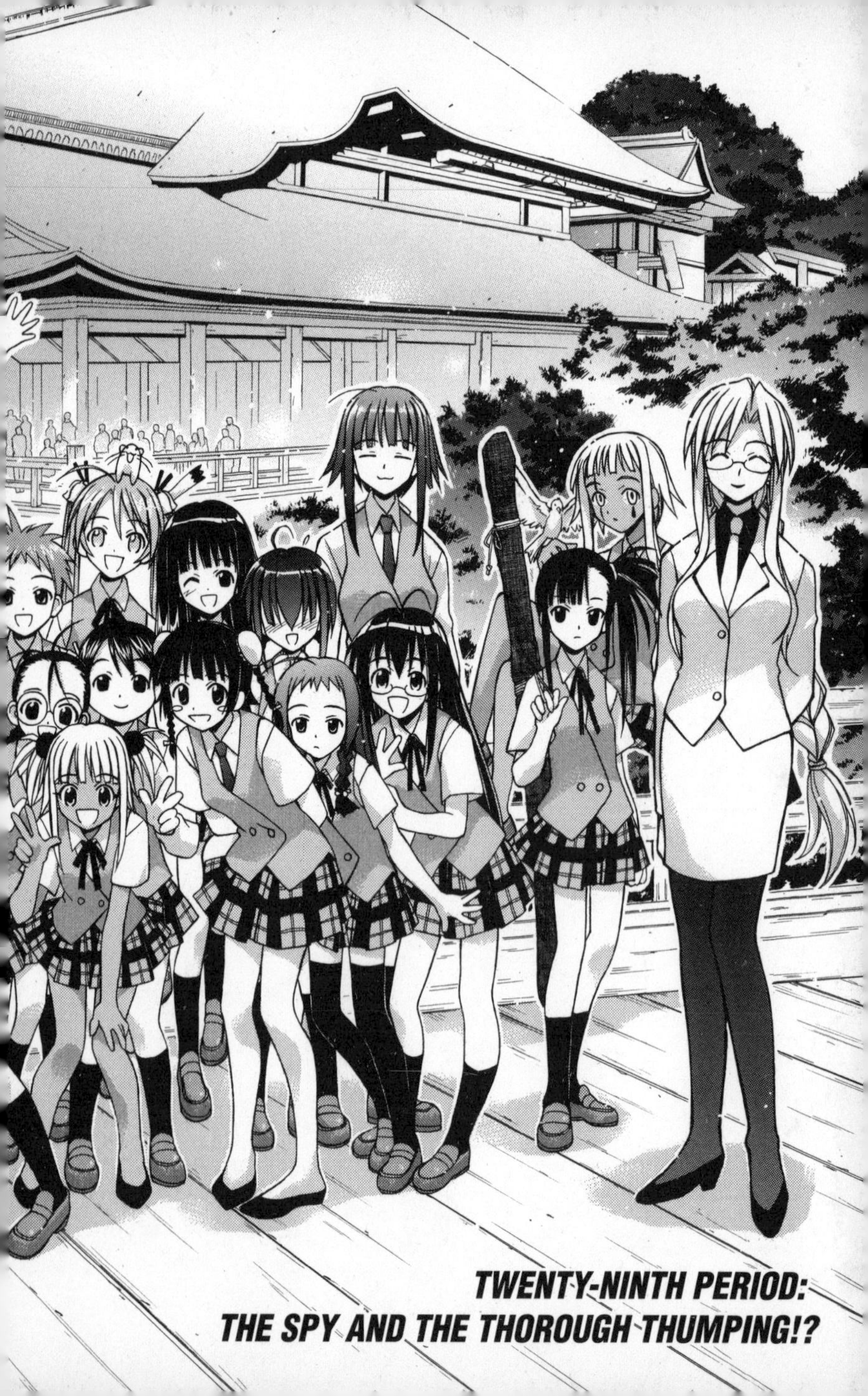
TWENTY-NINTH PERIOD:
THE SPY AND THE THOROUGH THUMPING!?

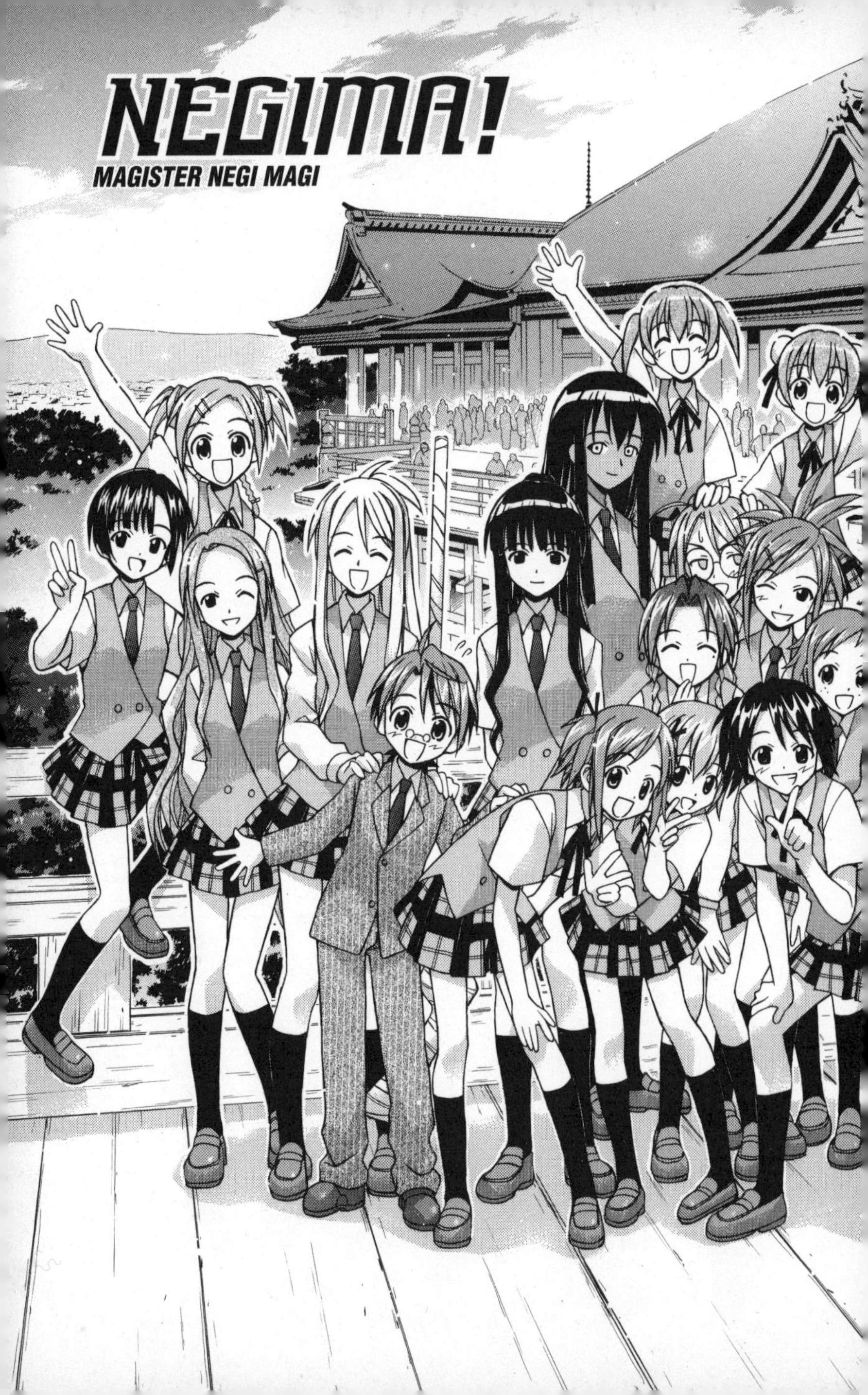
NEGIMA!
MAGISTER NEGI MAGI

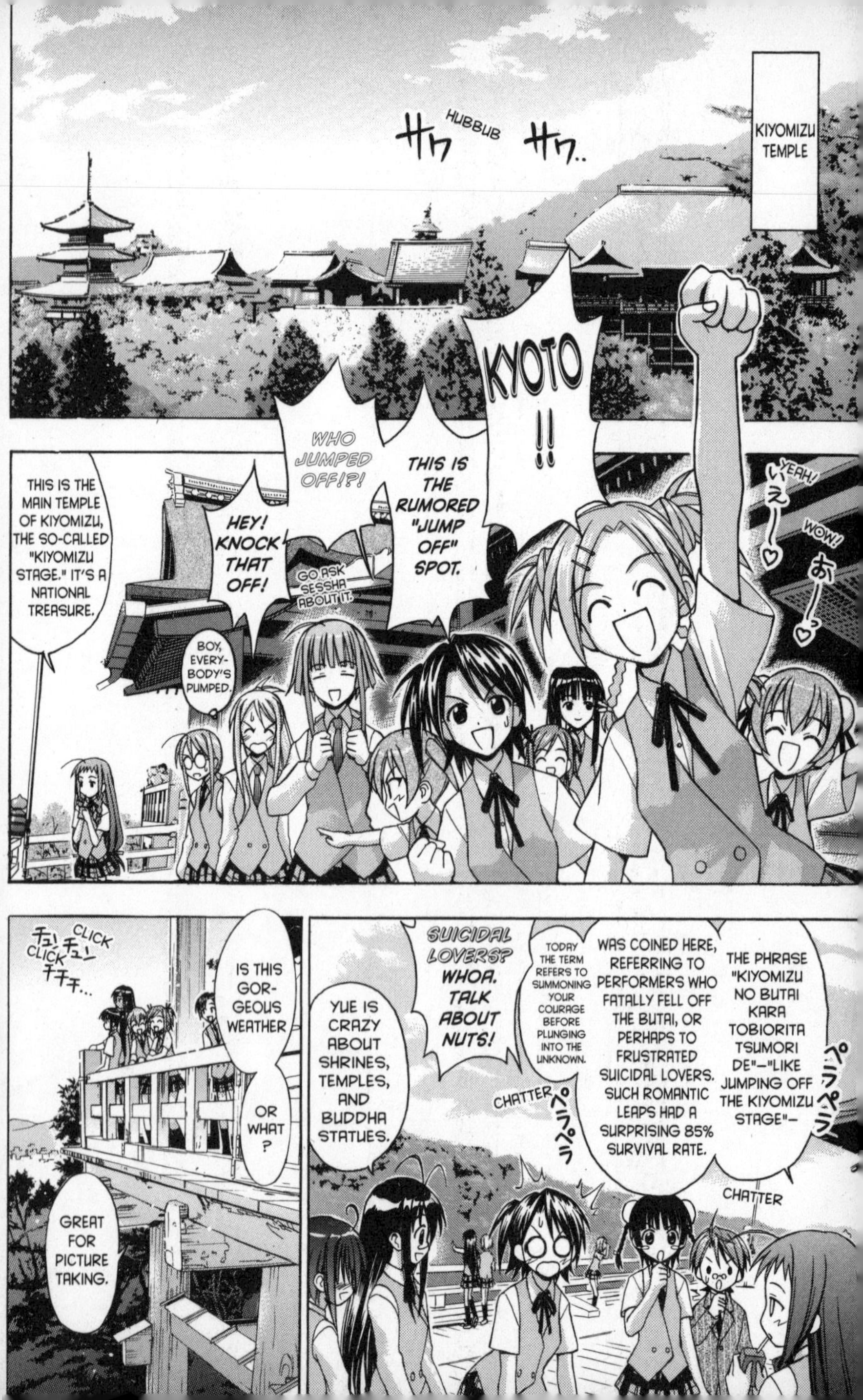
KIYOMIZU TEMPLE
サワ HUBBUB サワ..
KYOTO !!
YEAH! いぇー♡
WOW! おー♡
THIS IS THE RUMORED "JUMP OFF" SPOT.
WHO JUMPED OFF!?!
HEY! KNOCK THAT OFF!
GO ASK SESSHA ABOUT IT.
THIS IS THE MAIN TEMPLE OF KIYOMIZU, THE SO-CALLED "KIYOMIZU STAGE." IT'S A NATIONAL TREASURE.
BOY, EVERY-BODY'S PUMPED.
THE PHRASE "KIYOMIZU NO BUTAI KARA TOBIORITA TSUMORI DE"—"LIKE JUMPING OFF THE KIYOMIZU STAGE"—
WAS COINED HERE, REFERRING TO PERFORMERS WHO FATALLY FELL OFF THE BUTAI, OR PERHAPS TO FRUSTRATED SUICIDAL LOVERS. SUCH ROMANTIC LEAPS HAD A SURPRISING 85% SURVIVAL RATE.
TODAY THE TERM REFERS TO SUMMONING YOUR COURAGE BEFORE PLUNGING INTO THE UNKNOWN.
ペラペラ CHATTER
SUICIDAL LOVERS? WHOA. TALK ABOUT NUTS!
CHATTER ペラペラ
YUE IS CRAZY ABOUT SHRINES, TEMPLES, AND BUDDHA STATUES.
チュンチュン CLICK CLICK チチチ...
IS THIS GORGEOUS WEATHER
OR WHAT?
GREAT FOR PICTURE TAKING.

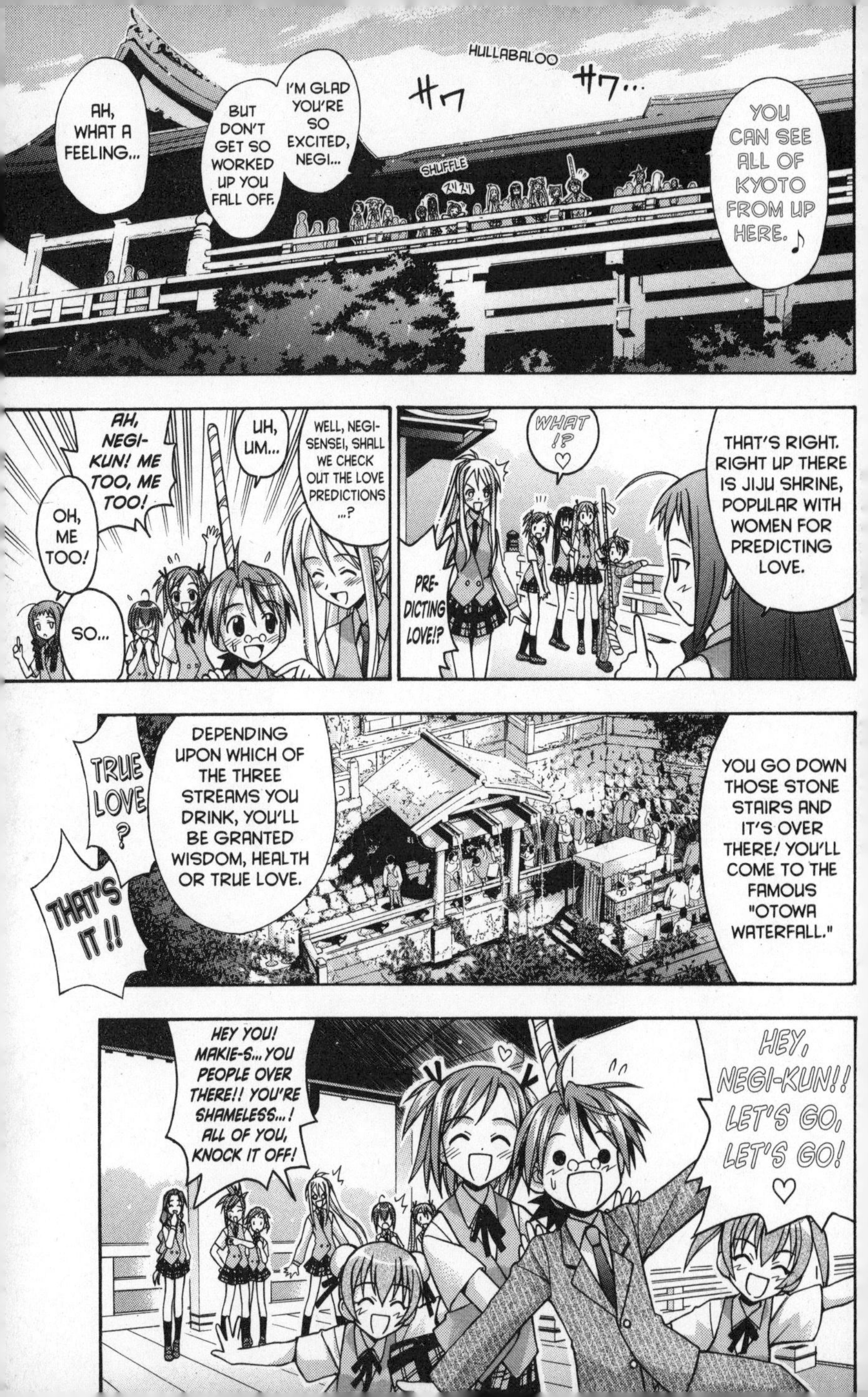
YOU CAN SEE ALL OF KYOTO FROM UP HERE. ♪
HULLABALOO
サワ
サワ...
SHUFFLE
I'M GLAD YOU'RE SO EXCITED, NEGI...
BUT DON'T GET SO WORKED UP YOU FALL OFF.
AH, WHAT A FEELING...
THAT'S RIGHT. RIGHT UP THERE IS JIJU SHRINE, POPULAR WITH WOMEN FOR PREDICTING LOVE.
WHAT !? ♡
PRE-DICTING LOVE!?
WELL, NEGI-SENSEI, SHALL WE CHECK OUT THE LOVE PREDICTIONS ...?
UH, UM...
AH, NEGI-KUN! ME TOO, ME TOO!
OH, ME TOO!
SO...
YOU GO DOWN THOSE STONE STAIRS AND IT'S OVER THERE! YOU'LL COME TO THE FAMOUS "OTOWA WATERFALL."
DEPENDING UPON WHICH OF THE THREE STREAMS YOU DRINK, YOU'LL BE GRANTED WISDOM, HEALTH OR TRUE LOVE.
TRUE LOVE ?
THAT'S IT !!
HEY, NEGI-KUN!! LET'S GO, LET'S GO! ♡
HEY YOU! MAKIE-S... YOU PEOPLE OVER THERE!! YOU'RE SHAMELESS...! ALL OF YOU, KNOCK IT OFF!

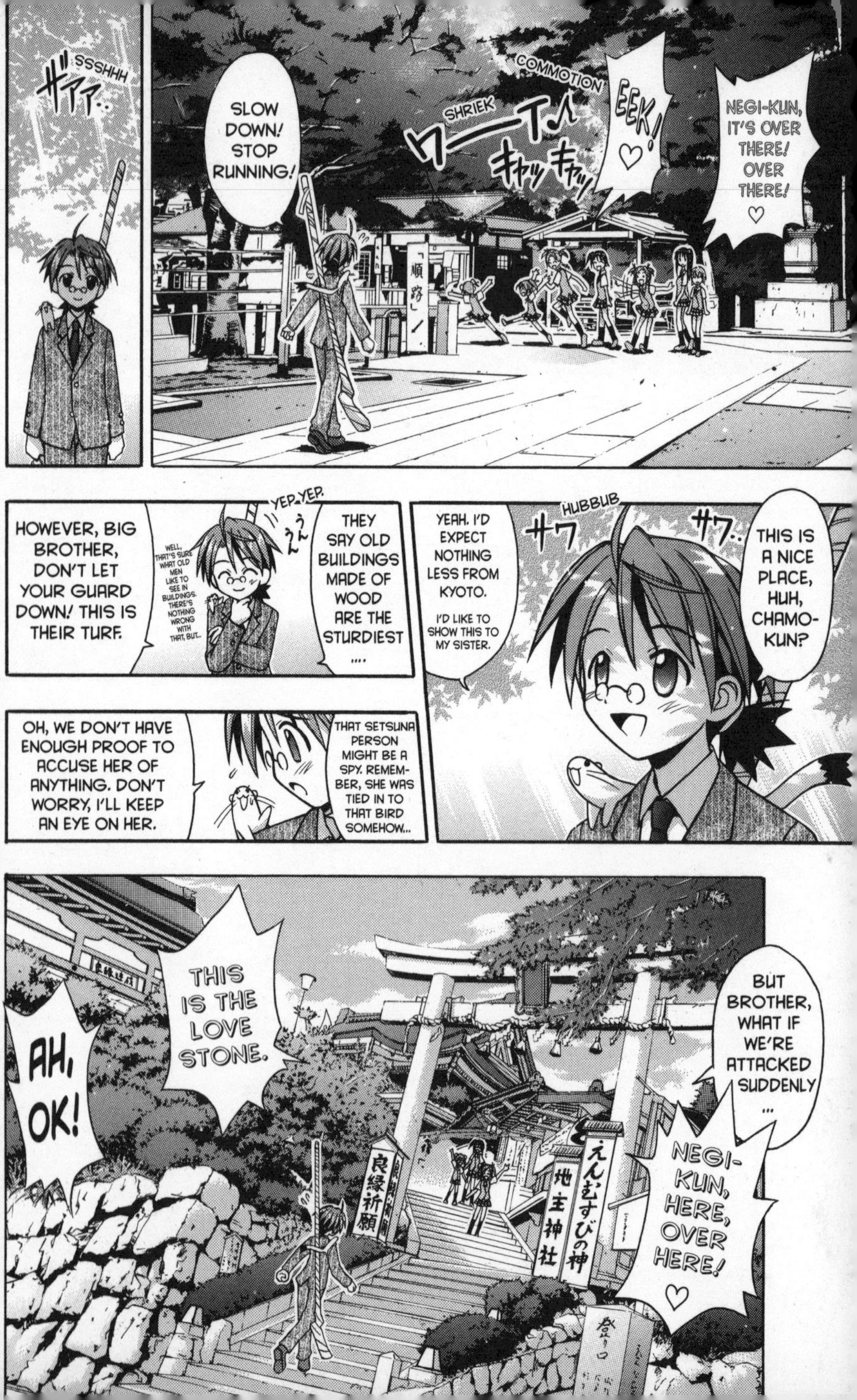
NEGI-KUN, IT'S OVER THERE! OVER THERE! ♡
EEK! ♡
COMMOTION
SHRIEK
SLOW DOWN! STOP RUNNING!
順路
SSSHHH
HUBBUB
THIS IS A NICE PLACE, HUH, CHAMO-KUN?
YEAH. I'D EXPECT NOTHING LESS FROM KYOTO.
I'D LIKE TO SHOW THIS TO MY SISTER.
THEY SAY OLD BUILDINGS MADE OF WOOD ARE THE STURDIEST ....
YEP YEP.
WELL, THAT'S SURE WHAT OLD MEN LIKE TO SEE IN BUILDINGS. THERE'S NOTHING WRONG WITH THAT, BUT...
HOWEVER, BIG BROTHER, DON'T LET YOUR GUARD DOWN! THIS IS THEIR TURF.
THAT SETSUNA PERSON MIGHT BE A SPY. REMEMBER, SHE WAS TIED IN TO THAT BIRD SOMEHOW...
OH, WE DON'T HAVE ENOUGH PROOF TO ACCUSE HER OF ANYTHING. DON'T WORRY, I'LL KEEP AN EYE ON HER.
BUT BROTHER, WHAT IF WE'RE ATTACKED SUDDENLY ...
NEGI-KUN, HERE, OVER HERE! ♡
えんむすびの神
地主神社
良縁祈願
THIS IS THE LOVE STONE.
AH, OK!

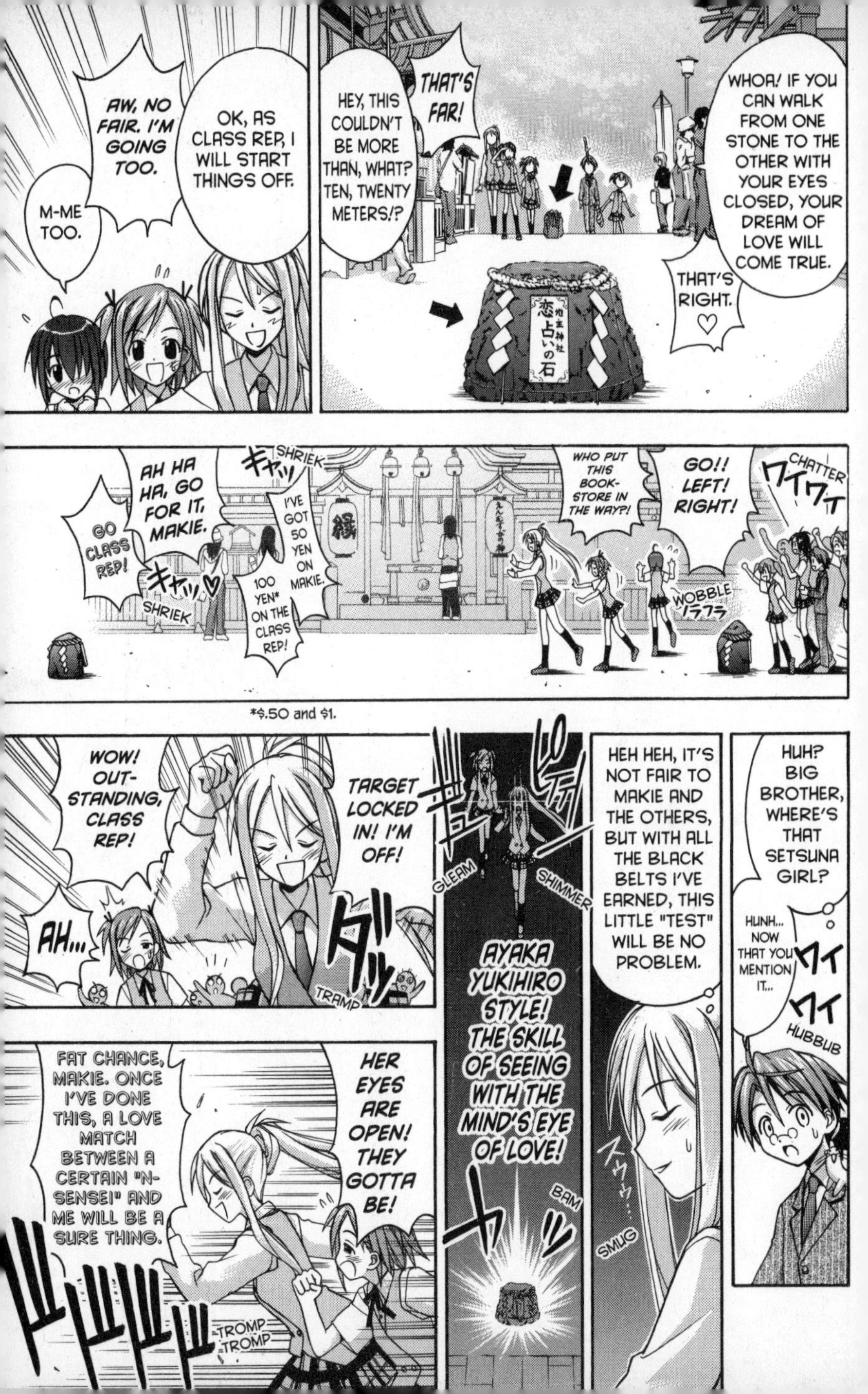

WHOA! IF YOU CAN WALK FROM ONE STONE TO THE OTHER WITH YOUR EYES CLOSED, YOUR DREAM OF LOVE WILL COME TRUE.
THAT'S RIGHT. ♡
THAT'S FAR!
HEY, THIS COULDN'T BE MORE THAN, WHAT? TEN, TWENTY METERS!?
地主神社 恋占いの石
OK, AS CLASS REP, I WILL START THINGS OFF.
AW, NO FAIR. I'M GOING TOO.
M-ME TOO.
CHATTER
GO!! LEFT! RIGHT!
WHO PUT THIS BOOK-STORE IN THE WAY?!
WOBBLE
I'VE GOT 50 YEN ON MAKIE.
100 YEN* ON THE CLASS REP!
SHRIEK
AH HA HA, GO FOR IT, MAKIE.
GO CLASS REP!
SHRIEK
HUH? BIG BROTHER, WHERE'S THAT SETSUNA GIRL?
HUNH... NOW THAT YOU MENTION IT...
HUBBUB
HEH HEH, IT'S NOT FAIR TO MAKIE AND THE OTHERS, BUT WITH ALL THE BLACK BELTS I'VE EARNED, THIS LITTLE "TEST" WILL BE NO PROBLEM.
GLEAM
SHIMMER
TARGET LOCKED IN! I'M OFF!
WOW! OUT-STANDING, CLASS REP!
AH...
TRAMP
SMUG
AYAKA YUKIHIRO STYLE! THE SKILL OF SEEING WITH THE MIND'S EYE OF LOVE!
BAM
HER EYES ARE OPEN! THEY GOTTA BE!
FAT CHANCE, MAKIE. ONCE I'VE DONE THIS, A LOVE MATCH BETWEEN A CERTAIN "N-SENSEI" AND ME WILL BE A SURE THING.
TROMP TROMP

*$.50 and $1.

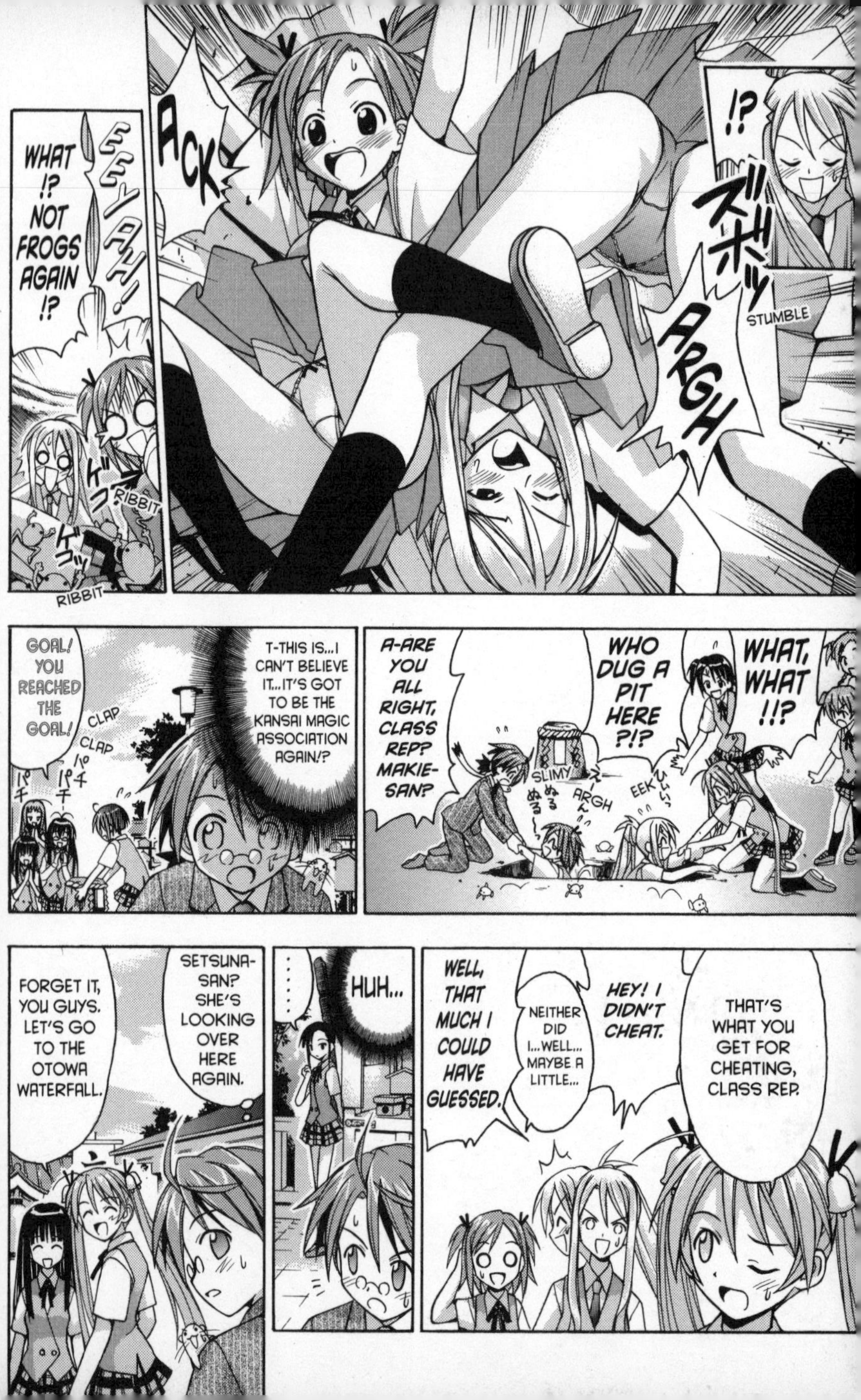
!?
ズボッ
STUMBLE
ARGH
ACK
EEYAAH!
WHAT!? NOT FROGS AGAIN!?
ゲコ
RIBBIT
ゲコッ
RIBBIT
WHAT, WHAT!!?
WHO DUG A PIT HERE?!?
A-ARE YOU ALL RIGHT, CLASS REP? MAKIE-SAN?
ひぃぃっ
EEK
えーん
ARGH
ぬるぬる
SLIMY
T-THIS IS...I CAN'T BELIEVE IT...IT'S GOT TO BE THE KANSAI MAGIC ASSOCIATION AGAIN!?
GOAL! YOU REACHED THE GOAL!
パチ
CLAP
パチ
CLAP
パチ
THAT'S WHAT YOU GET FOR CHEATING, CLASS REP.
HEY! I DIDN'T CHEAT.
NEITHER DID I...WELL... MAYBE A LITTLE...
WELL, THAT MUCH I COULD HAVE GUESSED.
HUH...
......
SETSUNA-SAN? SHE'S LOOKING OVER HERE AGAIN.
FORGET IT, YOU GUYS. LET'S GO TO THE OTOWA WATERFALL.

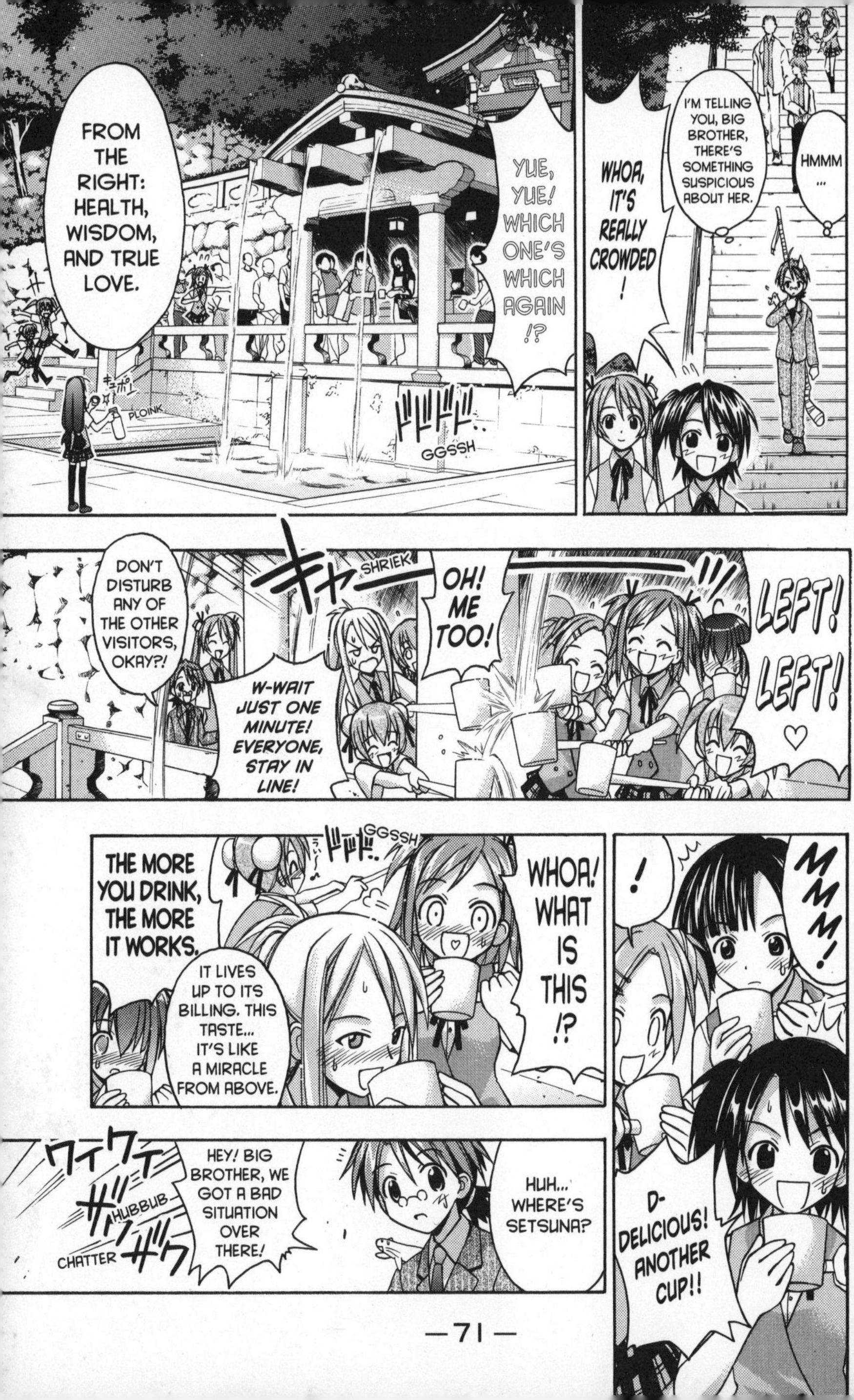
HMMM ...
I'M TELLING YOU, BIG BROTHER, THERE'S SOMETHING SUSPICIOUS ABOUT HER.
WHOA, IT'S REALLY CROWDED!
YUE, YUE! WHICH ONE'S WHICH AGAIN!?
FROM THE RIGHT: HEALTH, WISDOM, AND TRUE LOVE.
GGSSH
PLOINK
LEFT! LEFT!
OH! ME TOO!
SHRIEK
W-WAIT JUST ONE MINUTE! EVERYONE, STAY IN LINE!
DON'T DISTURB ANY OF THE OTHER VISITORS, OKAY?!
MMM!
!
D-DELICIOUS! ANOTHER CUP!!
WHOA! WHAT IS THIS!?
GGSSH
THE MORE YOU DRINK, THE MORE IT WORKS.
IT LIVES UP TO ITS BILLING. THIS TASTE... IT'S LIKE A MIRACLE FROM ABOVE.
HUH... WHERE'S SETSUNA?
HEY! BIG BROTHER, WE GOT A BAD SITUATION OVER THERE!
HUBBUB
CHATTER

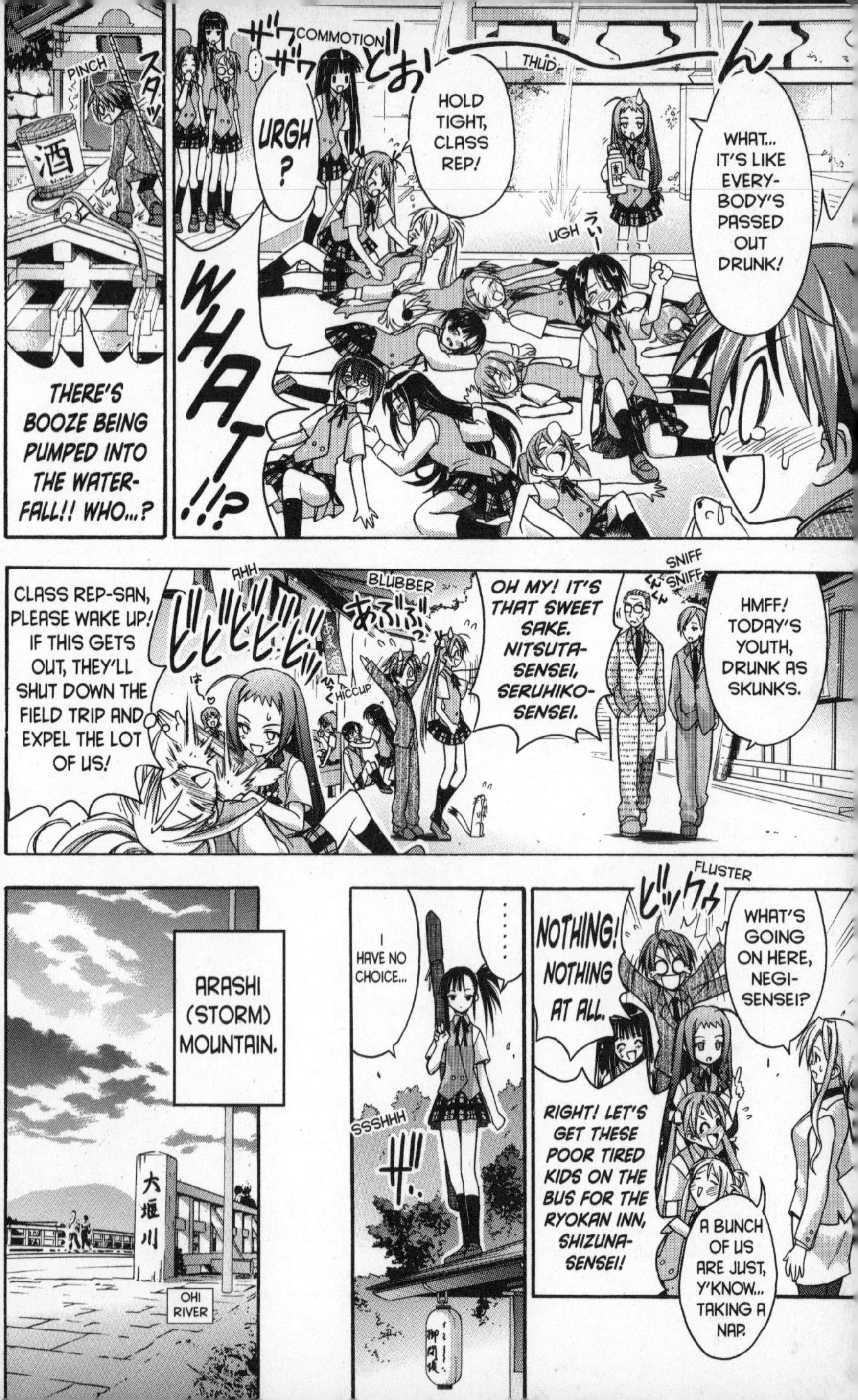

THUD
WHAT... IT'S LIKE EVERYBODY'S PASSED OUT DRUNK!
COMMOTION
HOLD TIGHT, CLASS REP!
URGH ?
UGH
WHAT!!?
PINCH
酒
THERE'S BOOZE BEING PUMPED INTO THE WATERFALL!! WHO...?
SNIFF SNIFF
HMFF! TODAY'S YOUTH, DRUNK AS SKUNKS.
OH MY! IT'S THAT SWEET SAKE. NITSUTA-SENSEI, SERUHIKO-SENSEI.
BLUBBER
HICCUP
AHH
CLASS REP-SAN, PLEASE WAKE UP! IF THIS GETS OUT, THEY'LL SHUT DOWN THE FIELD TRIP AND EXPEL THE LOT OF US!
FLUSTER
WHAT'S GOING ON HERE, NEGI-SENSEI?
NOTHING! NOTHING AT ALL.
A BUNCH OF US ARE JUST, Y'KNOW... TAKING A NAP.
RIGHT! LET'S GET THESE POOR TIRED KIDS ON THE BUS FOR THE RYOKAN INN, SHIZUNA-SENSEI!
......
I HAVE NO CHOICE...
SSSHHH
ARASHI (STORM) MOUNTAIN.
大堰川
OHI RIVER

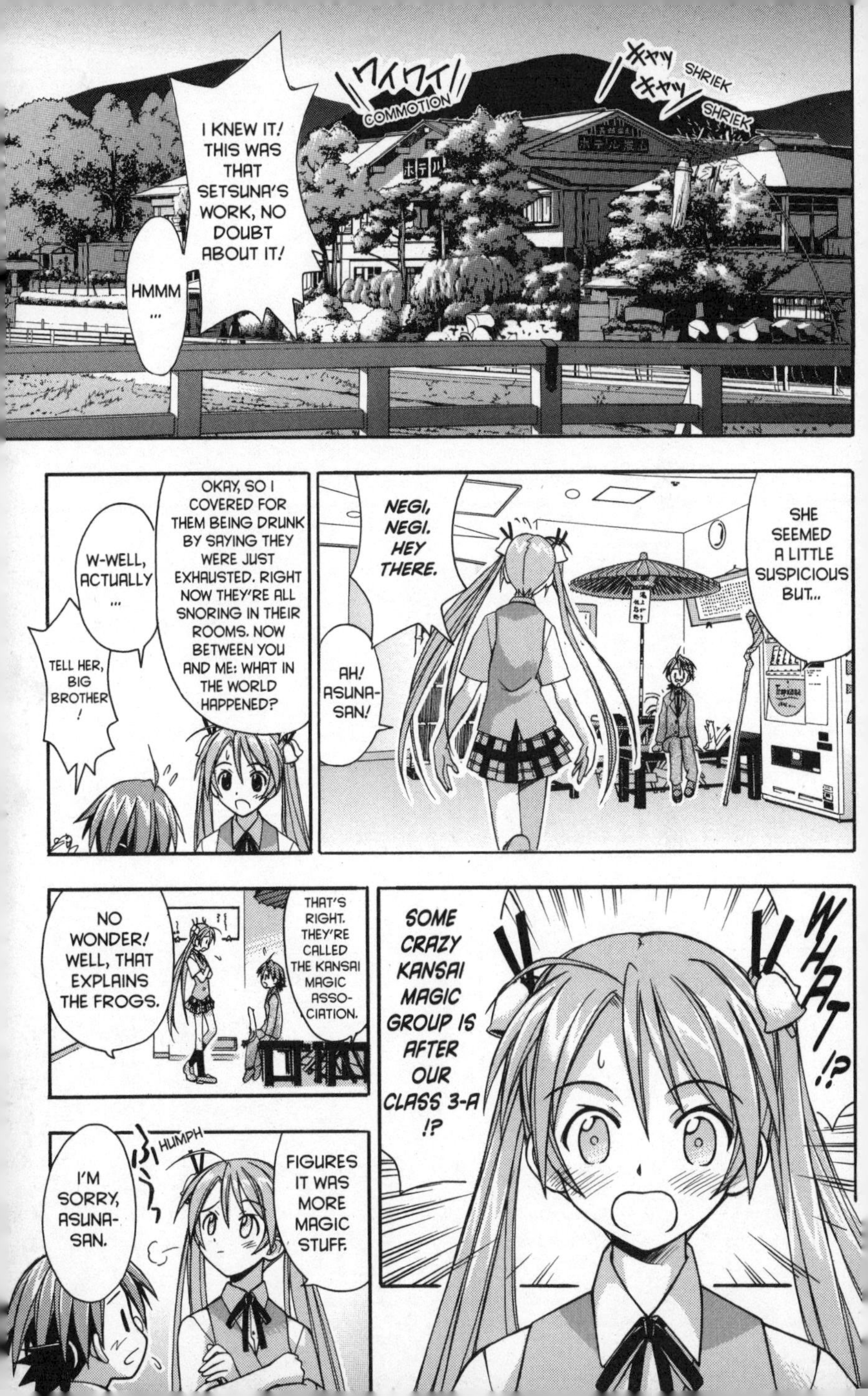
キャッ
SHRIEK
キャッ
SHRIEK
ワイワイ
COMMOTION
I KNEW IT! THIS WAS THAT SETSUNA'S WORK, NO DOUBT ABOUT IT!
HMMM ...
SHE SEEMED A LITTLE SUSPICIOUS BUT...
NEGI, NEGI. HEY THERE.
AH! ASUNA-SAN!
OKAY, SO I COVERED FOR THEM BEING DRUNK BY SAYING THEY WERE JUST EXHAUSTED. RIGHT NOW THEY'RE ALL SNORING IN THEIR ROOMS. NOW BETWEEN YOU AND ME: WHAT IN THE WORLD HAPPENED?
W-WELL, ACTUALLY ...
TELL HER, BIG BROTHER!
WHAT !?
SOME CRAZY KANSAI MAGIC GROUP IS AFTER OUR CLASS 3-A !?
THAT'S RIGHT. THEY'RE CALLED THE KANSAI MAGIC ASSO-CIATION.
NO WONDER! WELL, THAT EXPLAINS THE FROGS.
FIGURES IT WAS MORE MAGIC STUFF.
HUMPH
I'M SORRY, ASUNA-SAN.

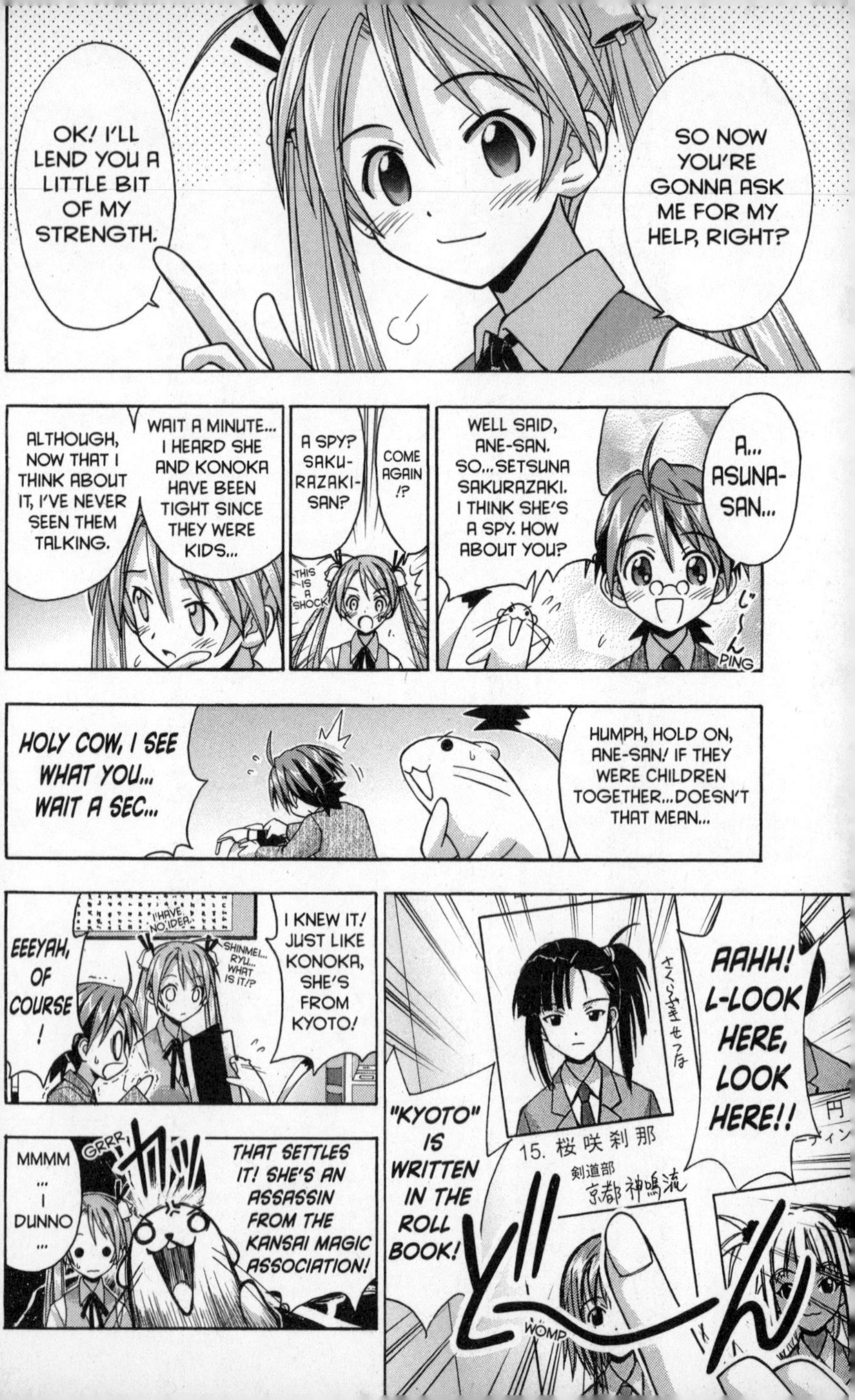
SO NOW YOU'RE GONNA ASK ME FOR MY HELP, RIGHT?
OK! I'LL LEND YOU A LITTLE BIT OF MY STRENGTH.
A... ASUNA-SAN...
じ~ん
PING
WELL SAID, ANE-SAN. SO... SETSUNA SAKURAZAKI. I THINK SHE'S A SPY. HOW ABOUT YOU?
COME AGAIN!?
A SPY? SAKU-RAZAKI-SAN?
THIS IS A SHOCK
WAIT A MINUTE... I HEARD SHE AND KONOKA HAVE BEEN TIGHT SINCE THEY WERE KIDS...
ALTHOUGH, NOW THAT I THINK ABOUT IT, I'VE NEVER SEEN THEM TALKING.
HUMPH, HOLD ON, ANE-SAN! IF THEY WERE CHILDREN TOGETHER...DOESN'T THAT MEAN...
HOLY COW, I SEE WHAT YOU... WAIT A SEC...
AAHH! L-LOOK HERE, LOOK HERE!!
さくらざきせつな
15. 桜咲刹那
剣道部
京都神鳴流
"KYOTO" IS WRITTEN IN THE ROLL BOOK!
WOMP
I KNEW IT! JUST LIKE KONOKA, SHE'S FROM KYOTO!
SHINMEI... RYU... WHAT IS IT!?
I HAVE NO IDEA.
EEEYAH, OF COURSE!
THAT SETTLES IT! SHE'S AN ASSASSIN FROM THE KANSAI MAGIC ASSOCIATION!
GRRR
MMMM ... I DUNNO ...

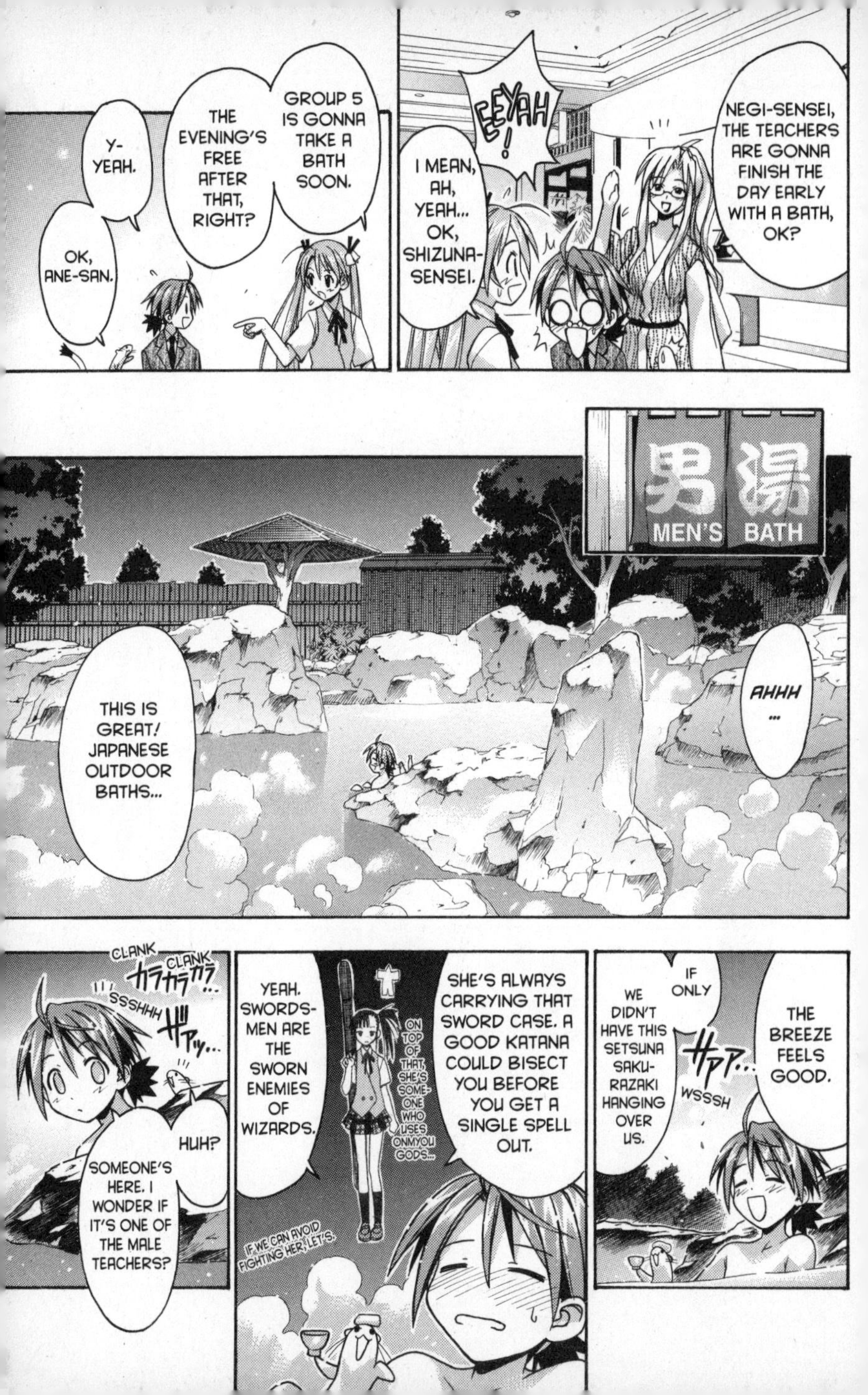
NEGI-SENSEI, THE TEACHERS ARE GONNA FINISH THE DAY EARLY WITH A BATH, OK?
EEYAH!
I MEAN, AH, YEAH... OK, SHIZUNA-SENSEI.
GROUP 5 IS GONNA TAKE A BATH SOON.
THE EVENING'S FREE AFTER THAT, RIGHT?
Y-YEAH.
OK, ANE-SAN.
男湯
MEN'S BATH
AHHH...
THIS IS GREAT! JAPANESE OUTDOOR BATHS...
THE BREEZE FEELS GOOD.
IF ONLY WE DIDN'T HAVE THIS SETSUNA SAKURAZAKI HANGING OVER US.
WSSSH
SHE'S ALWAYS CARRYING THAT SWORD CASE. A GOOD KATANA COULD BISECT YOU BEFORE YOU GET A SINGLE SPELL OUT.
YEAH. SWORDSMEN ARE THE SWORN ENEMIES OF WIZARDS.
ON TOP OF THAT, SHE'S SOMEONE WHO USES ONMYOU GODS...
IF WE CAN AVOID FIGHTING HER, LET'S.
CLANK CLANK
SSSHHH
HUH?
SOMEONE'S HERE. I WONDER IF IT'S ONE OF THE MALE TEACHERS?

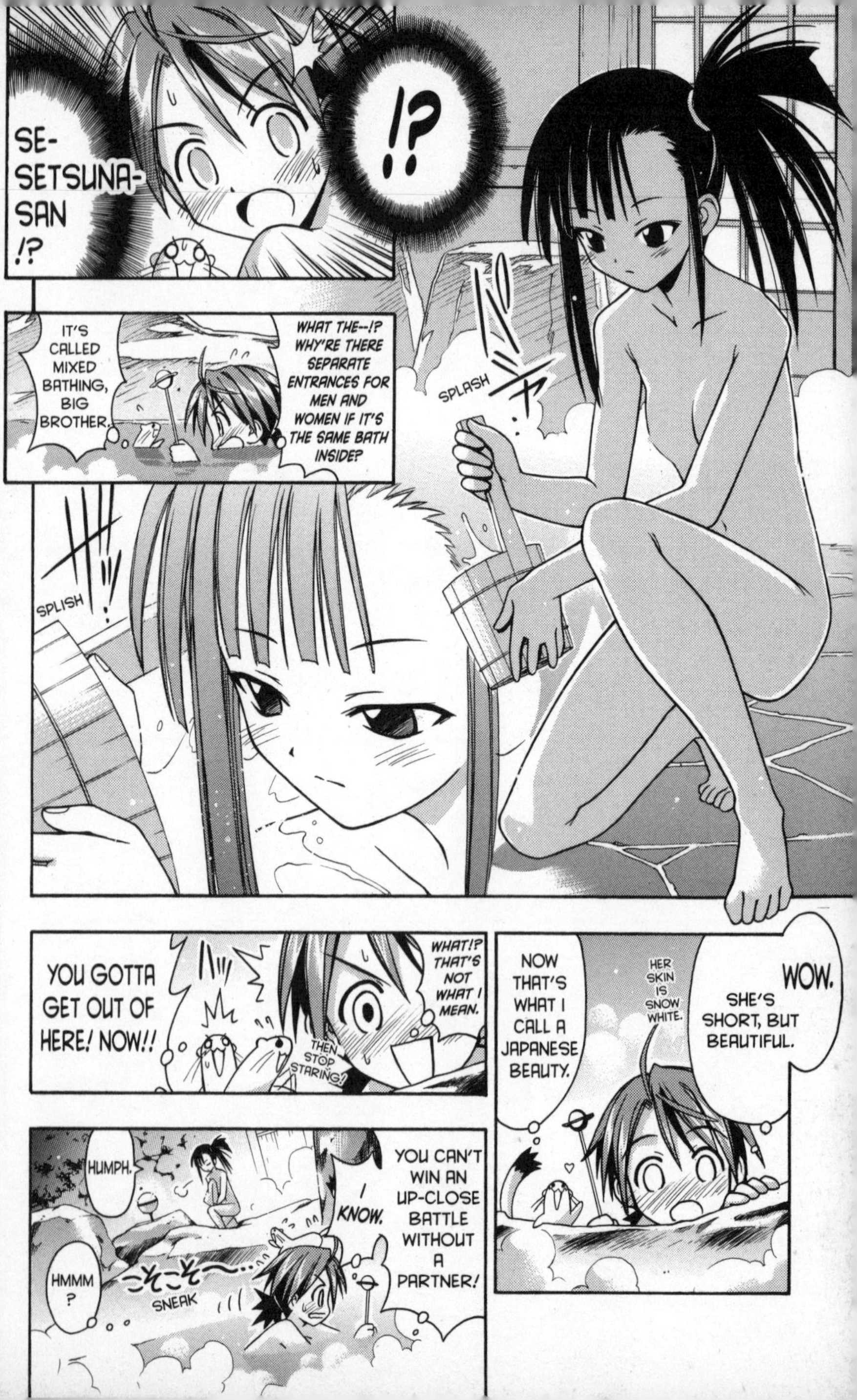
!?
SE-SETSUNA-SAN !?
SPLASH
WHAT THE--!? WHY'RE THERE SEPARATE ENTRANCES FOR MEN AND WOMEN IF IT'S THE SAME BATH INSIDE?
IT'S CALLED MIXED BATHING, BIG BROTHER.
SPLISH
WOW.
SHE'S SHORT, BUT BEAUTIFUL.
HER SKIN IS SNOW WHITE.
NOW THAT'S WHAT I CALL A JAPANESE BEAUTY.
WHAT!? THAT'S NOT WHAT I MEAN.
THEN STOP STARING!
YOU GOTTA GET OUT OF HERE! NOW!!
YOU CAN'T WIN AN UP-CLOSE BATTLE WITHOUT A PARTNER!
I KNOW.
HUMPH.
HMMM ?
こそこそ〜…
SNEAK

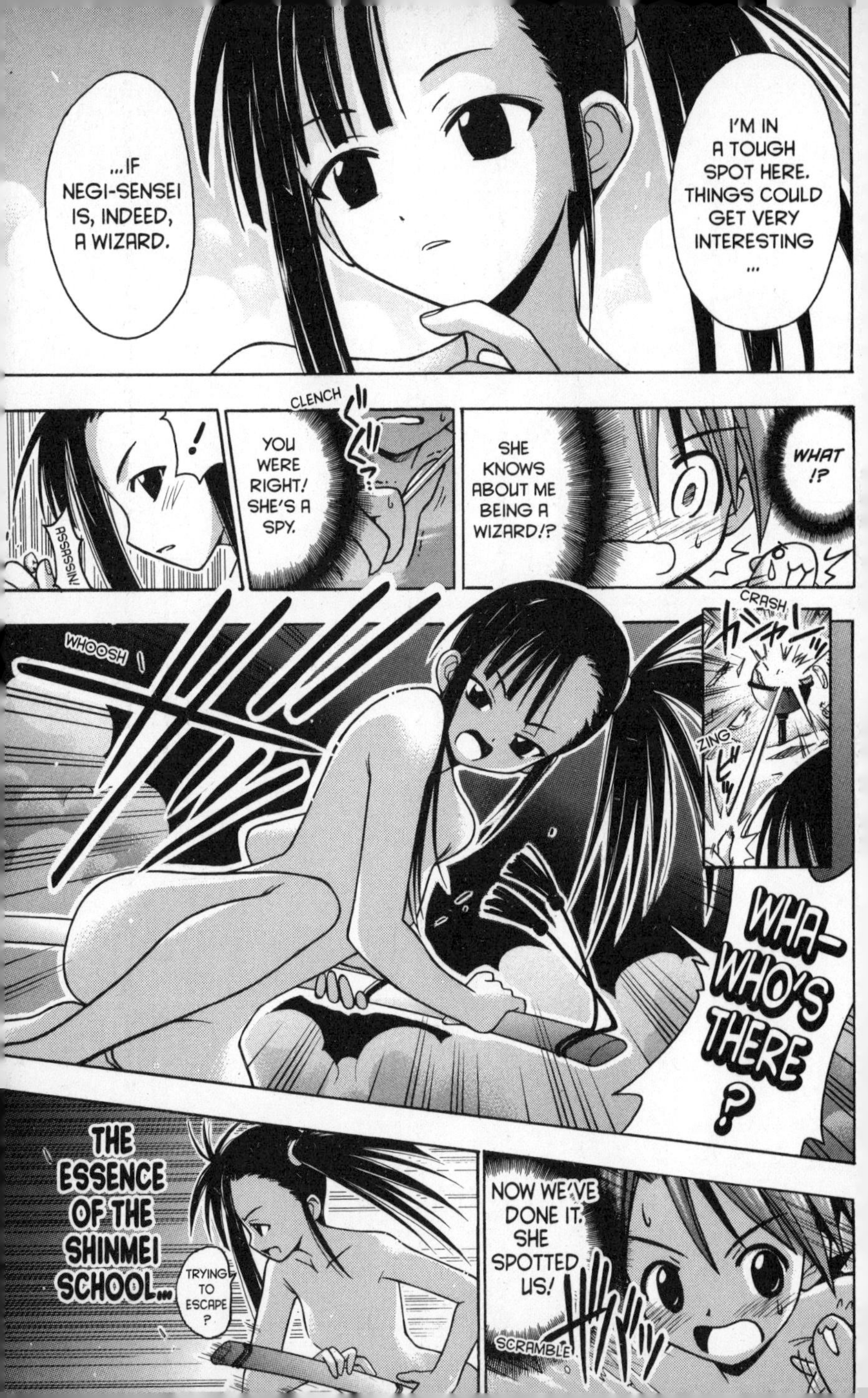

I'M IN A TOUGH SPOT HERE. THINGS COULD GET VERY INTERESTING ...
...IF NEGI-SENSEI IS, INDEED, A WIZARD.
WHAT !?
SHE KNOWS ABOUT ME BEING A WIZARD!?
CLENCH
YOU WERE RIGHT! SHE'S A SPY.
!
ASSASSIN!
CRASH
ZING
WHOOSH
WHA-WHO'S THERE ?
NOW WE'VE DONE IT. SHE SPOTTED US!
SCRAMBLE
TRYING TO ESCAPE ?
THE ESSENCE OF THE SHINMEI SCHOOL...

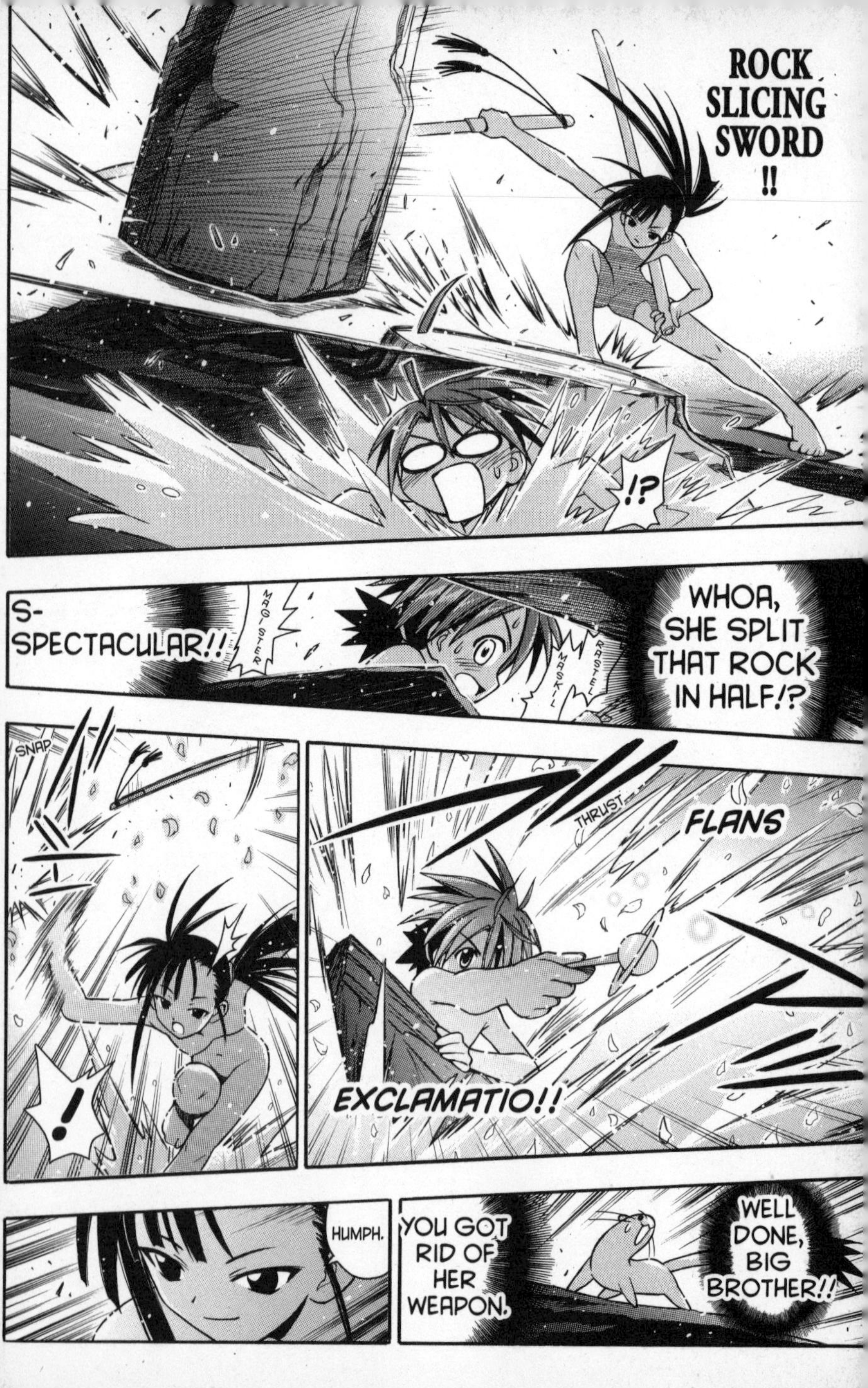
ROCK SLICING SWORD !!
!?
WHOA, SHE SPLIT THAT ROCK IN HALF!?
RASTEL MASKIL
MAGISTER
S- SPECTACULAR!!
THRUST
FLANS
EXCLAMATIO!!
SNAP
!
WELL DONE, BIG BROTHER!!
YOU GOT RID OF HER WEAPON.
HUMPH.

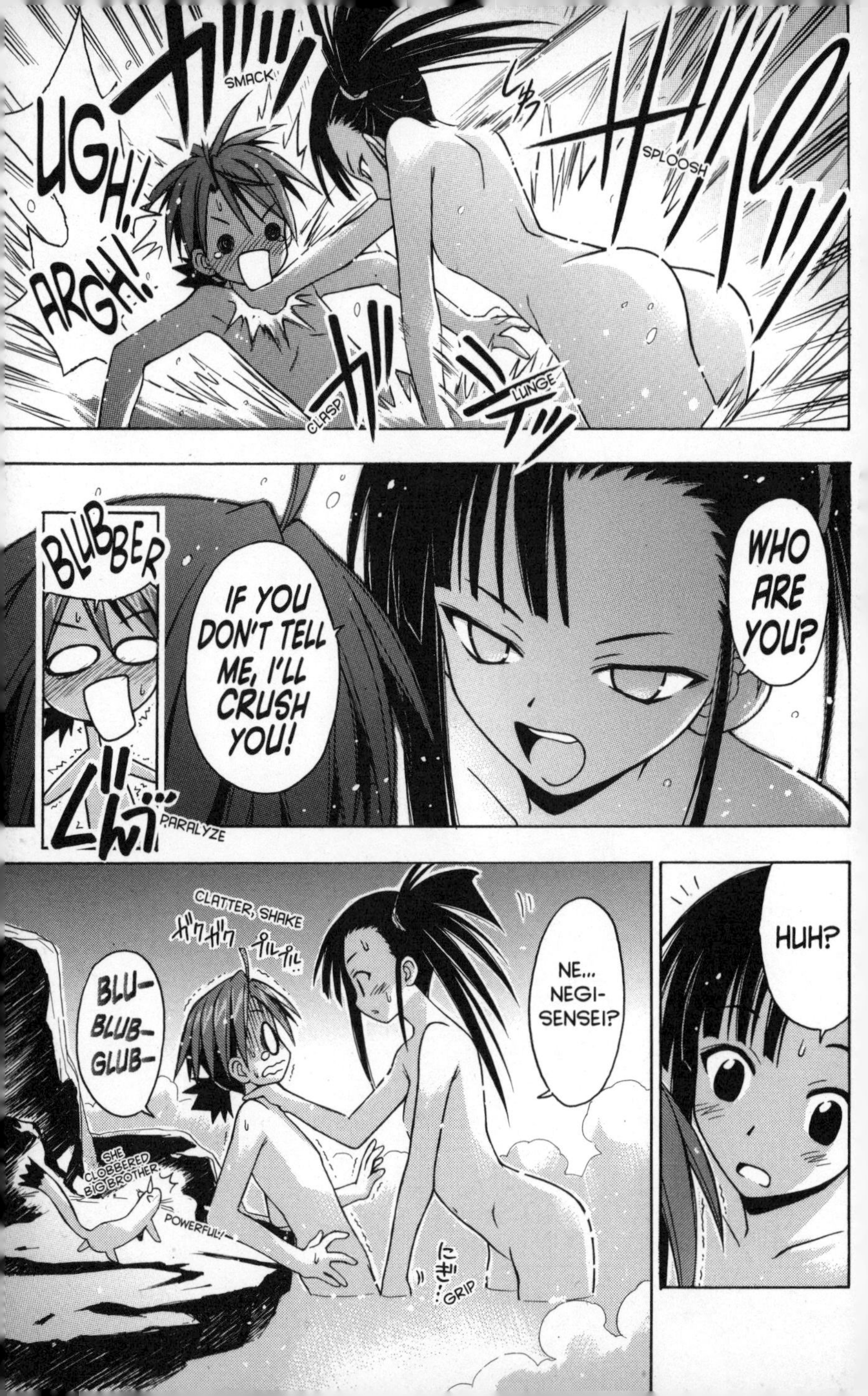
SPLOOSH
SMACK
UGH!!
ARGH!!
LUNGE
CLASP
WHO ARE YOU?
IF YOU DON'T TELL ME, I'LL CRUSH YOU!
BLUBBER
PARALYZE
HUH?
NE... NEGI-SENSEI?
CLATTER, SHAKE
BLU-BLUB-GLUB-
SHE CLOBBERED BIG BROTHER
POWERFUL!
にぎ...GRIP

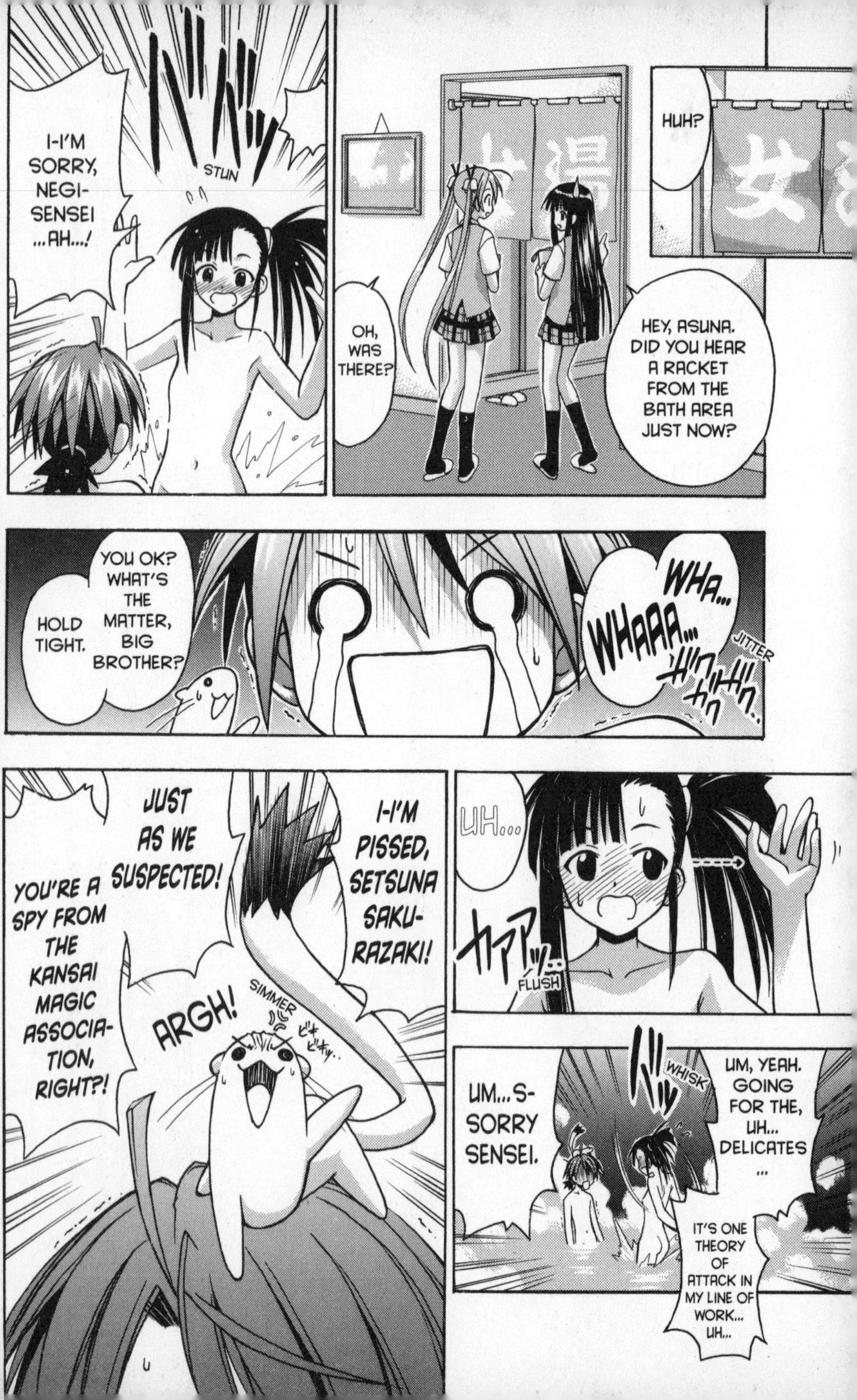
HUH?
HEY, ASUNA. DID YOU HEAR A RACKET FROM THE BATH AREA JUST NOW?
OH, WAS THERE?
STUN
I-I'M SORRY, NEGI-SENSEI ...AH...!
WHA... WHAAA...
JITTER
YOU OK? WHAT'S THE MATTER, BIG BROTHER?
HOLD TIGHT.
UH...
FLUSH
UM, YEAH. GOING FOR THE, UH... DELICATES ...
WHISK
UM... S-SORRY SENSEI.
IT'S ONE THEORY OF ATTACK IN MY LINE OF WORK... UH...
I-I'M PISSED, SETSUNA SAKU-RAZAKI!
JUST AS WE SUSPECTED!
YOU'RE A SPY FROM THE KANSAI MAGIC ASSOCIA-TION, RIGHT?!
ARGH!
SIMMER

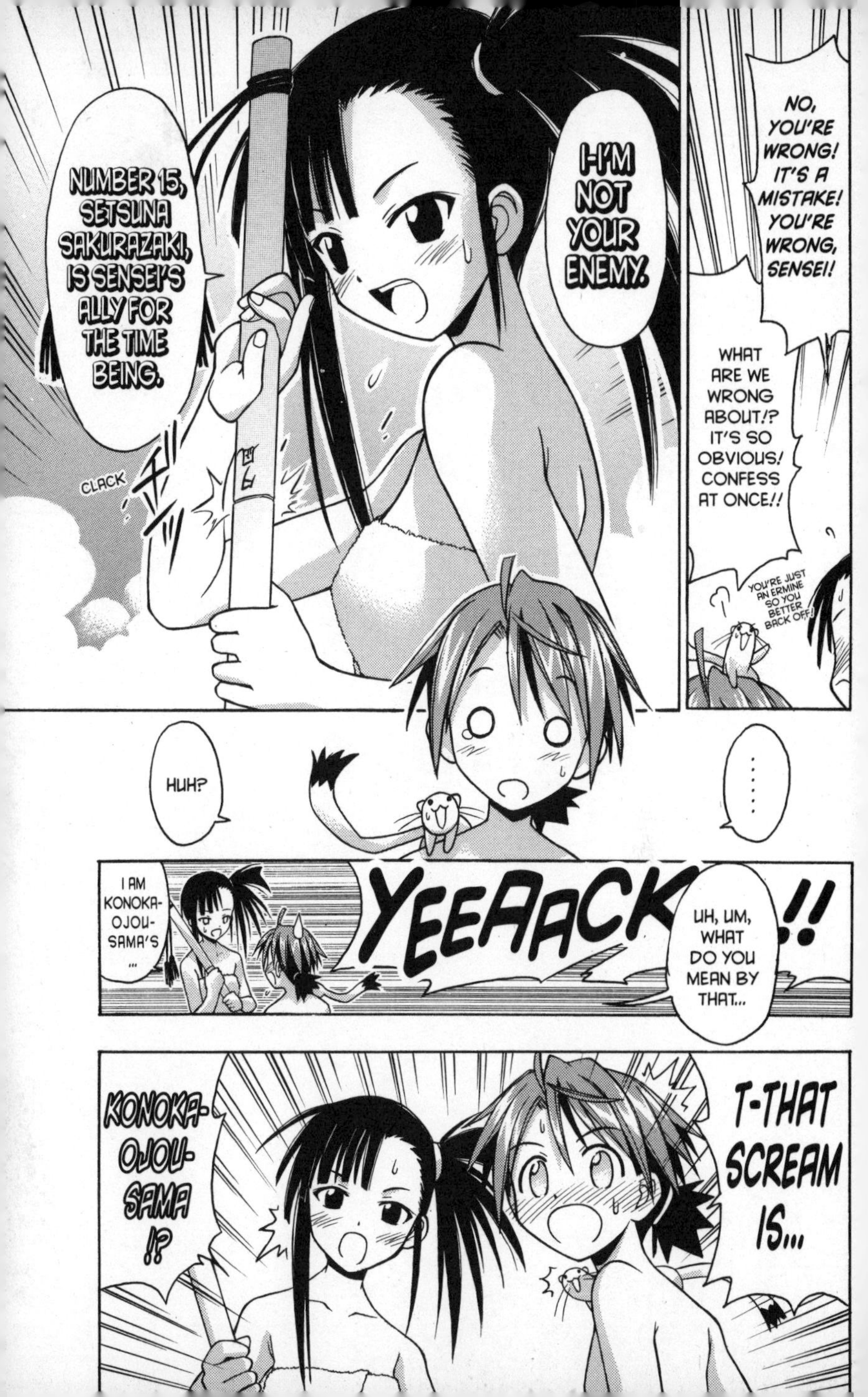
NO, YOU'RE WRONG! IT'S A MISTAKE! YOU'RE WRONG, SENSEI!
WHAT ARE WE WRONG ABOUT!? IT'S SO OBVIOUS! CONFESS AT ONCE!!
YOU'RE JUST AN ERMINE SO YOU BETTER BACK OFF!
I-I'M NOT YOUR ENEMY.
NUMBER 15, SETSUNA SAKURAZAKI, IS SENSEI'S ALLY FOR THE TIME BEING.
CLACK
......
HUH?
UH, UM, WHAT DO YOU MEAN BY THAT...
YEEAACK!!
I AM KONOKA-OJOU-SAMA'S ...
T-THAT SCREAM IS...
KONOKA-OJOU-SAMA!?

3-A FIELD TRIP GROUP NUMBER 1

(GROUP LEADER)
MISA KAKIZAKI

MADOKA KUGIMIYA
SAKURAKO SHIINA
FUKA NARUTAKI
FUMIKA NARUTAKI

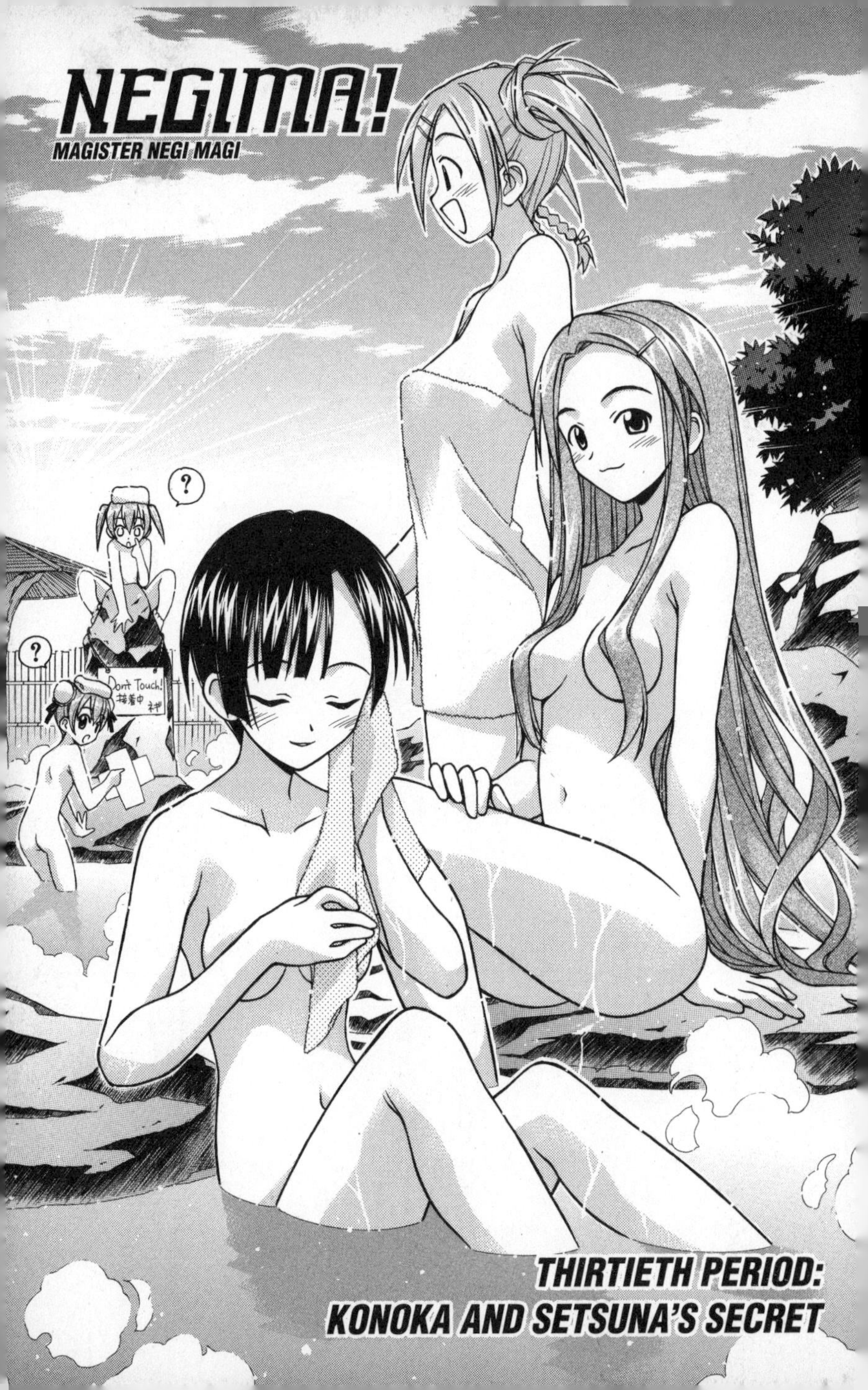
NEGIMA!
MAGISTER NEGI MAGI
?
?
Don't Touch!
接着中
THIRTIETH PERIOD:
KONOKA AND SETSUNA'S SECRET

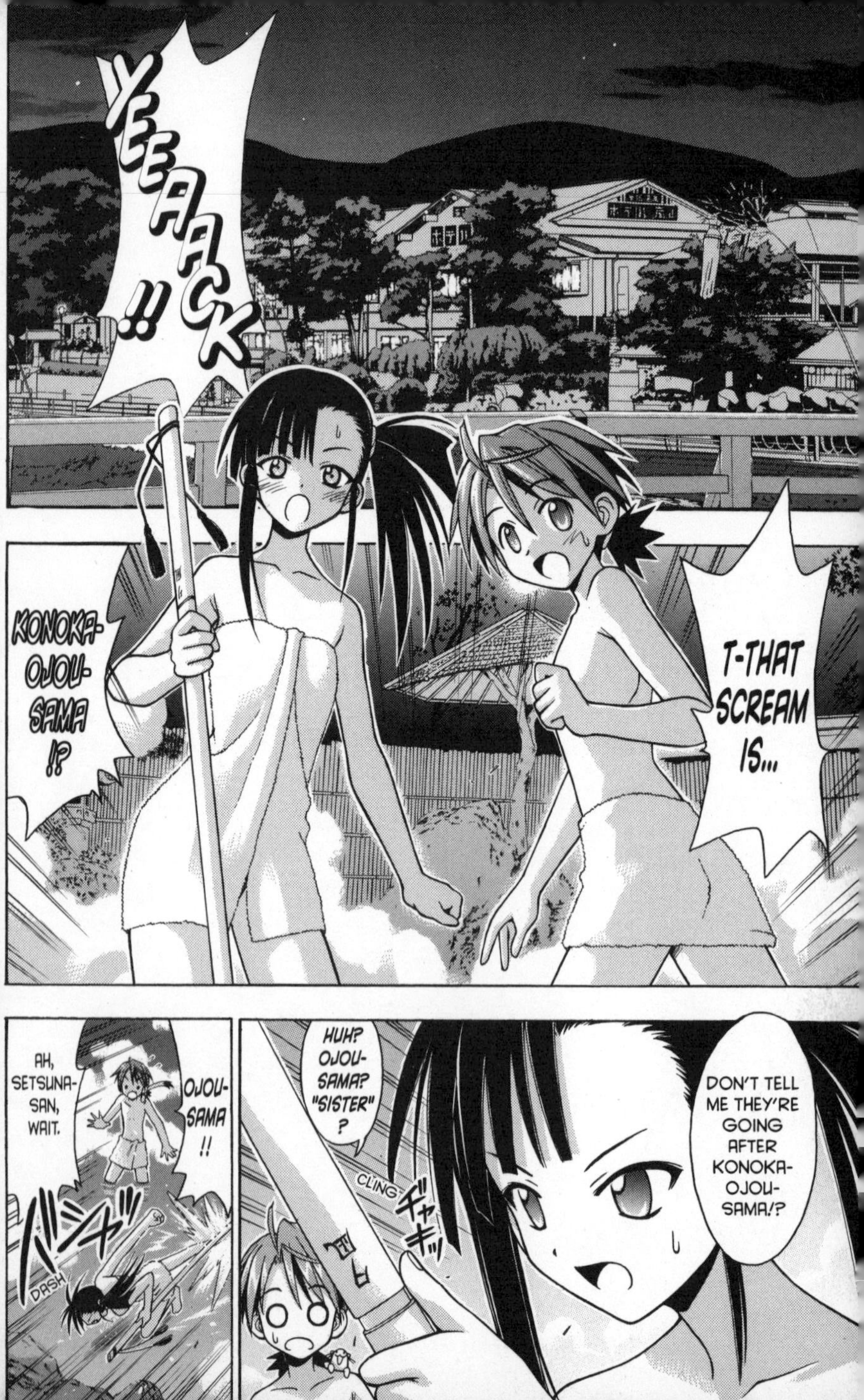
YEEAAACK!!
T-THAT SCREAM IS...
KONOKA-OJOU-SAMA!?
DON'T TELL ME THEY'RE GOING AFTER KONOKA-OJOU-SAMA!?
HUH? OJOU-SAMA? "SISTER"?
CLING
OJOU-SAMA!!
AH, SETSUNA-SAN, WAIT.
DASH

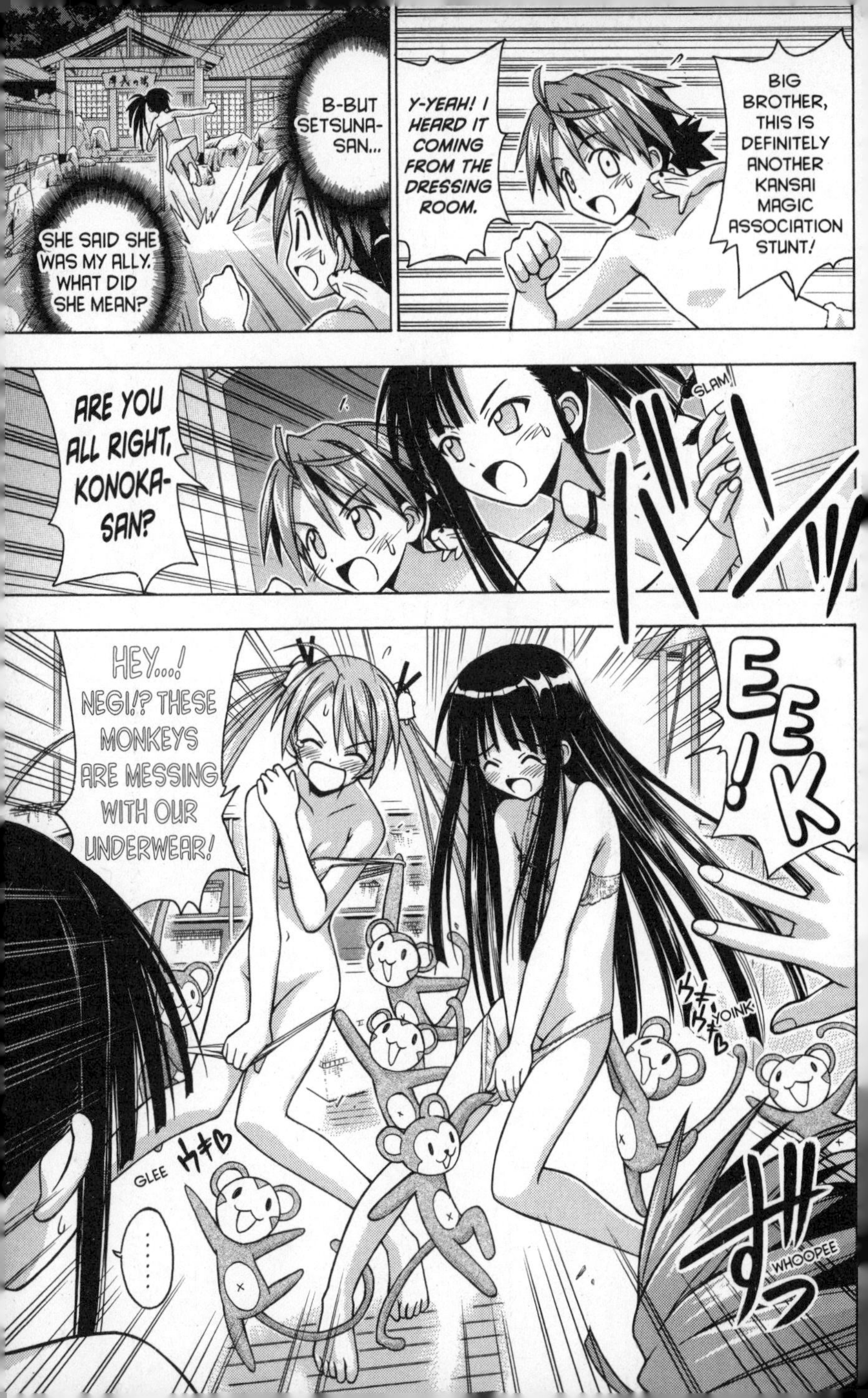
BIG BROTHER, THIS IS DEFINITELY ANOTHER KANSAI MAGIC ASSOCIATION STUNT!
Y-YEAH! I HEARD IT COMING FROM THE DRESSING ROOM.
B-BUT SETSUNA-SAN...
SHE SAID SHE WAS MY ALLY. WHAT DID SHE MEAN?
SLAM!
ARE YOU ALL RIGHT, KONOKA-SAN?
EEEK!
HEY...! NEGI!? THESE MONKEYS ARE MESSING WITH OUR UNDERWEAR!
YOINK
GLEE
WHOOPEE
......

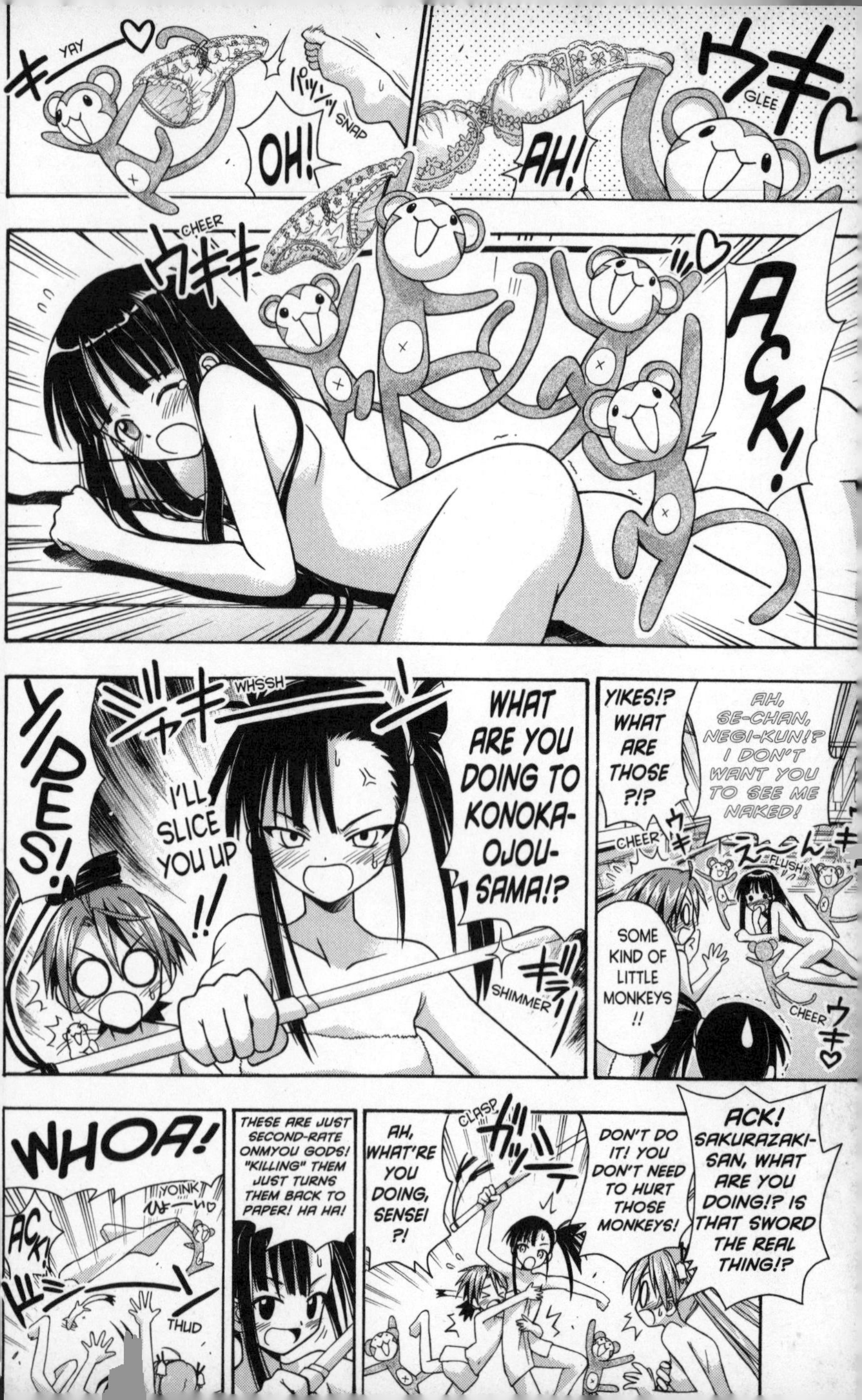

GLEE
AH!
YAY
SNAP
OH!
CHEER
ACK!
AH, SE-CHAN, NEGI-KUN!? I DON'T WANT YOU TO SEE ME NAKED!
YIKES!? WHAT ARE THOSE ?!?
CHEER
FLUSH
SOME KIND OF LITTLE MONKEYS !!
CHEER
WHAT ARE YOU DOING TO KONOKA-OJOU-SAMA!?
WHSSH
I'LL SLICE YOU UP !!
SHIMMER
YIPES!
ACK! SAKURAZAKI-SAN, WHAT ARE YOU DOING!? IS THAT SWORD THE REAL THING!?
DON'T DO IT! YOU DON'T NEED TO HURT THOSE MONKEYS!
CLASP
AH, WHAT'RE YOU DOING, SENSEI ?!
THESE ARE JUST SECOND-RATE ONMYOU GODS! "KILLING" THEM JUST TURNS THEM BACK TO PAPER! HA HA!
WHOA!
YOINK
ACK!
THUD

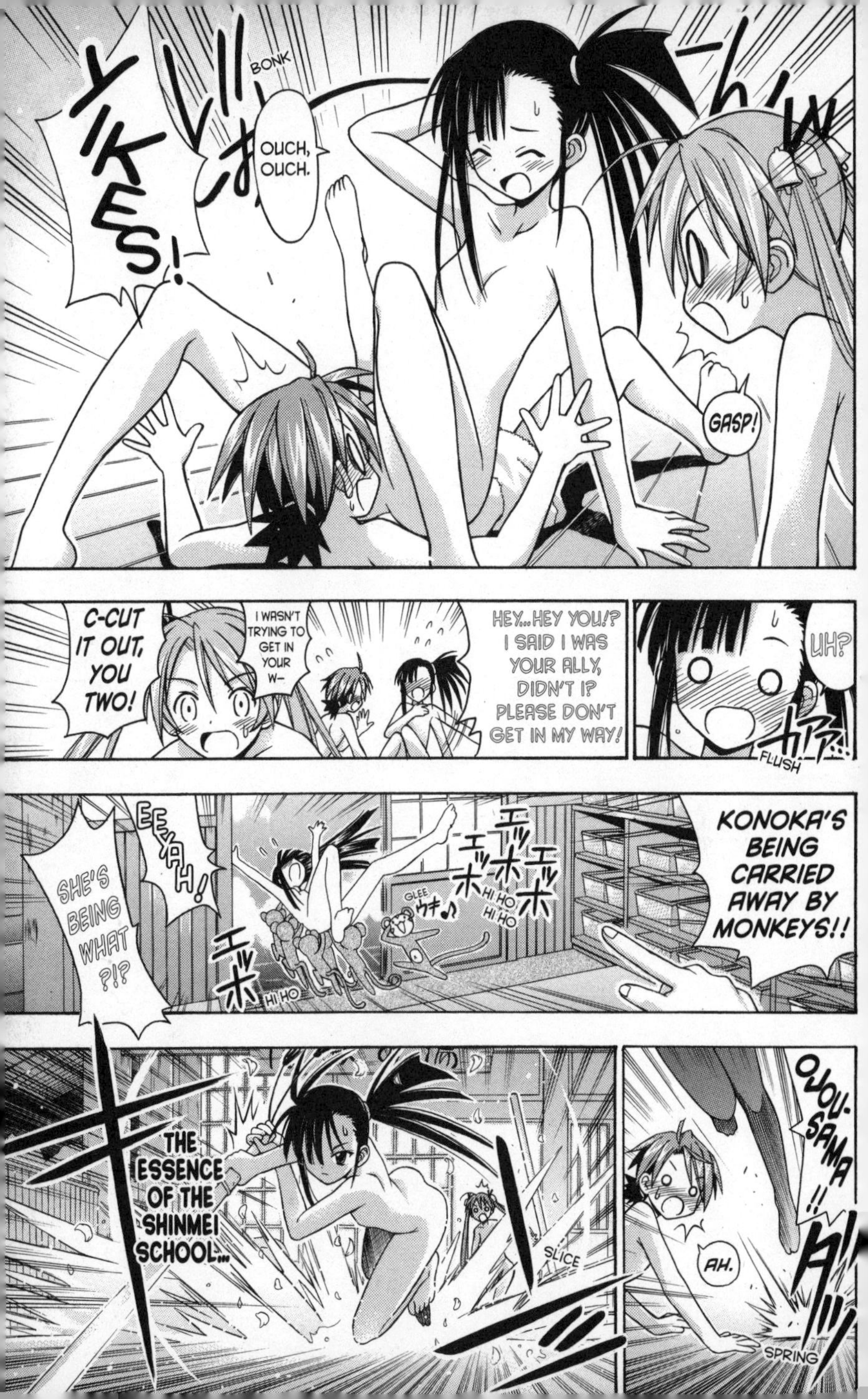

BONK
OUCH, OUCH.
YIKES!
GASP!
UH?
FLUSH
HEY...HEY YOU!? I SAID I WAS YOUR ALLY, DIDN'T I? PLEASE DON'T GET IN MY WAY!
I WASN'T TRYING TO GET IN YOUR W–
C-CUT IT OUT, YOU TWO!
KONOKA'S BEING CARRIED AWAY BY MONKEYS!!
HI HO HI HO
GLEE
HI HO
EEYAAH!
SHE'S BEING WHAT?!?
OJOU-SAMA!!
AH.
SPRING
SLICE
THE ESSENCE OF THE SHINMEI SCHOOL...

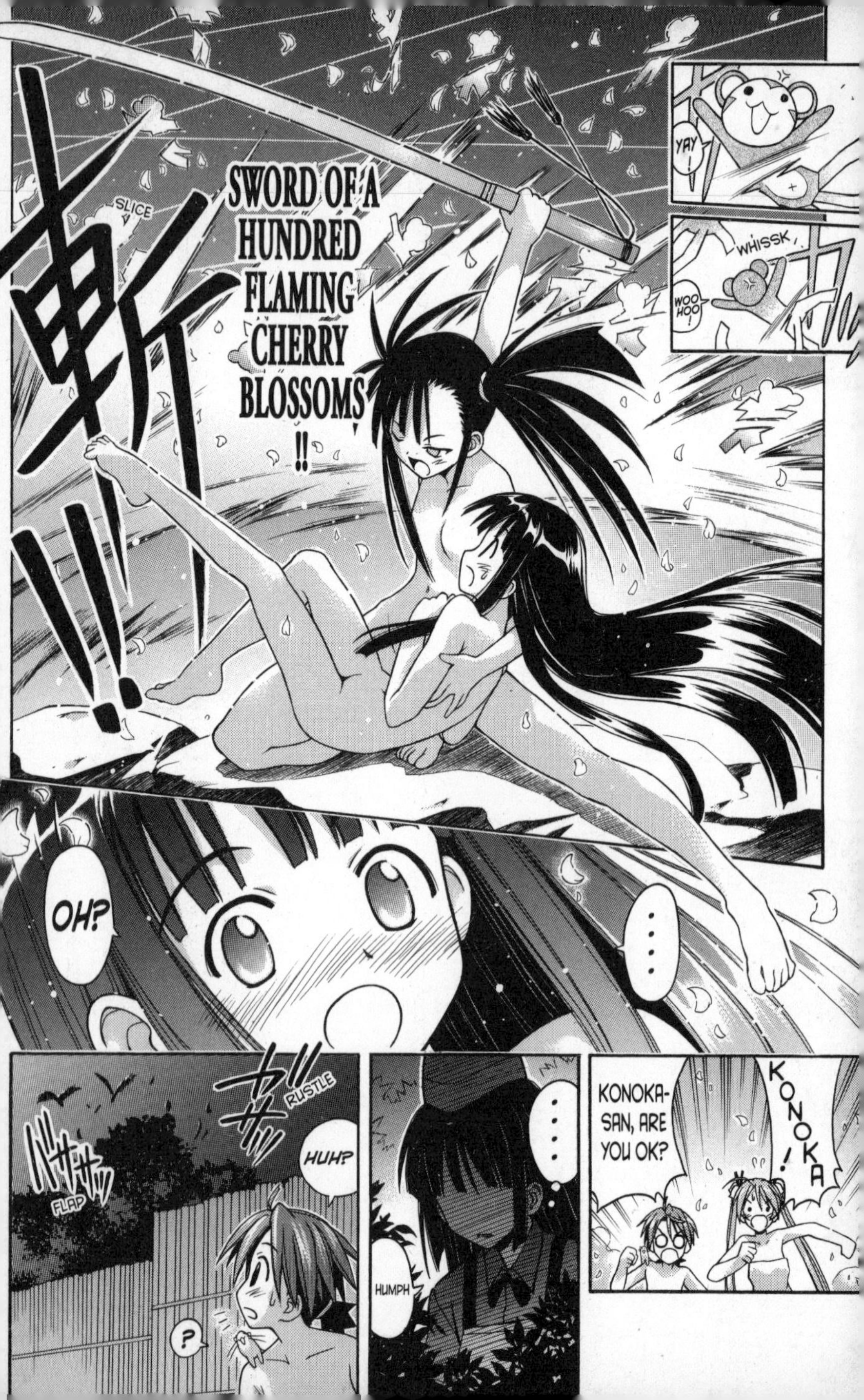
YAY!
WHISSK
WOO HOO!
SLICE
SWORD OF A HUNDRED FLAMING CHERRY BLOSSOMS!!
....
OH?
KONOKA-SAN, ARE YOU OK?
KONOKA!
....
HUMPH
RUSTLE
HUH?
FLAP
?

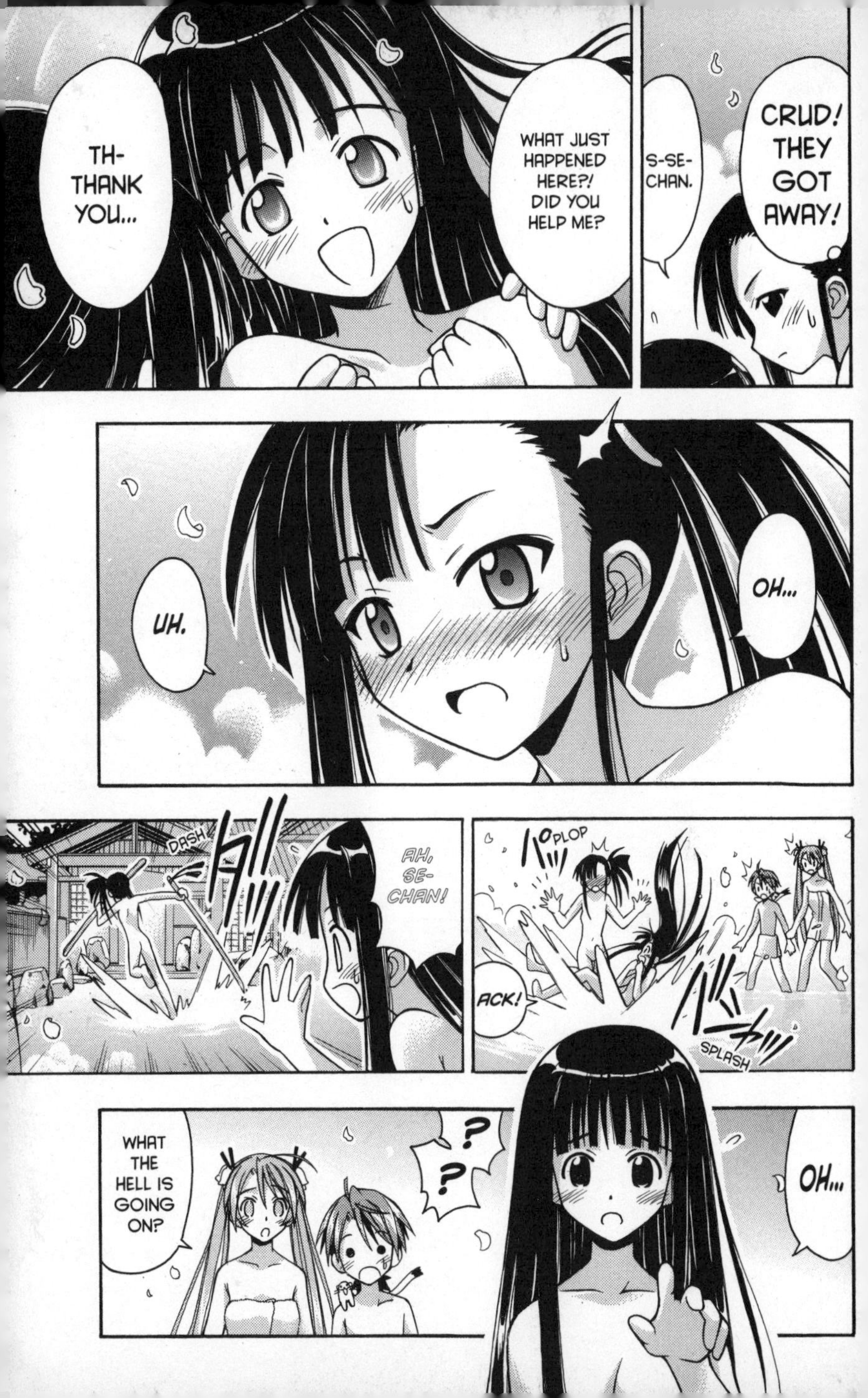
CRUD! THEY GOT AWAY!
S-SE-CHAN.
WHAT JUST HAPPENED HERE?! DID YOU HELP ME?
TH-THANK YOU...
OH...
UH.
PLOP
ACK!
SPLASH
DASH
AH, SE-CHAN!
OH...
? ?
WHAT THE HELL IS GOING ON?

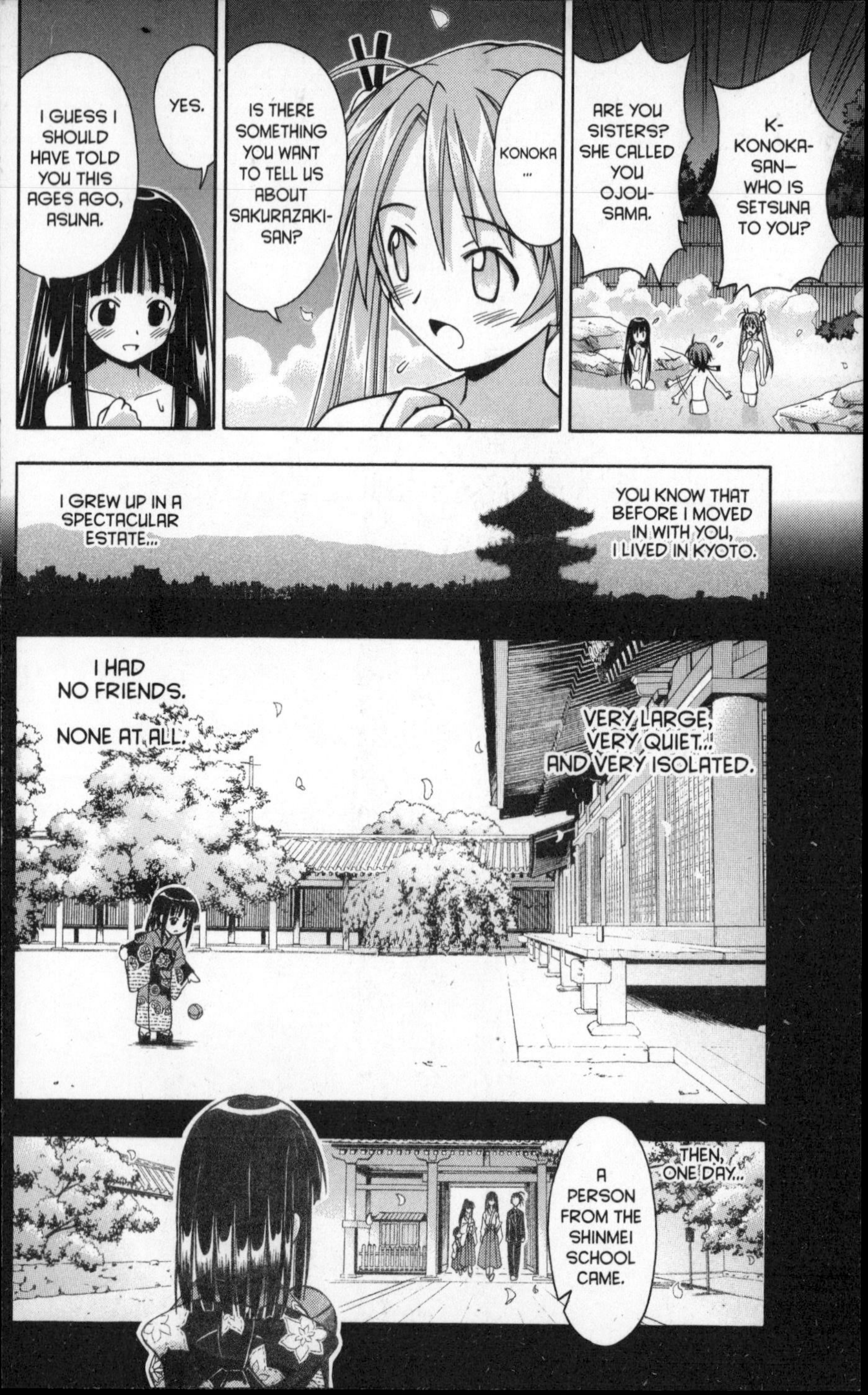
K-KONOKA-SAN—WHO IS SETSUNA TO YOU?
ARE YOU SISTERS? SHE CALLED YOU OJOU-SAMA.
KONOKA...
IS THERE SOMETHING YOU WANT TO TELL US ABOUT SAKURAZAKI-SAN?
YES.
I GUESS I SHOULD HAVE TOLD YOU THIS AGES AGO, ASUNA.
YOU KNOW THAT BEFORE I MOVED IN WITH YOU, I LIVED IN KYOTO.
I GREW UP IN A SPECTACULAR ESTATE...
VERY LARGE, VERY QUIET... AND VERY ISOLATED.
I HAD NO FRIENDS.
NONE AT ALL.
THEN, ONE DAY...
A PERSON FROM THE SHINMEI SCHOOL CAME.

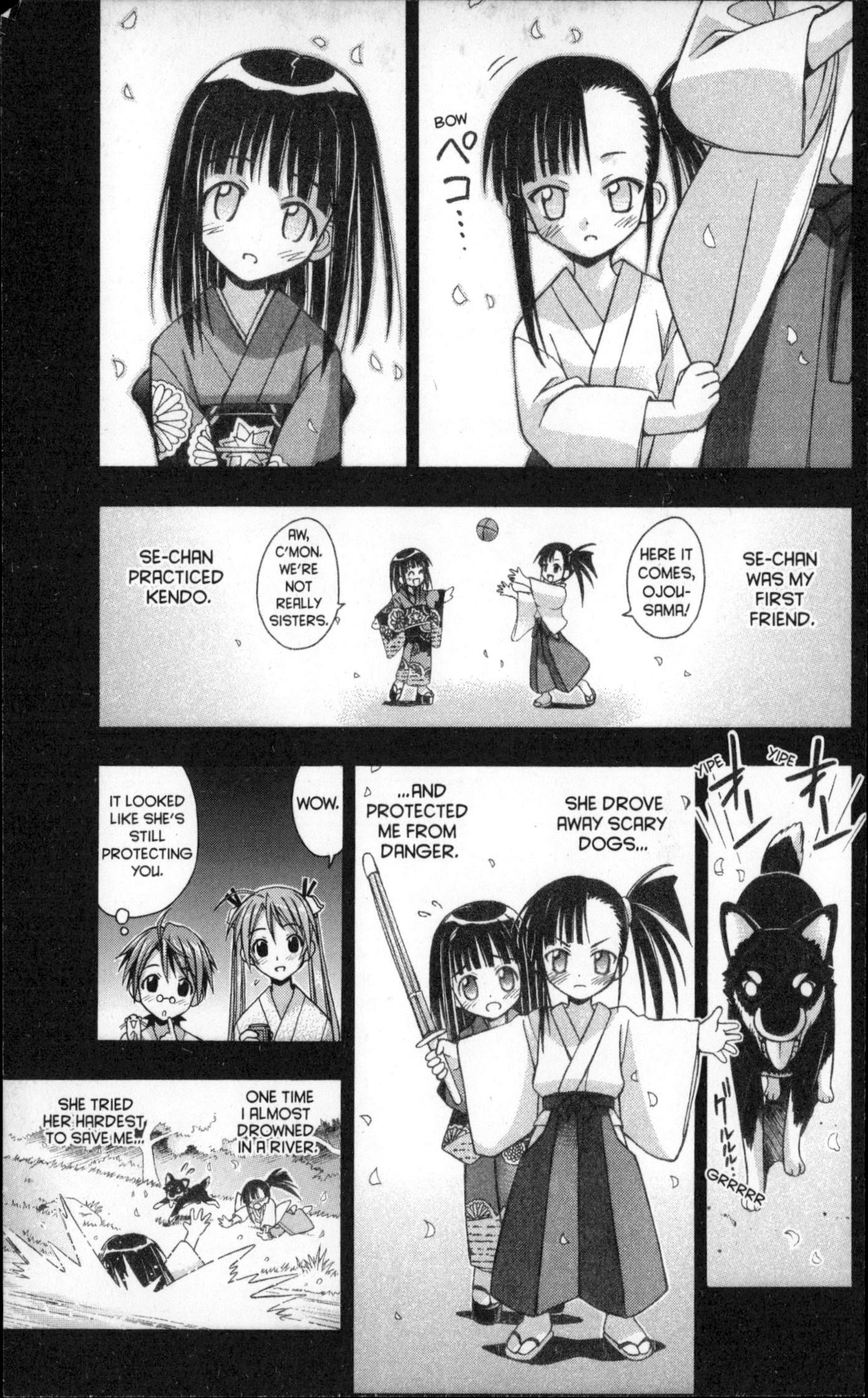
BOW
ペコ…
SE-CHAN WAS MY FIRST FRIEND.
HERE IT COMES, OJOU-SAMA!
AW, C'MON. WE'RE NOT REALLY SISTERS.
SE-CHAN PRACTICED KENDO.
YIPE
YIPE
オン オン
グルルル…
GRRRRR
SHE DROVE AWAY SCARY DOGS...
...AND PROTECTED ME FROM DANGER.
WOW.
IT LOOKED LIKE SHE'S STILL PROTECTING YOU.
ONE TIME I ALMOST DROWNED IN A RIVER.
SHE TRIED HER HARDEST TO SAVE ME...

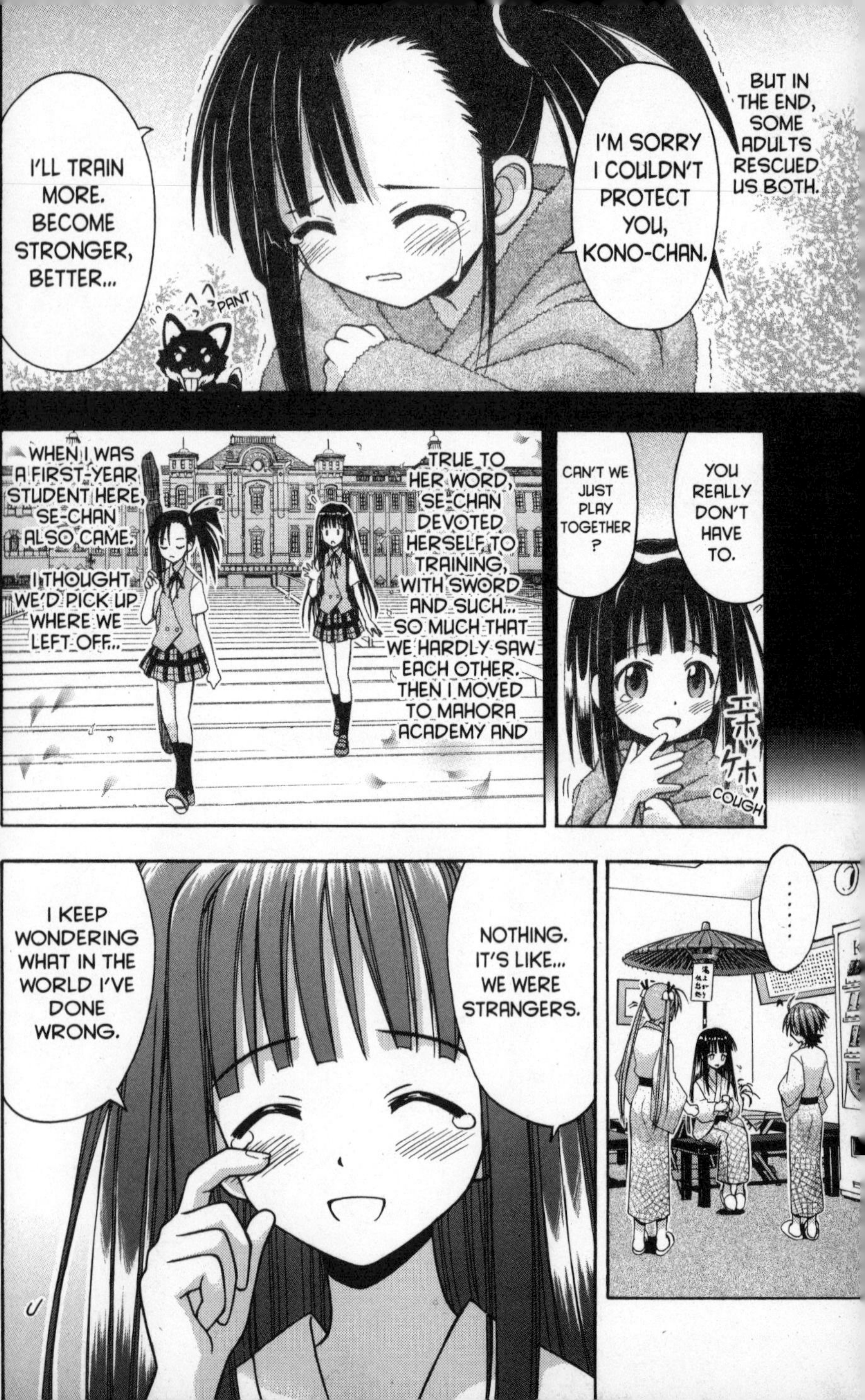
BUT IN THE END, SOME ADULTS RESCUED US BOTH.
I'M SORRY I COULDN'T PROTECT YOU, KONO-CHAN.
I'LL TRAIN MORE. BECOME STRONGER, BETTER...
PANT
YOU REALLY DON'T HAVE TO.
CAN'T WE JUST PLAY TOGETHER ?
COUGH
TRUE TO HER WORD, SE-CHAN DEVOTED HERSELF TO TRAINING, WITH SWORD AND SUCH... SO MUCH THAT WE HARDLY SAW EACH OTHER. THEN I MOVED TO MAHORA ACADEMY AND
WHEN I WAS A FIRST-YEAR STUDENT HERE, SE-CHAN ALSO CAME.
I THOUGHT WE'D PICK UP WHERE WE LEFT OFF...
......
NOTHING. IT'S LIKE... WE WERE STRANGERS.
I KEEP WONDERING WHAT IN THE WORLD I'VE DONE WRONG.

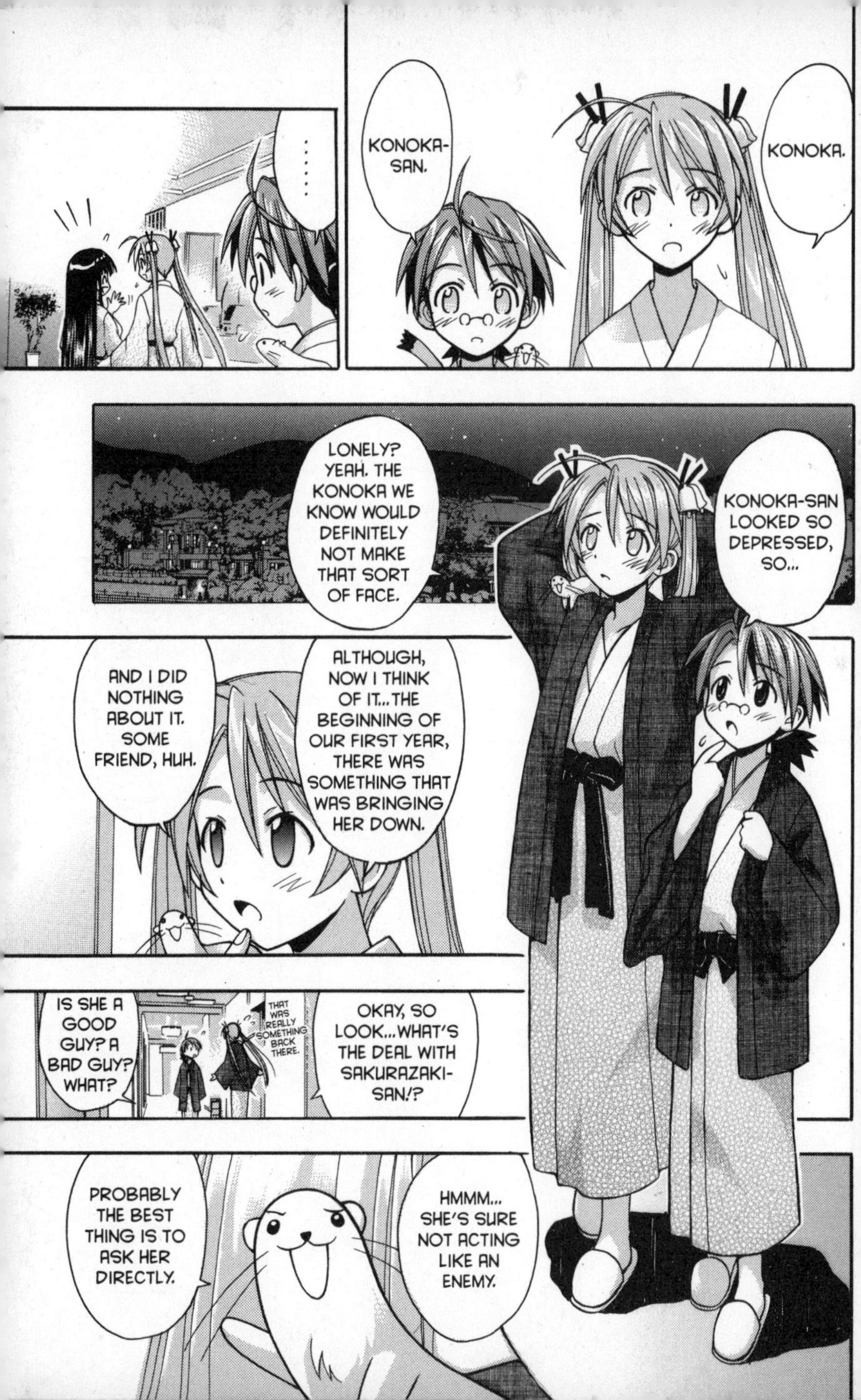
KONOKA.
KONOKA-SAN.
......
KONOKA-SAN LOOKED SO DEPRESSED, SO...
LONELY? YEAH. THE KONOKA WE KNOW WOULD DEFINITELY NOT MAKE THAT SORT OF FACE.
ALTHOUGH, NOW I THINK OF IT... THE BEGINNING OF OUR FIRST YEAR, THERE WAS SOMETHING THAT WAS BRINGING HER DOWN.
AND I DID NOTHING ABOUT IT. SOME FRIEND, HUH.
OKAY, SO LOOK...WHAT'S THE DEAL WITH SAKURAZAKI-SAN!?
THAT WAS REALLY SOMETHING BACK THERE.
IS SHE A GOOD GUY? A BAD GUY? WHAT?
HMMM... SHE'S SURE NOT ACTING LIKE AN ENEMY.
PROBABLY THE BEST THING IS TO ASK HER DIRECTLY.

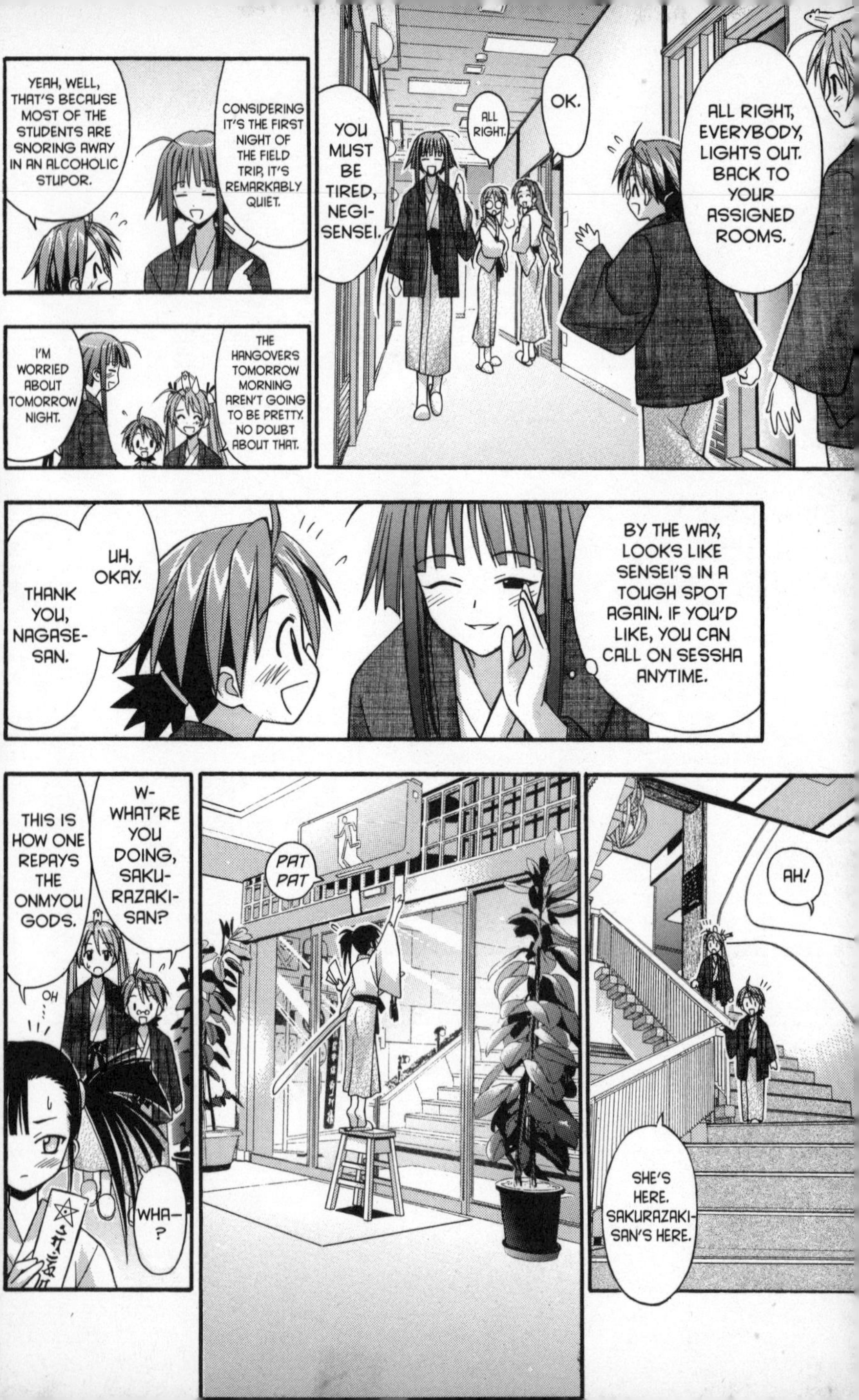
ALL RIGHT, EVERYBODY, LIGHTS OUT. BACK TO YOUR ASSIGNED ROOMS.
OK.
ALL RIGHT.
YOU MUST BE TIRED, NEGI-SENSEI.
CONSIDERING IT'S THE FIRST NIGHT OF THE FIELD TRIP, IT'S REMARKABLY QUIET.
YEAH, WELL, THAT'S BECAUSE MOST OF THE STUDENTS ARE SNORING AWAY IN AN ALCOHOLIC STUPOR.
THE HANGOVERS TOMORROW MORNING AREN'T GOING TO BE PRETTY. NO DOUBT ABOUT THAT.
I'M WORRIED ABOUT TOMORROW NIGHT.
BY THE WAY, LOOKS LIKE SENSEI'S IN A TOUGH SPOT AGAIN. IF YOU'D LIKE, YOU CAN CALL ON SESSHA ANYTIME.
UH, OKAY.
THANK YOU, NAGASE-SAN.
AH!
SHE'S HERE. SAKURAZAKI-SAN'S HERE.
PAT PAT
W-WHAT'RE YOU DOING, SAKURAZAKI-SAN?
THIS IS HOW ONE REPAYS THE ONMYOU GODS.
OH...
WHA-?

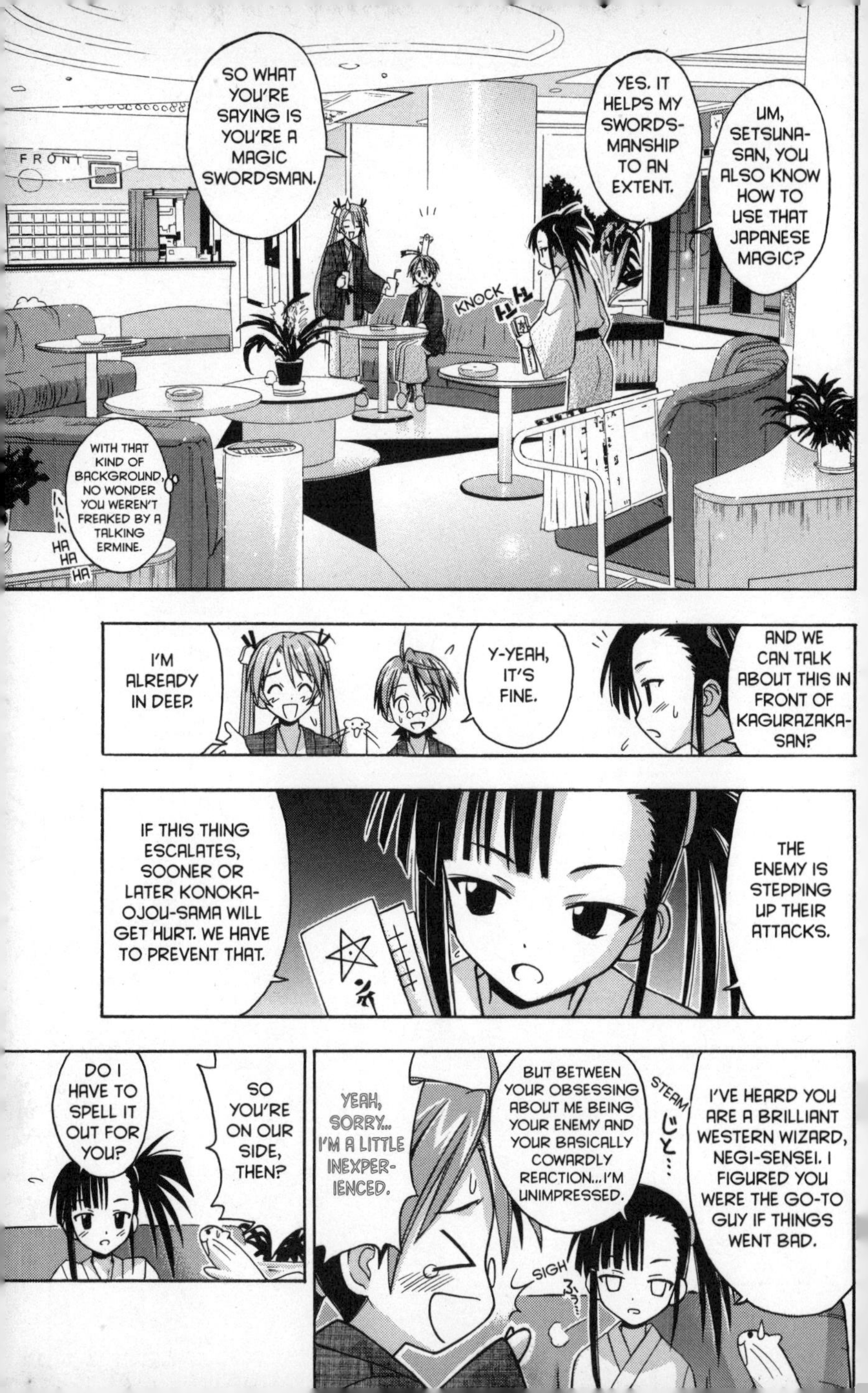
FRONT
UM, SETSUNA-SAN, YOU ALSO KNOW HOW TO USE THAT JAPANESE MAGIC?
YES. IT HELPS MY SWORDS-MANSHIP TO AN EXTENT.
SO WHAT YOU'RE SAYING IS YOU'RE A MAGIC SWORDSMAN.
KNOCK
WITH THAT KIND OF BACKGROUND, NO WONDER YOU WEREN'T FREAKED BY A TALKING ERMINE.
HA HA HA
AND WE CAN TALK ABOUT THIS IN FRONT OF KAGURAZAKA-SAN?
Y-YEAH, IT'S FINE.
I'M ALREADY IN DEEP.
THE ENEMY IS STEPPING UP THEIR ATTACKS.
IF THIS THING ESCALATES, SOONER OR LATER KONOKA-OJOU-SAMA WILL GET HURT. WE HAVE TO PREVENT THAT.
I'VE HEARD YOU ARE A BRILLIANT WESTERN WIZARD, NEGI-SENSEI. I FIGURED YOU WERE THE GO-TO GUY IF THINGS WENT BAD.
STEAM
BUT BETWEEN YOUR OBSESSING ABOUT ME BEING YOUR ENEMY AND YOUR BASICALLY COWARDLY REACTION...I'M UNIMPRESSED.
YEAH, SORRY... I'M A LITTLE INEXPER-IENCED.
SIGH
SO YOU'RE ON OUR SIDE, THEN?
DO I HAVE TO SPELL IT OUT FOR YOU?

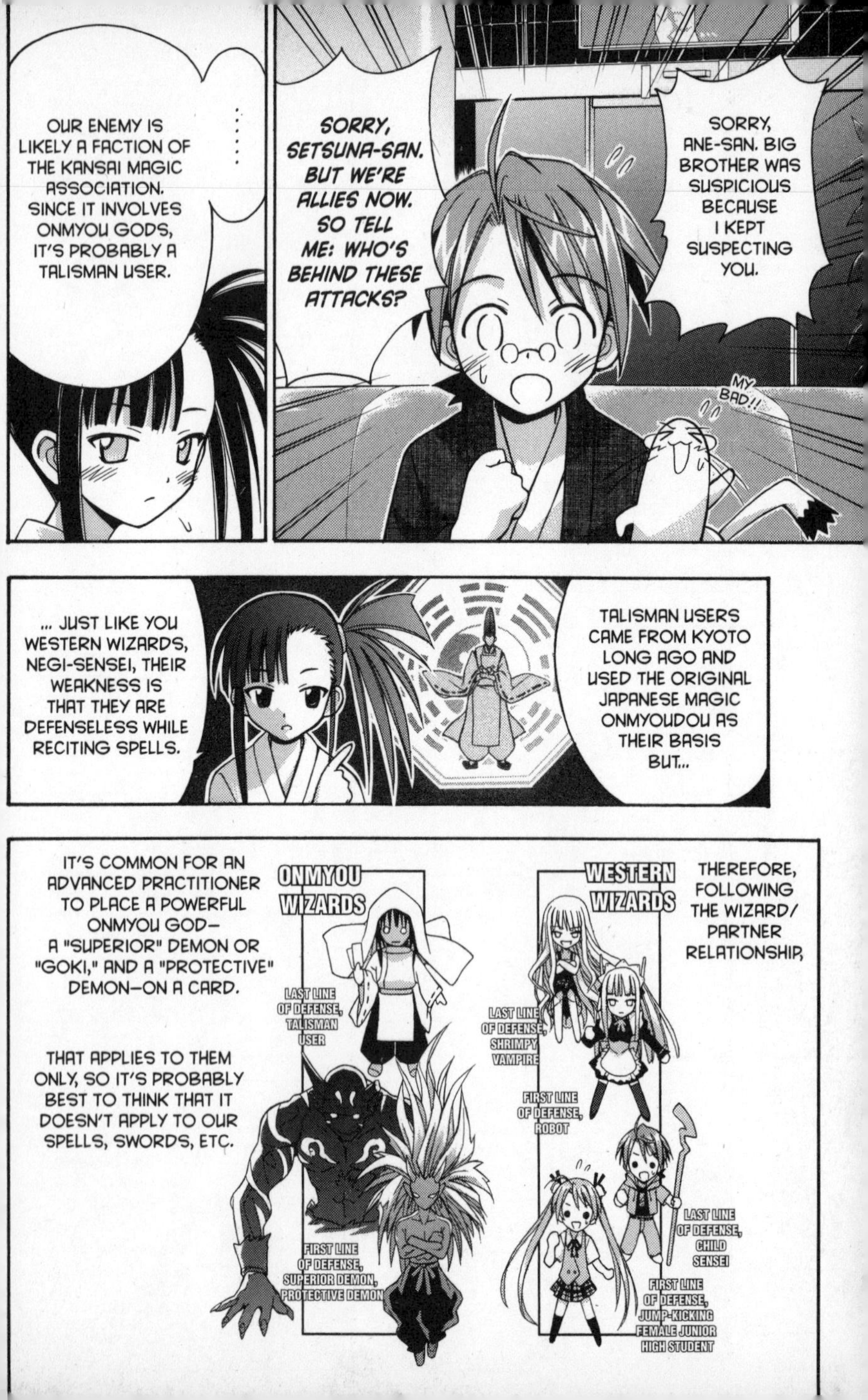

SORRY, ANE-SAN. BIG BROTHER WAS SUSPICIOUS BECAUSE I KEPT SUSPECTING YOU.
MY BAD!!
SORRY, SETSUNA-SAN. BUT WE'RE ALLIES NOW. SO TELL ME: WHO'S BEHIND THESE ATTACKS?
......
OUR ENEMY IS LIKELY A FACTION OF THE KANSAI MAGIC ASSOCIATION. SINCE IT INVOLVES ONMYOU GODS, IT'S PROBABLY A TALISMAN USER.
TALISMAN USERS CAME FROM KYOTO LONG AGO AND USED THE ORIGINAL JAPANESE MAGIC ONMYOUDOU AS THEIR BASIS BUT...
... JUST LIKE YOU WESTERN WIZARDS, NEGI-SENSEI, THEIR WEAKNESS IS THAT THEY ARE DEFENSELESS WHILE RECITING SPELLS.
THEREFORE, FOLLOWING THE WIZARD/PARTNER RELATIONSHIP,
IT'S COMMON FOR AN ADVANCED PRACTITIONER TO PLACE A POWERFUL ONMYOU GOD– A "SUPERIOR" DEMON OR "GOKI," AND A "PROTECTIVE" DEMON–ON A CARD.
THAT APPLIES TO THEM ONLY, SO IT'S PROBABLY BEST TO THINK THAT IT DOESN'T APPLY TO OUR SPELLS, SWORDS, ETC.
WESTERN WIZARDS
LAST LINE OF DEFENSE, SHRIMPY VAMPIRE
FIRST LINE OF DEFENSE, ROBOT
LAST LINE OF DEFENSE, CHILD SENSEI
FIRST LINE OF DEFENSE, JUMP-KICKING FEMALE JUNIOR HIGH STUDENT
ONMYOU WIZARDS
LAST LINE OF DEFENSE, TALISMAN USER
FIRST LINE OF DEFENSE, SUPERIOR DEMON, PROTECTIVE DEMON

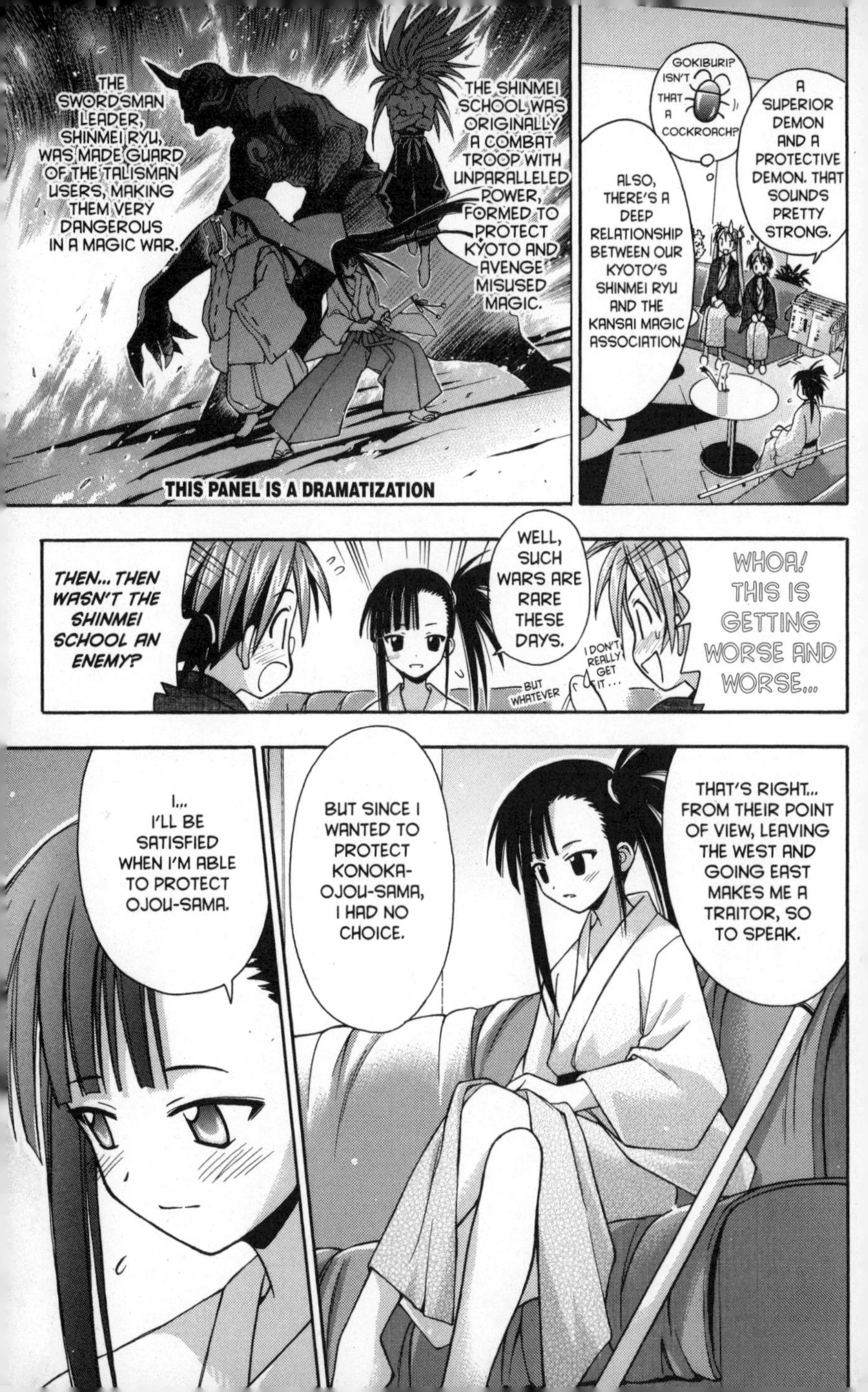
A SUPERIOR DEMON AND A PROTECTIVE DEMON. THAT SOUNDS PRETTY STRONG.
GOKIBURI? ISN'T THAT A COCKROACH?
ALSO, THERE'S A DEEP RELATIONSHIP BETWEEN OUR KYOTO'S SHINMEI RYU AND THE KANSAI MAGIC ASSOCIATION.
THE SHINMEI SCHOOL WAS ORIGINALLY A COMBAT TROOP WITH UNPARALLELED POWER, FORMED TO PROTECT KYOTO AND AVENGE MISUSED MAGIC.
THE SWORDSMAN LEADER, SHINMEI RYU, WAS MADE GUARD OF THE TALISMAN USERS, MAKING THEM VERY DANGEROUS IN A MAGIC WAR.
THIS PANEL IS A DRAMATIZATION
THEN... THEN WASN'T THE SHINMEI SCHOOL AN ENEMY?
WELL, SUCH WARS ARE RARE THESE DAYS.
I DON'T REALLY GET IT...
BUT WHATEVER
WHOA! THIS IS GETTING WORSE AND WORSE...
THAT'S RIGHT... FROM THEIR POINT OF VIEW, LEAVING THE WEST AND GOING EAST MAKES ME A TRAITOR, SO TO SPEAK.
BUT SINCE I WANTED TO PROTECT KONOKA-OJOU-SAMA, I HAD NO CHOICE.
I... I'LL BE SATISFIED WHEN I'M ABLE TO PROTECT OJOU-SAMA.

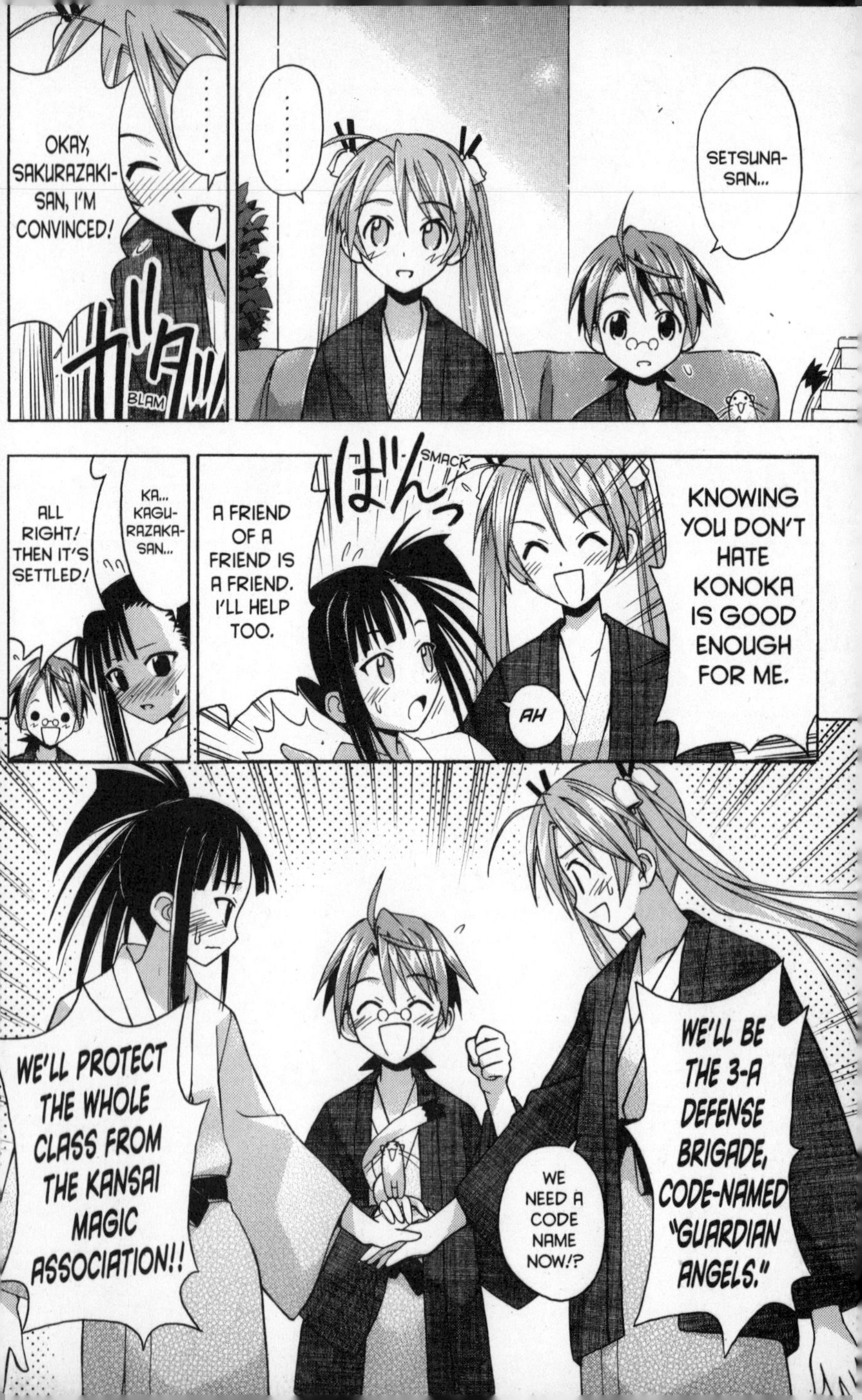
SETSUNA-SAN...
...
...
OKAY, SAKURAZAKI-SAN, I'M CONVINCED!
BLAM
KNOWING YOU DON'T HATE KONOKA IS GOOD ENOUGH FOR ME.
ばんっ
SMACK
AH
A FRIEND OF A FRIEND IS A FRIEND. I'LL HELP TOO.
KA... KAGU-RAZAKA-SAN...
ALL RIGHT! THEN IT'S SETTLED!
WE'LL BE THE 3-A DEFENSE BRIGADE, CODE-NAMED "GUARDIAN ANGELS."
WE NEED A CODE NAME NOW!?
WE'LL PROTECT THE WHOLE CLASS FROM THE KANSAI MAGIC ASSOCIATION!!

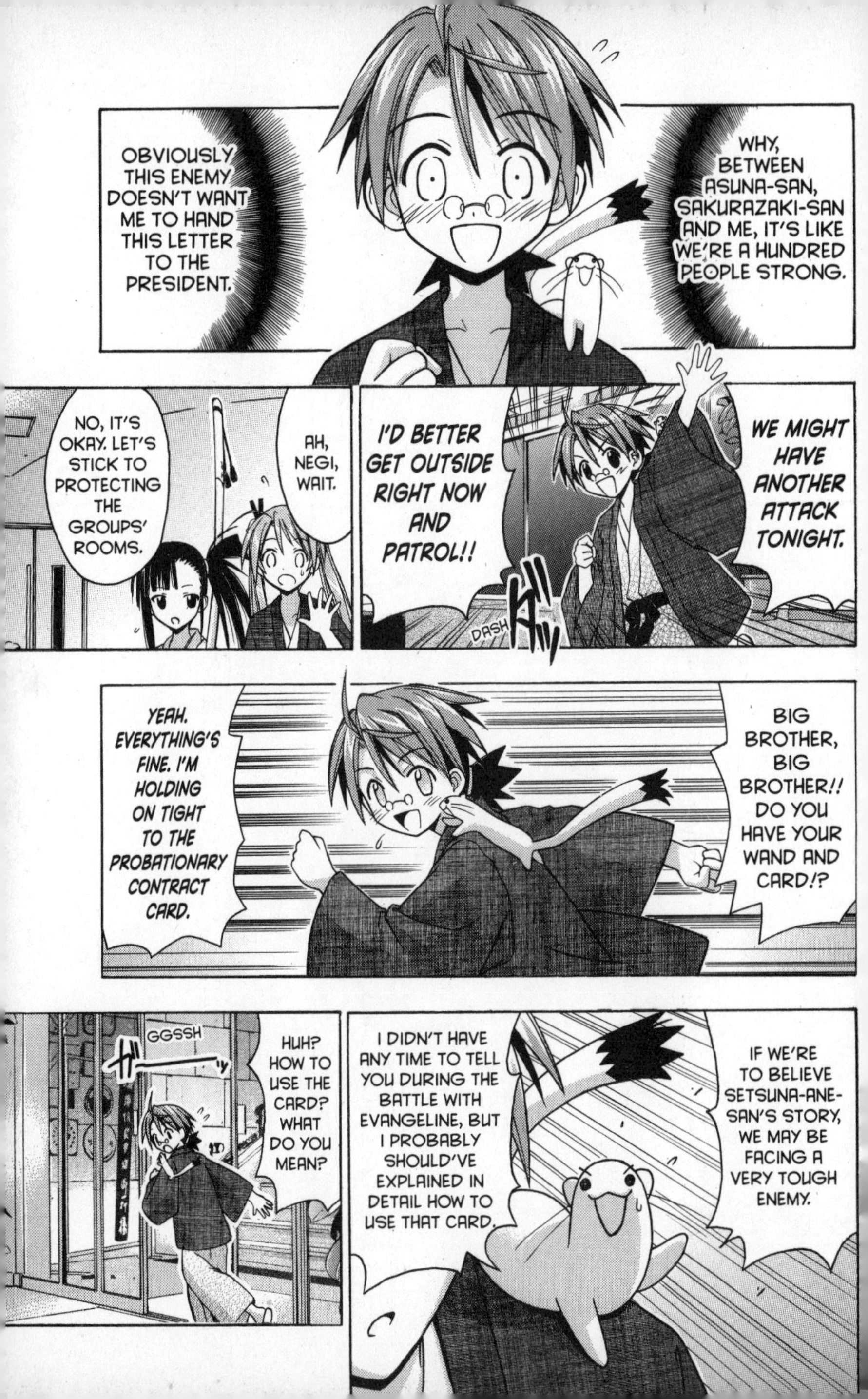
WHY, BETWEEN ASUNA-SAN, SAKURAZAKI-SAN AND ME, IT'S LIKE WE'RE A HUNDRED PEOPLE STRONG.
OBVIOUSLY THIS ENEMY DOESN'T WANT ME TO HAND THIS LETTER TO THE PRESIDENT.
WE MIGHT HAVE ANOTHER ATTACK TONIGHT.
I'D BETTER GET OUTSIDE RIGHT NOW AND PATROL!!
DASH
AH, NEGI, WAIT.
NO, IT'S OKAY. LET'S STICK TO PROTECTING THE GROUPS' ROOMS.
BIG BROTHER, BIG BROTHER!! DO YOU HAVE YOUR WAND AND CARD!?
YEAH. EVERYTHING'S FINE. I'M HOLDING ON TIGHT TO THE PROBATIONARY CONTRACT CARD.
IF WE'RE TO BELIEVE SETSUNA-ANE-SAN'S STORY, WE MAY BE FACING A VERY TOUGH ENEMY.
I DIDN'T HAVE ANY TIME TO TELL YOU DURING THE BATTLE WITH EVANGELINE, BUT I PROBABLY SHOULD'VE EXPLAINED IN DETAIL HOW TO USE THAT CARD.
HUH? HOW TO USE THE CARD? WHAT DO YOU MEAN?
GGGSH

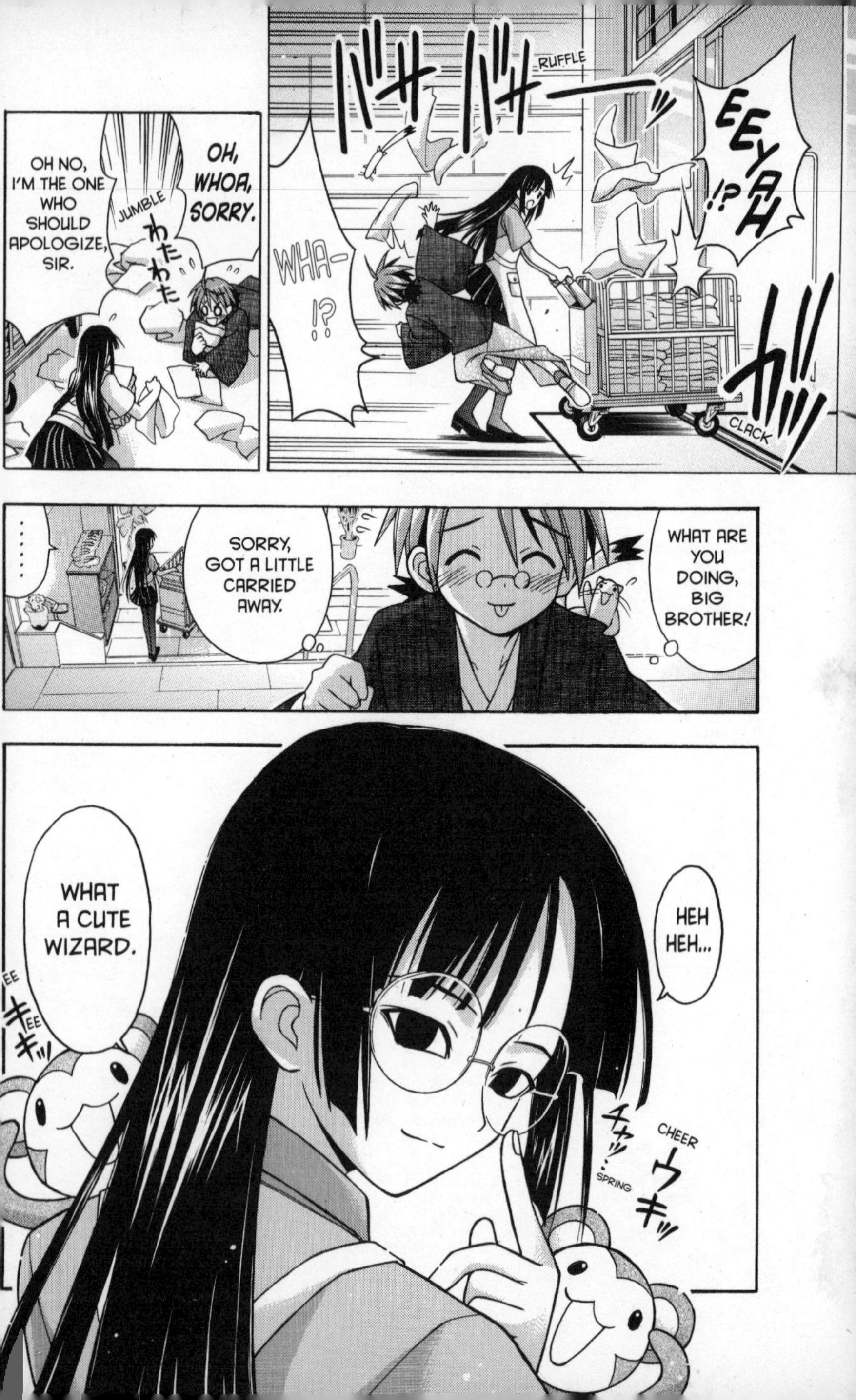

RUFFLE
EEYAAH!?
CLACK
WHA- !?
OH, WHOA, SORRY.
JUMBLE
わたわた
OH NO, I'M THE ONE WHO SHOULD APOLOGIZE, SIR.
WHAT ARE YOU DOING, BIG BROTHER!
SORRY, GOT A LITTLE CARRIED AWAY.
......
HEH HEH...
WHAT A CUTE WIZARD.
CHEER
ウキッ
SPRING
EE EE

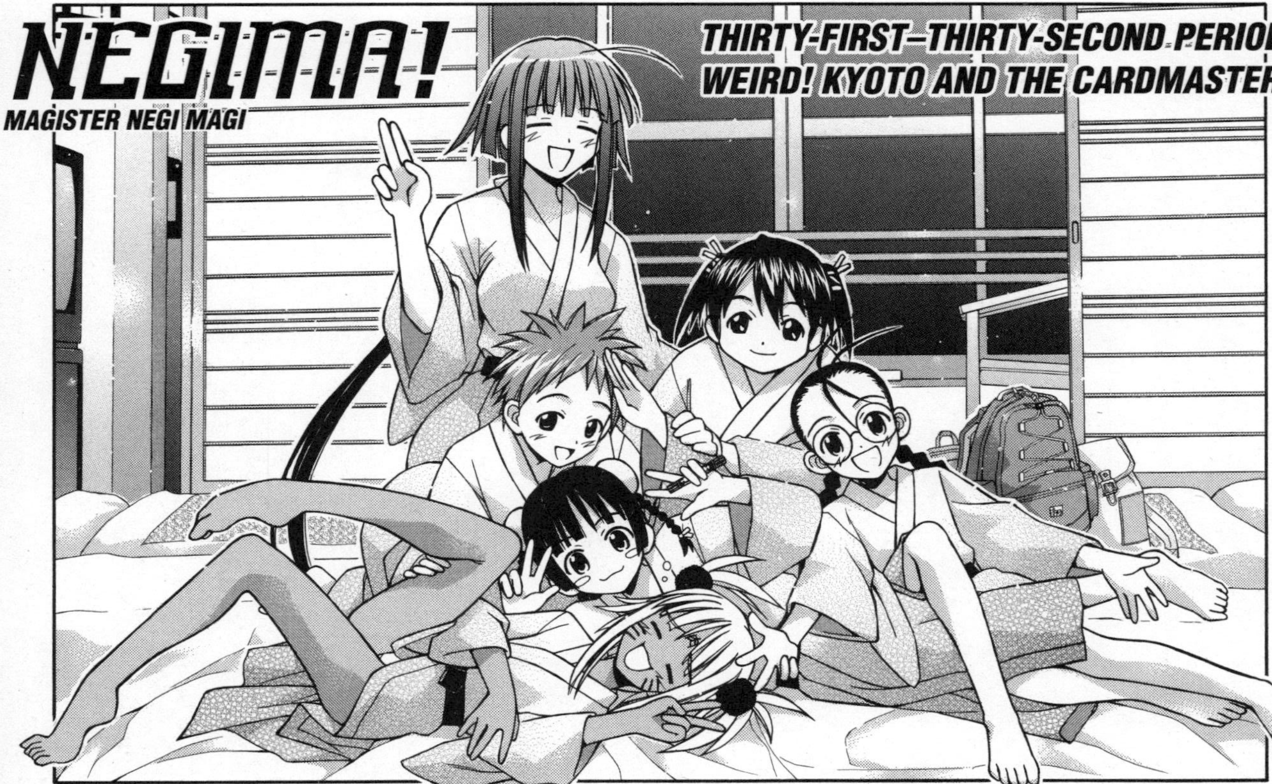
NEGIMA!
MAGISTER NEGI MAGI
THIRTY-FIRST–THIRTY-SECOND PERIODS:
WEIRD! KYOTO AND THE CARDMASTER!!

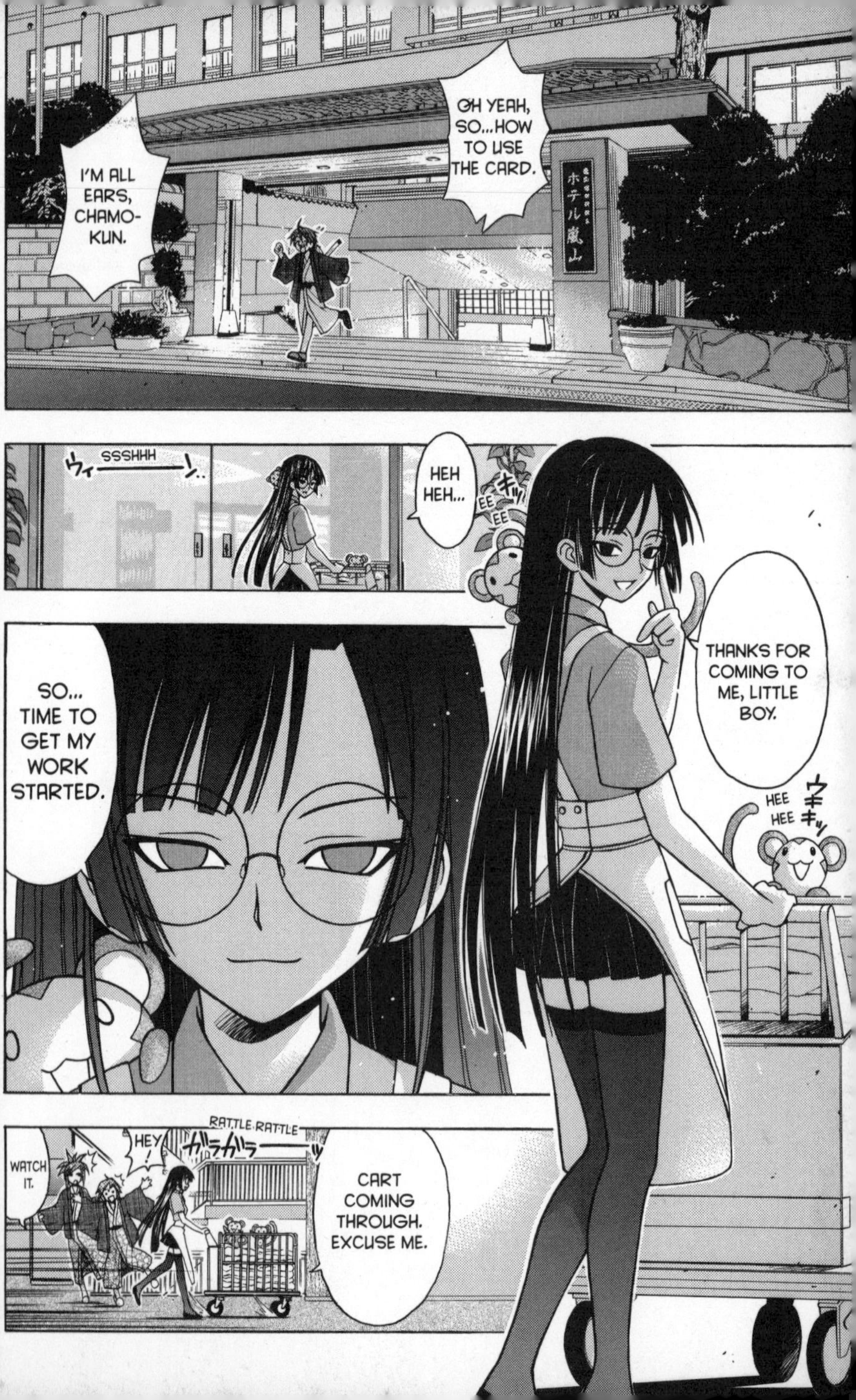
OH YEAH, SO...HOW TO USE THE CARD.
I'M ALL EARS, CHAMO-KUN.
ホテル嵐山
SSSHHH
ウィーン..
HEH HEH...
EE EE
キッ
THANKS FOR COMING TO ME, LITTLE BOY.
HEE HEE
ウキキッ
SO... TIME TO GET MY WORK STARTED.
RATTLE RATTLE
ガラガラ
CART COMING THROUGH. EXCUSE ME.
HEY!
WATCH IT.

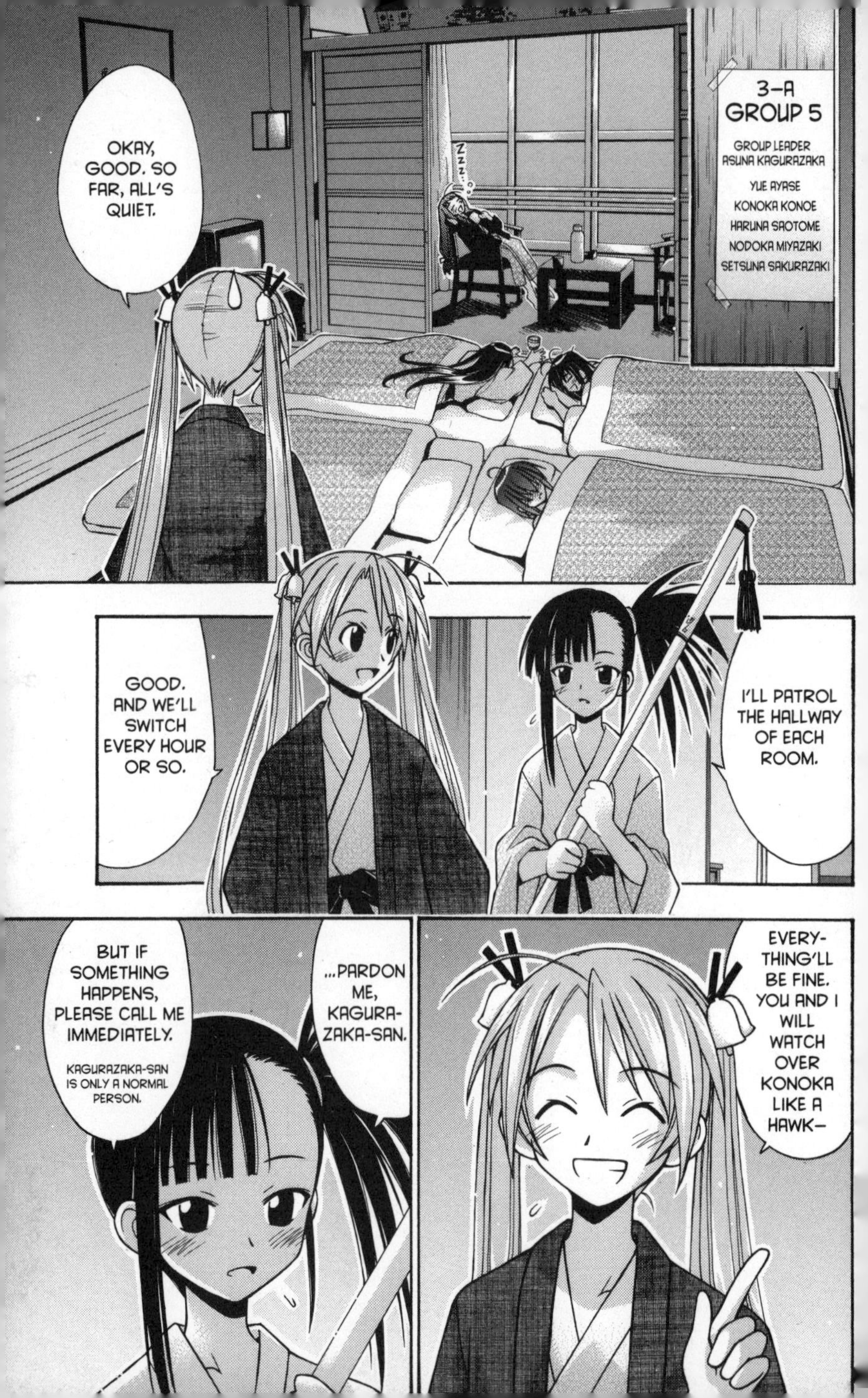
3–A
GROUP 5
GROUP LEADER
ASUNA KAGURAZAKA
YUE AYASE
KONOKA KONOE
HARUNA SAOTOME
NODOKA MIYAZAKI
SETSUNA SAKURAZAKI
ZZZ...
OKAY, GOOD. SO FAR, ALL'S QUIET.
I'LL PATROL THE HALLWAY OF EACH ROOM.
GOOD. AND WE'LL SWITCH EVERY HOUR OR SO.
EVERY-THING'LL BE FINE. YOU AND I WILL WATCH OVER KONOKA LIKE A HAWK–
...PARDON ME, KAGURA-ZAKA-SAN.
BUT IF SOMETHING HAPPENS, PLEASE CALL ME IMMEDIATELY.
KAGURAZAKA-SAN IS ONLY A NORMAL PERSON.

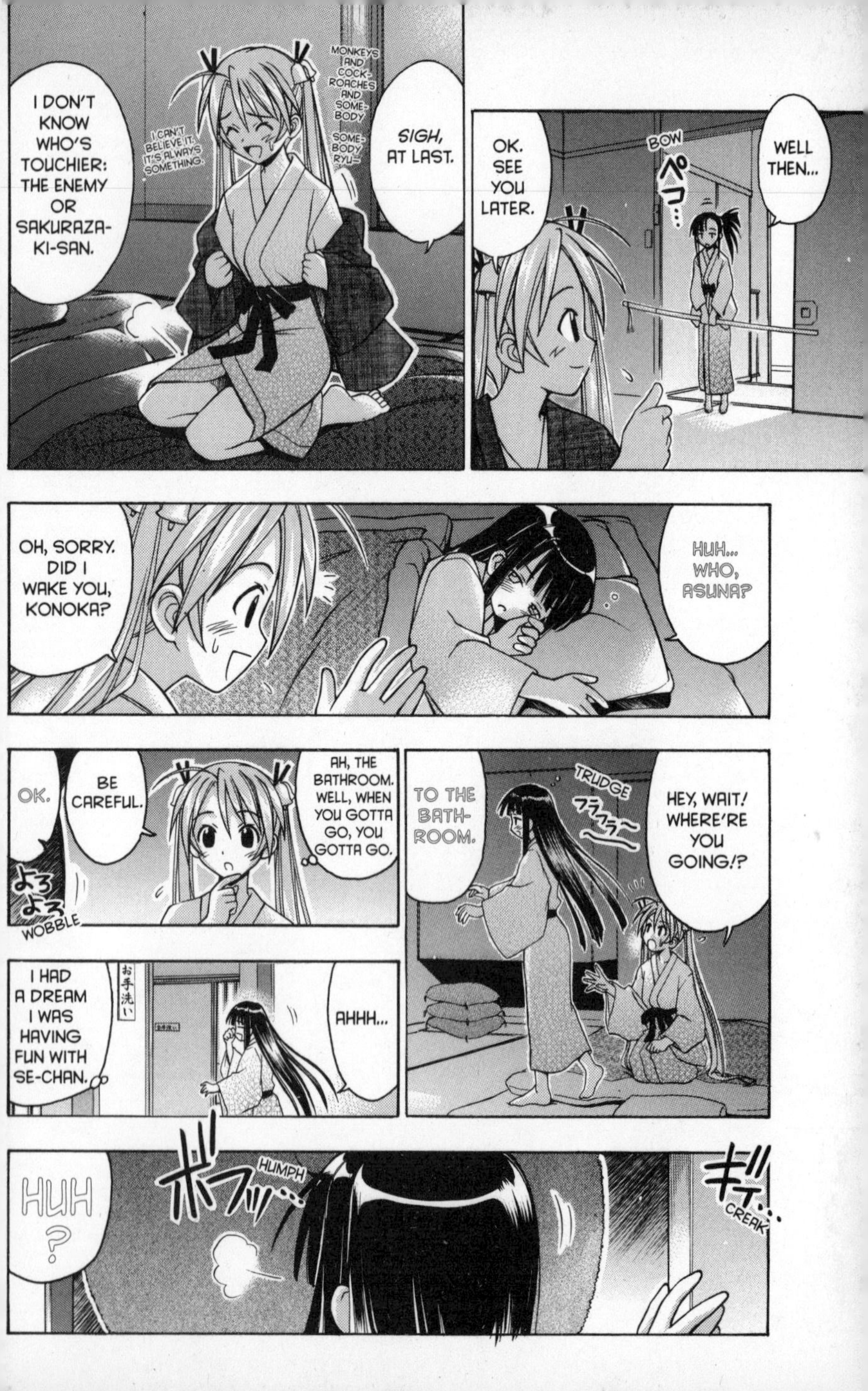
WELL THEN...
BOW
ペコ...
OK. SEE YOU LATER.
SIGH, AT LAST.
MONKEYS AND COCK-ROACHES AND SOME-BODY SOME-BODY RYU—
I CAN'T BELIEVE IT. IT'S ALWAYS SOMETHING.
I DON'T KNOW WHO'S TOUCHIER: THE ENEMY OR SAKURAZA-KI-SAN.
HUH... WHO, ASUNA?
OH, SORRY. DID I WAKE YOU, KONOKA?
HEY, WAIT! WHERE'RE YOU GOING!?
TRUDGE
フラフラ~
TO THE BATH-ROOM.
AH, THE BATHROOM. WELL, WHEN YOU GOTTA GO, YOU GOTTA GO.
BE CAREFUL.
OK.
よろよろ
WOBBLE
AHHH...
お手洗い
I HAD A DREAM I WAS HAVING FUN WITH SE-CHAN.
ギィ...
CREAK
ボフッ...
HUMPH
HUH?

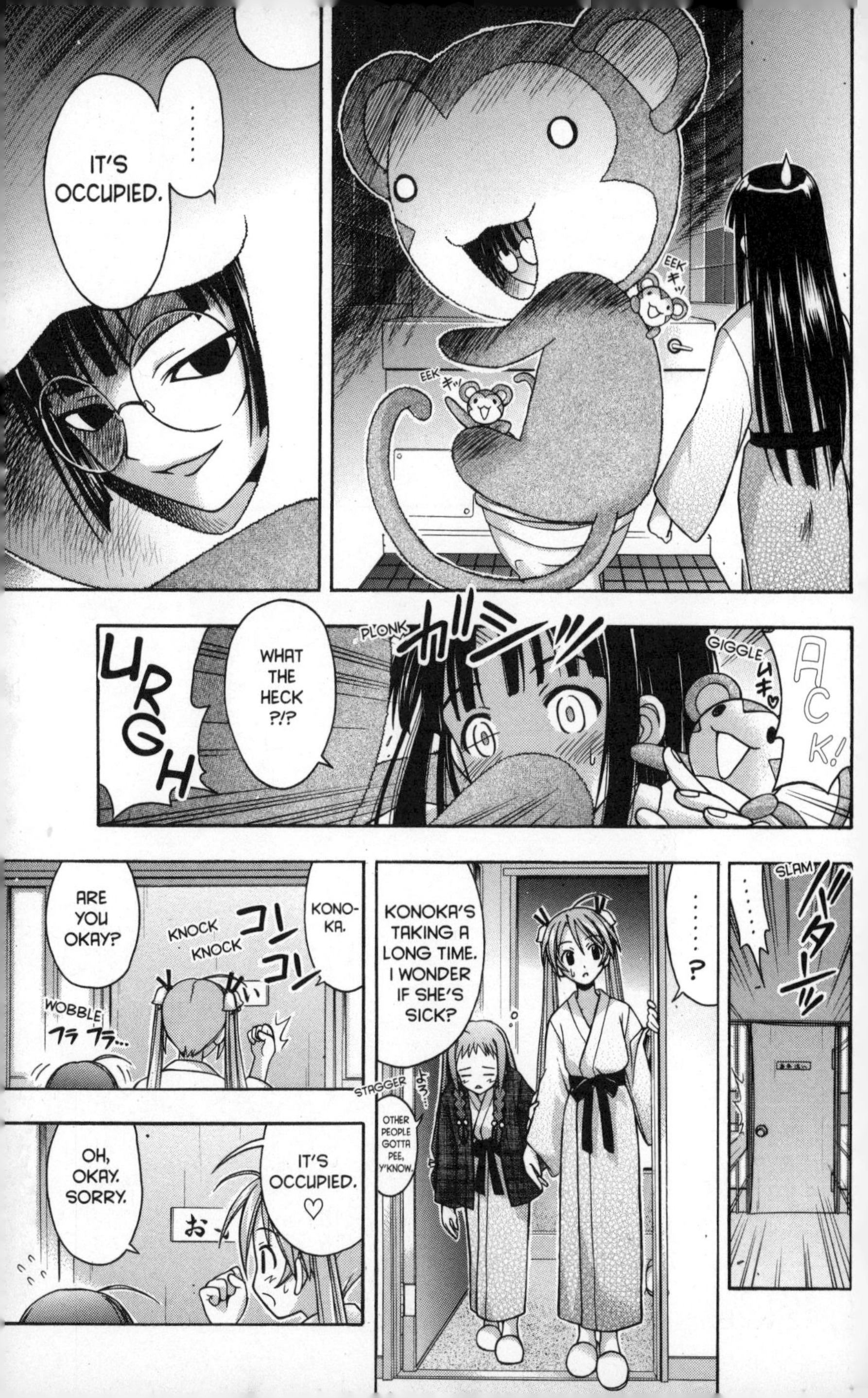
EEK キッ
EEK キッ
......
IT'S OCCUPIED.
ACK!
GIGGLE うき♥
PLONK ガシッ
WHAT THE HECK ?!?
URGH
SLAM バターン
......
......?
KONOKA'S TAKING A LONG TIME. I WONDER IF SHE'S SICK?
STAGGER よろ...
OTHER PEOPLE GOTTA PEE, Y'KNOW.
KONO-KA.
KNOCK KNOCK コンコン
ARE YOU OKAY?
WOBBLE フラフラ...
IT'S OCCUPIED. ♡
OH, OKAY. SORRY.

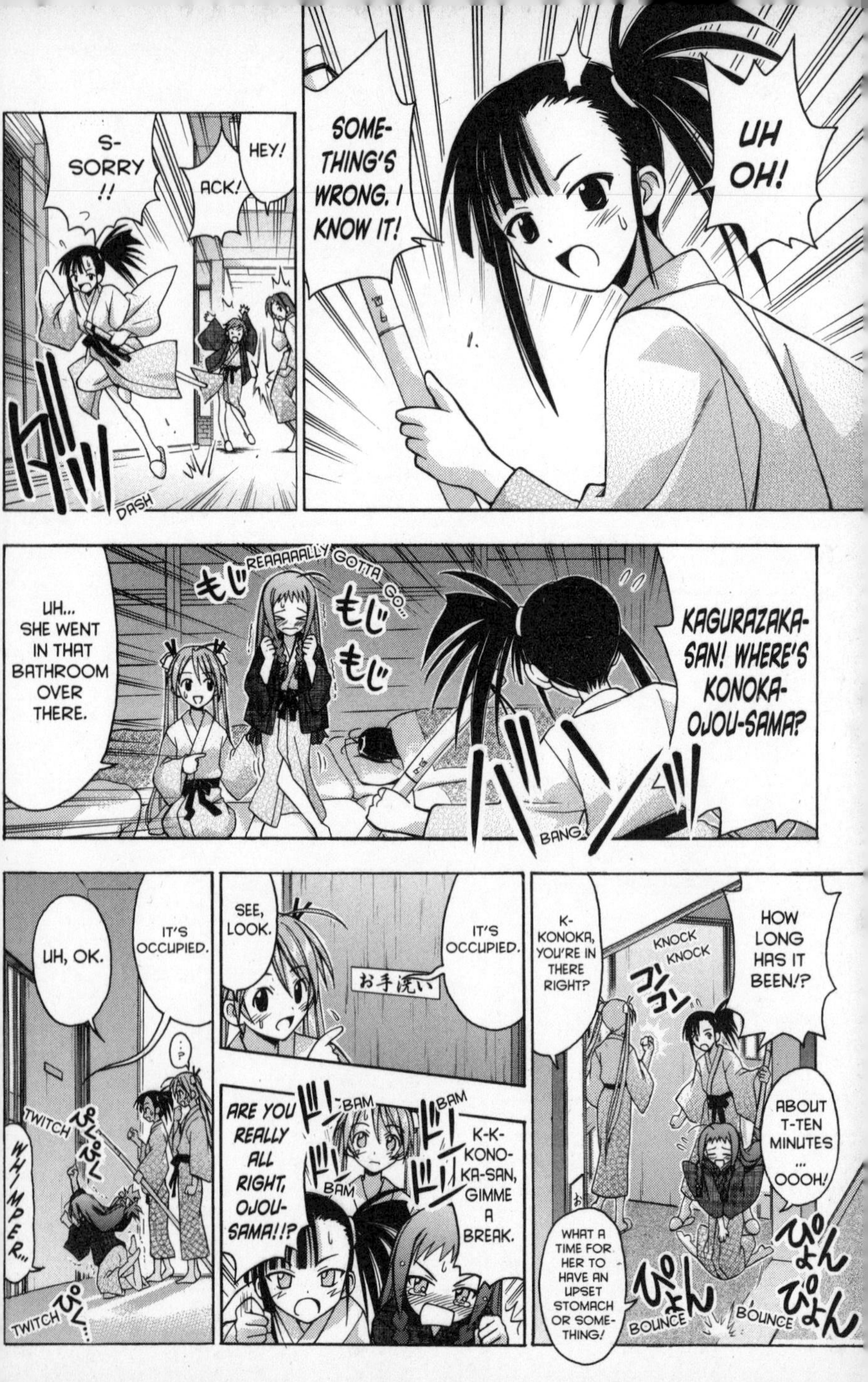
UH OH!
SOME-THING'S WRONG. I KNOW IT!
HEY!
ACK!
S-SORRY!!
DASH
KAGURAZAKA-SAN! WHERE'S KONOKA-OJOU-SAMA?
BANG
REAAAAALLY GOTTA GO...
もじ もじ もじ
UH... SHE WENT IN THAT BATHROOM OVER THERE.
HOW LONG HAS IT BEEN!?
K-KONOKA, YOU'RE IN THERE RIGHT?
KNOCK KNOCK
ABOUT T-TEN MINUTES ... OOOH!
WHAT A TIME FOR HER TO HAVE AN UPSET STOMACH OR SOME-THING!
ぴょん ぴょん ぴょん
BOUNCE
BOUNCE
IT'S OCCUPIED.
お手洗い
SEE, LOOK.
K-K-KONO-KA-SAN, GIMME A BREAK.
BAM
BAM
BAM
ARE YOU REALLY ALL RIGHT, OJOU-SAMA!!?
IT'S OCCUPIED.
UH, OK.
...?
ぴくぴく
TWITCH
WHIMPER...
ぴく...
TWITCH

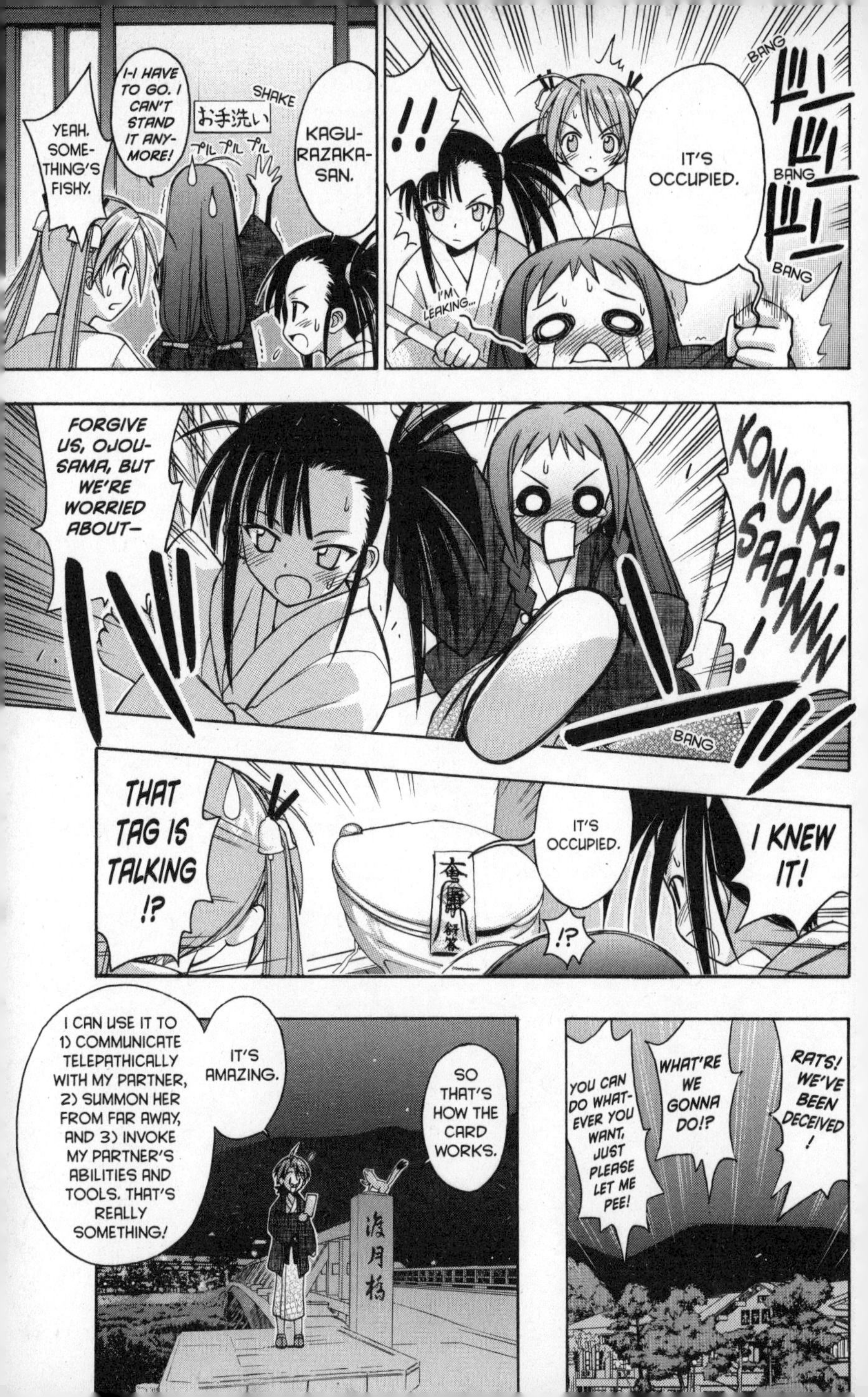
BANG
BANG
BANG
IT'S OCCUPIED.
!!
I'M LEAKING...
KAGU-RAZAKA-SAN.
SHAKE
お手洗い
プルプルプル
I-I HAVE TO GO. I CAN'T STAND IT ANYMORE!
YEAH. SOME-THING'S FISHY.
KONOKA-SAANNN!
FORGIVE US, OJOU-SAMA, BUT WE'RE WORRIED ABOUT—
BANG
I KNEW IT!
IT'S OCCUPIED.
!?
THAT TAG IS TALKING!?
RATS! WE'VE BEEN DECEIVED!
WHAT'RE WE GONNA DO!?
YOU CAN DO WHAT-EVER YOU WANT, JUST PLEASE LET ME PEE!
SO THAT'S HOW THE CARD WORKS.
IT'S AMAZING.
I CAN USE IT TO 1) COMMUNICATE TELEPATHICALLY WITH MY PARTNER, 2) SUMMON HER FROM FAR AWAY, AND 3) INVOKE MY PARTNER'S ABILITIES AND TOOLS. THAT'S REALLY SOMETHING!
渡月橋

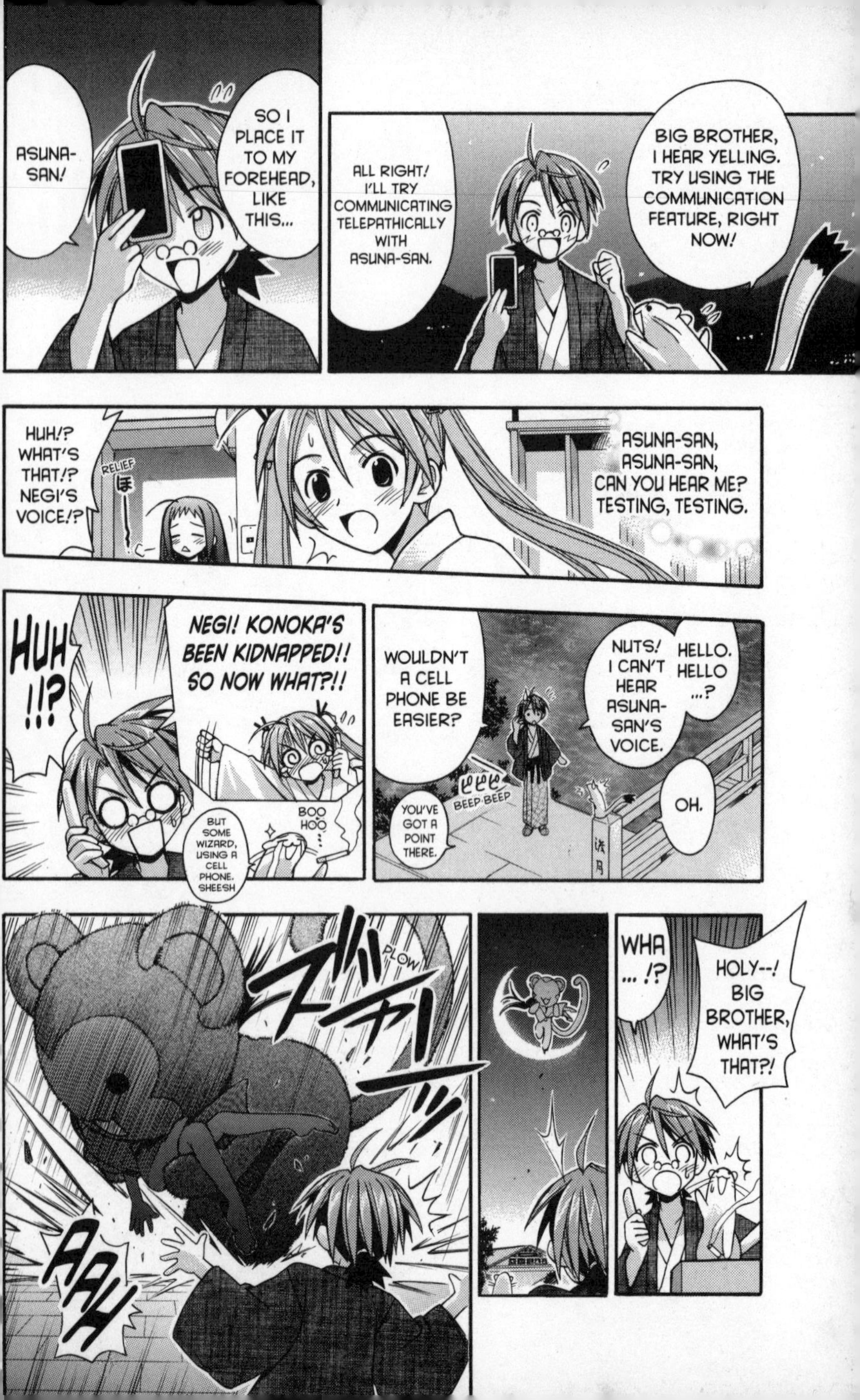
BIG BROTHER, I HEAR YELLING. TRY USING THE COMMUNICATION FEATURE, RIGHT NOW!
ALL RIGHT! I'LL TRY COMMUNICATING TELEPATHICALLY WITH ASUNA-SAN.
SO I PLACE IT TO MY FOREHEAD, LIKE THIS...
ASUNA-SAN!
ASUNA-SAN, ASUNA-SAN, CAN YOU HEAR ME? TESTING, TESTING.
RELIEF
HUH!? WHAT'S THAT!? NEGI'S VOICE!?
HELLO. HELLO ...?
NUTS! I CAN'T HEAR ASUNA-SAN'S VOICE.
OH.
WOULDN'T A CELL PHONE BE EASIER?
ピピピ BEEP BEEP
YOU'VE GOT A POINT THERE.
NEGI! KONOKA'S BEEN KIDNAPPED!! SO NOW WHAT?!!
HUH !!?
BOO HOO...
BUT SOME WIZARD, USING A CELL PHONE. SHEESH
HOLY--! BIG BROTHER, WHAT'S THAT?!
WHA ... !?
PLOW
AAH

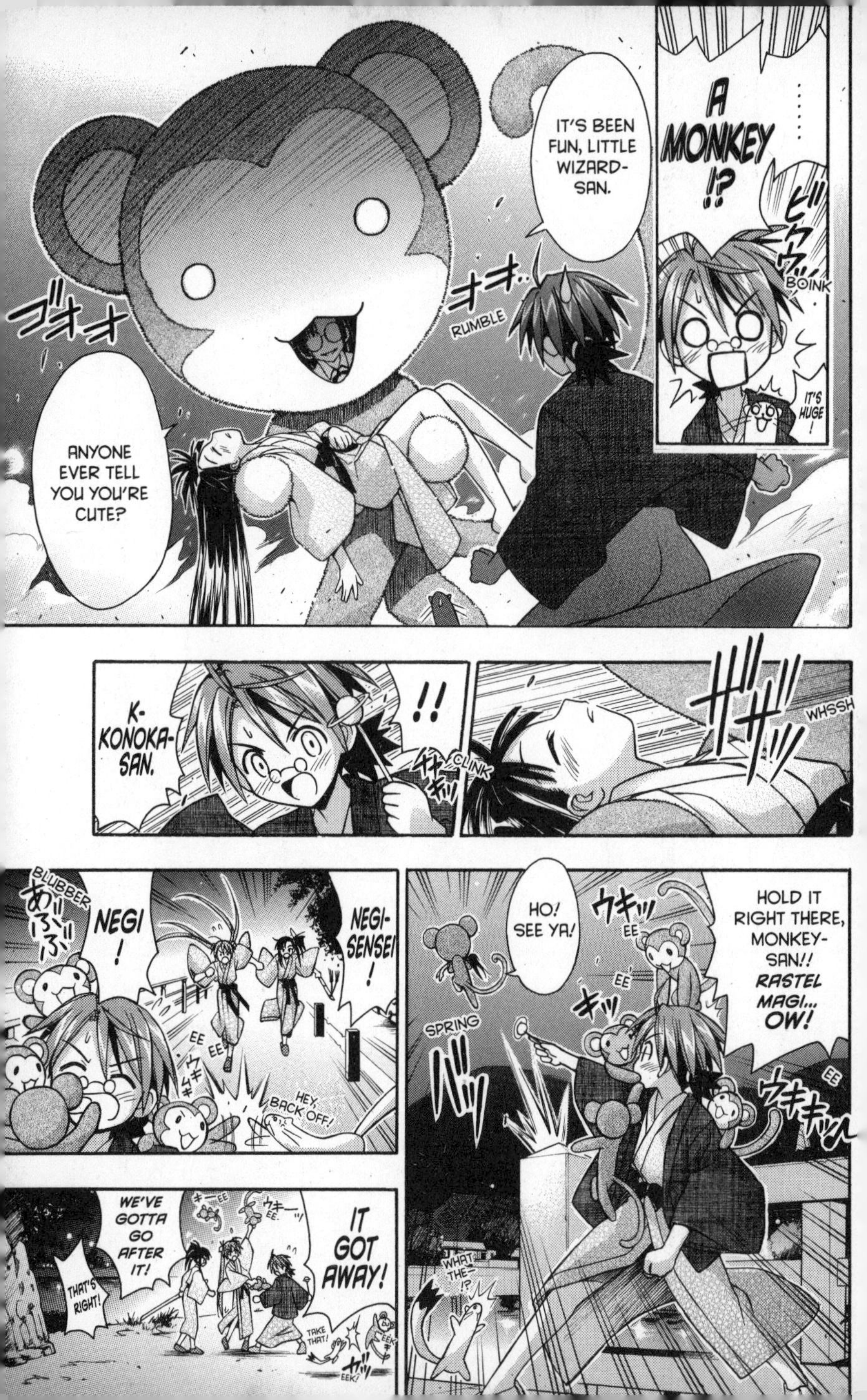

A MONKEY !?
......
BOINK
IT'S HUGE!
IT'S BEEN FUN, LITTLE WIZARD-SAN.
RUMBLE
ANYONE EVER TELL YOU YOU'RE CUTE?
WHSSH
!!
CLINK
K-KONOKA-SAN.
HOLD IT RIGHT THERE, MONKEY-SAN!! RASTEL MAGI... OW!
EE
HO! SEE YA!
EE
EE
SPRING
WHAT THE-!?
NEGI-SENSEI!
NEGI!
BLUBBER
EE
EE
HEY, BACK OFF!
IT GOT AWAY!
EE
EE
WE'VE GOTTA GO AFTER IT!
THAT'S RIGHT!
TAKE THAT!
EEK
EEK!

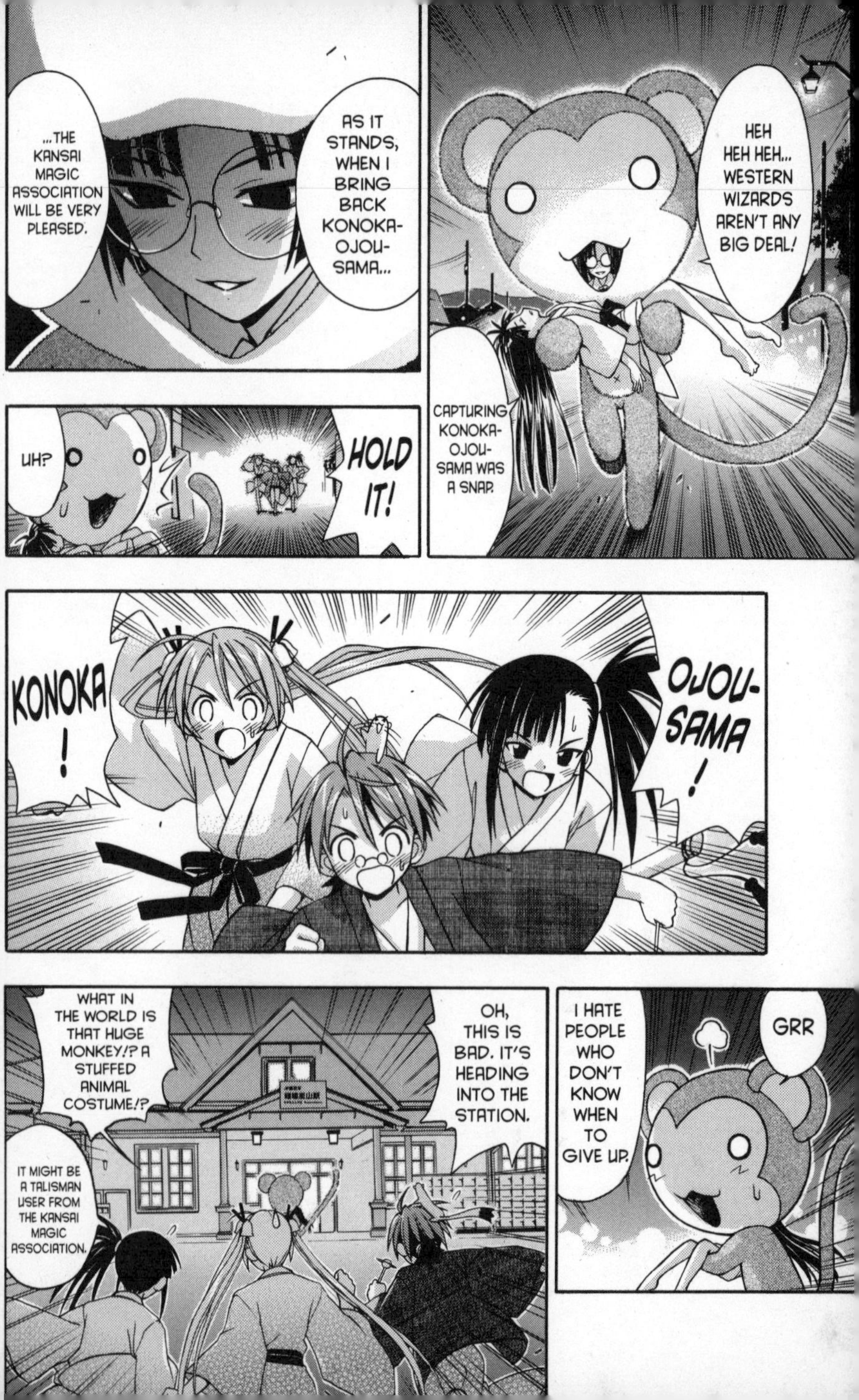
HEH HEH HEH... WESTERN WIZARDS AREN'T ANY BIG DEAL!
CAPTURING KONOKA-OJOU-SAMA WAS A SNAP.
AS IT STANDS, WHEN I BRING BACK KONOKA-OJOU-SAMA...
...THE KANSAI MAGIC ASSOCIATION WILL BE VERY PLEASED.
HOLD IT!
UH?
OJOU-SAMA!
KONOKA!
GRR
I HATE PEOPLE WHO DON'T KNOW WHEN TO GIVE UP.
OH, THIS IS BAD. IT'S HEADING INTO THE STATION.
WHAT IN THE WORLD IS THAT HUGE MONKEY!? A STUFFED ANIMAL COSTUME!?
IT MIGHT BE A TALISMAN USER FROM THE KANSAI MAGIC ASSOCIATION.

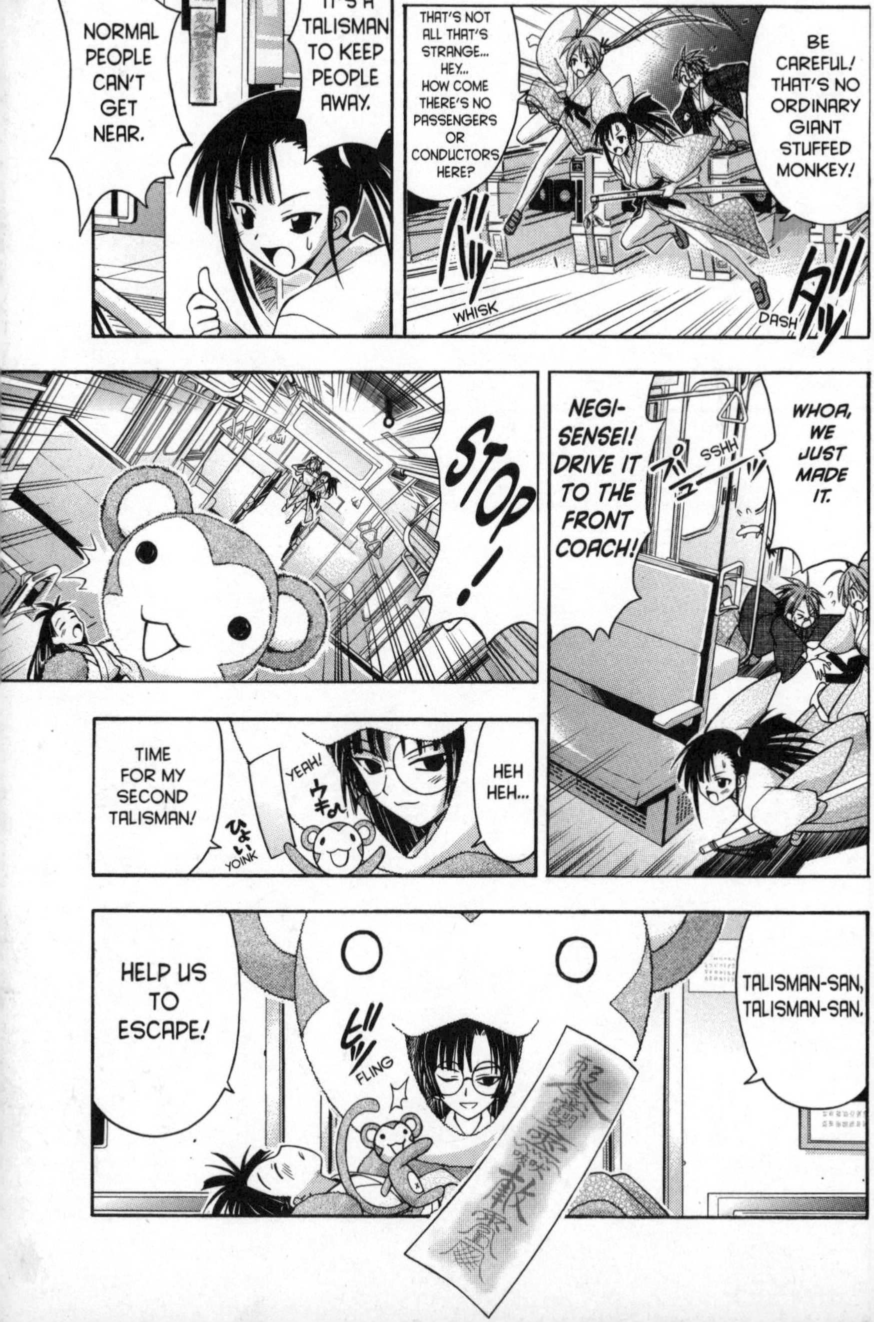
BE CAREFUL! THAT'S NO ORDINARY GIANT STUFFED MONKEY!
DASH
THAT'S NOT ALL THAT'S STRANGE... HEY... HOW COME THERE'S NO PASSENGERS OR CONDUCTORS HERE?
WHISK
IT'S A TALISMAN TO KEEP PEOPLE AWAY.
NORMAL PEOPLE CAN'T GET NEAR.
WHOA, WE JUST MADE IT.
SSHH
NEGI-SENSEI! DRIVE IT TO THE FRONT COACH!
STOP!
HEH HEH...
YEAH!
TIME FOR MY SECOND TALISMAN!
YOINK
TALISMAN-SAN, TALISMAN-SAN.
FLING
HELP US TO ESCAPE!

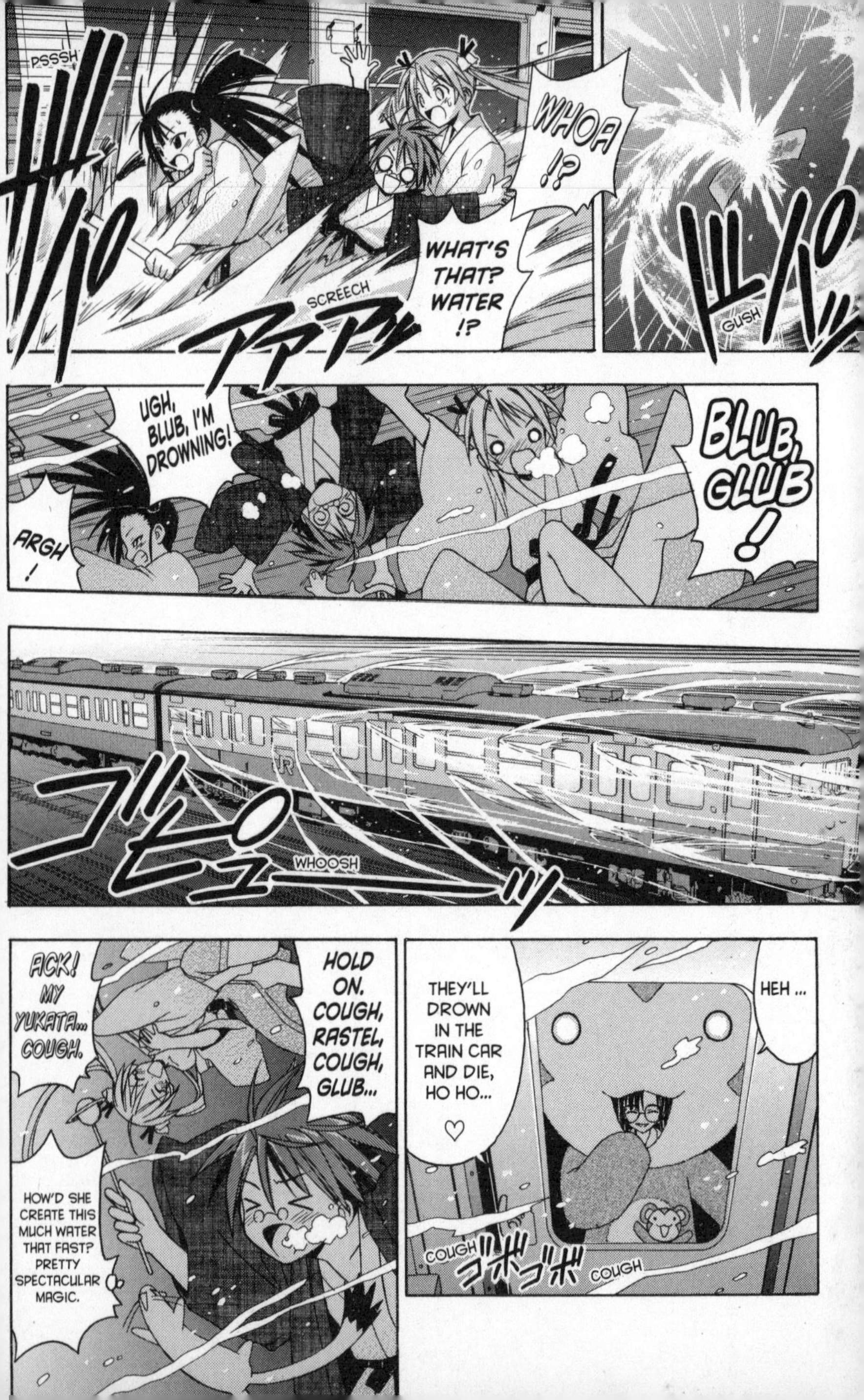
GUSH
WHOA !?
WHAT'S THAT? WATER !?
SCREECH
PSSSH
BLUB, GLUB !
UGH, BLUB, I'M DROWNING!
ARGH !
WHOOSH
HEH ...
THEY'LL DROWN IN THE TRAIN CAR AND DIE, HO HO... ♡
COUGH
COUGH
HOLD ON. COUGH, RASTEL, COUGH, GLUB...
ACK! MY YUKATA... COUGH.
HOW'D SHE CREATE THIS MUCH WATER THAT FAST? PRETTY SPECTACULAR MAGIC.

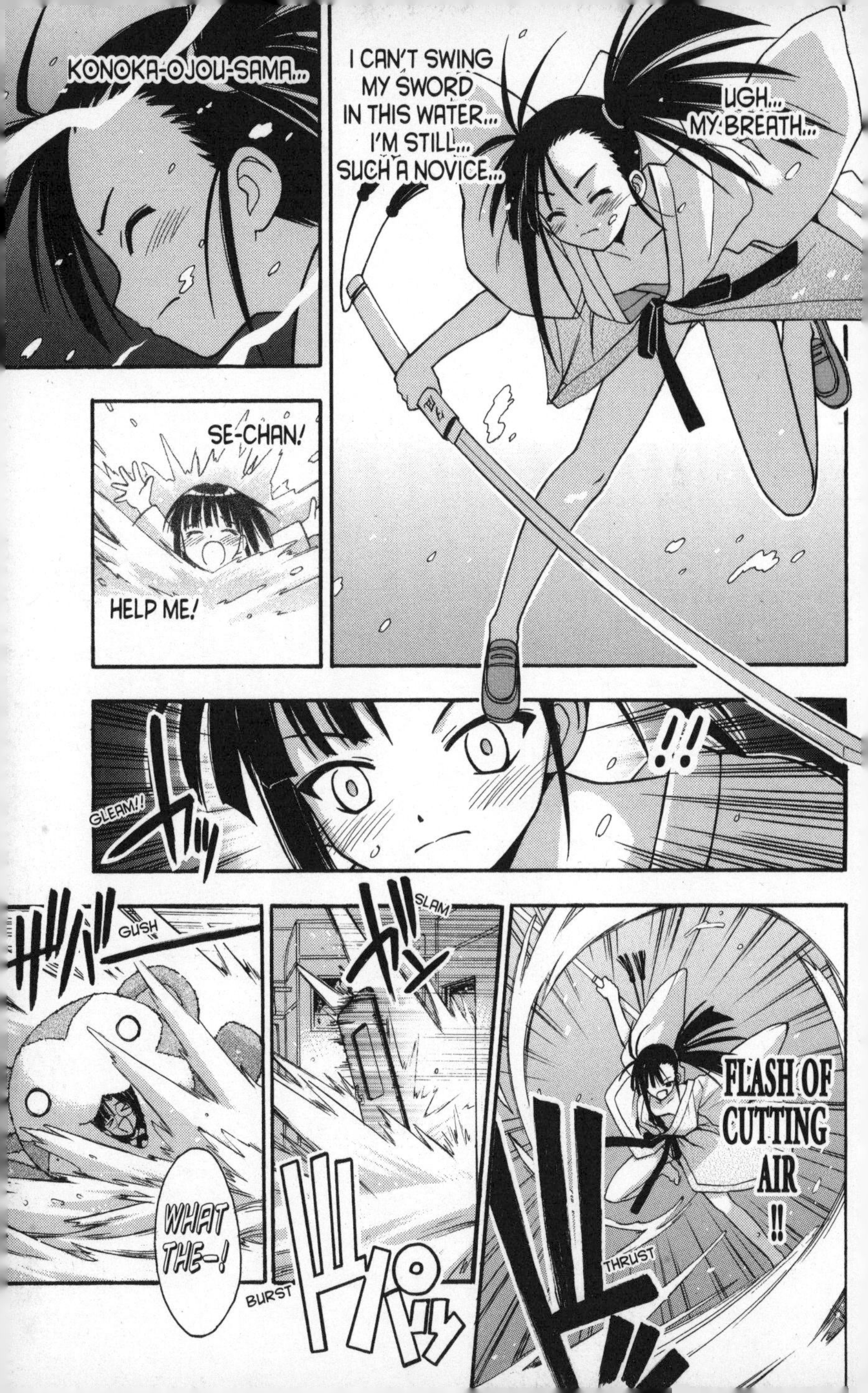
UGH... MY BREATH...
I CAN'T SWING MY SWORD IN THIS WATER... I'M STILL... SUCH A NOVICE...
KONOKA-OJOU-SAMA...
SE-CHAN!
HELP ME!
!!
GLEAM!!
FLASH OF CUTTING AIR!!
THRUST
SLAM
BURST
WHAT THE-!
GUSH

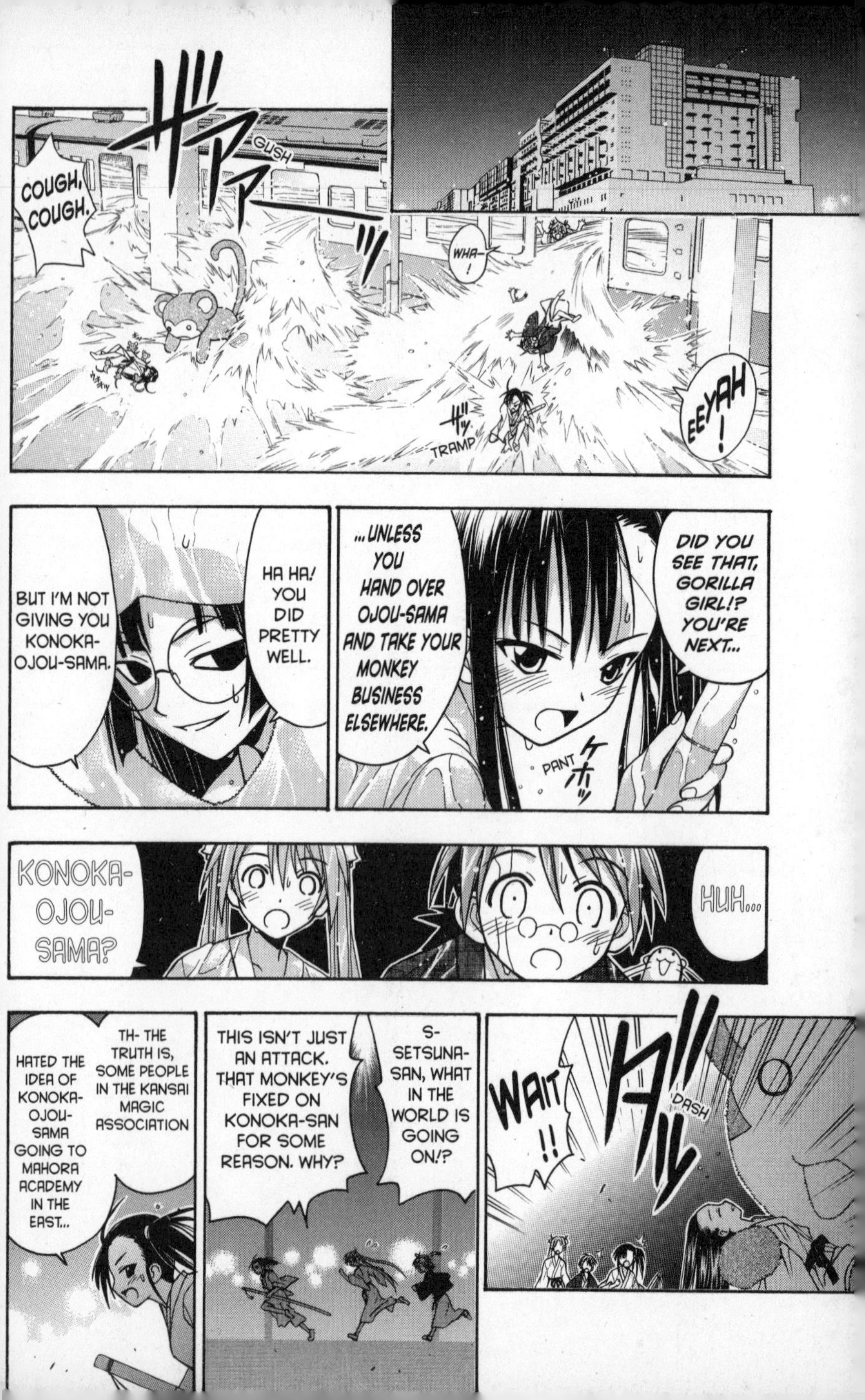

GUSH
COUGH, COUGH.
WHA-!
EEYAH!
TRAMP
DID YOU SEE THAT, GORILLA GIRL!? YOU'RE NEXT...
...UNLESS YOU HAND OVER OJOU-SAMA AND TAKE YOUR MONKEY BUSINESS ELSEWHERE.
PANT
HA HA! YOU DID PRETTY WELL.
BUT I'M NOT GIVING YOU KONOKA-OJOU-SAMA.
HUH...
KONOKA-OJOU-SAMA?
WAIT!!
DASH
S-SETSUNA-SAN, WHAT IN THE WORLD IS GOING ON!?
THIS ISN'T JUST AN ATTACK. THAT MONKEY'S FIXED ON KONOKA-SAN FOR SOME REASON. WHY?
TH- THE TRUTH IS, SOME PEOPLE IN THE KANSAI MAGIC ASSOCIATION
HATED THE IDEA OF KONOKA-OJOU-SAMA GOING TO MAHORA ACADEMY IN THE EAST...

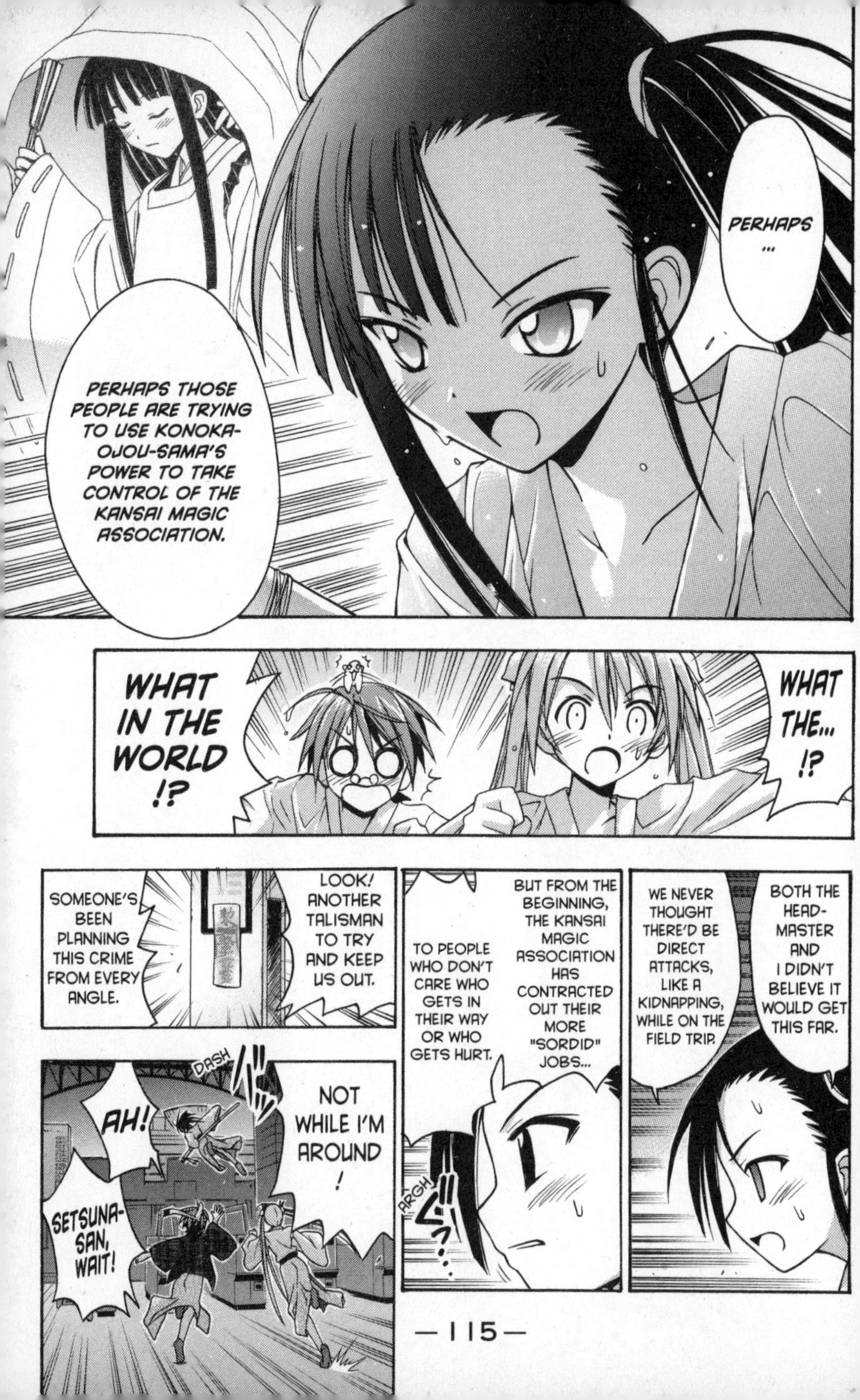
PERHAPS ...
PERHAPS THOSE PEOPLE ARE TRYING TO USE KONOKA-OJOU-SAMA'S POWER TO TAKE CONTROL OF THE KANSAI MAGIC ASSOCIATION.
WHAT THE... !?
WHAT IN THE WORLD !?
BOTH THE HEAD-MASTER AND I DIDN'T BELIEVE IT WOULD GET THIS FAR.
WE NEVER THOUGHT THERE'D BE DIRECT ATTACKS, LIKE A KIDNAPPING, WHILE ON THE FIELD TRIP.
BUT FROM THE BEGINNING, THE KANSAI MAGIC ASSOCIATION HAS CONTRACTED OUT THEIR MORE "SORDID" JOBS...
TO PEOPLE WHO DON'T CARE WHO GETS IN THEIR WAY OR WHO GETS HURT.
ARGH
LOOK! ANOTHER TALISMAN TO TRY AND KEEP US OUT.
SOMEONE'S BEEN PLANNING THIS CRIME FROM EVERY ANGLE.
NOT WHILE I'M AROUND!
DASH
AH!
SETSUNA-SAN, WAIT!

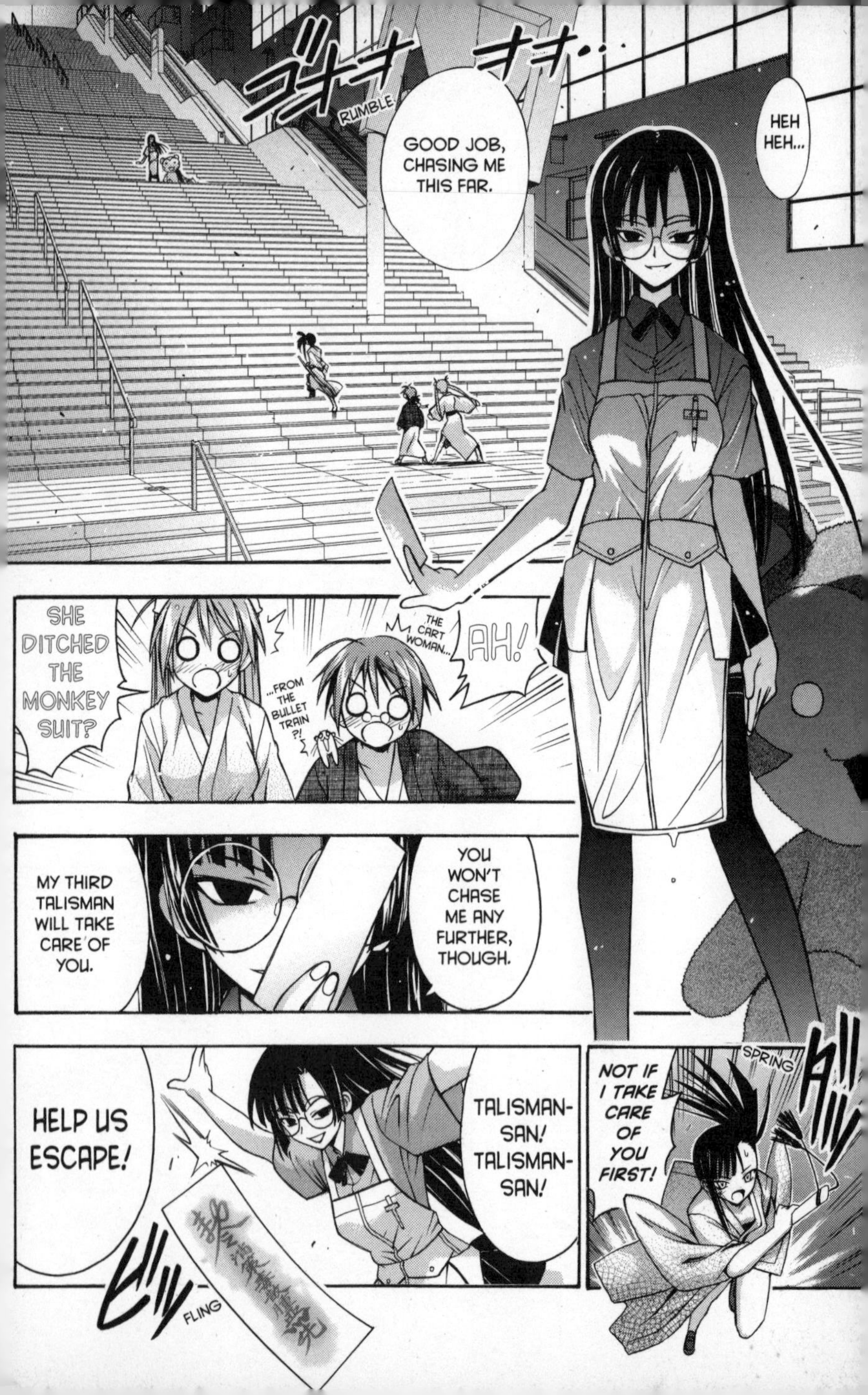

RUMBLE
HEH HEH...
GOOD JOB, CHASING ME THIS FAR.
AH!
THE CART WOMAN...
...FROM THE BULLET TRAIN?!
SHE DITCHED THE MONKEY SUIT?
YOU WON'T CHASE ME ANY FURTHER, THOUGH.
MY THIRD TALISMAN WILL TAKE CARE OF YOU.
SPRING
NOT IF I TAKE CARE OF YOU FIRST!
TALISMAN-SAN! TALISMAN-SAN!
HELP US ESCAPE!
FLING

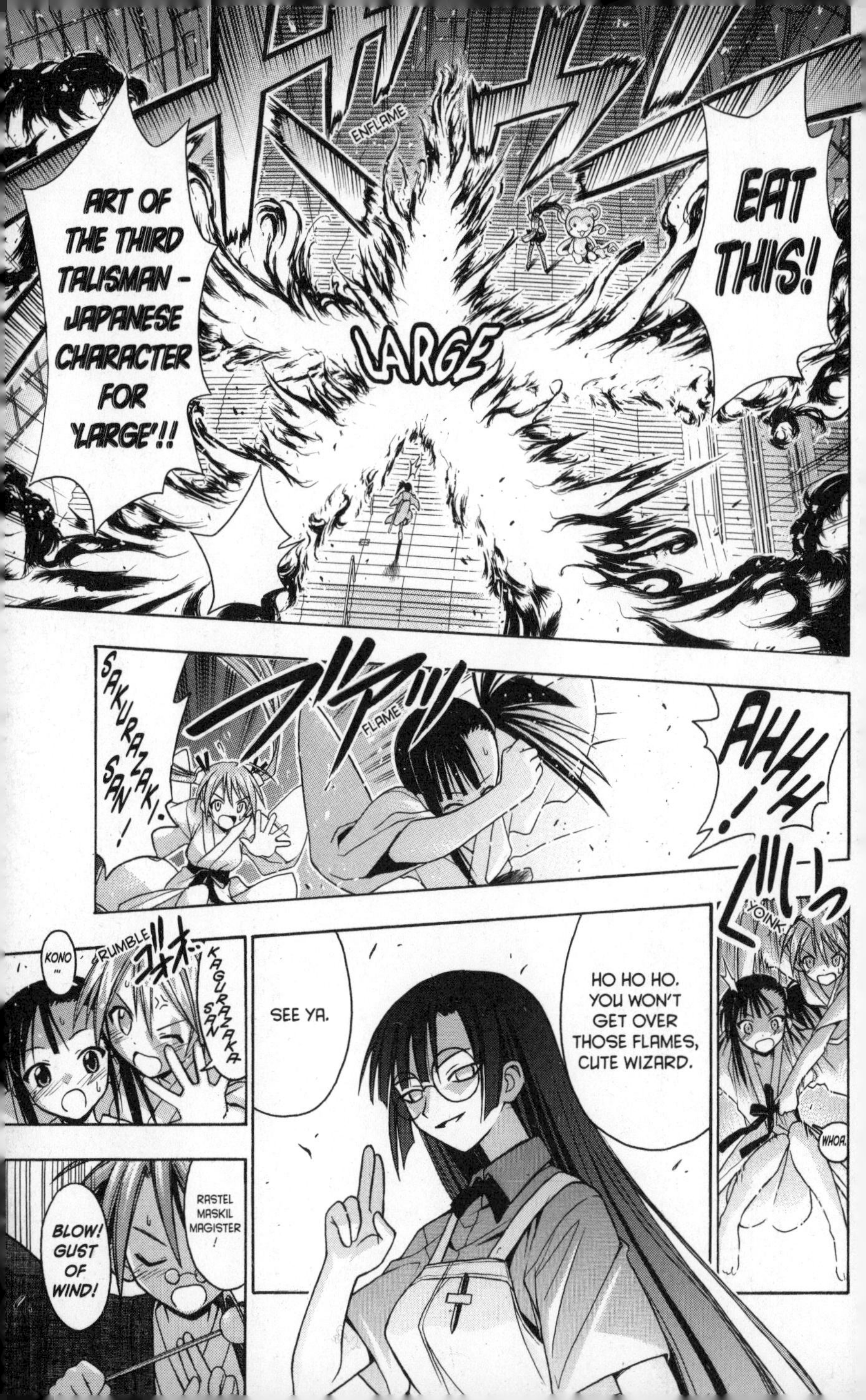
EAT THIS!
ENFLAME
LARGE
ART OF THE THIRD TALISMAN - JAPANESE CHARACTER FOR 'LARGE'!!
AHHH!
FLAME
SAKURAZAKI-SAN!
YOINK
WHOA.
HO HO HO. YOU WON'T GET OVER THOSE FLAMES, CUTE WIZARD.
SEE YA.
KAGURAZAKA-SAN
RUMBLE
KONO...
RASTEL MASKIL MAGISTER!
BLOW! GUST OF WIND!

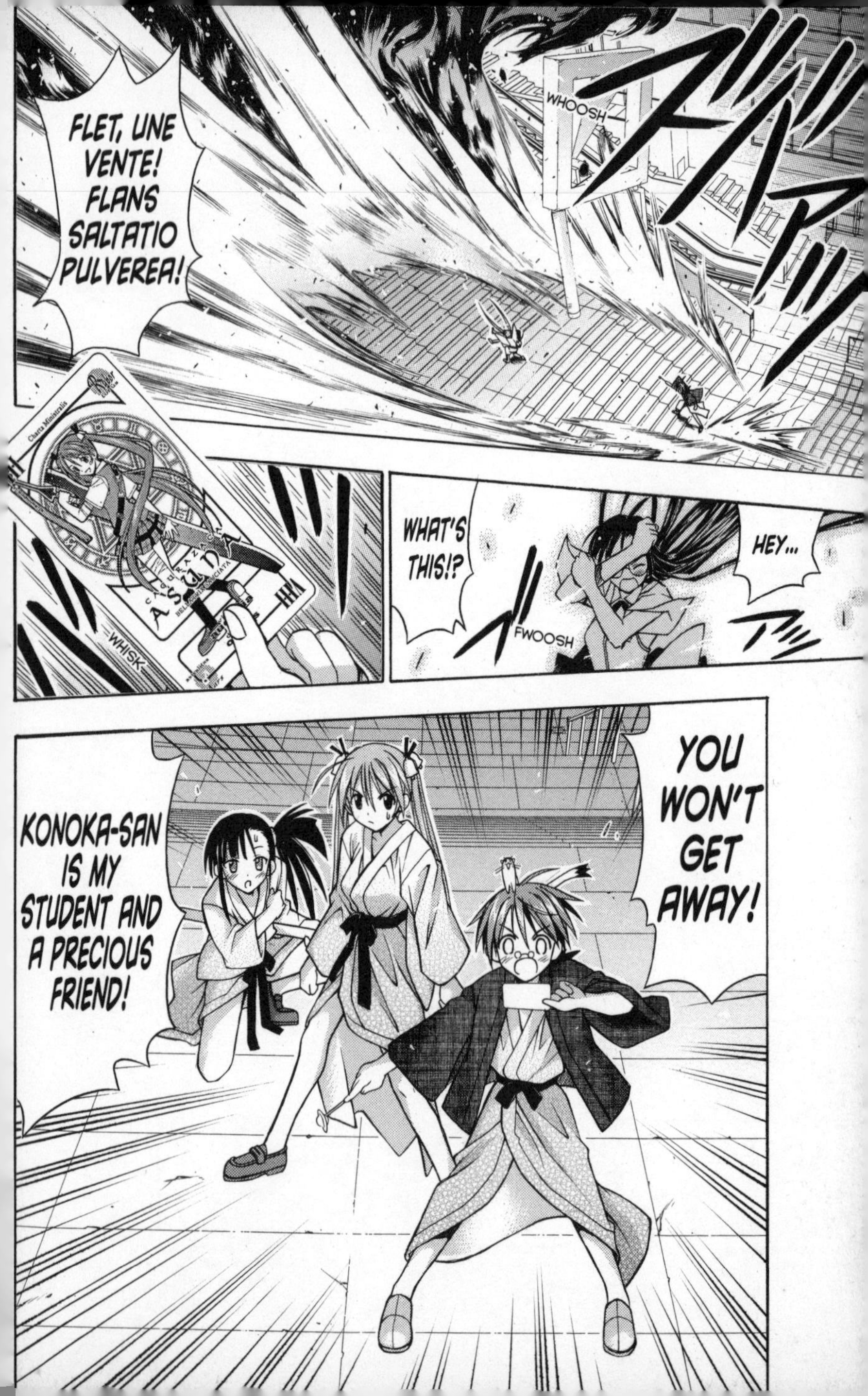
WHOOSH
FLET, UNE VENTE! FLANS SALTATIO PULVEREA!
HEY...
WHAT'S THIS!?
FWOOSH
WHISK
YOU WON'T GET AWAY!
KONOKA-SAN IS MY STUDENT AND A PRECIOUS FRIEND!

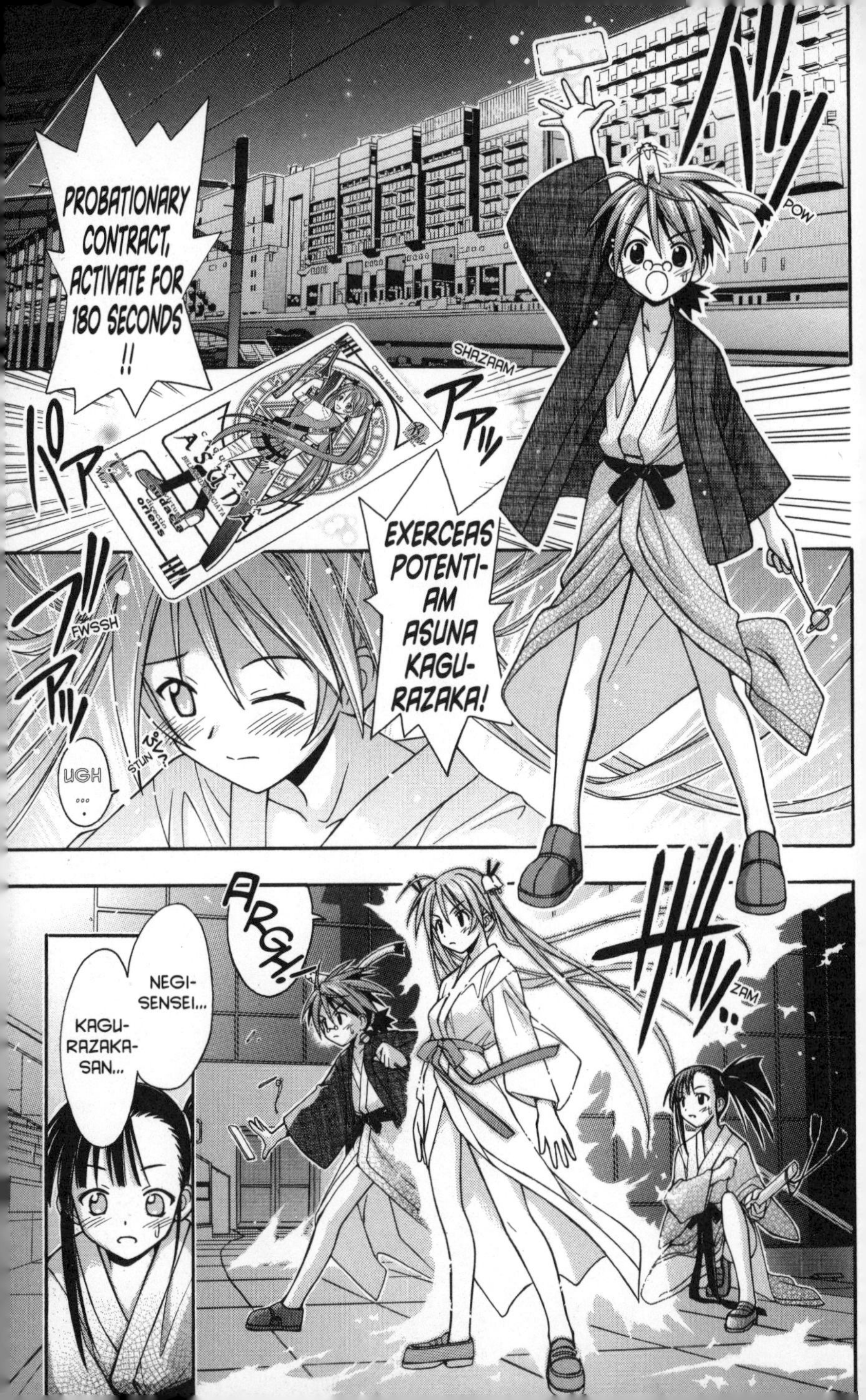

POW
PROBATIONARY CONTRACT, ACTIVATE FOR 180 SECONDS !!
SHAZAAM
EXERCEAS POTENTI-AM ASUNA KAGU-RAZAKA!
FWSSH
STUN
UGH ...
ZAM
ARGH!
NEGI-SENSEI...
KAGU-RAZAKA-SAN...

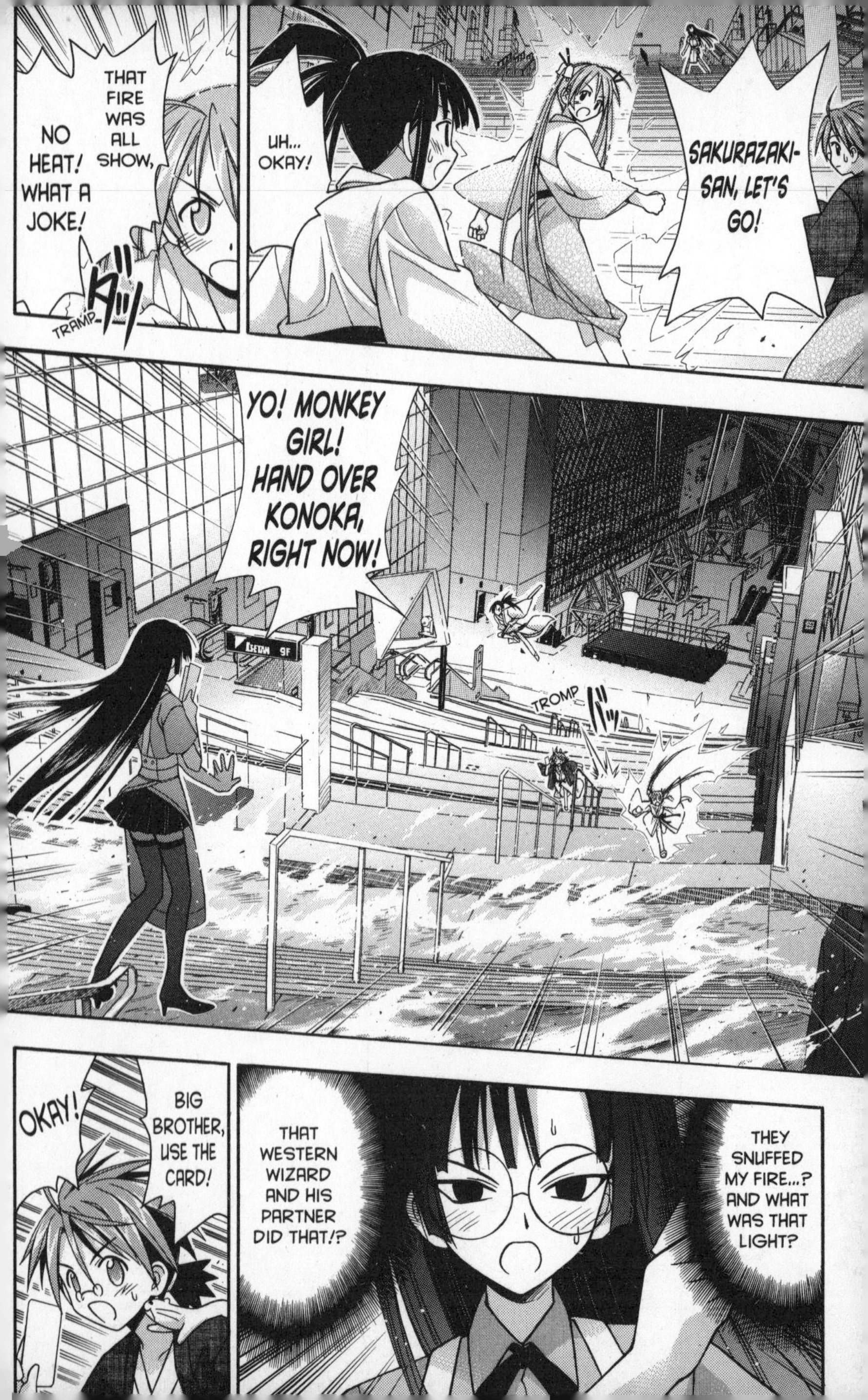
SAKURAZAKI-SAN, LET'S GO!
UH... OKAY!
THAT FIRE WAS ALL SHOW,
NO HEAT! WHAT A JOKE!
TRAMP
YO! MONKEY GIRL! HAND OVER KONOKA, RIGHT NOW!
ISETAN 9F
TROMP
THEY SNUFFED MY FIRE...? AND WHAT WAS THAT LIGHT?
THAT WESTERN WIZARD AND HIS PARTNER DID THAT!?
BIG BROTHER, USE THE CARD!
OKAY!

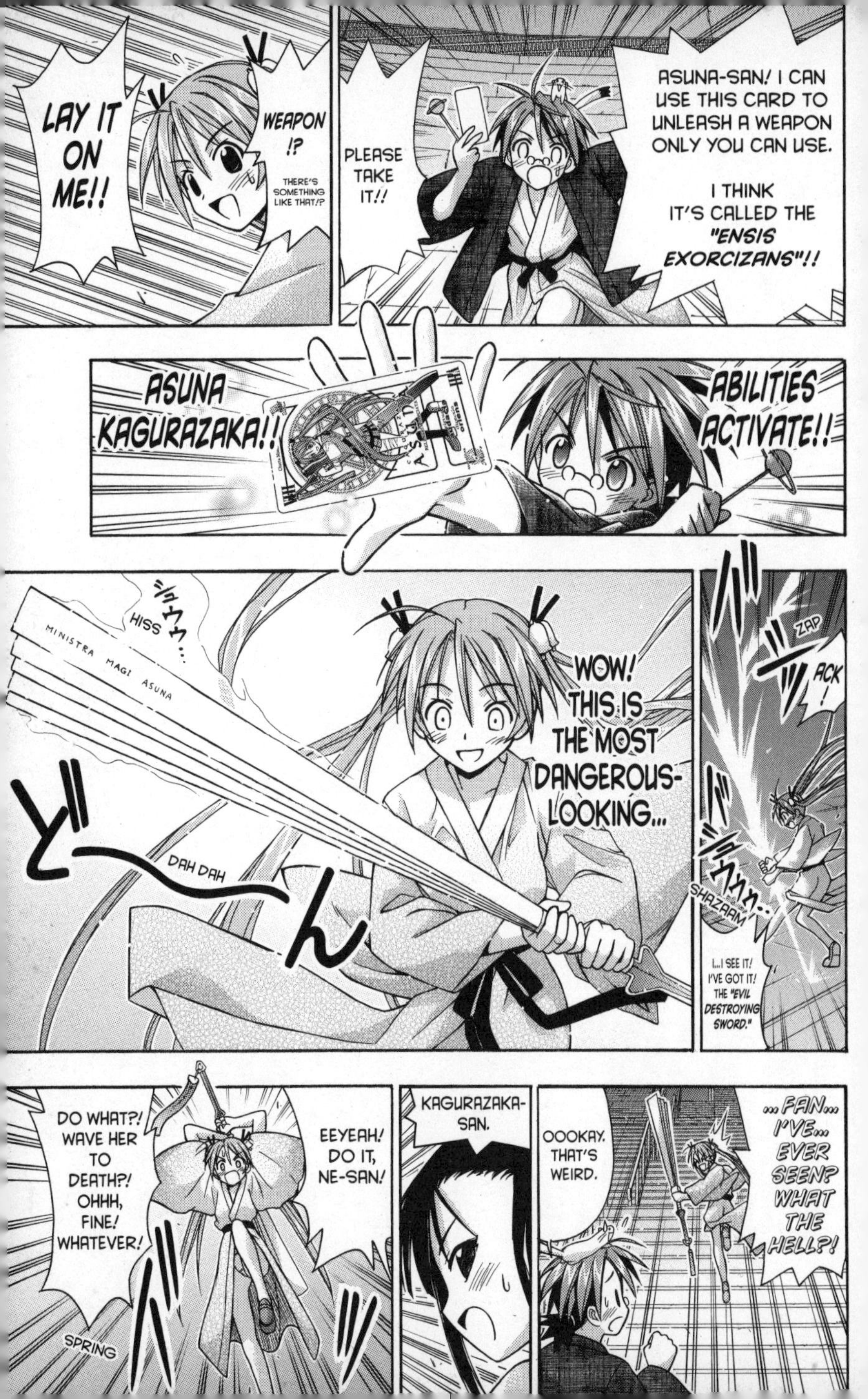
ASUNA-SAN! I CAN USE THIS CARD TO UNLEASH A WEAPON ONLY YOU CAN USE.
I THINK IT'S CALLED THE "ENSIS EXORCIZANS"!!
PLEASE TAKE IT!!
WEAPON !?
THERE'S SOMETHING LIKE THAT!?
LAY IT ON ME!!
ASUNA KAGURAZAKA!!
ABILITIES ACTIVATE!!
ZAP
ACK !
SHAZAAM
I...I SEE IT! I'VE GOT IT! THE "EVIL DESTROYING SWORD."
HISS
MINISTRA MAGI ASUNA
WOW! THIS IS THE MOST DANGEROUS-LOOKING...
DAH DAH
...FAN... I'VE... EVER SEEN? WHAT THE HELL?!
OOOKAY. THAT'S WEIRD.
KAGURAZAKA-SAN.
EEYEAH! DO IT, NE-SAN!
DO WHAT?! WAVE HER TO DEATH?! OHHH, FINE! WHATEVER!
SPRING

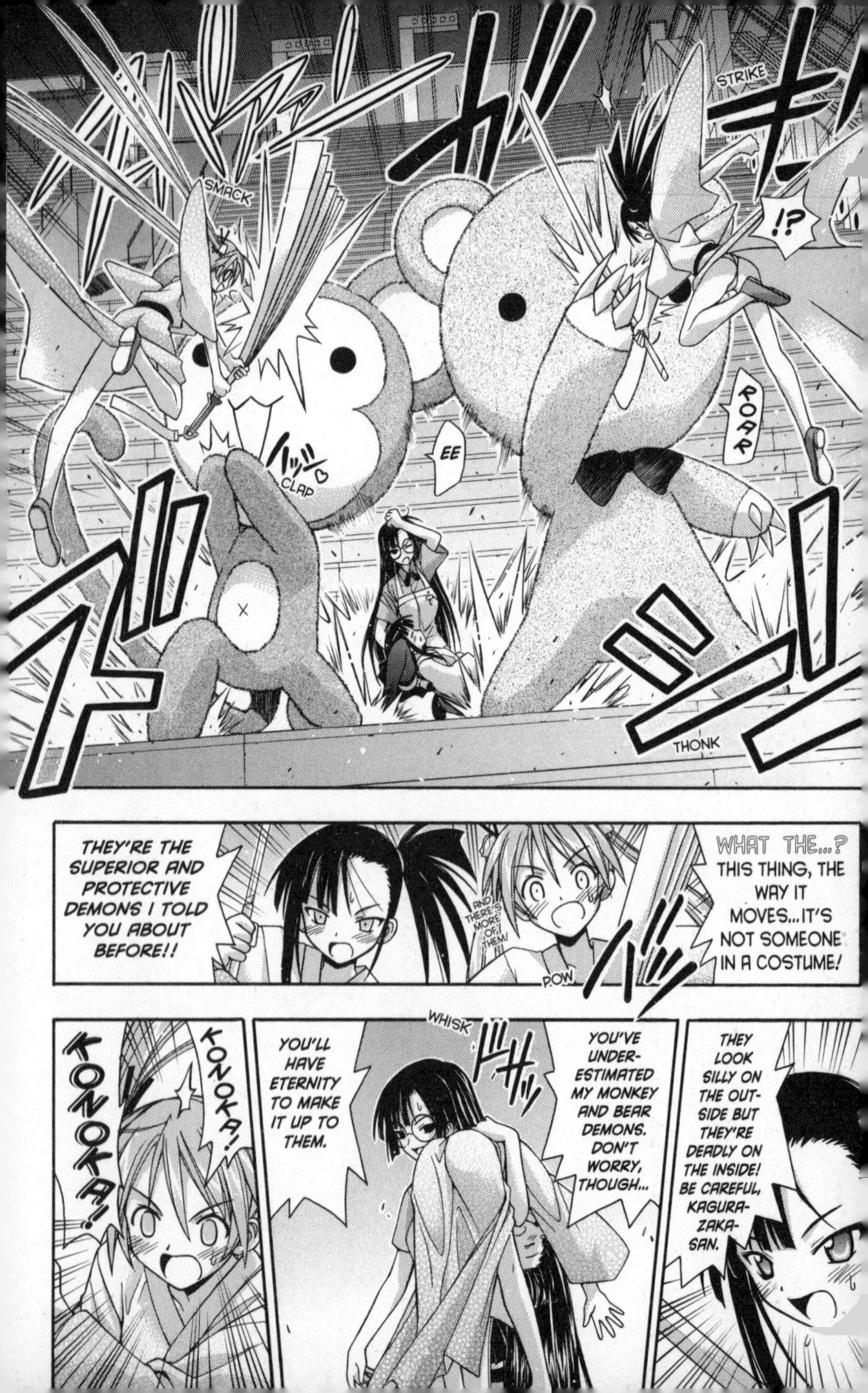
STRIKE
!?
SMACK
ROAR
EE
ハッ♡
CLAP
THONK
WHAT THE...? THIS THING, THE WAY IT MOVES...IT'S NOT SOMEONE IN A COSTUME!
AND THERE'S MORE OF THEM!
POW
THEY'RE THE SUPERIOR AND PROTECTIVE DEMONS I TOLD YOU ABOUT BEFORE!!
THEY LOOK SILLY ON THE OUT-SIDE BUT THEY'RE DEADLY ON THE INSIDE! BE CAREFUL, KAGURA-ZAKA-SAN.
WHISK
YOU'VE UNDER-ESTIMATED MY MONKEY AND BEAR DEMONS. DON'T WORRY, THOUGH...
YOU'LL HAVE ETERNITY TO MAKE IT UP TO THEM.
KONOKA!
KONOKA!

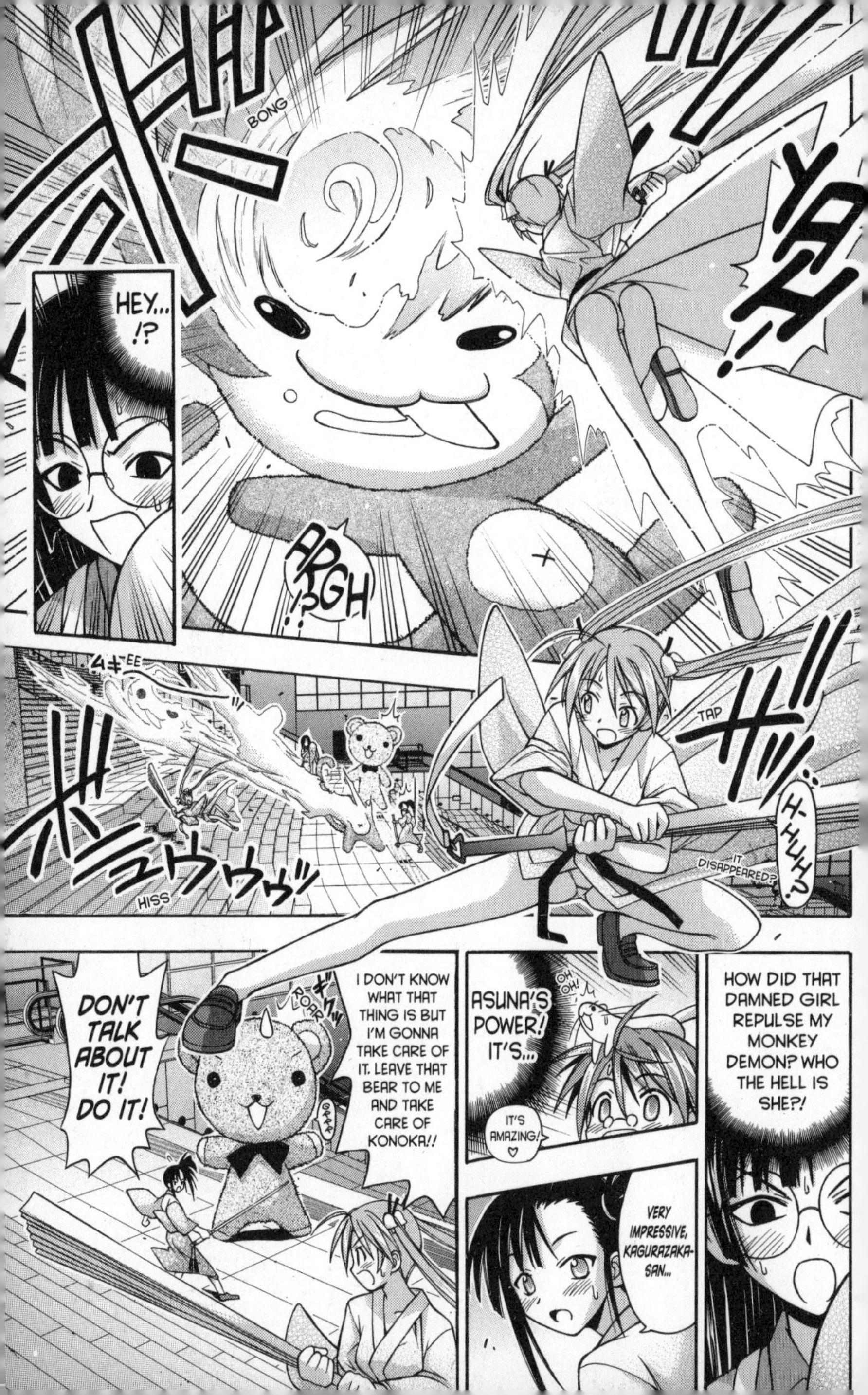
BONG
HEY... !?
ARGH !?
TAP
H-HUH?
IT DISAPPEARED?
HISS
HOW DID THAT DAMNED GIRL REPULSE MY MONKEY DEMON? WHO THE HELL IS SHE?!
ASUNA'S POWER! IT'S...
OH OH!
IT'S AMAZING! ♡
I DON'T KNOW WHAT THAT THING IS BUT I'M GONNA TAKE CARE OF IT. LEAVE THAT BEAR TO ME AND TAKE CARE OF KONOKA!!
ROAR
DON'T TALK ABOUT IT! DO IT!
VERY IMPRESSIVE, KAGURAZAKA-SAN...

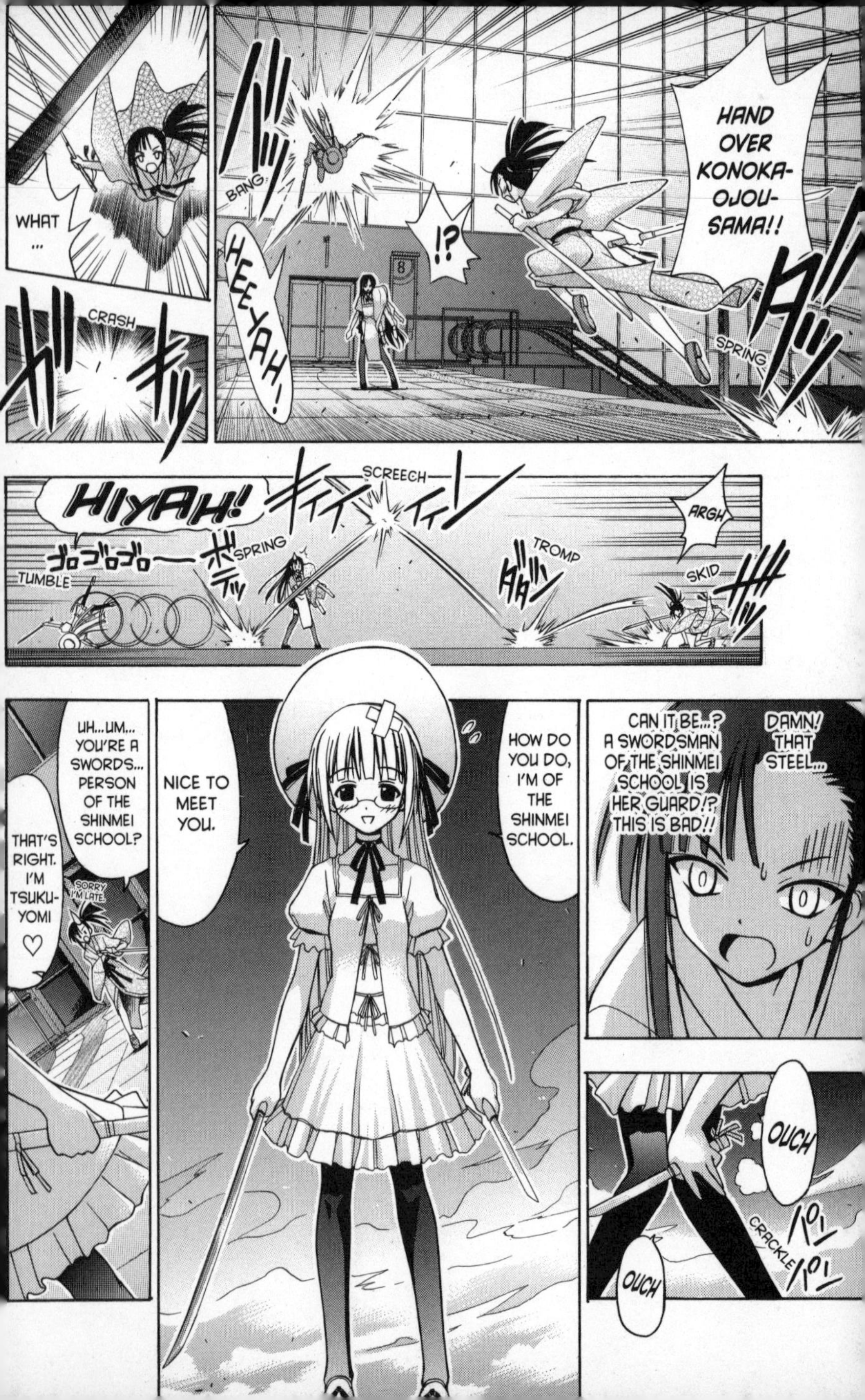
HAND OVER KONOKA-OJOUSAMA!!
SPRING
!?
HEEYAH!
BANG
WHAT ...
CRASH
SCREECH
ARGH
SKID
TROMP
SPRING
HIYAH!
TUMBLE
DAMN! THAT STEEL...
CAN IT BE...? A SWORDSMAN OF THE SHINMEI SCHOOL IS HER GUARD!? THIS IS BAD!!
OUCH
CRACKLE
OUCH
HOW DO YOU DO, I'M OF THE SHINMEI SCHOOL.
NICE TO MEET YOU.
UH...UM... YOU'RE A SWORDS... PERSON OF THE SHINMEI SCHOOL?
THAT'S RIGHT. I'M TSUKUYOMI ♡
SORRY I'M LATE

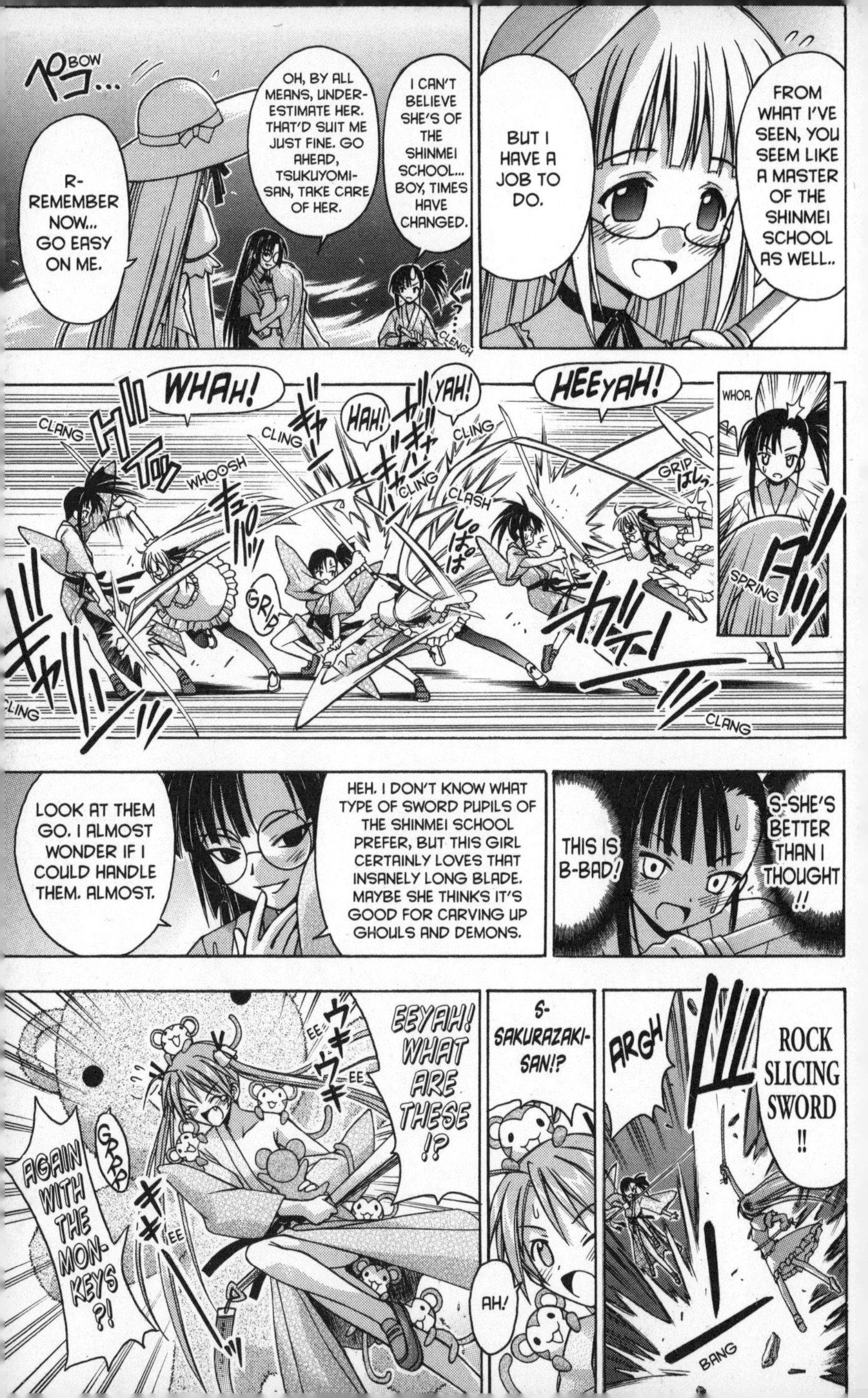
FROM WHAT I'VE SEEN, YOU SEEM LIKE A MASTER OF THE SHINMEI SCHOOL AS WELL..
BUT I HAVE A JOB TO DO.
I CAN'T BELIEVE SHE'S OF THE SHINMEI SCHOOL... BOY, TIMES HAVE CHANGED.
CLENCH
OH, BY ALL MEANS, UNDER-ESTIMATE HER. THAT'D SUIT ME JUST FINE. GO AHEAD, TSUKUYOMI-SAN, TAKE CARE OF HER.
R-REMEMBER NOW... GO EASY ON ME.
BOW
WHOA.
SPRING
HEEYAH!
GRIP
CLING
YAH!
CLASH
CLING
HAH!
CLING
WHAH!
WHOOSH
CLANG
GRIP
CLING
CLANG
S-SHE'S BETTER THAN I THOUGHT!!
THIS IS B-BAD!
HEH. I DON'T KNOW WHAT TYPE OF SWORD PUPILS OF THE SHINMEI SCHOOL PREFER, BUT THIS GIRL CERTAINLY LOVES THAT INSANELY LONG BLADE. MAYBE SHE THINKS IT'S GOOD FOR CARVING UP GHOULS AND DEMONS.
LOOK AT THEM GO. I ALMOST WONDER IF I COULD HANDLE THEM. ALMOST.
ROCK SLICING SWORD!!
ARGH
BANG
S-SAKURAZAKI-SAN!?
AH!
EEYAH! WHAT ARE THESE!?
EE
EE
GRRR
EE
AGAIN WITH THE MON-KEYS?!

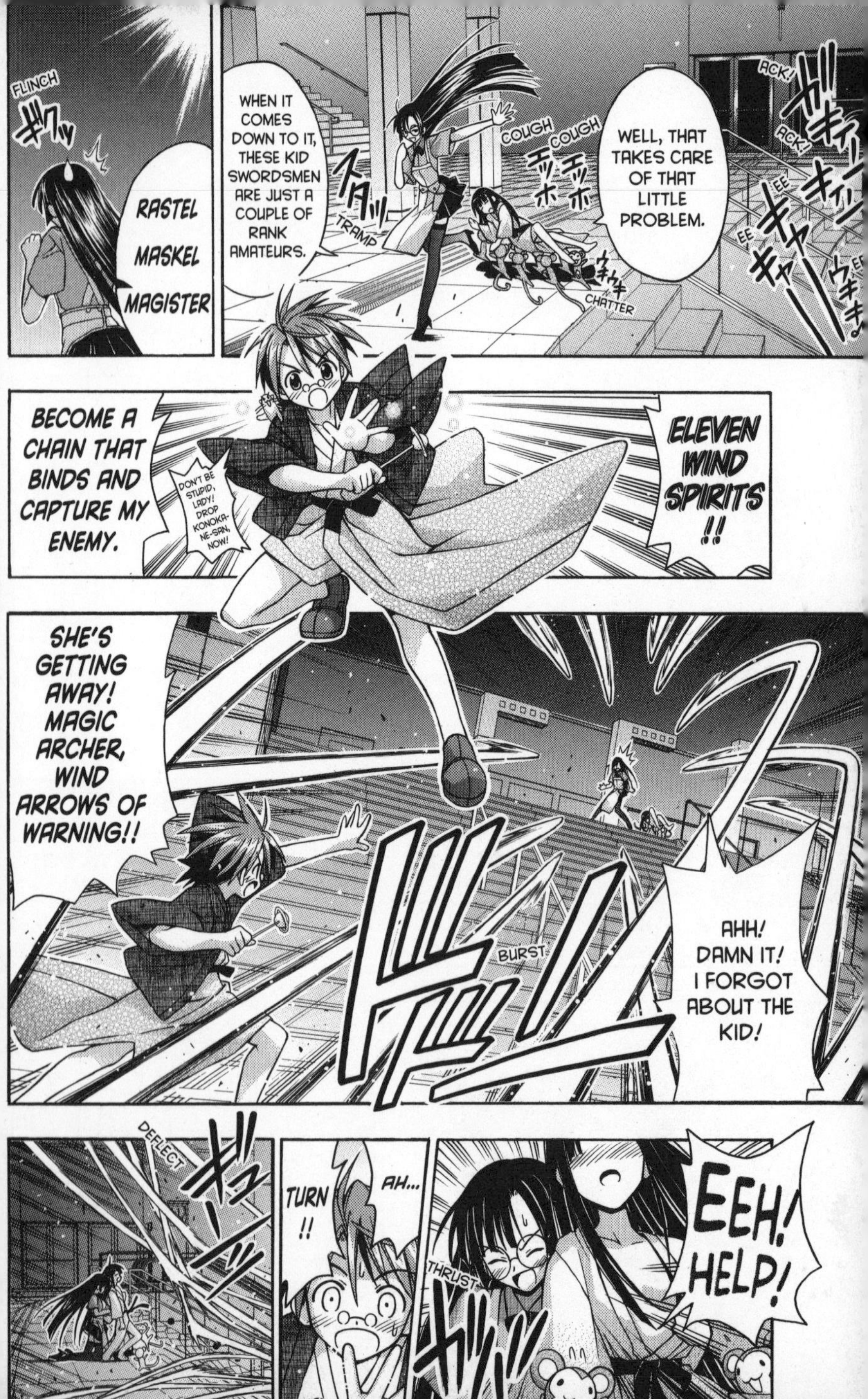
ACK!
ACK!
EE
EE
EE
WELL, THAT TAKES CARE OF THAT LITTLE PROBLEM.
CHATTER
COUGH
COUGH
TRAMP
WHEN IT COMES DOWN TO IT, THESE KID SWORDSMEN ARE JUST A COUPLE OF RANK AMATEURS.
FLINCH
RASTEL MASKEL MAGISTER
ELEVEN WIND SPIRITS!!
DON'T BE STUPID, LADY! DROP KONOKA-NE-SAN, NOW!
BECOME A CHAIN THAT BINDS AND CAPTURE MY ENEMY.
AHH! DAMN IT! I FORGOT ABOUT THE KID!
BURST
SHE'S GETTING AWAY! MAGIC ARCHER, WIND ARROWS OF WARNING!!
EEH! HELP!
THRUST
AH...
TURN!!
DEFLECT

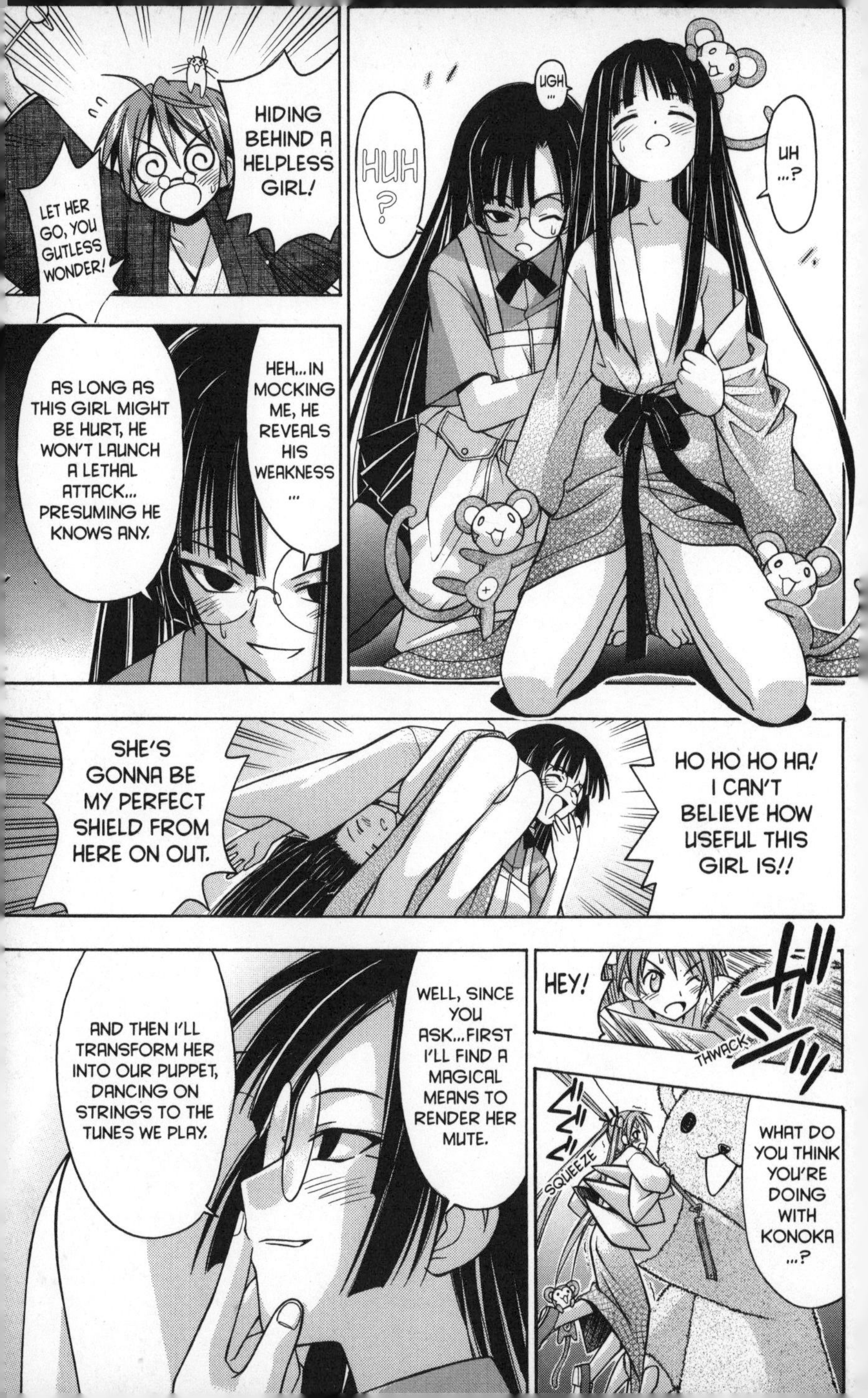
UH ...?
UGH ...
HUH ?
HIDING BEHIND A HELPLESS GIRL!
LET HER GO, YOU GUTLESS WONDER!
HEH...IN MOCKING ME, HE REVEALS HIS WEAKNESS ...
AS LONG AS THIS GIRL MIGHT BE HURT, HE WON'T LAUNCH A LETHAL ATTACK... PRESUMING HE KNOWS ANY.
HO HO HO HA! I CAN'T BELIEVE HOW USEFUL THIS GIRL IS!!
SHE'S GONNA BE MY PERFECT SHIELD FROM HERE ON OUT.
HEY!
THWACK
SQUEEZE
WHAT DO YOU THINK YOU'RE DOING WITH KONOKA ...?
WELL, SINCE YOU ASK...FIRST I'LL FIND A MAGICAL MEANS TO RENDER HER MUTE.
AND THEN I'LL TRANSFORM HER INTO OUR PUPPET, DANCING ON STRINGS TO THE TUNES WE PLAY.

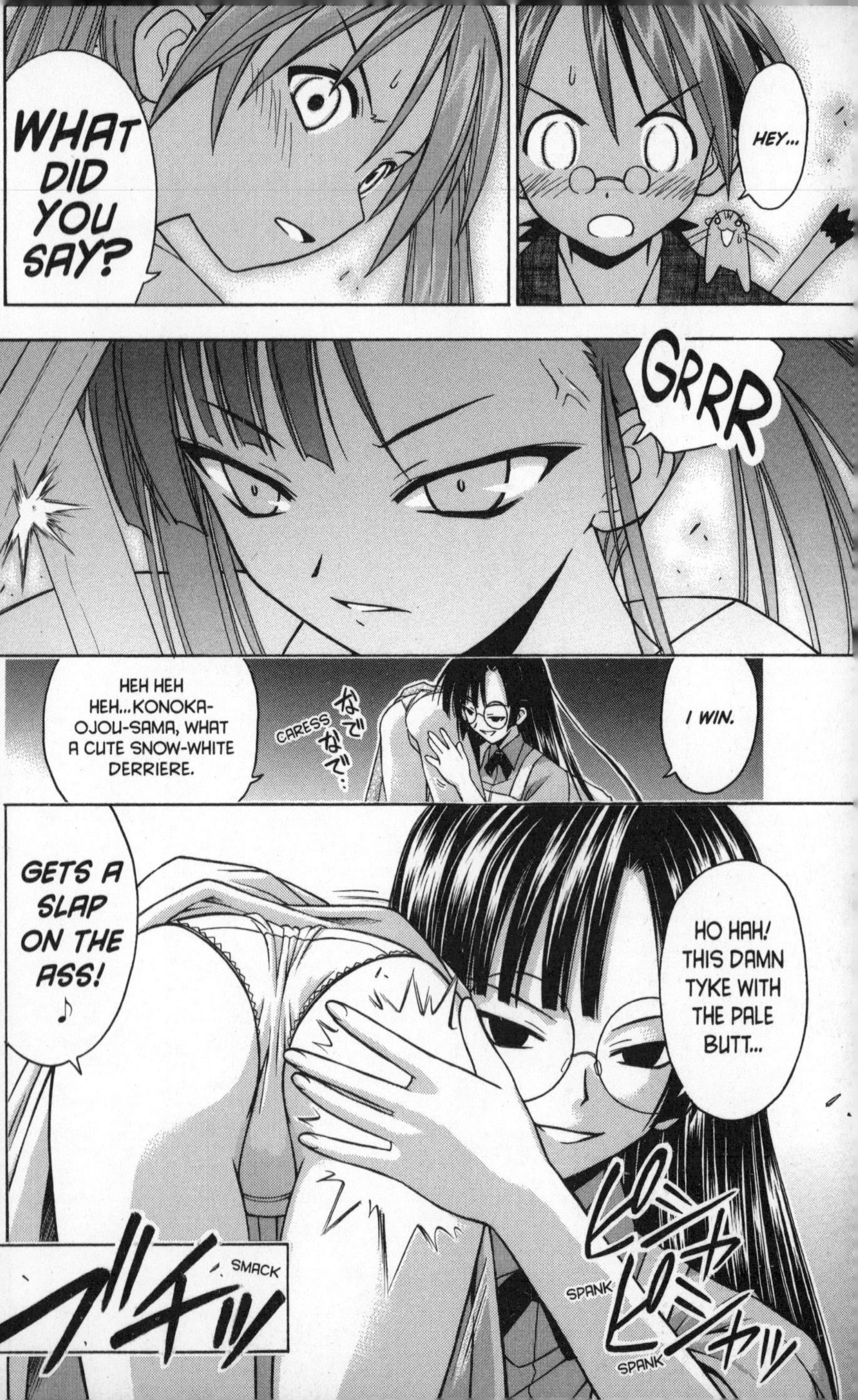
HEY...
WHAT DID YOU SAY?
GRRR
I WIN.
なでなで...
CARESS
HEH HEH HEH...KONOKA-OJOU-SAMA, WHAT A CUTE SNOW-WHITE DERRIERE.
HO HAH! THIS DAMN TYKE WITH THE PALE BUTT...
GETS A SLAP ON THE ASS! ♪
SMACK
SPANK
SPANK

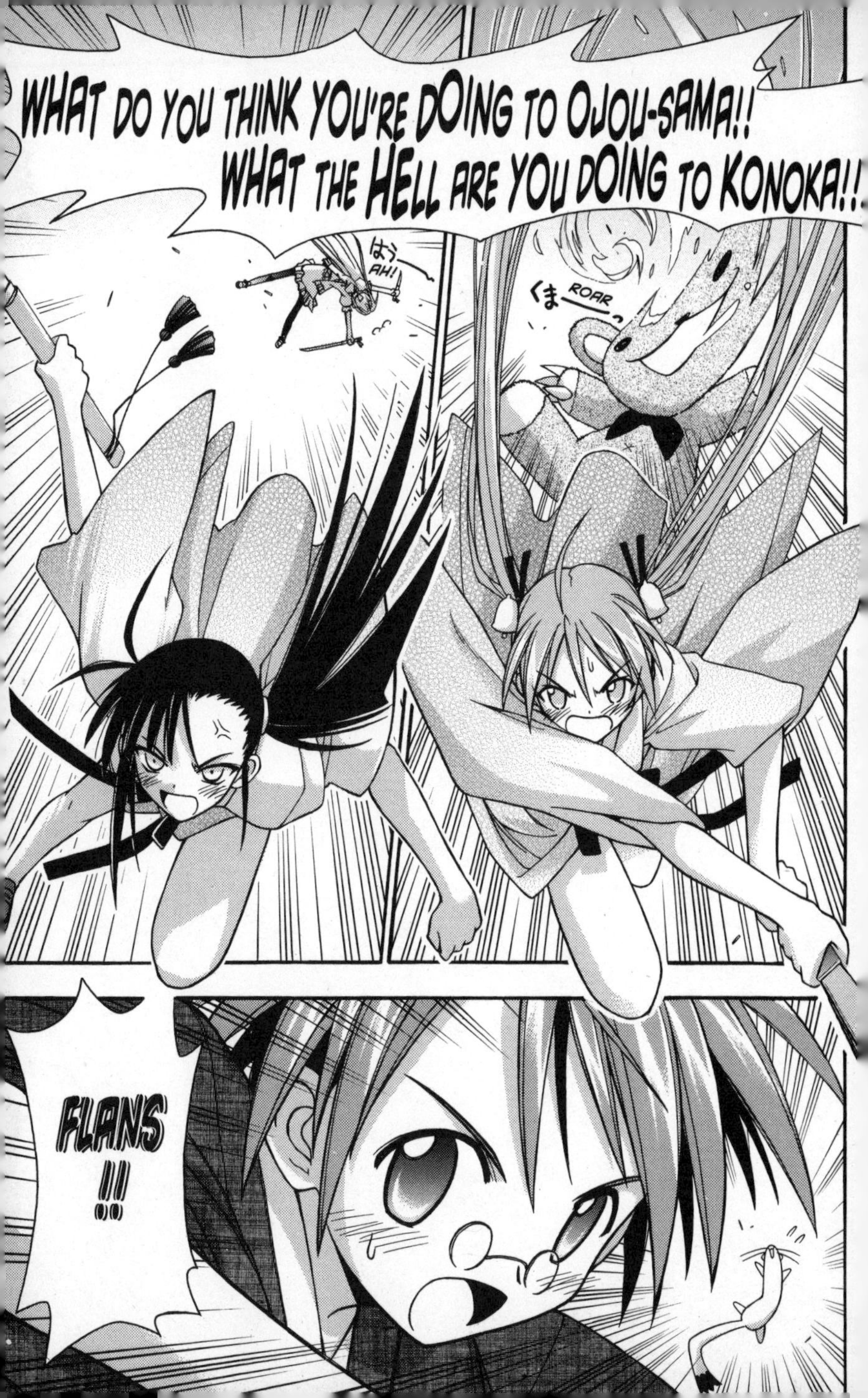
WHAT DO YOU THINK YOU'RE DOING TO OJOU-SAMA!!
WHAT THE HELL ARE YOU DOING TO KONOKA!!
はう AH!
くま ROAR
FLANS !!

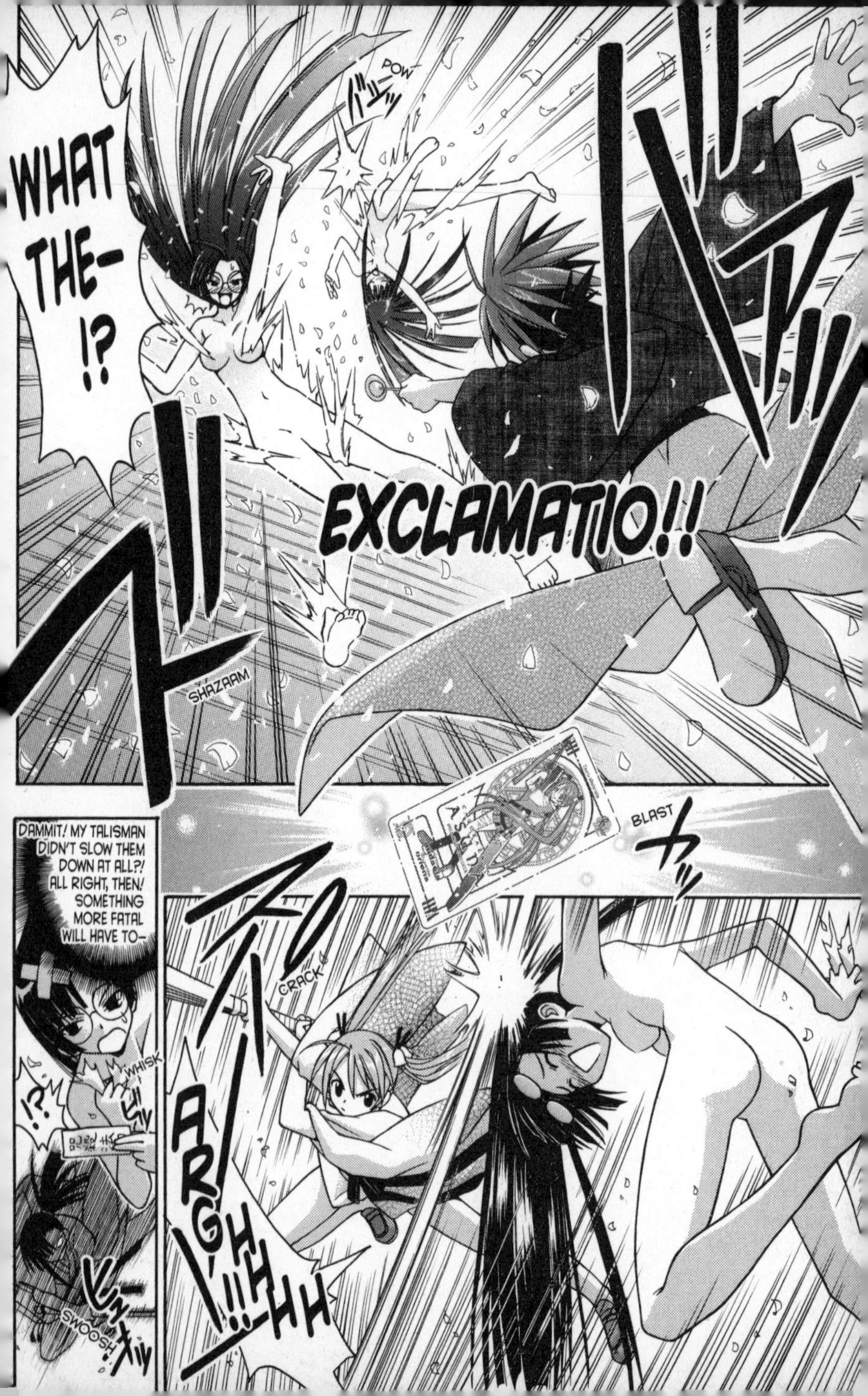

POW
WHAT THE-!?
EXCLAMATIO!!
SHAZAAM
BLAST
DAMMIT! MY TALISMAN DIDN'T SLOW THEM DOWN AT ALL?! ALL RIGHT, THEN! SOMETHING MORE FATAL WILL HAVE TO—
CRACK
WHISK
!?
ARGHHHHH!!!
SWOOSH

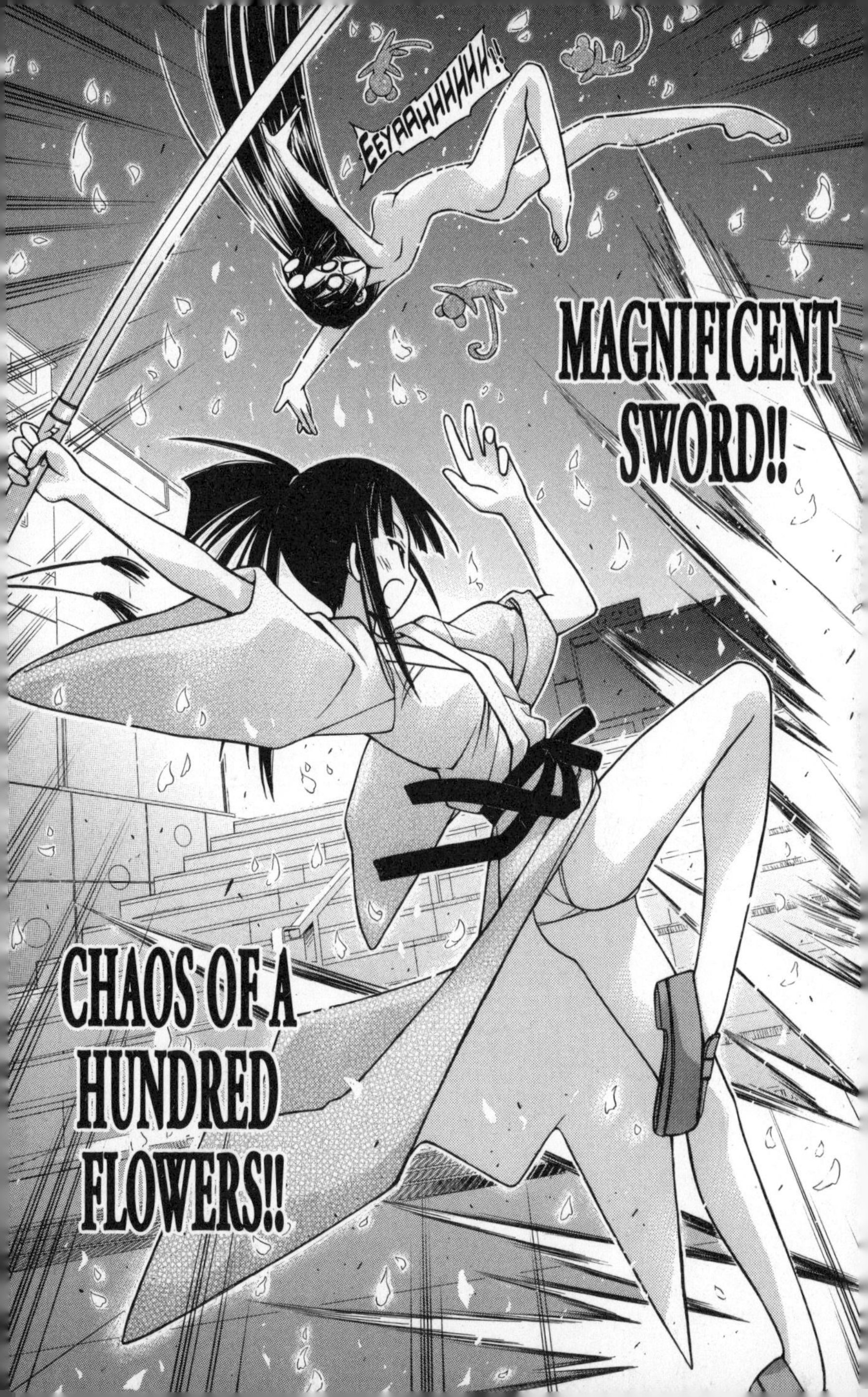
EEYAAHHHHHH!!
MAGNIFICENT SWORD!!
CHAOS OF A HUNDRED FLOWERS!!

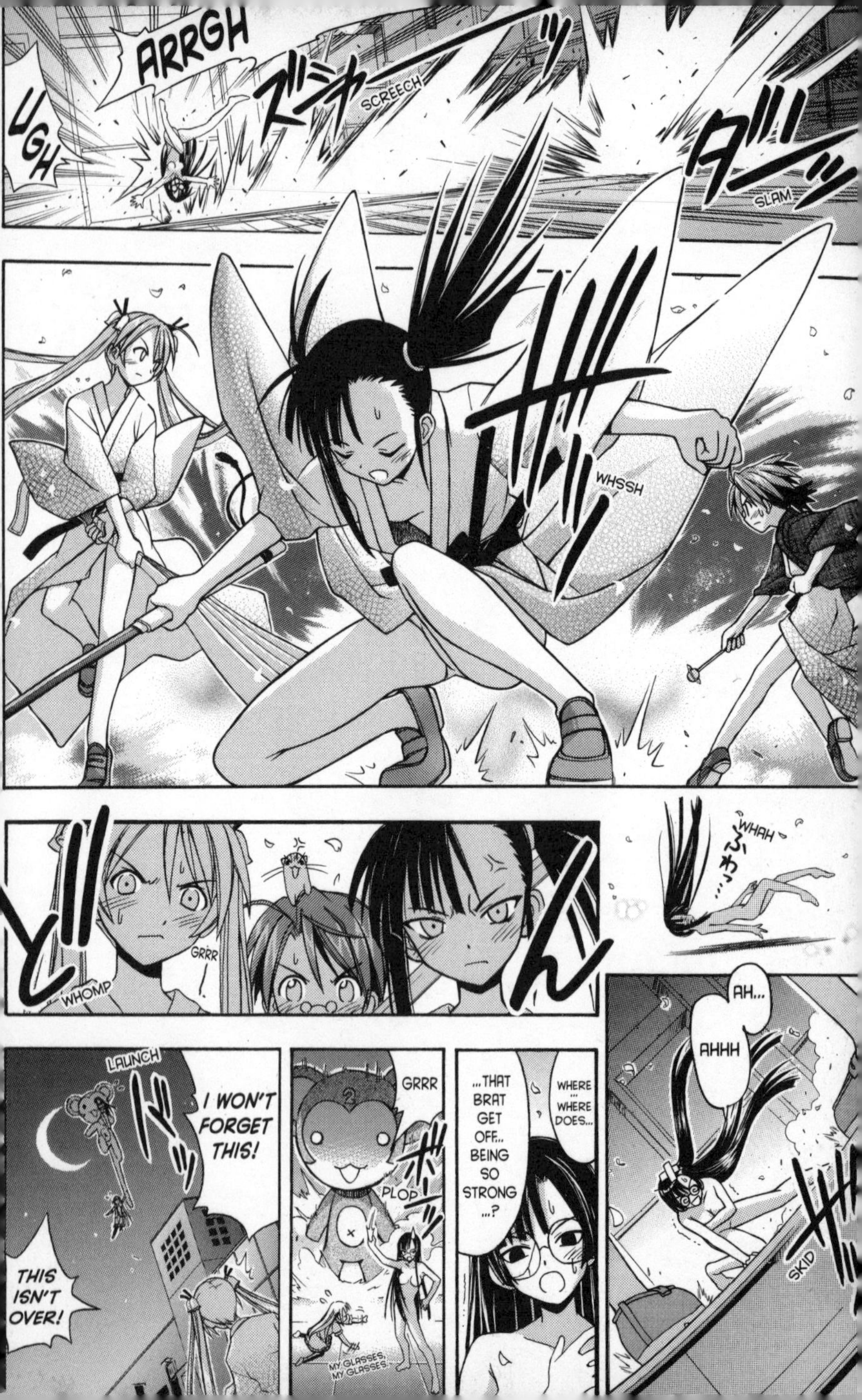

SLAM
SCREECH
ARRGH
UGH
WHSSH
WHAH
GRRR
WHOMP
AH...
AHHH
SKID
WHERE... WHERE DOES...
...THAT BRAT GET OFF... BEING SO STRONG ...?
GRRR
PLOP
MY GLASSES, MY GLASSES
LAUNCH
I WON'T FORGET THIS!
THIS ISN'T OVER!

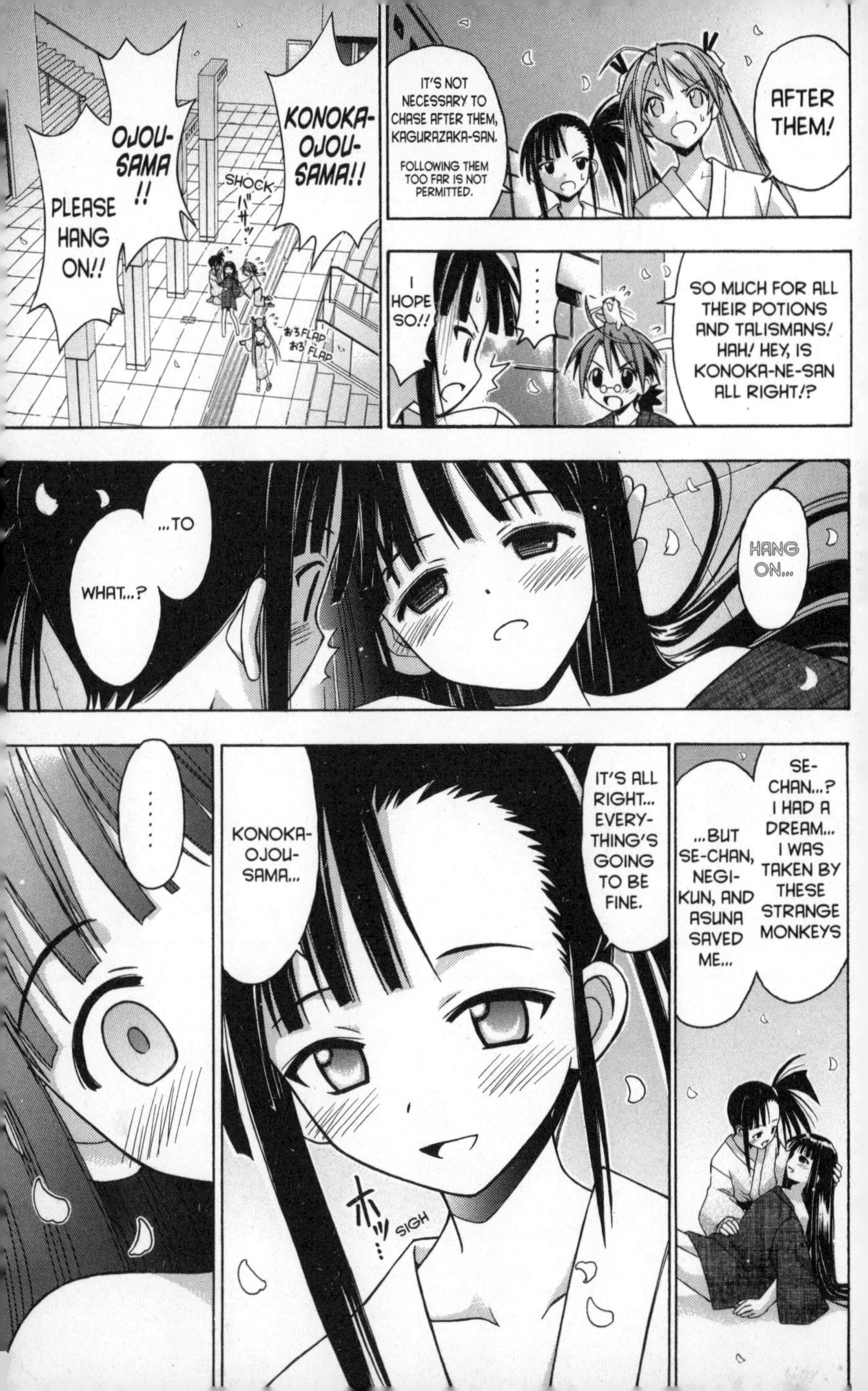
AFTER THEM!
IT'S NOT NECESSARY TO CHASE AFTER THEM, KAGURAZAKA-SAN.
FOLLOWING THEM TOO FAR IS NOT PERMITTED.
KONOKA-OJOU-SAMA!!
OJOU-SAMA!!
SHOCK
PLEASE HANG ON!!
FLAP FLAP
SO MUCH FOR ALL THEIR POTIONS AND TALISMANS! HAH! HEY, IS KONOKA-NE-SAN ALL RIGHT!?
......
I HOPE SO!!
HANG ON...
...TO WHAT...?
SE-CHAN...? I HAD A DREAM... I WAS TAKEN BY THESE STRANGE MONKEYS
...BUT SE-CHAN, NEGI-KUN, AND ASUNA SAVED ME...
IT'S ALL RIGHT... EVERY-THING'S GOING TO BE FINE.
KONOKA-OJOU-SAMA...
SIGH
......

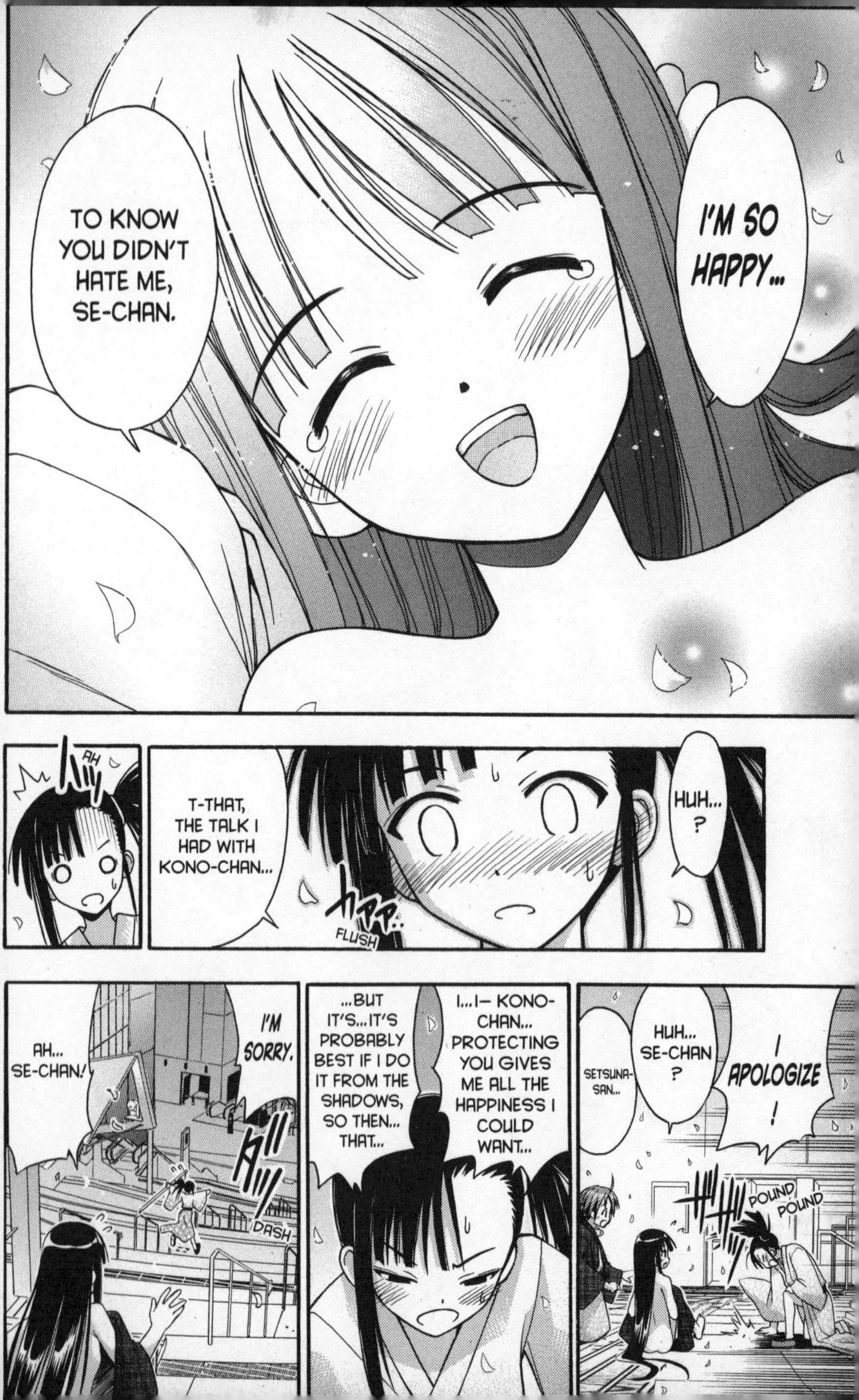
I'M SO HAPPY...
TO KNOW YOU DIDN'T HATE ME, SE-CHAN.
HUH...?
T-THAT, THE TALK I HAD WITH KONO-CHAN...
FLUSH
AH
I APOLOGIZE!
HUH... SE-CHAN?
SETSUNA-SAN...
POUND POUND
I...I– KONO-CHAN... PROTECTING YOU GIVES ME ALL THE HAPPINESS I COULD WANT...
...BUT IT'S...IT'S PROBABLY BEST IF I DO IT FROM THE SHADOWS, SO THEN... THAT...
I'M SORRY.
AH... SE-CHAN!
DASH

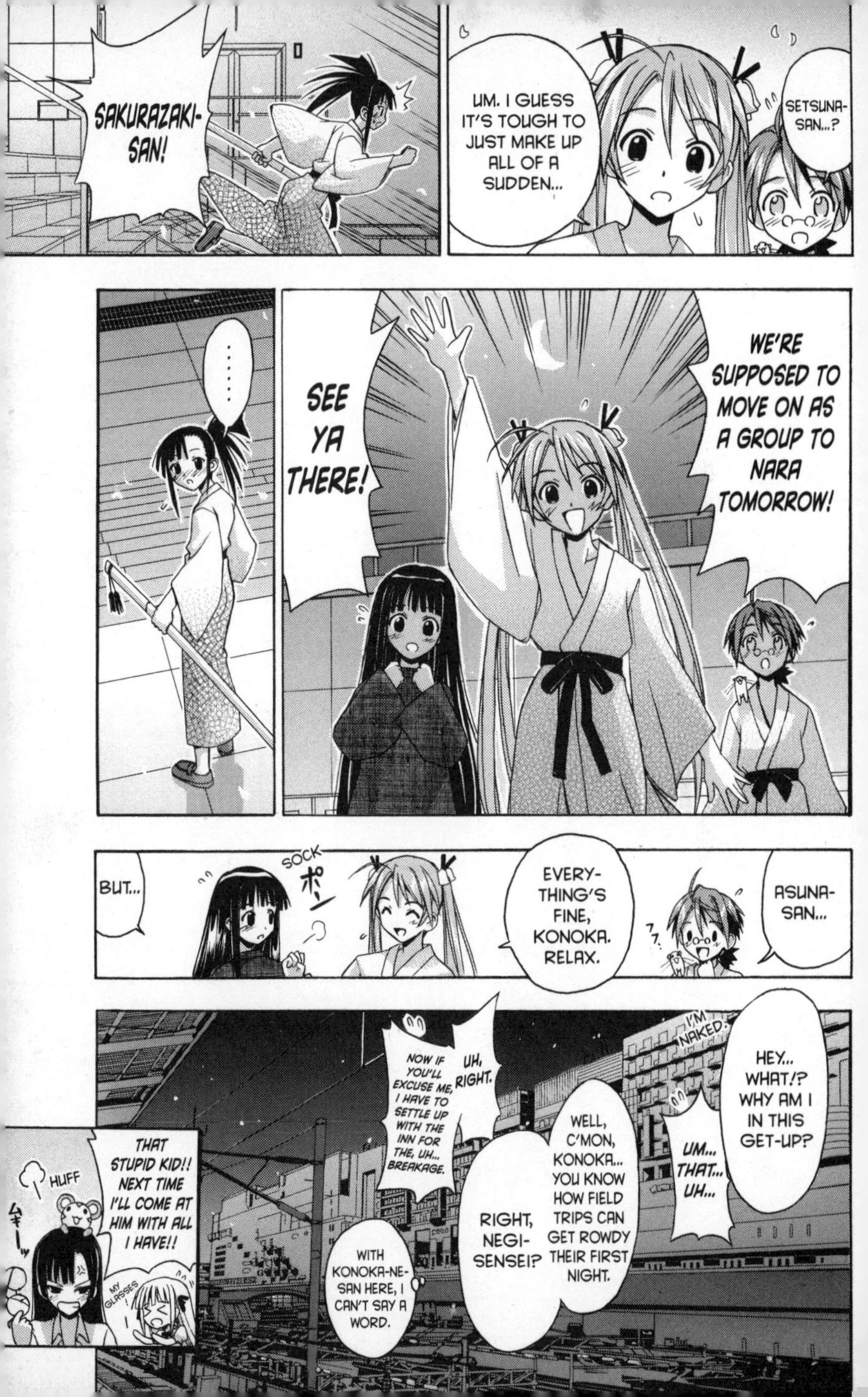
SETSUNA-SAN...?
UM. I GUESS IT'S TOUGH TO JUST MAKE UP ALL OF A SUDDEN...
SAKURAZAKI-SAN!
WE'RE SUPPOSED TO MOVE ON AS A GROUP TO NARA TOMORROW!
SEE YA THERE!
......
ASUNA-SAN...
EVERY-THING'S FINE, KONOKA. RELAX.
SOCK
BUT...
HEY... WHAT!? WHY AM I IN THIS GET-UP?
I'M NAKED.
UM... THAT... UH...
WELL, C'MON, KONOKA... YOU KNOW HOW FIELD TRIPS CAN GET ROWDY THEIR FIRST NIGHT.
RIGHT, NEGI-SENSEI!?
UH, RIGHT.
NOW IF YOU'LL EXCUSE ME, I HAVE TO SETTLE UP WITH THE INN FOR THE, UH... BREAKAGE.
WITH KONOKA-NE-SAN HERE, I CAN'T SAY A WORD.
THAT STUPID KID!! NEXT TIME I'LL COME AT HIM WITH ALL I HAVE!!
HUFF
MY GLASSES!

3-A FIELD TRIP GROUPS 2 AND 3

GROUP 2

(GROUP LEADER)
FEI KU

MISORA KASUGA
SHEN RIN
KAEDE NAGASE
SATOMI HAKASE
SATSUKI YOTSUBA

GROUP 3

(GROUP LEADER)
AYAKA YUKIHIRO

KAZUMI ASAKURA
CHITSURU NABA
CHISAME HASEGAWA
NATSUMI MURAKAMI
ZAZIE RAINYDAY

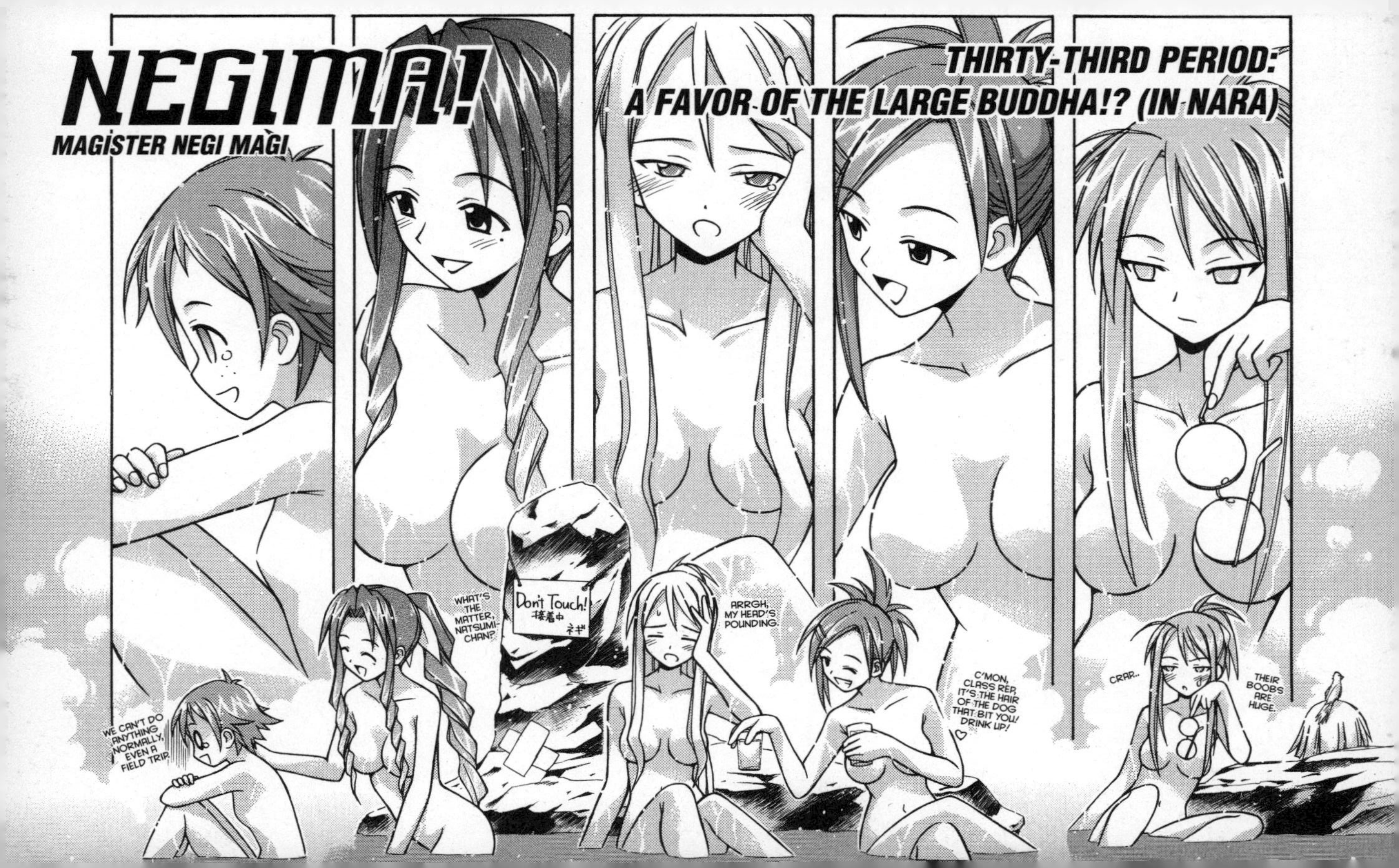
NEGIMA!
MAGISTER NEGI MAGI
THIRTY-THIRD PERIOD:
A FAVOR OF THE LARGE BUDDHA!? (IN NARA)
THEIR BOOBS ARE HUGE.
CRAP...
C'MON, CLASS REP, IT'S THE HAIR OF THE DOG THAT BIT YOU! DRINK UP!
ARRGH, MY HEAD'S POUNDING.
Don't Touch!
接着中
ネギ
WHAT'S THE MATTER, NATSUMI-CHAN?
WE CAN'T DO ANYTHING NORMALLY, EVEN A FIELD TRIP.

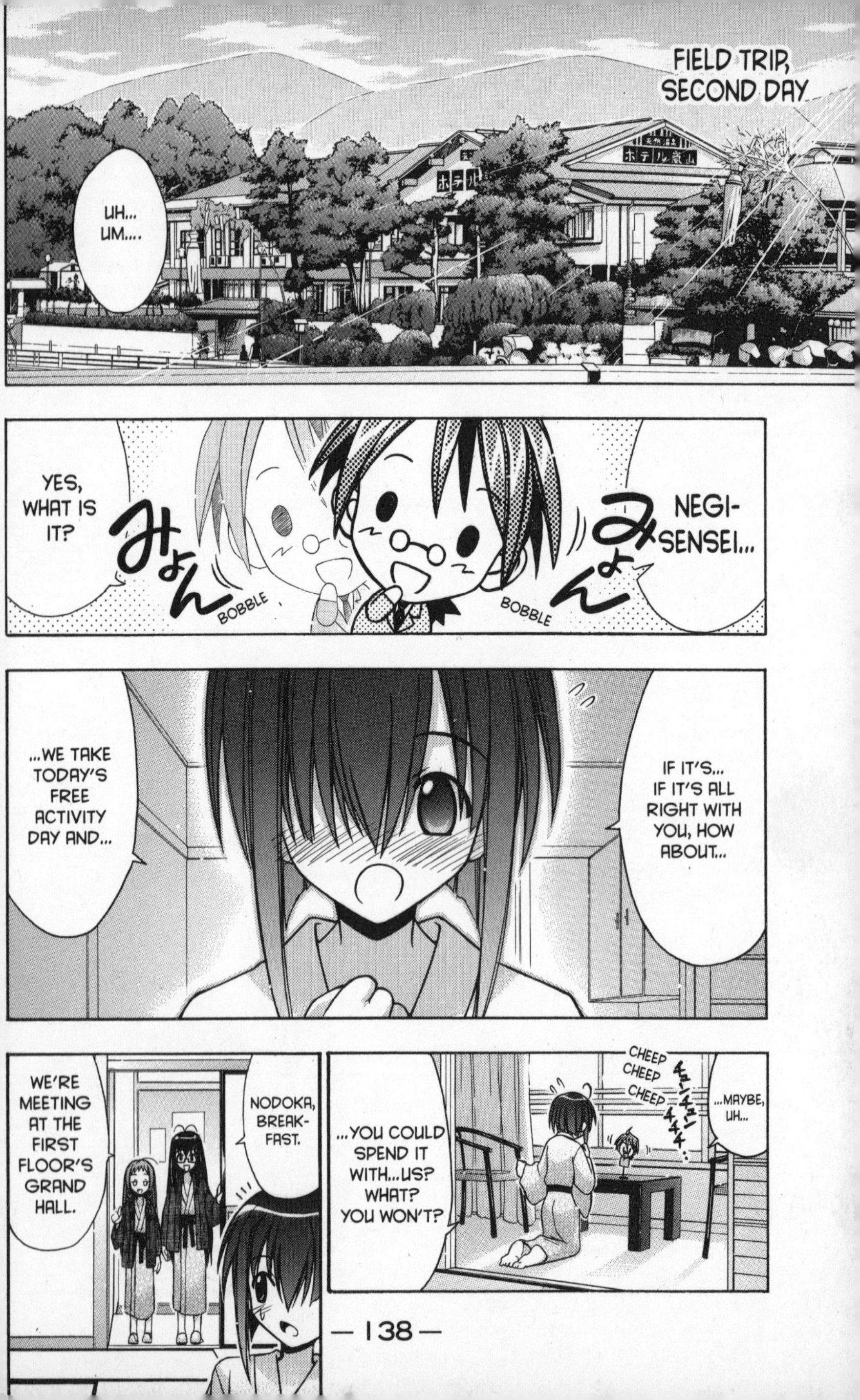
FIELD TRIP, SECOND DAY
UH... UM....
NEGI-SENSEI...
みょん
BOBBLE
みょん
BOBBLE
YES, WHAT IS IT?
IF IT'S... IF IT'S ALL RIGHT WITH YOU, HOW ABOUT...
...WE TAKE TODAY'S FREE ACTIVITY DAY AND...
...MAYBE, UH...
CHEEP CHEEP CHEEP
チュンチュン チチチ...
...YOU COULD SPEND IT WITH...US? WHAT? YOU WON'T?
NODOKA, BREAK-FAST.
WE'RE MEETING AT THE FIRST FLOOR'S GRAND HALL.

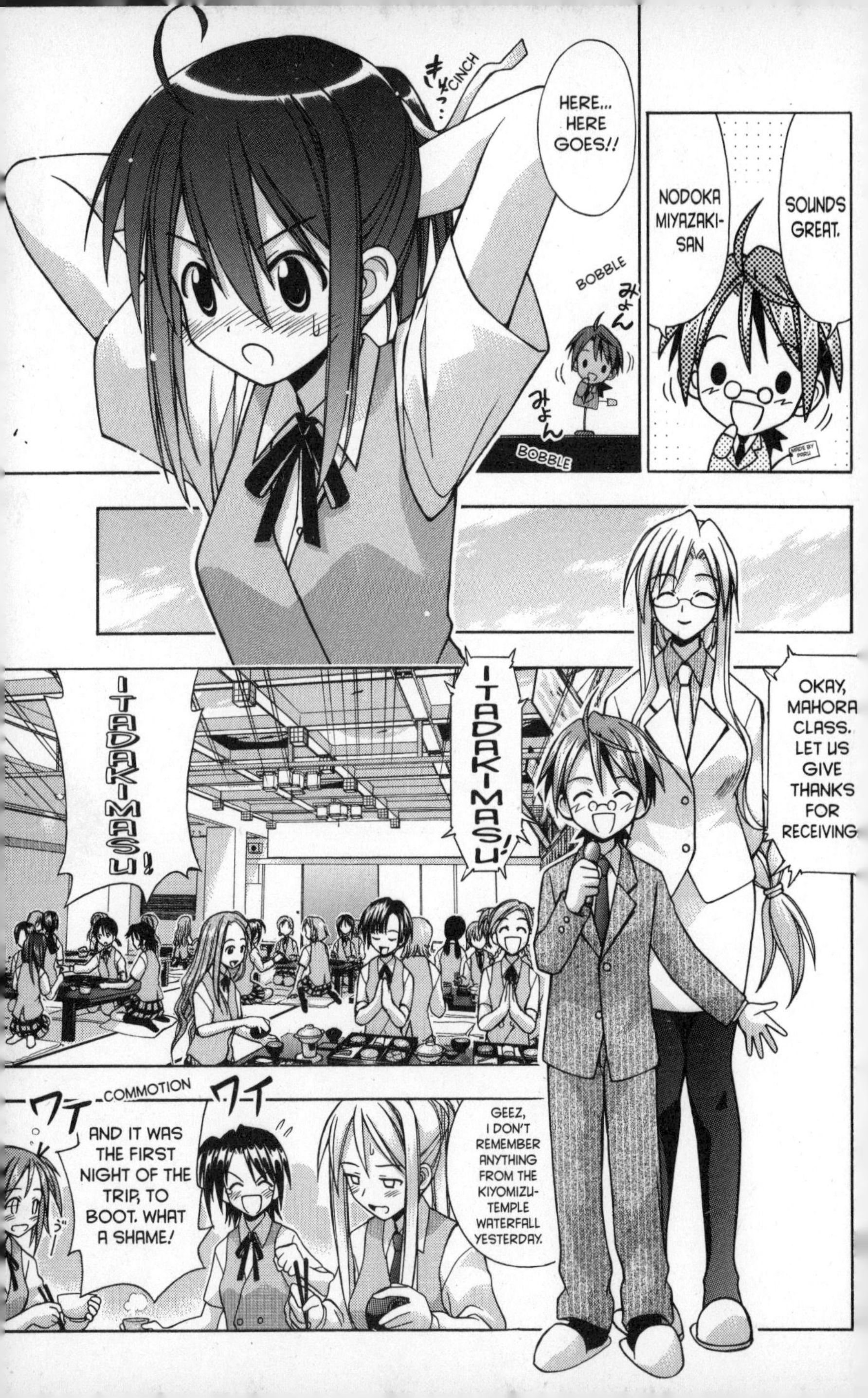
SOUNDS GREAT.
NODOKA MIYAZAKI-SAN
MADE BY PARU
BOBBLE
みょん
みょん
BOBBLE
HERE... HERE GOES!!
CINCH
OKAY, MAHORA CLASS. LET US GIVE THANKS FOR RECEIVING
ITADAKIMASU!
ITADAKIMASU!!
GEEZ, I DON'T REMEMBER ANYTHING FROM THE KIYOMIZU-TEMPLE WATERFALL YESTERDAY.
ワイ
COMMOTION
ワイ
AND IT WAS THE FIRST NIGHT OF THE TRIP, TO BOOT. WHAT A SHAME!

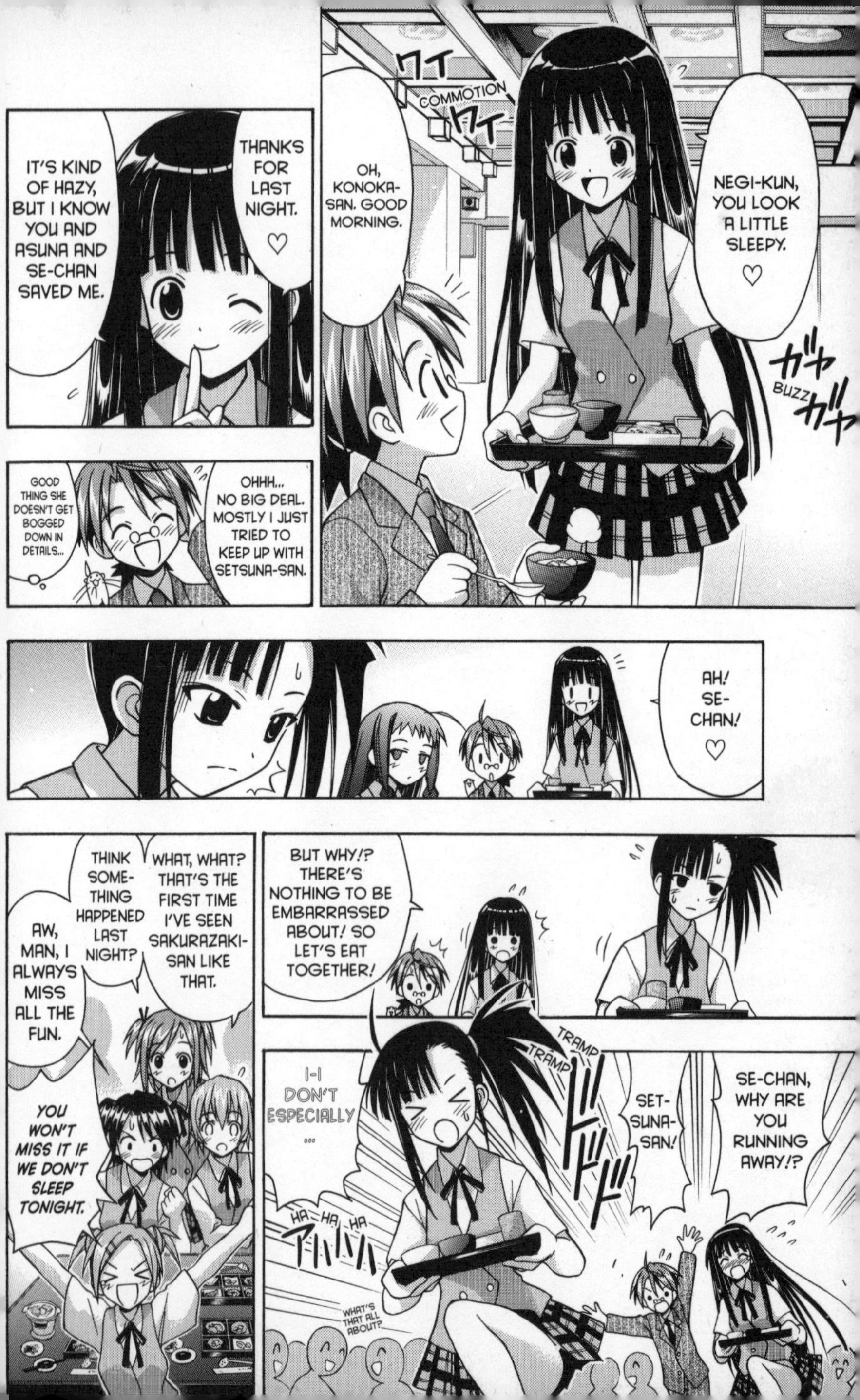
ワイ
COMMOTION
ワイ
NEGI-KUN, YOU LOOK A LITTLE SLEEPY. ♡
ガヤ
BUZZ
ガヤ
OH, KONOKA-SAN. GOOD MORNING.
THANKS FOR LAST NIGHT. ♡
IT'S KIND OF HAZY, BUT I KNOW YOU AND ASUNA AND SE-CHAN SAVED ME.
OHHH... NO BIG DEAL. MOSTLY I JUST TRIED TO KEEP UP WITH SETSUNA-SAN.
GOOD THING SHE DOESN'T GET BOGGED DOWN IN DETAILS...
AH! SE-CHAN! ♡
BUT WHY!? THERE'S NOTHING TO BE EMBARRASSED ABOUT! SO LET'S EAT TOGETHER!
SE-CHAN, WHY ARE YOU RUNNING AWAY!?
SET-SUNA-SAN!
TRAMP TRAMP
ドドド
I-I DON'T ESPECIALLY...
HA HA HA
アハハハ
WHAT'S THAT ALL ABOUT?
WHAT, WHAT? THAT'S THE FIRST TIME I'VE SEEN SAKURAZAKI-SAN LIKE THAT.
THINK SOMETHING HAPPENED LAST NIGHT?
AW, MAN, I ALWAYS MISS ALL THE FUN.
YOU WON'T MISS IT IF WE DON'T SLEEP TONIGHT.

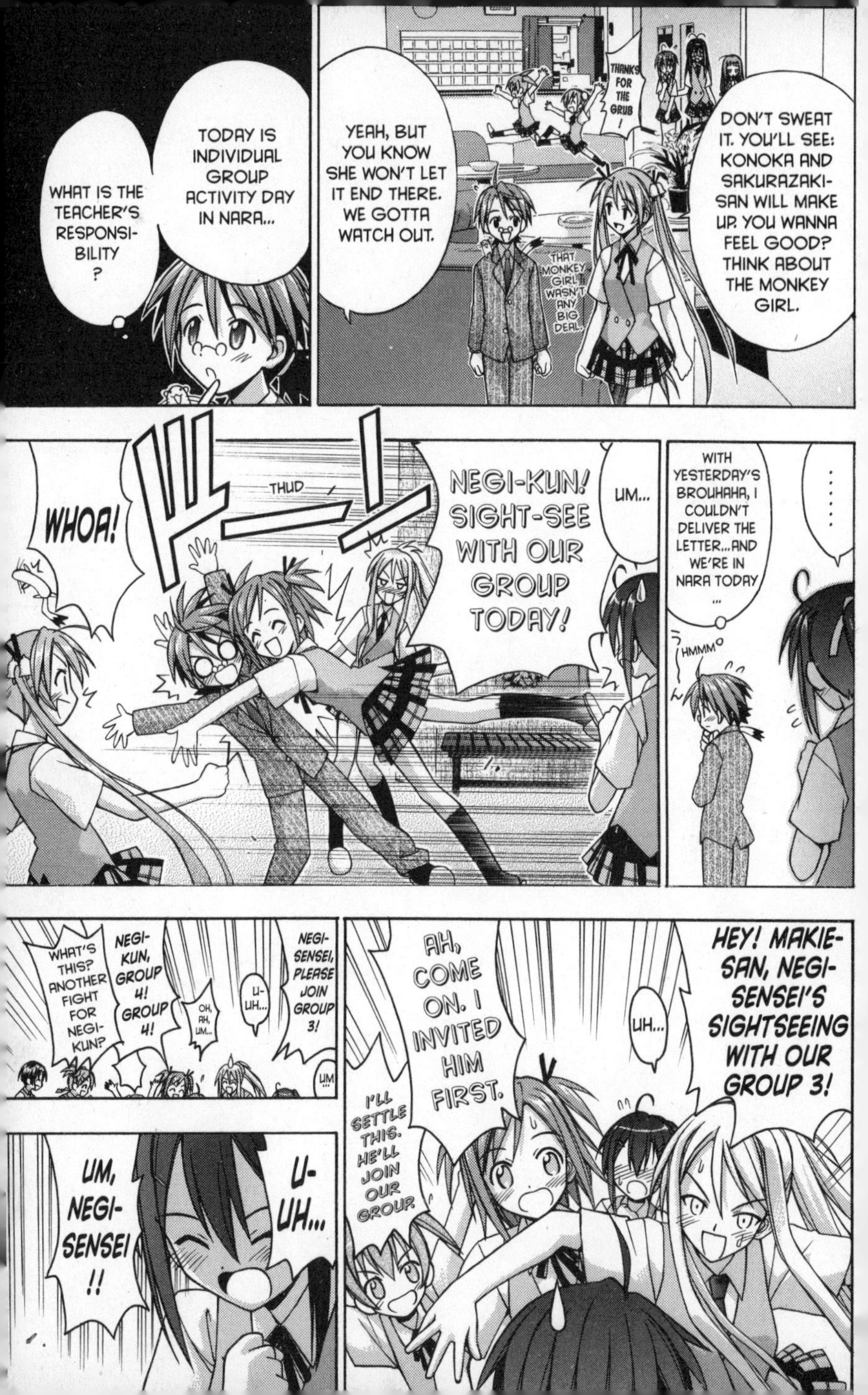
THANKS FOR THE GRUB!
DON'T SWEAT IT. YOU'LL SEE: KONOKA AND SAKURAZAKI-SAN WILL MAKE UP. YOU WANNA FEEL GOOD? THINK ABOUT THE MONKEY GIRL.
THAT MONKEY GIRL WASN'T ANY BIG DEAL.
YEAH, BUT YOU KNOW SHE WON'T LET IT END THERE. WE GOTTA WATCH OUT.
TODAY IS INDIVIDUAL GROUP ACTIVITY DAY IN NARA...
WHAT IS THE TEACHER'S RESPONSIBILITY?
......
WITH YESTERDAY'S BROUHAHA, I COULDN'T DELIVER THE LETTER...AND WE'RE IN NARA TODAY...
HMMM
UM...
NEGI-KUN! SIGHT-SEE WITH OUR GROUP TODAY!
THUD
WHOA!
HEY! MAKIE-SAN, NEGI-SENSEI'S SIGHTSEEING WITH OUR GROUP 3!
UH...
AH, COME ON. I INVITED HIM FIRST.
I'LL SETTLE THIS. HE'LL JOIN OUR GROUP.
UM...
NEGI-SENSEI, PLEASE JOIN GROUP 3!
U-UH...
OH, AH, UM...
NEGI-KUN, GROUP 4! GROUP 4!
WHAT'S THIS? ANOTHER FIGHT FOR NEGI-KUN?
U-UH...
UM, NEGI-SENSEI!!

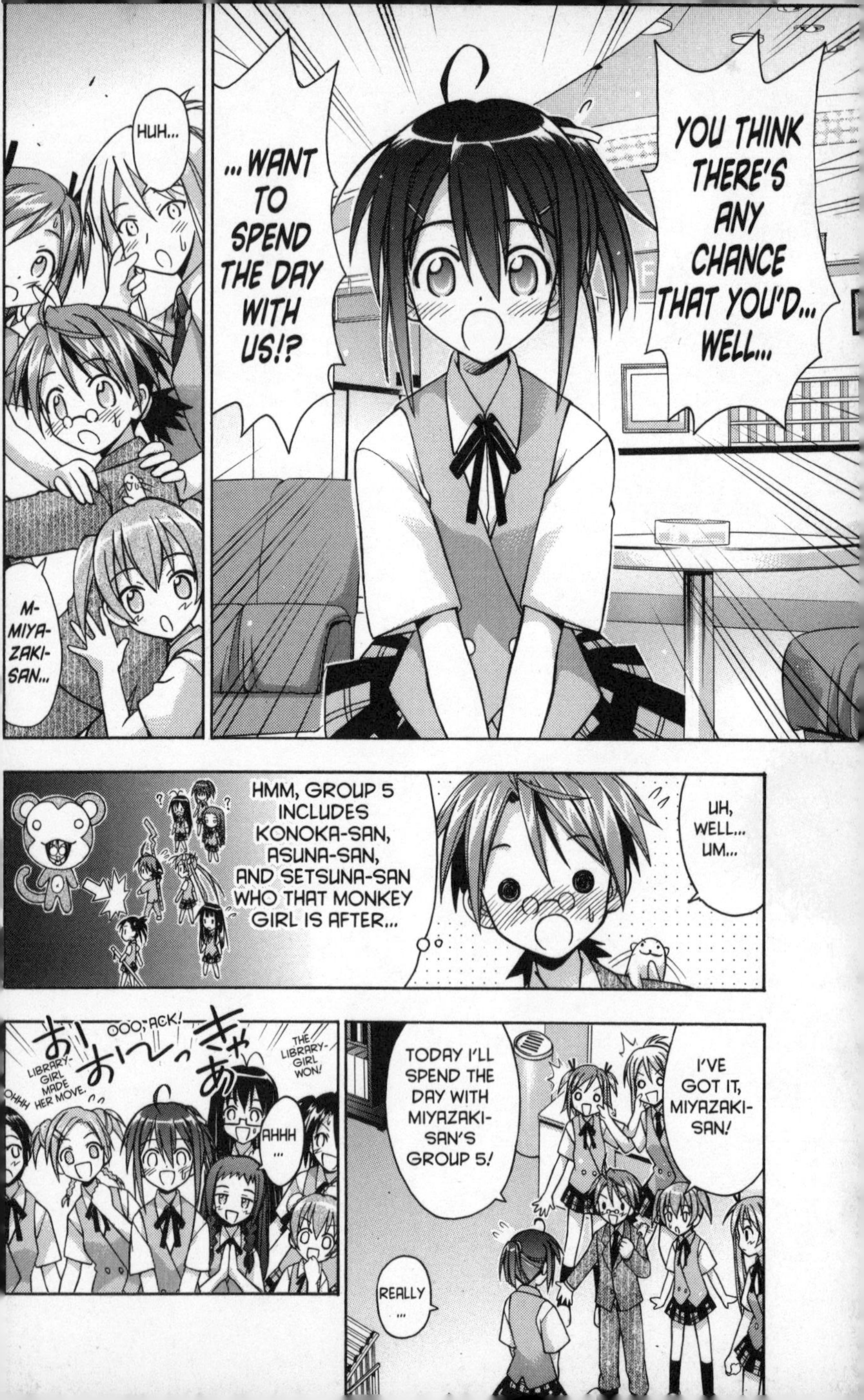
YOU THINK THERE'S ANY CHANCE THAT YOU'D... WELL...
...WANT TO SPEND THE DAY WITH US!?
HUH...
M-MIYAZAKI-SAN...
UH, WELL... UM...
HMM, GROUP 5 INCLUDES KONOKA-SAN, ASUNA-SAN, AND SETSUNA-SAN WHO THAT MONKEY GIRL IS AFTER...
I'VE GOT IT, MIYAZAKI-SAN!
TODAY I'LL SPEND THE DAY WITH MIYAZAKI-SAN'S GROUP 5!
REALLY...
きゃあ
THE LIBRARY-GIRL WON!
OOO, ACK!
AHHH ...
お！おお〜っ
LIBRARY-GIRL MADE HER MOVE.
OHHH

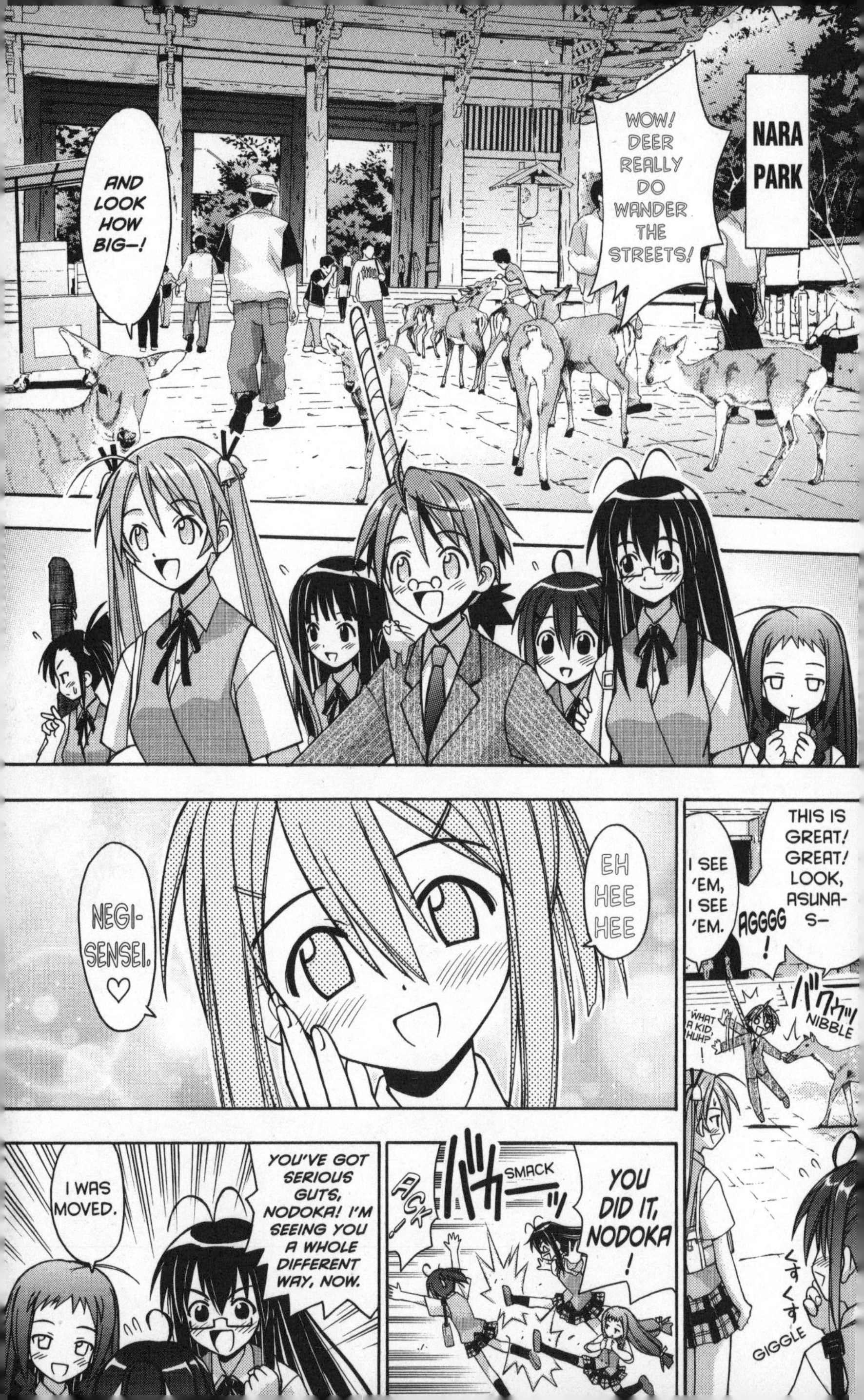
NARA PARK
WOW! DEER REALLY DO WANDER THE STREETS!
AND LOOK HOW BIG—!
THIS IS GREAT! GREAT! LOOK, ASUNA-S—
I SEE 'EM, I SEE 'EM.
AGGGG!
バクッ
NIBBLE
WHAT A KID, HUH?!
くすくす
GIGGLE
EH HEE HEE
NEGI-SENSEI. ♡
YOU DID IT, NODOKA!
バカーッ
SMACK
ACK!
YOU'VE GOT SERIOUS GUTS, NODOKA! I'M SEEING YOU A WHOLE DIFFERENT WAY, NOW.
I WAS MOVED.

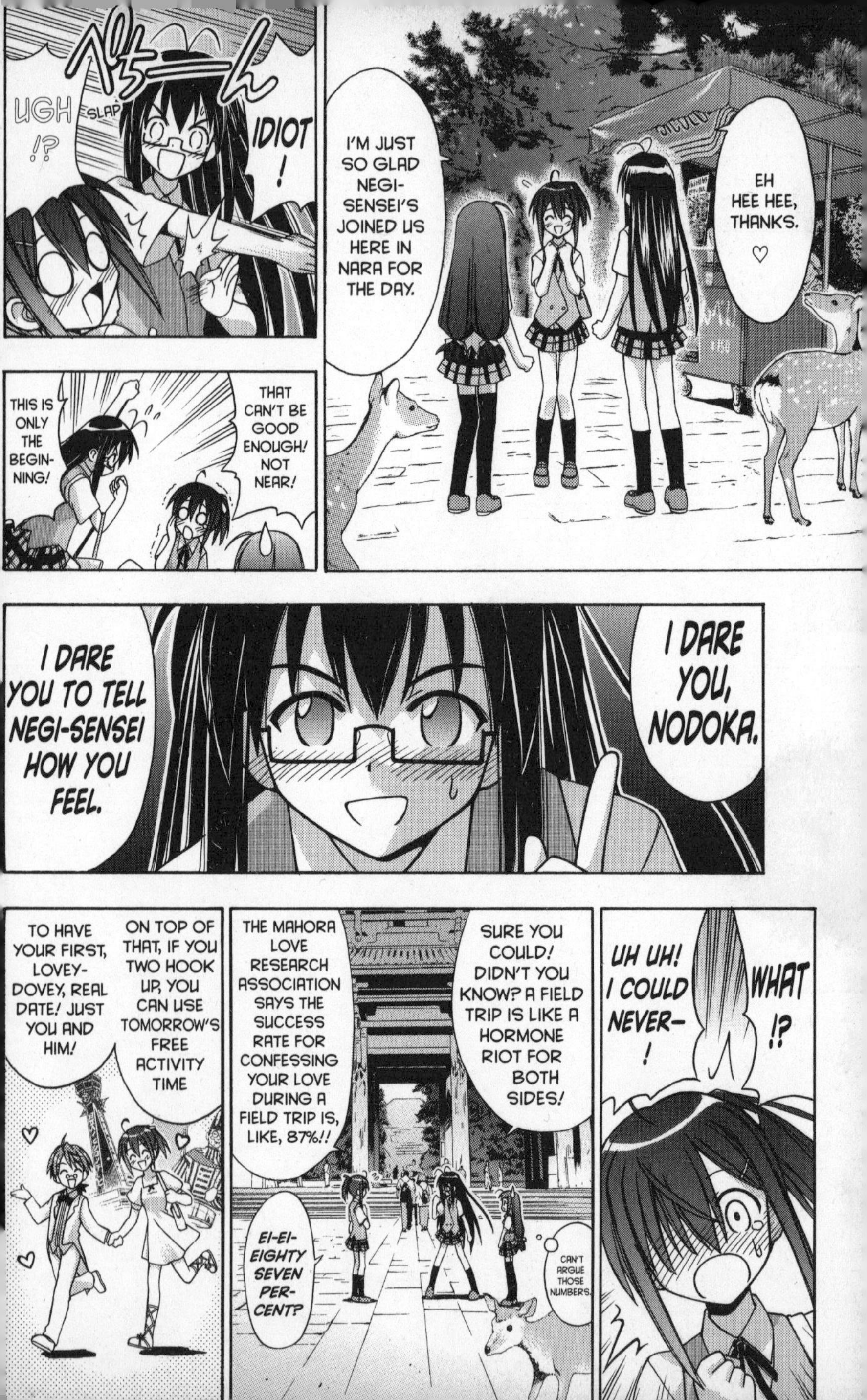
EH HEE HEE, THANKS. ♡
I'M JUST SO GLAD NEGI-SENSEI'S JOINED US HERE IN NARA FOR THE DAY.
IDIOT!
SLAP
UGH !?
THAT CAN'T BE GOOD ENOUGH! NOT NEAR!
THIS IS ONLY THE BEGIN-NING!
I DARE YOU, NODOKA.
I DARE YOU TO TELL NEGI-SENSEI HOW YOU FEEL.
WHAT !?
UH UH! I COULD NEVER—!
SURE YOU COULD! DIDN'T YOU KNOW? A FIELD TRIP IS LIKE A HORMONE RIOT FOR BOTH SIDES!
THE MAHORA LOVE RESEARCH ASSOCIATION SAYS THE SUCCESS RATE FOR CONFESSING YOUR LOVE DURING A FIELD TRIP IS, LIKE, 87%!!
EI-EI-EIGHTY SEVEN PER-CENT?
CAN'T ARGUE THOSE NUMBERS.
ON TOP OF THAT, IF YOU TWO HOOK UP, YOU CAN USE TOMORROW'S FREE ACTIVITY TIME
TO HAVE YOUR FIRST, LOVEY-DOVEY, REAL DATE! JUST YOU AND HIM!

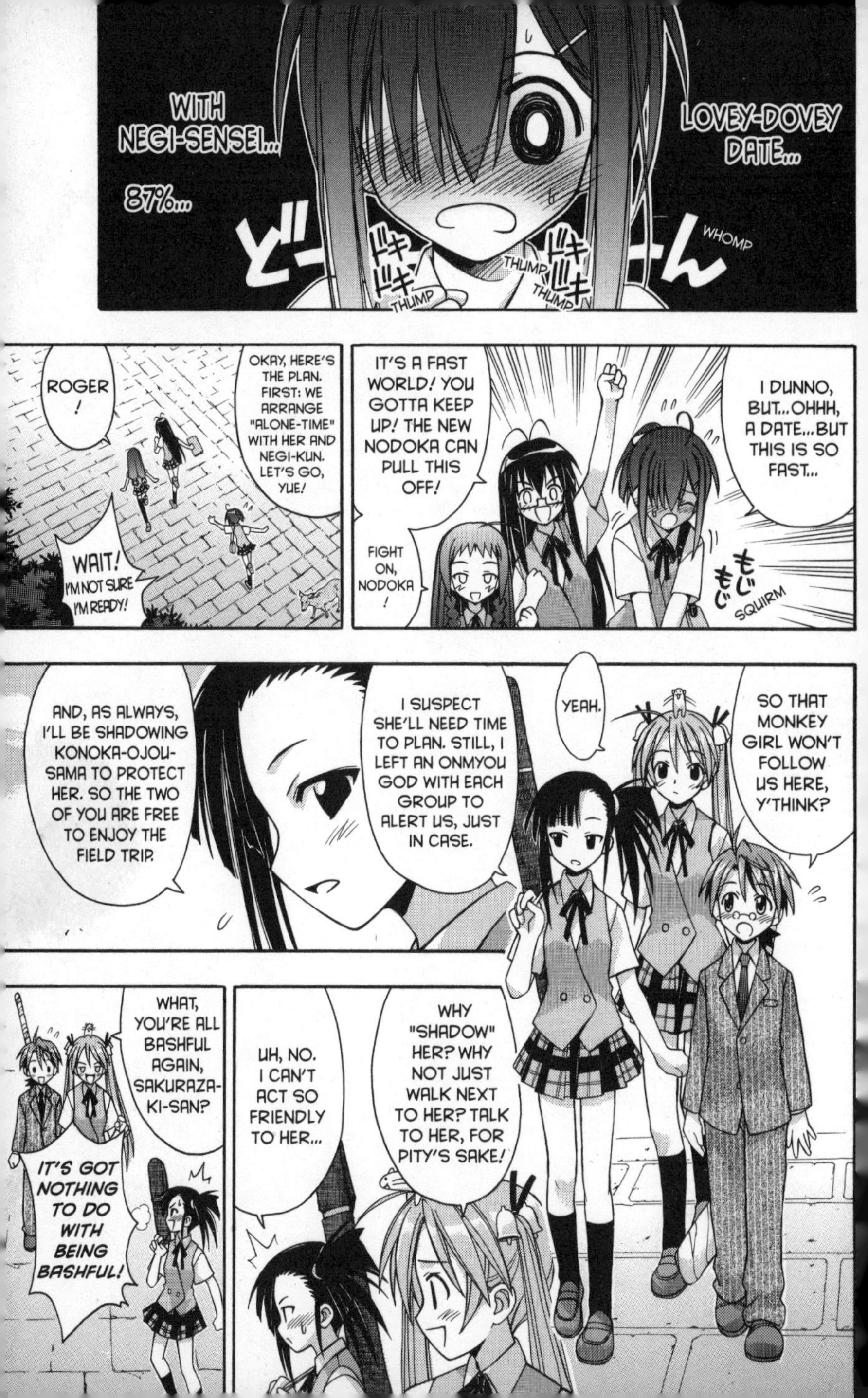
LOVEY-DOVEY DATE...
WITH NEGI-SENSEI...
87%...
ドーん
WHOMP
ドキドキ
THUMP
THUMP
ドキドキ
THUMP
THUMP
I DUNNO, BUT...OHHH, A DATE...BUT THIS IS SO FAST...
もじもじ
SQUIRM
IT'S A FAST WORLD! YOU GOTTA KEEP UP! THE NEW NODOKA CAN PULL THIS OFF!
FIGHT ON, NODOKA!
OKAY, HERE'S THE PLAN. FIRST: WE ARRANGE "ALONE-TIME" WITH HER AND NEGI-KUN. LET'S GO, YUE!
ROGER!
WAIT! I'M NOT SURE I'M READY!
SO THAT MONKEY GIRL WON'T FOLLOW US HERE, Y'THINK?
YEAH.
I SUSPECT SHE'LL NEED TIME TO PLAN. STILL, I LEFT AN ONMYOU GOD WITH EACH GROUP TO ALERT US, JUST IN CASE.
AND, AS ALWAYS, I'LL BE SHADOWING KONOKA-OJOU-SAMA TO PROTECT HER. SO THE TWO OF YOU ARE FREE TO ENJOY THE FIELD TRIP.
WHY "SHADOW" HER? WHY NOT JUST WALK NEXT TO HER? TALK TO HER, FOR PITY'S SAKE!
UH, NO. I CAN'T ACT SO FRIENDLY TO HER...
WHAT, YOU'RE ALL BASHFUL AGAIN, SAKURAZAKI-SAN?
IT'S GOT NOTHING TO DO WITH BEING BASHFUL!

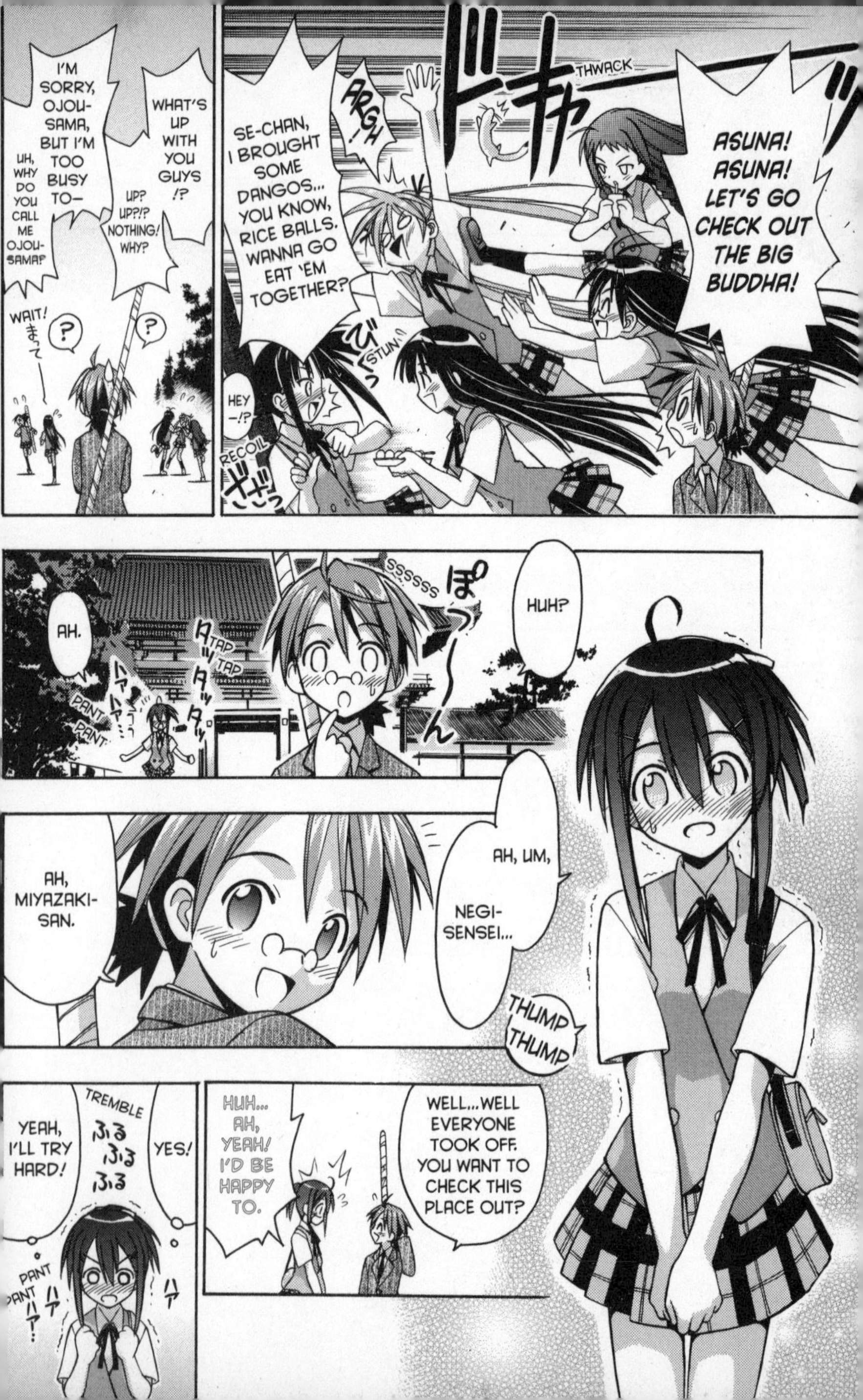
ASUNA! ASUNA! LET'S GO CHECK OUT THE BIG BUDDHA!
ドギャ
THWACK
ARGH!
SE-CHAN, I BROUGHT SOME DANGOS... YOU KNOW, RICE BALLS. WANNA GO EAT 'EM TOGETHER?
びくっ
STUN
HEY—!?
ズざっ
RECOIL
WHAT'S UP WITH YOU GUYS!?
I'M SORRY, OJOU-SAMA, BUT I'M TOO BUSY TO—
UP? UP?!? NOTHING! WHY?
UH, WHY DO YOU CALL ME OJOU-SAMA!?
WAIT! まって—
?
?
HUH?
ぽつ～ん
SSSSSS
タッタッタッ
TAP TAP
ハァハァ
PANT PANT
AH.
AH, UM,
NEGI-SENSEI...
THUMP THUMP
AH, MIYAZAKI-SAN.
WELL...WELL EVERYONE TOOK OFF. YOU WANT TO CHECK THIS PLACE OUT?
HUH... AH, YEAH! I'D BE HAPPY TO.
YES!
ふる ふる ふる
TREMBLE
YEAH, I'LL TRY HARD!
ハァ ハァ
PANT PANT

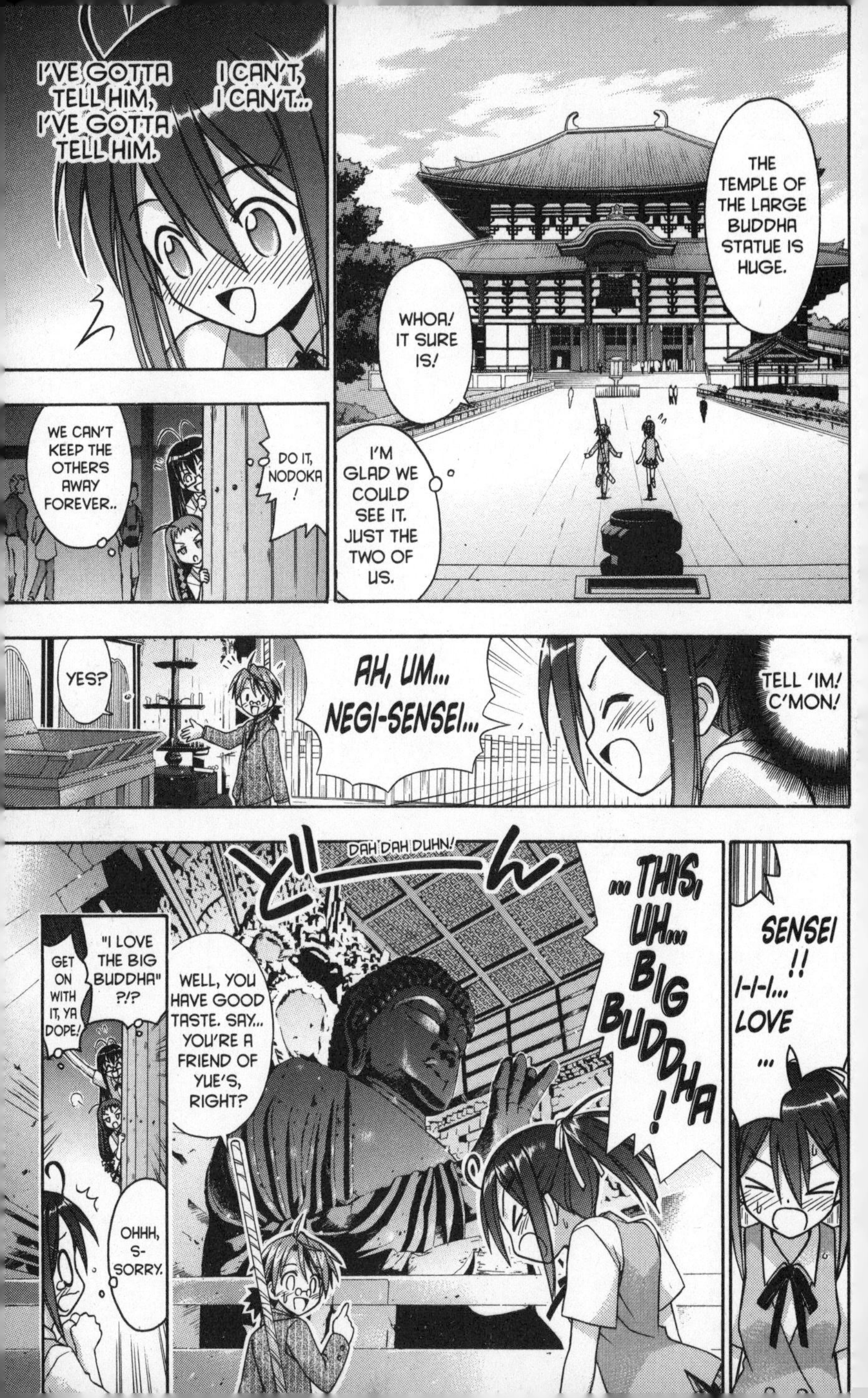
THE TEMPLE OF THE LARGE BUDDHA STATUE IS HUGE.
WHOA! IT SURE IS!
I'M GLAD WE COULD SEE IT. JUST THE TWO OF US.
I CAN'T, I CAN'T...
I'VE GOTTA TELL HIM, I'VE GOTTA TELL HIM.
DO IT, NODOKA!
WE CAN'T KEEP THE OTHERS AWAY FOREVER..
TELL 'IM! C'MON!
AH, UM... NEGI-SENSEI...
YES?
SENSEI!!
I-I-I... LOVE ...
DAH DAH DUHN!
...THIS, UH... BIG BUDDHA!
WELL, YOU HAVE GOOD TASTE. SAY... YOU'RE A FRIEND OF YUE'S, RIGHT?
OHHH, S-SORRY.
"I LOVE THE BIG BUDDHA" ?!?
GET ON WITH IT, YA DOPE!

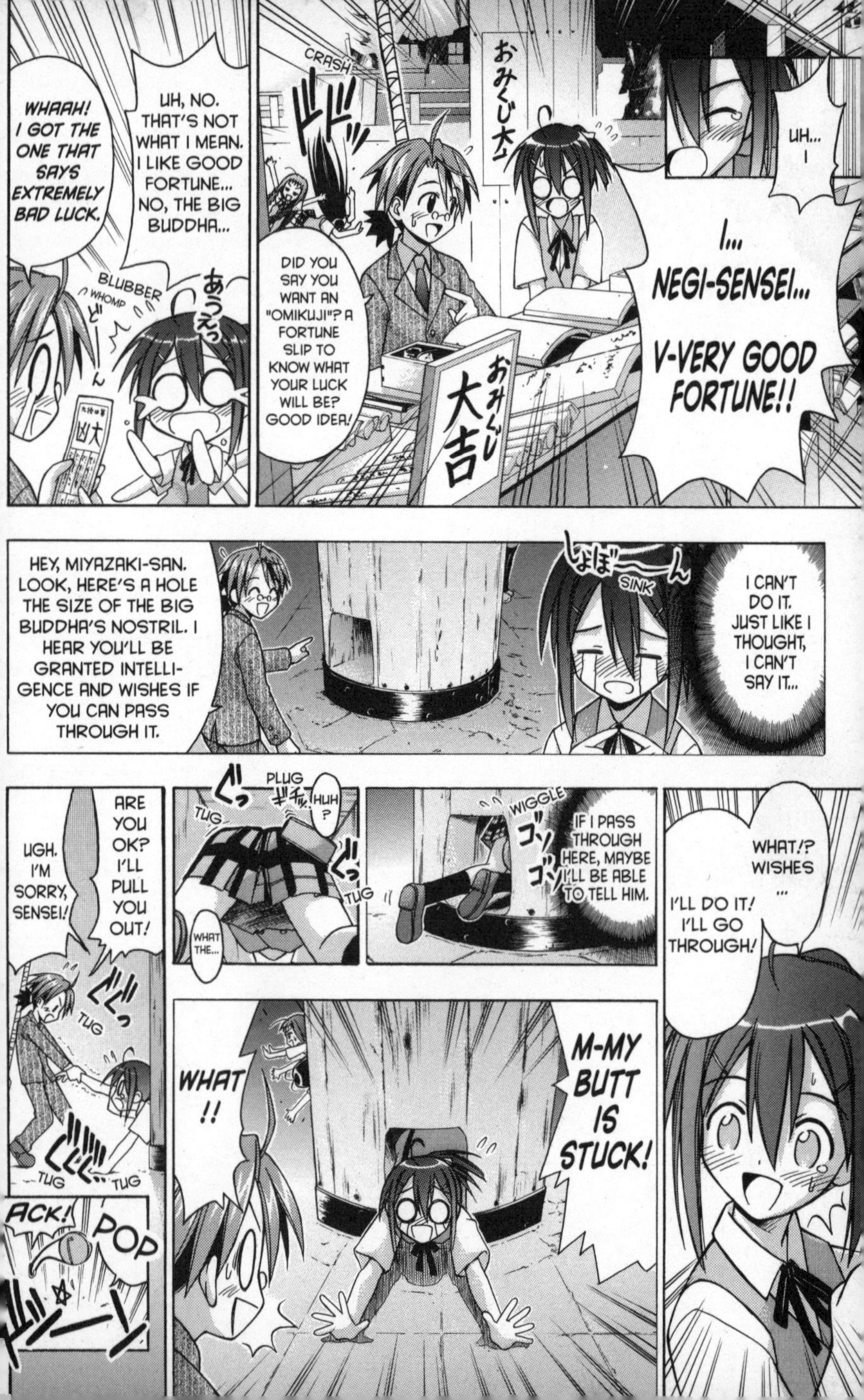

UH... I
I... NEGI-SENSEI... V-VERY GOOD FORTUNE!!
CRASH
ドドッ
おみくじ大吉
DID YOU SAY YOU WANT AN "OMIKUJI"? A FORTUNE SLIP TO KNOW WHAT YOUR LUCK WILL BE? GOOD IDEA!
おみくじ
大吉
UH, NO. THAT'S NOT WHAT I MEAN. I LIKE GOOD FORTUNE... NO, THE BIG BUDDHA...
WHAAH! I GOT THE ONE THAT SAYS EXTREMELY BAD LUCK.
BLUBBER
あうえっ
WHOMP
どーん
しょぼーん
SINK
I CAN'T DO IT. JUST LIKE I THOUGHT, I CAN'T SAY IT...
HEY, MIYAZAKI-SAN. LOOK, HERE'S A HOLE THE SIZE OF THE BIG BUDDHA'S NOSTRIL. I HEAR YOU'LL BE GRANTED INTELLIGENCE AND WISHES IF YOU CAN PASS THROUGH IT.
WHAT!? WISHES ...
I'LL DO IT! I'LL GO THROUGH!
WIGGLE
ゴソゴソ
IF I PASS THROUGH HERE, MAYBE I'LL BE ABLE TO TELL HIM.
PLUG
ギチッ
HUH?
ぐっ
TUG
ぐっ
TUG
WHAT THE...
ARE YOU OK? I'LL PULL YOU OUT!
UGH. I'M SORRY, SENSEI!
ぐぐっ
TUG
ぐぐぐ...
TUG
TUG
M-MY BUTT IS STUCK!
WHAT !!
ACK!
POP

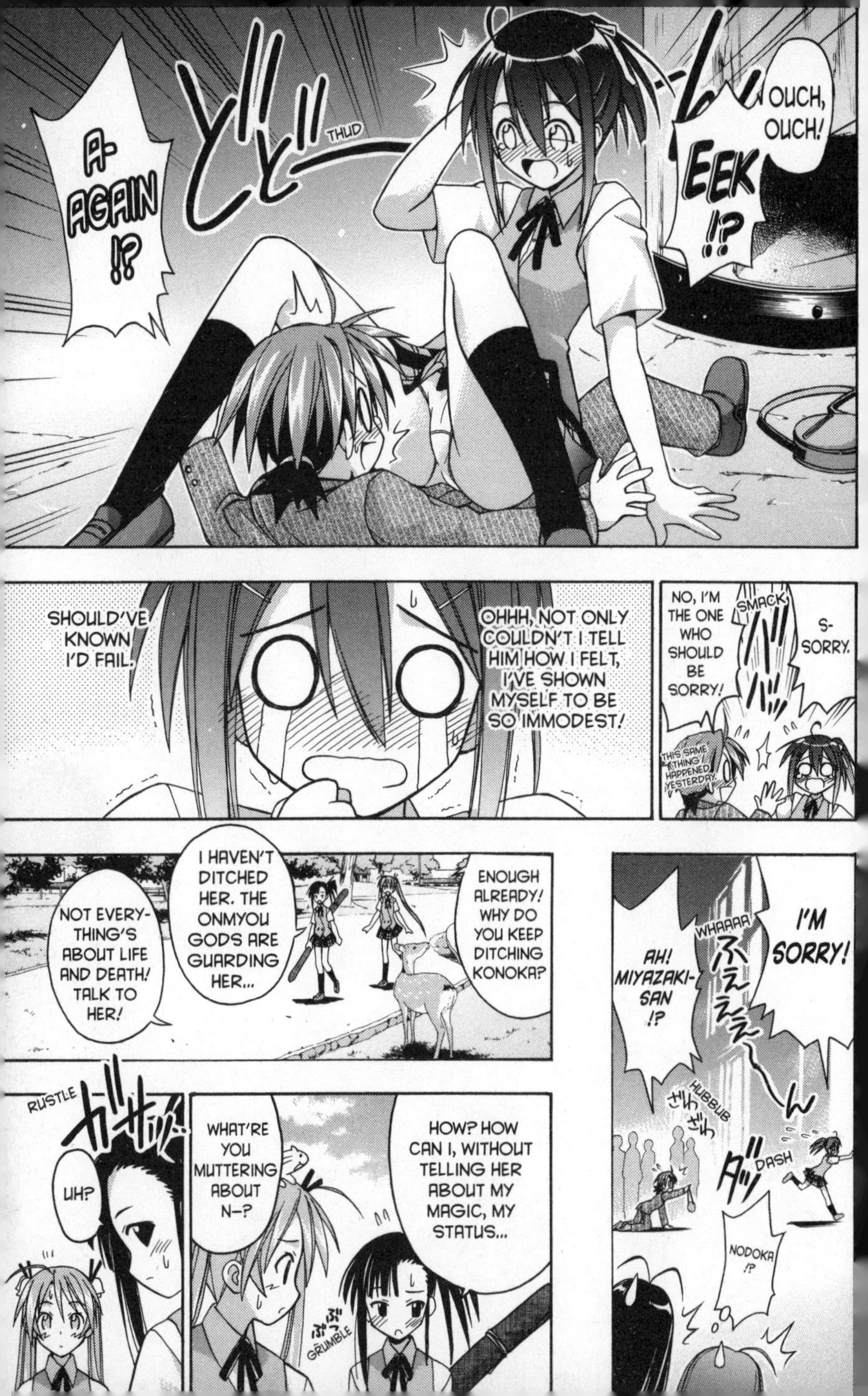
OUCH, OUCH!
EEK !?
THUD
A-AGAIN !?
S-SORRY.
SMACK
NO, I'M THE ONE WHO SHOULD BE SORRY!
THIS SAME THING HAPPENED YESTERDAY.
OHHH, NOT ONLY COULDN'T I TELL HIM HOW I FELT, I'VE SHOWN MYSELF TO BE SO IMMODEST!
SHOULD'VE KNOWN I'D FAIL.
I'M SORRY!
WHAAAA
AH! MIYAZAKI-SAN !?
HUBBUB
DASH
NODOKA !?
ENOUGH ALREADY! WHY DO YOU KEEP DITCHING KONOKA?
I HAVEN'T DITCHED HER. THE ONMYOU GODS ARE GUARDING HER...
NOT EVERYTHING'S ABOUT LIFE AND DEATH! TALK TO HER!
HOW? HOW CAN I, WITHOUT TELLING HER ABOUT MY MAGIC, MY STATUS...
GRUMBLE
WHAT'RE YOU MUTTERING ABOUT N-?
RUSTLE
UH?

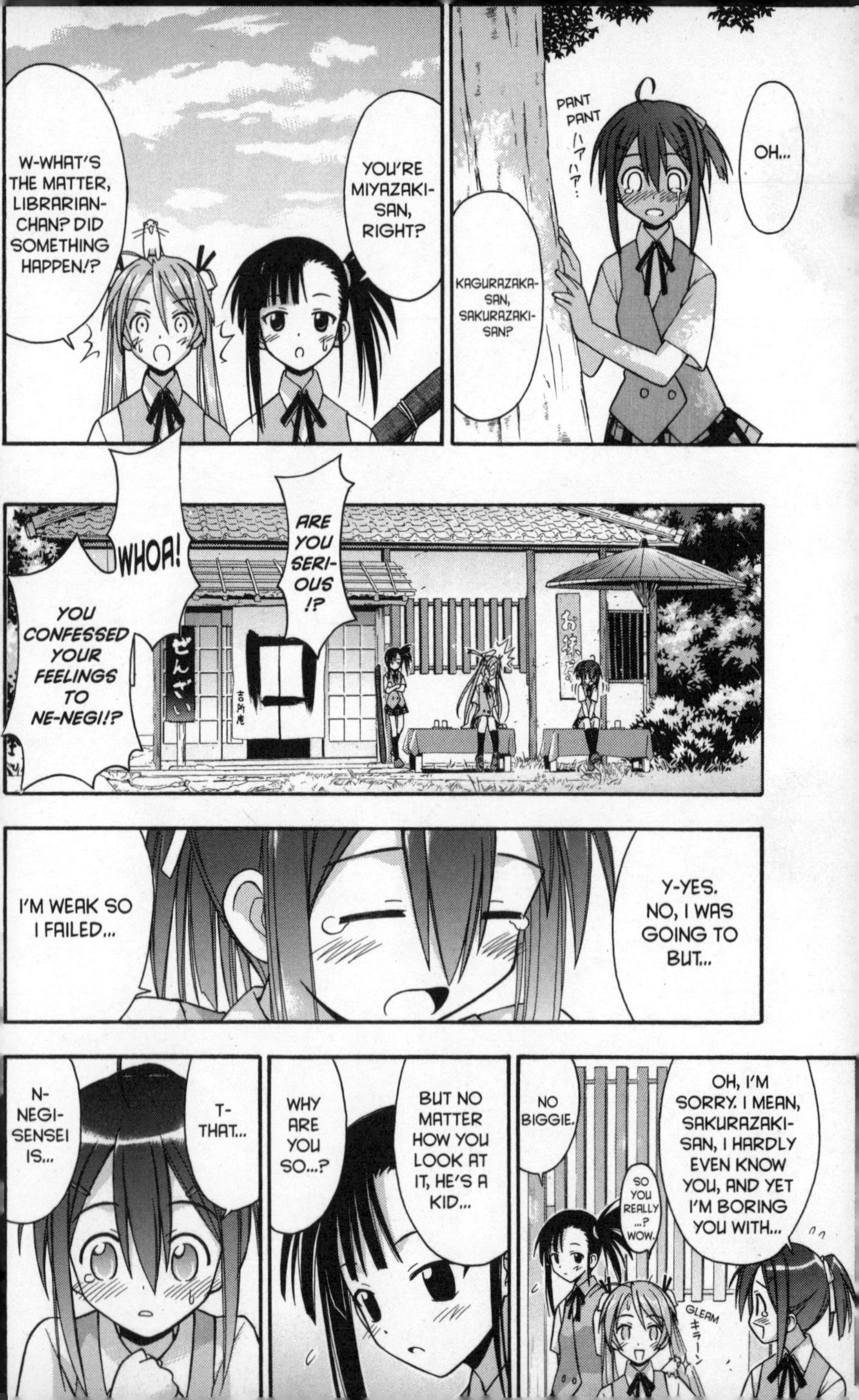
PANT PANT ハァハァ…
OH...
KAGURAZAKA-SAN, SAKURAZAKI-SAN?
YOU'RE MIYAZAKI-SAN, RIGHT?
W-WHAT'S THE MATTER, LIBRARIAN-CHAN? DID SOMETHING HAPPEN!?
ARE YOU SERI-OUS!?
WHOA!
YOU CONFESSED YOUR FEELINGS TO NE-NEGI!?
ぜんざい
Y-YES. NO, I WAS GOING TO BUT...
I'M WEAK SO I FAILED...
OH, I'M SORRY. I MEAN, SAKURAZAKI-SAN, I HARDLY EVEN KNOW YOU, AND YET I'M BORING YOU WITH...
SO YOU REALLY ...? WOW.
NO BIGGIE.
GLEAM キラーン
BUT NO MATTER HOW YOU LOOK AT IT, HE'S A KID...
WHY ARE YOU SO...?
T-THAT...
N-NEGI-SENSEI IS...

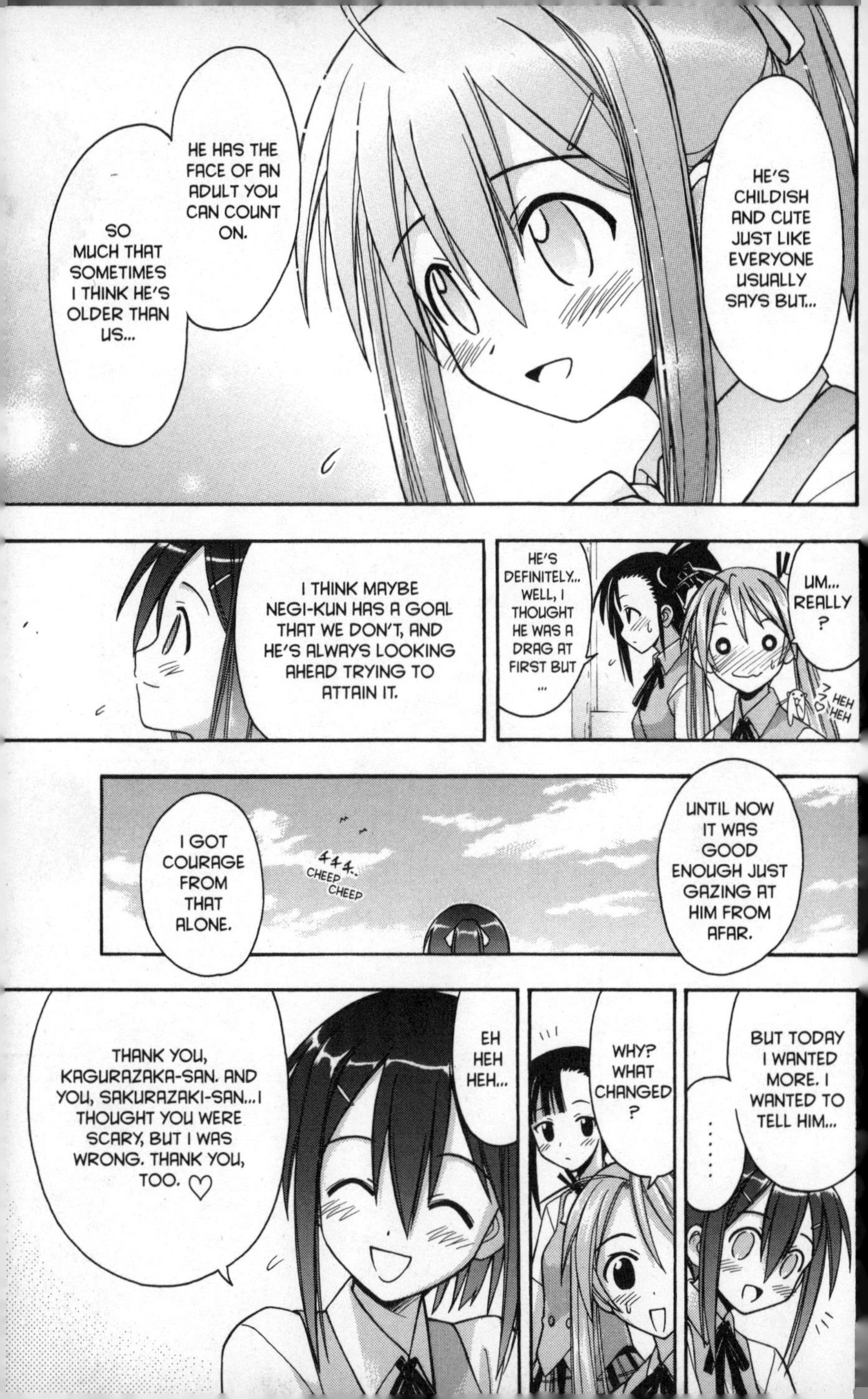
HE'S CHILDISH AND CUTE JUST LIKE EVERYONE USUALLY SAYS BUT...
HE HAS THE FACE OF AN ADULT YOU CAN COUNT ON.
SO MUCH THAT SOMETIMES I THINK HE'S OLDER THAN US...
UM... REALLY?
HEH HEH
HE'S DEFINITELY... WELL, I THOUGHT HE WAS A DRAG AT FIRST BUT ...
I THINK MAYBE NEGI-KUN HAS A GOAL THAT WE DON'T, AND HE'S ALWAYS LOOKING AHEAD TRYING TO ATTAIN IT.
UNTIL NOW IT WAS GOOD ENOUGH JUST GAZING AT HIM FROM AFAR.
CHEEP CHEEP
I GOT COURAGE FROM THAT ALONE.
BUT TODAY I WANTED MORE. I WANTED TO TELL HIM...
......
WHY? WHAT CHANGED?
EH HEH HEH...
THANK YOU, KAGURAZAKA-SAN. AND YOU, SAKURAZAKI-SAN...I THOUGHT YOU WERE SCARY, BUT I WAS WRONG. THANK YOU, TOO. ♡

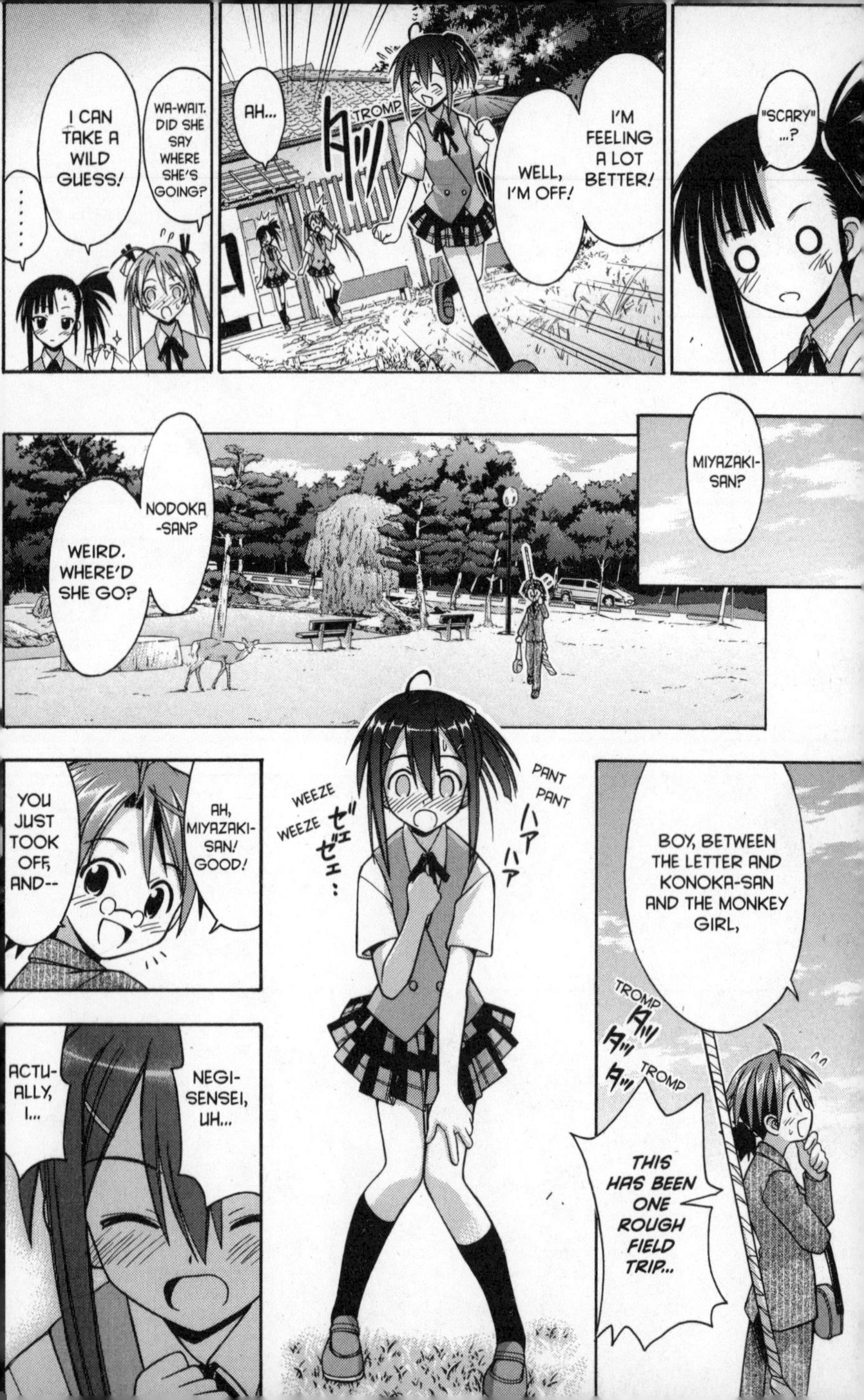
"SCARY" ...?
I'M FEELING A LOT BETTER!
WELL, I'M OFF!
TROMP
AH...
WA-WAIT. DID SHE SAY WHERE SHE'S GOING?
I CAN TAKE A WILD GUESS!
......
MIYAZAKI-SAN?
NODOKA-SAN?
WEIRD. WHERE'D SHE GO?
BOY, BETWEEN THE LETTER AND KONOKA-SAN AND THE MONKEY GIRL,
TROMP
TROMP
THIS HAS BEEN ONE ROUGH FIELD TRIP...
PANT PANT
WEEZE WEEZE
AH, MIYAZAKI-SAN! GOOD!
YOU JUST TOOK OFF, AND--
NEGI-SENSEI, UH...
ACTU-ALLY, I...

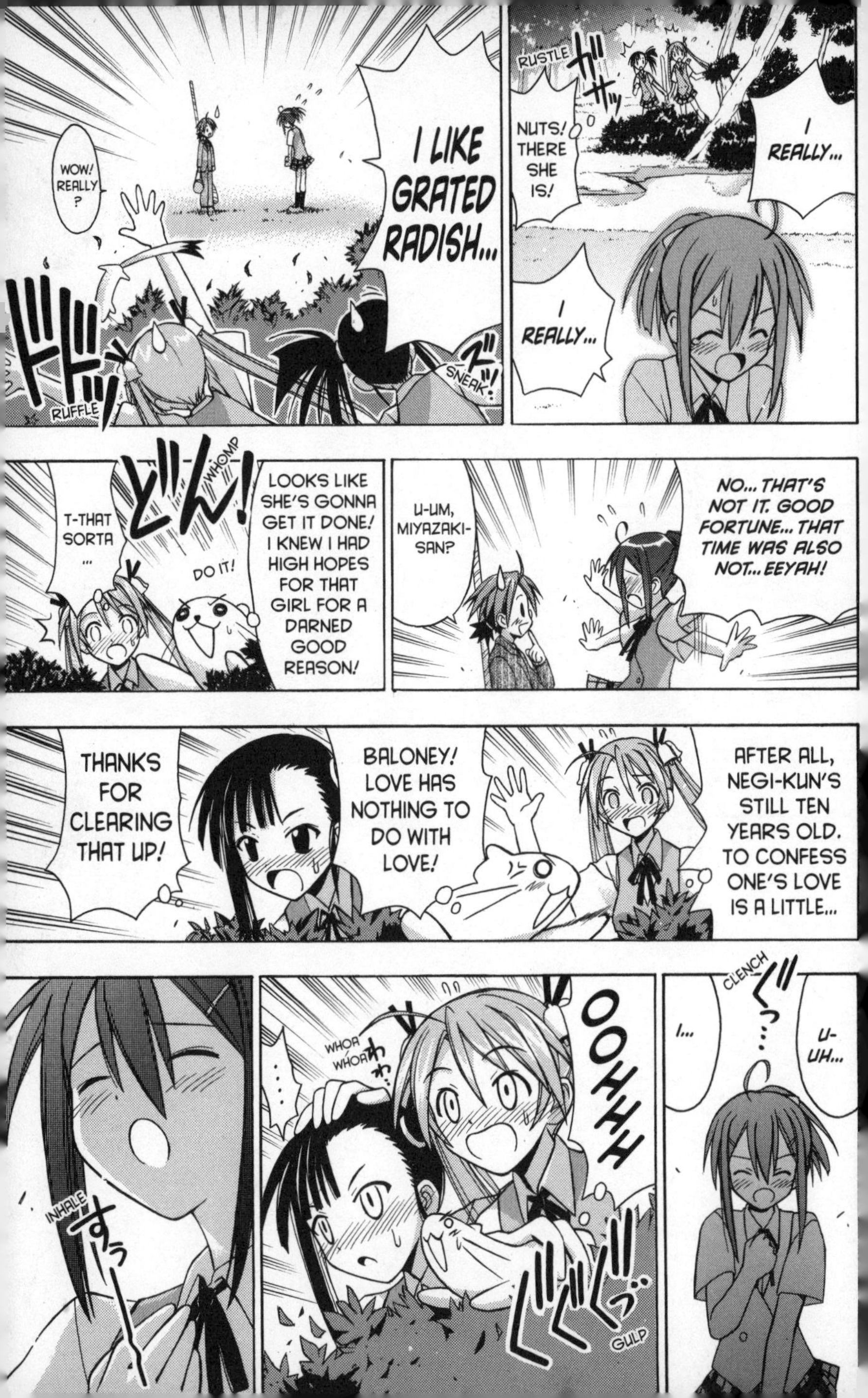
RUSTLE
NUTS! THERE SHE IS!
I REALLY...
I REALLY...
I LIKE GRATED RADISH...
WOW! REALLY?
RUFFLE
SNEAK
NO... THAT'S NOT IT. GOOD FORTUNE... THAT TIME WAS ALSO NOT... EEYAH!
U-UM, MIYAZAKI-SAN?
LOOKS LIKE SHE'S GONNA GET IT DONE! I KNEW I HAD HIGH HOPES FOR THAT GIRL FOR A DARNED GOOD REASON!
WHOMP
DO IT!
T-THAT SORTA ...
AFTER ALL, NEGI-KUN'S STILL TEN YEARS OLD. TO CONFESS ONE'S LOVE IS A LITTLE...
BALONEY! LOVE HAS NOTHING TO DO WITH LOVE!
THANKS FOR CLEARING THAT UP!
CLENCH
U-UH...
I...
OOHHHH
WHOA WHOA
GULP
INHALE

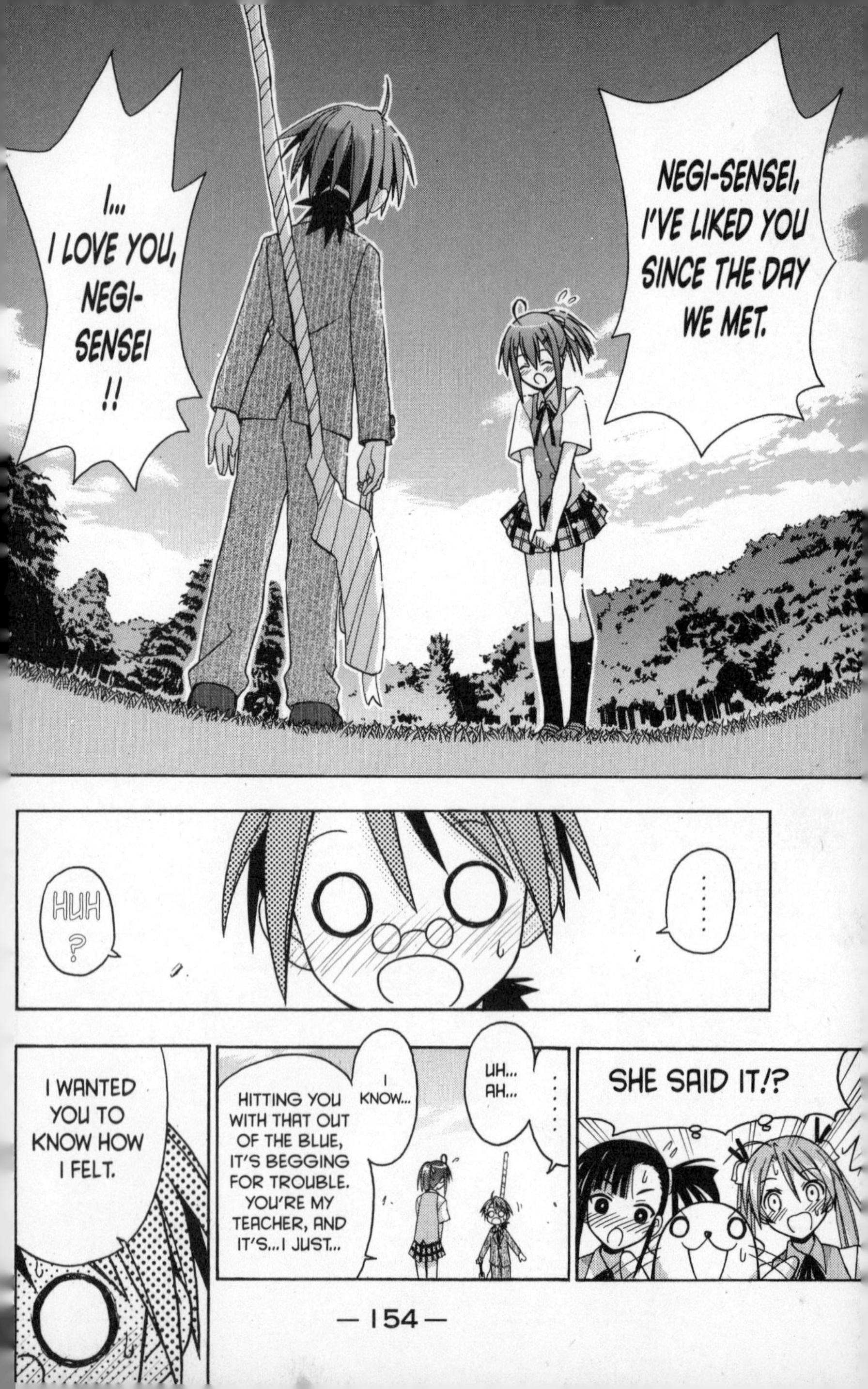
NEGI-SENSEI, I'VE LIKED YOU SINCE THE DAY WE MET.
I... I LOVE YOU, NEGI-SENSEI!!
......
HUH?
SHE SAID IT!?
UH... AH...
......
I KNOW...
HITTING YOU WITH THAT OUT OF THE BLUE, IT'S BEGGING FOR TROUBLE. YOU'RE MY TEACHER, AND IT'S...I JUST...
I WANTED YOU TO KNOW HOW I FELT.

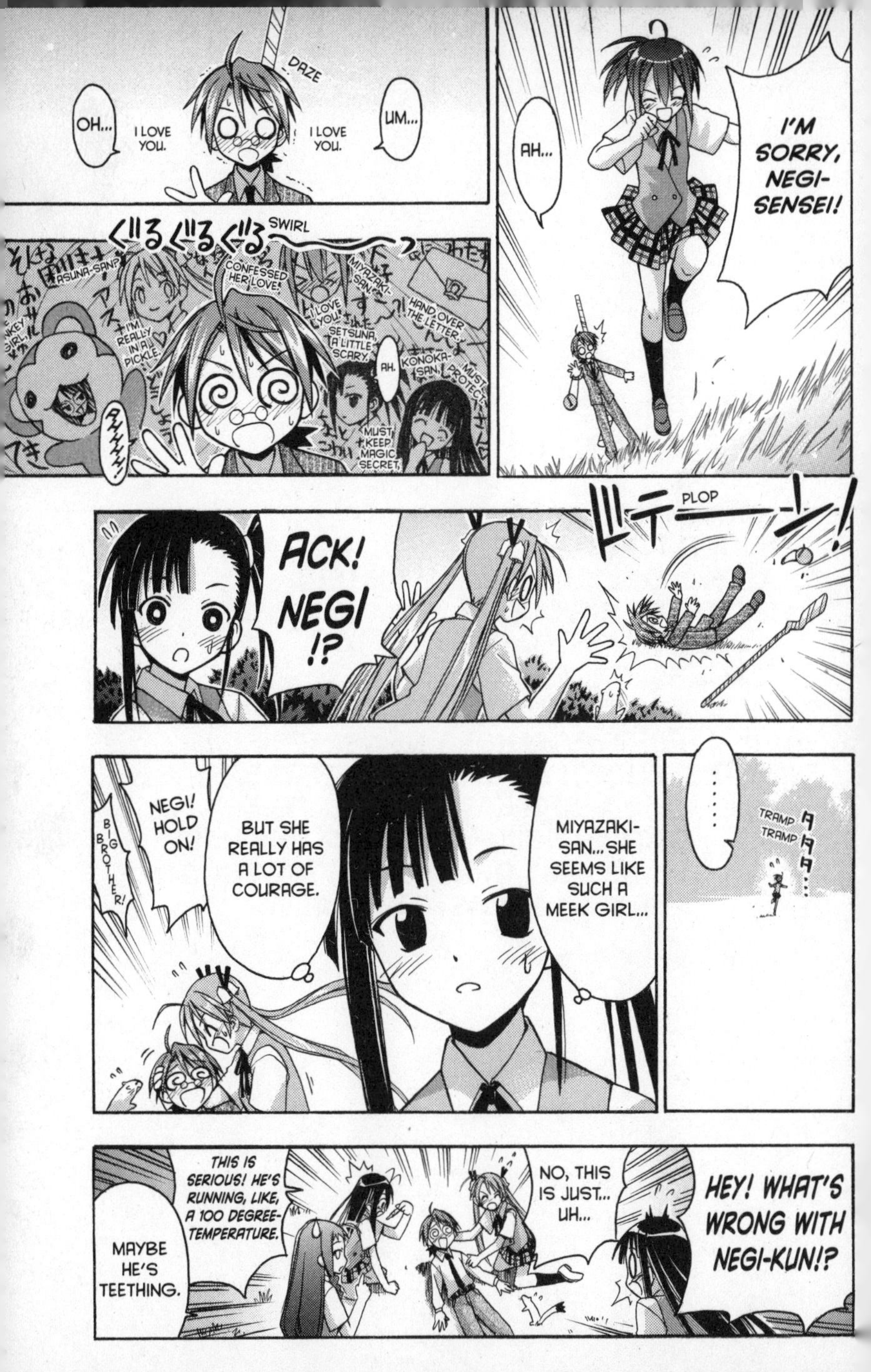

I'M SORRY, NEGI-SENSEI!
AH...
UM...
I LOVE YOU.
DAZE
I LOVE YOU.
OH...
ぐるぐるぐる
SWIRL
MIYAZAKI-SAN.
HAND OVER THE LETTER.
CONFESSED HER LOVE.
I LOVE YOU!
ASUNA-SAN?
I'M REALLY IN A PICKLE.
SETSUNA, A LITTLE SCARY.
AH.
KONOKA-SAN.
MUST PROTECT.
MUST KEEP MAGIC SECRET.
PLOP
ACK! NEGI!?
...
TRAMP TRAMP
MIYAZAKI-SAN... SHE SEEMS LIKE SUCH A MEEK GIRL...
BUT SHE REALLY HAS A LOT OF COURAGE.
NEGI! HOLD ON!
BIG BROTHER!
HEY! WHAT'S WRONG WITH NEGI-KUN!?
NO, THIS IS JUST... UH...
THIS IS SERIOUS! HE'S RUNNING, LIKE, A 100 DEGREE-TEMPERATURE.
MAYBE HE'S TEETHING.

STUDENT NUMBER 3
KAZUMI ASAKURA

BORN: JANUARY 10, 1989
BLOOD TYPE: O
ASTROLOGICAL SIGN: CAPRICORN
LIKES: THE BIG SCOOP, HUMAN-INTEREST
      STORIES, CAMERAS
DISLIKES: GREAT EVIL
AFFILIATIONS: JOURNALISM CLUB, REPORTER
      FOR THE MAHORA NEWSPAPER
NOTES: KNOWN AS THE HUMAN DATABASE
      OF 3-A, SHE HAS A TALENT FOR
      GATHERING INFORMATION. SHE HAS
      EXCELLENT GRADES AND THE FOURTH
      LARGEST BREASTS IN CLASS.

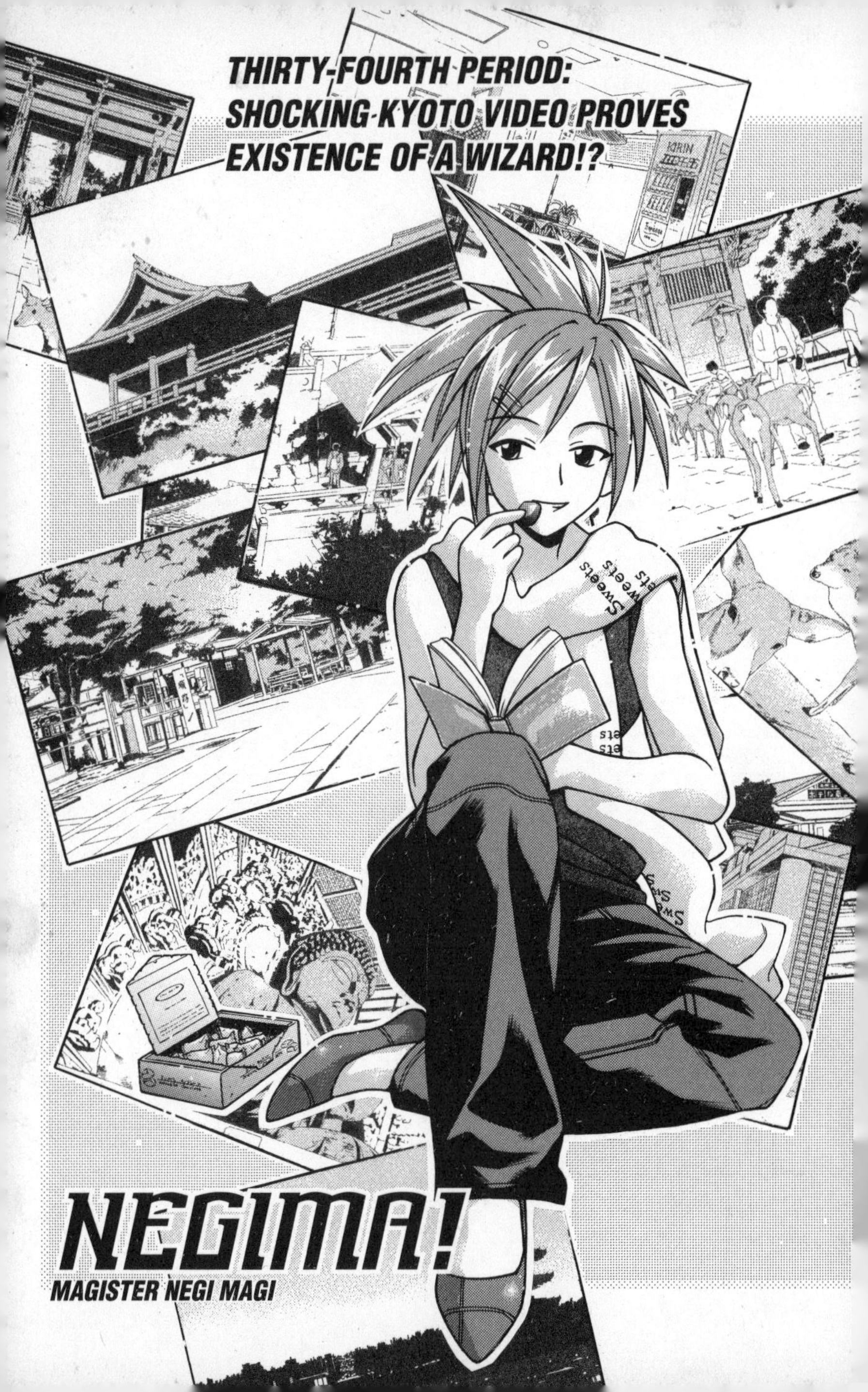
THIRTY-FOURTH PERIOD:
SHOCKING KYOTO VIDEO PROVES
EXISTENCE OF A WIZARD!?
NEGIMA!
MAGISTER NEGI MAGI

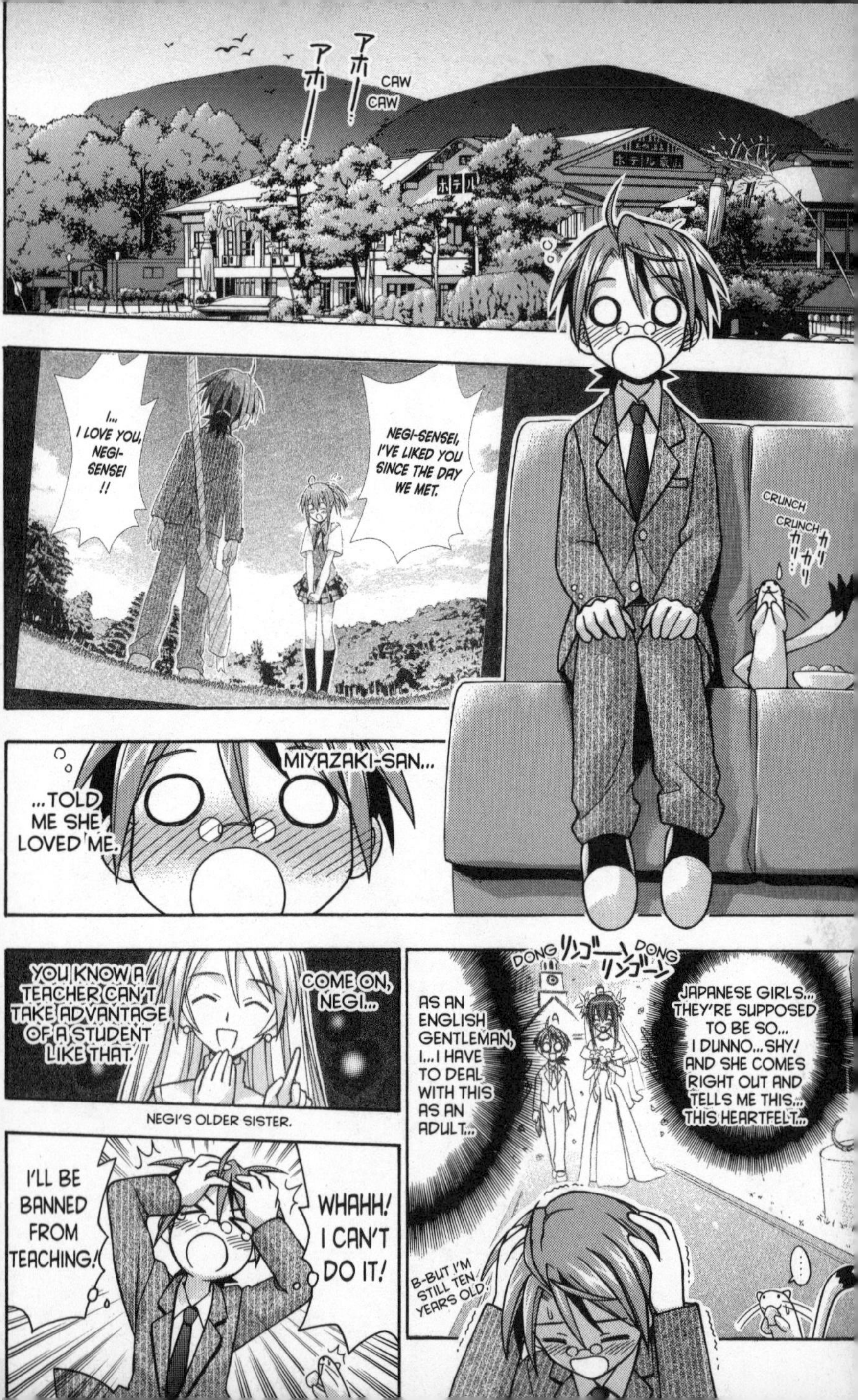
アホー!
アホー!
CAW
CAW
ホテル
NEGI-SENSEI, I'VE LIKED YOU SINCE THE DAY WE MET.
I... I LOVE YOU, NEGI-SENSEI!!
CRUNCH
CRUNCH
カリ
カリ
MIYAZAKI-SAN...
...TOLD ME SHE LOVED ME.
COME ON, NEGI...
YOU KNOW A TEACHER CAN'T TAKE ADVANTAGE OF A STUDENT LIKE THAT.
NEGI'S OLDER SISTER.
DONG
リンゴーン
DONG
リンゴーン
JAPANESE GIRLS... THEY'RE SUPPOSED TO BE SO... I DUNNO... SHY! AND SHE COMES RIGHT OUT AND TELLS ME THIS... THIS HEARTFELT...
AS AN ENGLISH GENTLEMAN, I... I HAVE TO DEAL WITH THIS AS AN ADULT...
WHAHH! I CAN'T DO IT!
I'LL BE BANNED FROM TEACHING!
B-BUT I'M STILL TEN YEARS OLD.

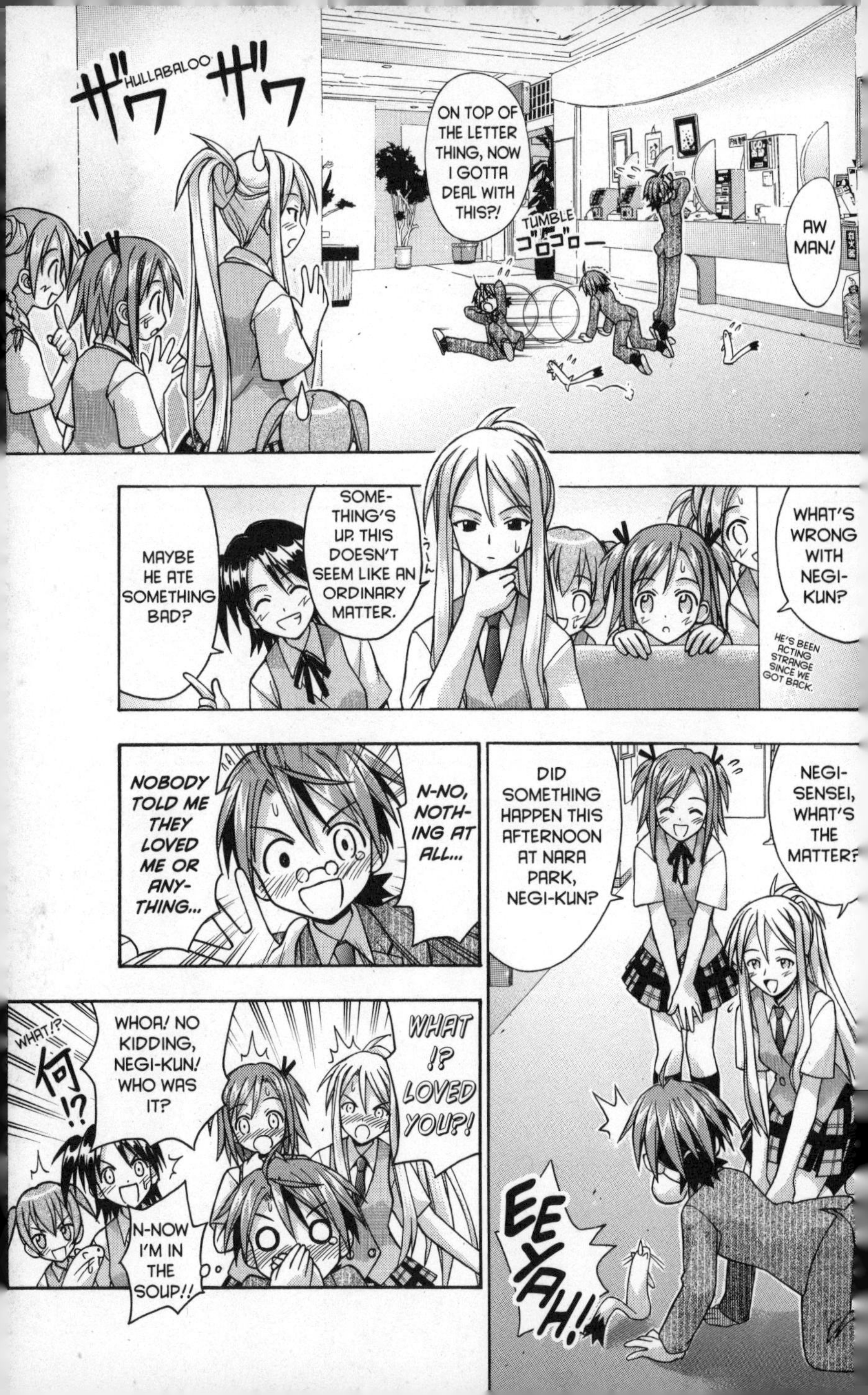
AW MAN!
ON TOP OF THE LETTER THING, NOW I GOTTA DEAL WITH THIS?!
TUMBLE
ゴロゴロー
HULLABALOO
ザワ ザワ
WHAT'S WRONG WITH NEGI-KUN?
HE'S BEEN ACTING STRANGE SINCE WE GOT BACK.
SOME-THING'S UP. THIS DOESN'T SEEM LIKE AN ORDINARY MATTER.
MAYBE HE ATE SOMETHING BAD?
NEGI-SENSEI, WHAT'S THE MATTER?
DID SOMETHING HAPPEN THIS AFTERNOON AT NARA PARK, NEGI-KUN?
N-NO, NOTH-ING AT ALL...
NOBODY TOLD ME THEY LOVED ME OR ANY-THING...
EEYAH!
WHAT !? LOVED YOU?!
WHOA! NO KIDDING, NEGI-KUN! WHO WAS IT?
WHAT!?
何!?
N-NOW I'M IN THE SOUP!!

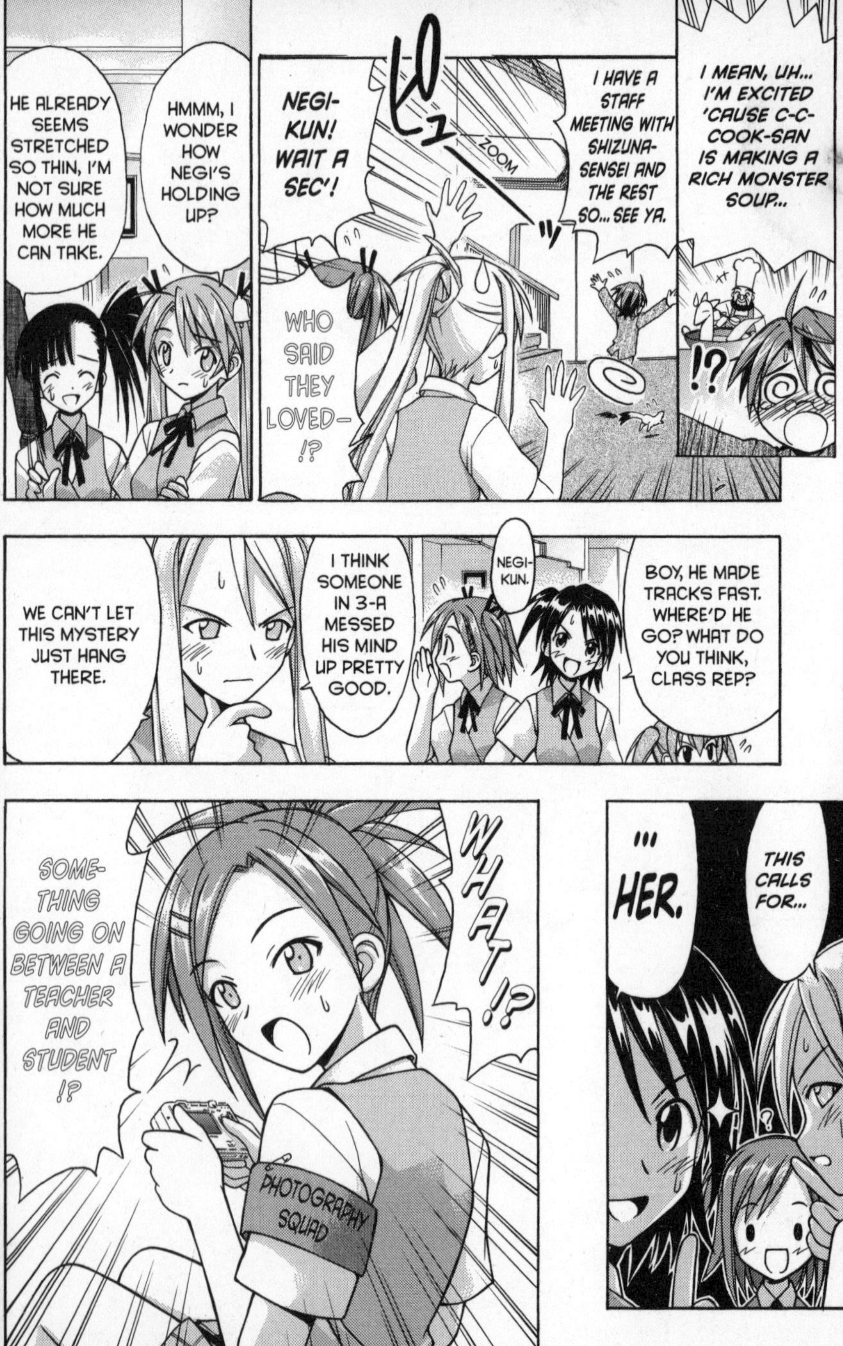
I MEAN, UH... I'M EXCITED 'CAUSE C-C-COOK-SAN IS MAKING A RICH MONSTER SOUP...
!?
I HAVE A STAFF MEETING WITH SHIZUNA-SENSEI AND THE REST SO... SEE YA.
ZOOM
NEGI-KUN! WAIT A SEC'!
WHO SAID THEY LOVED—!?
HMMM, I WONDER HOW NEGI'S HOLDING UP?
HE ALREADY SEEMS STRETCHED SO THIN, I'M NOT SURE HOW MUCH MORE HE CAN TAKE.
BOY, HE MADE TRACKS FAST. WHERE'D HE GO? WHAT DO YOU THINK, CLASS REP?
NEGI-KUN.
I THINK SOMEONE IN 3-A MESSED HIS MIND UP PRETTY GOOD.
WE CAN'T LET THIS MYSTERY JUST HANG THERE.
THIS CALLS FOR...
...HER.
WHAT!?
SOMETHING GOING ON BETWEEN A TEACHER AND STUDENT!?
PHOTOGRAPHY SQUAD

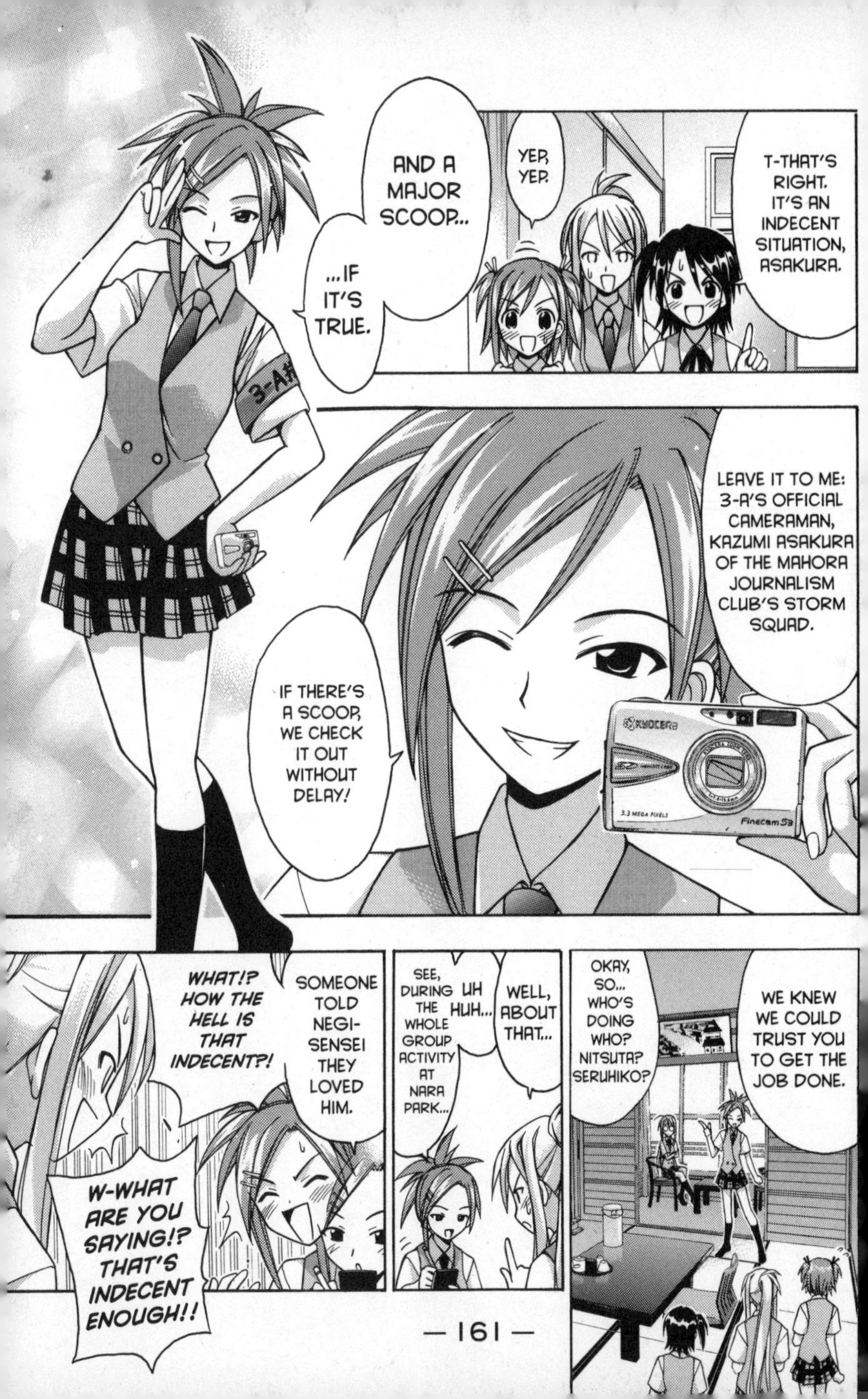
T-THAT'S RIGHT. IT'S AN INDECENT SITUATION, ASAKURA.
YEP, YEP.
AND A MAJOR SCOOP...
...IF IT'S TRUE.
LEAVE IT TO ME: 3-A'S OFFICIAL CAMERAMAN, KAZUMI ASAKURA OF THE MAHORA JOURNALISM CLUB'S STORM SQUAD.
IF THERE'S A SCOOP, WE CHECK IT OUT WITHOUT DELAY!
KYOCERA
3.3 MEGA PIXELS
Finecam S3
3-A
WE KNEW WE COULD TRUST YOU TO GET THE JOB DONE.
OKAY, SO... WHO'S DOING WHO? NITSUTA? SERUHIKO?
WELL, ABOUT THAT...
UH HUH...
SEE, DURING THE WHOLE GROUP ACTIVITY AT NARA PARK...
SOMEONE TOLD NEGI-SENSEI THEY LOVED HIM.
WHAT!? HOW THE HELL IS THAT INDECENT?!
W-WHAT ARE YOU SAYING!? THAT'S INDECENT ENOUGH!!

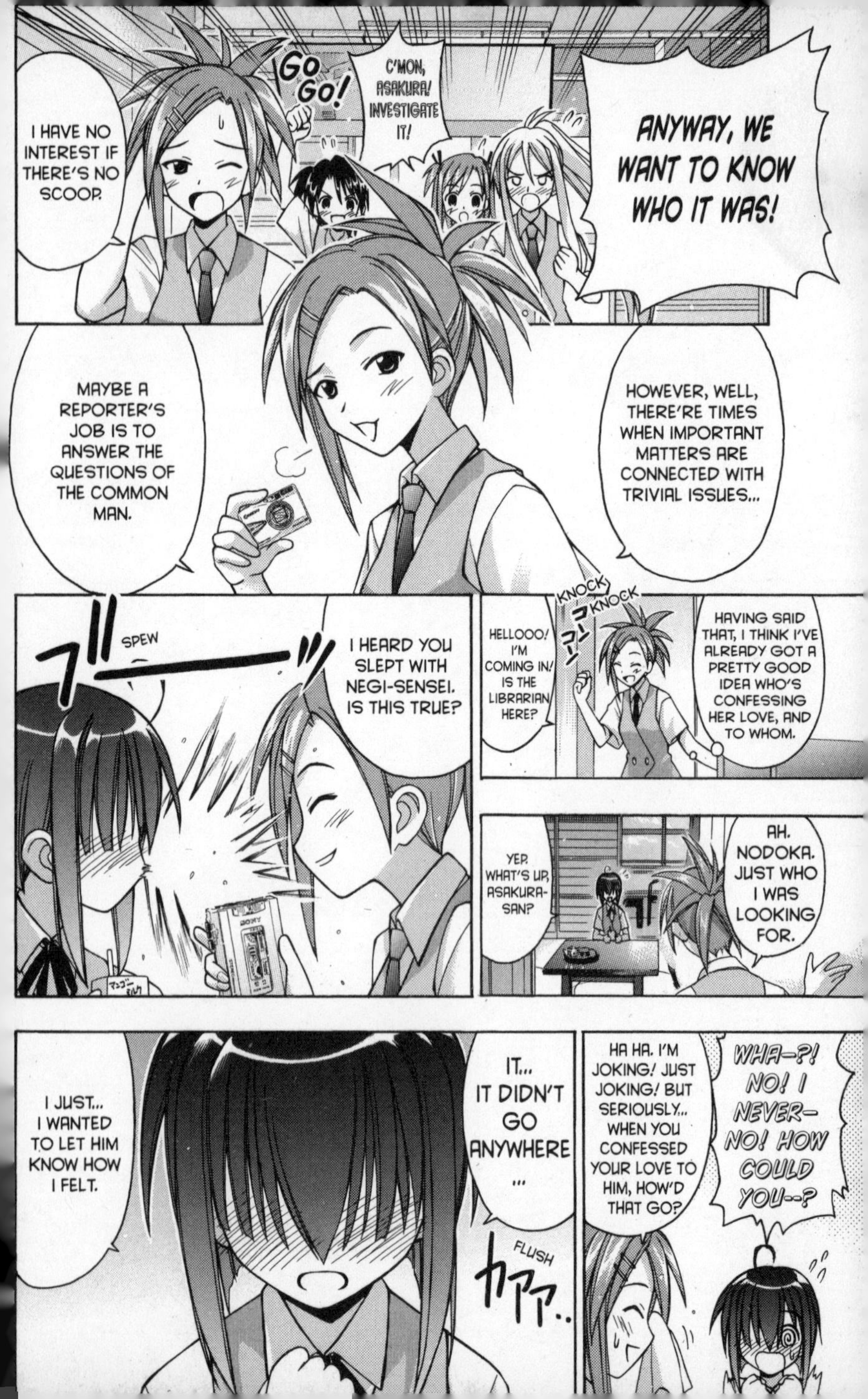
ANYWAY, WE WANT TO KNOW WHO IT WAS!
C'MON, ASAKURA! INVESTIGATE IT!
GO GO!
I HAVE NO INTEREST IF THERE'S NO SCOOP.
HOWEVER, WELL, THERE'RE TIMES WHEN IMPORTANT MATTERS ARE CONNECTED WITH TRIVIAL ISSUES...
MAYBE A REPORTER'S JOB IS TO ANSWER THE QUESTIONS OF THE COMMON MAN.
HAVING SAID THAT, I THINK I'VE ALREADY GOT A PRETTY GOOD IDEA WHO'S CONFESSING HER LOVE, AND TO WHOM.
KNOCK KNOCK
HELLOOO! I'M COMING IN! IS THE LIBRARIAN HERE?
AH. NODOKA. JUST WHO I WAS LOOKING FOR.
YEP. WHAT'S UP, ASAKURA-SAN?
I HEARD YOU SLEPT WITH NEGI-SENSEI. IS THIS TRUE?
SPEW
WHA--?! NO! I NEVER-- NO! HOW COULD YOU--?
HA HA. I'M JOKING! JUST JOKING! BUT SERIOUSLY... WHEN YOU CONFESSED YOUR LOVE TO HIM, HOW'D THAT GO?
IT... IT DIDN'T GO ANYWHERE...
FLUSH
I JUST... I WANTED TO LET HIM KNOW HOW I FELT.

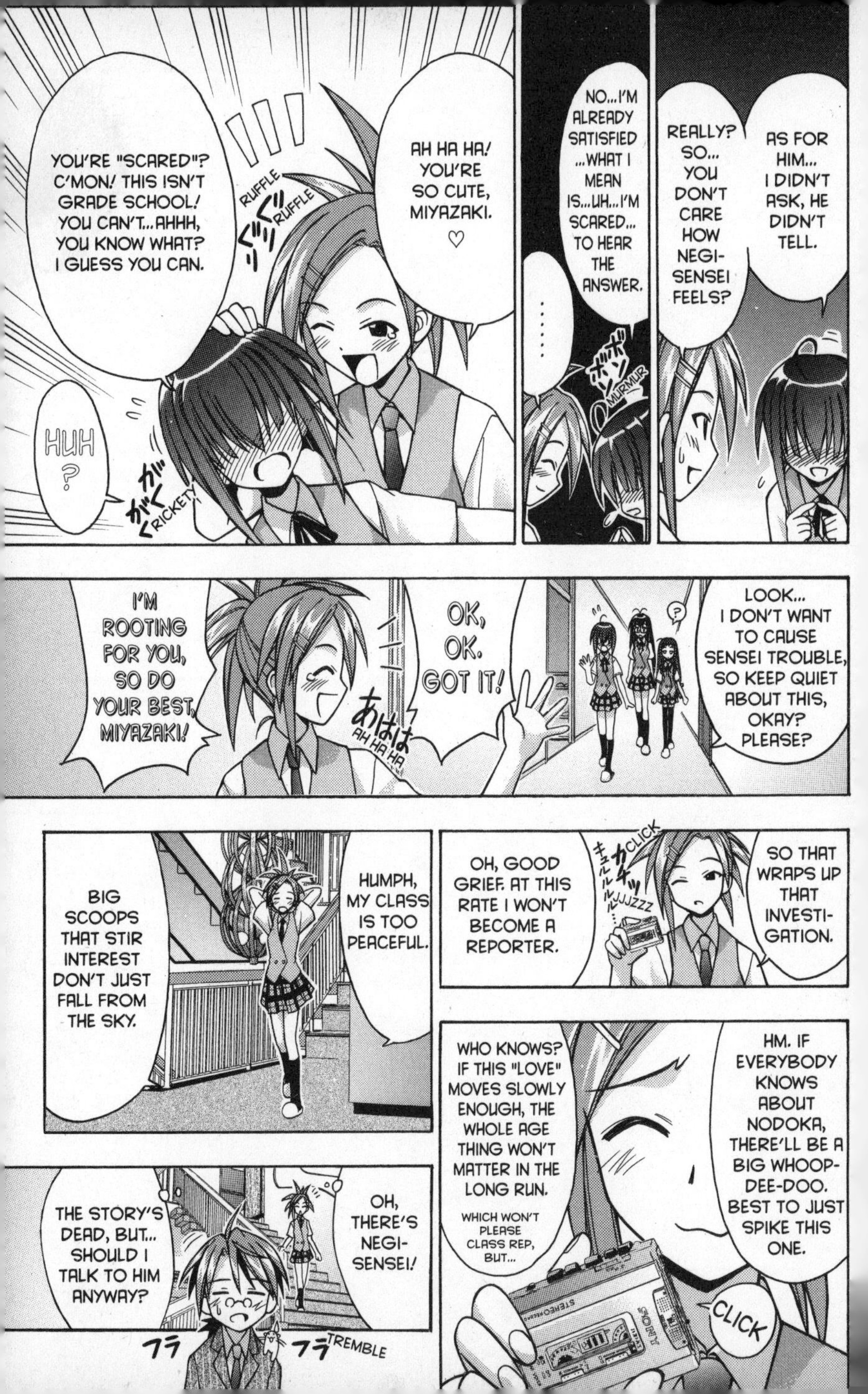
AS FOR HIM... I DIDN'T ASK, HE DIDN'T TELL.
REALLY? SO... YOU DON'T CARE HOW NEGI-SENSEI FEELS?
NO...I'M ALREADY SATISFIED ...WHAT I MEAN IS...UH...I'M SCARED... TO HEAR THE ANSWER.
MURMUR
......
AH HA HA! YOU'RE SO CUTE, MIYAZAKI. ♡
RUFFLE RUFFLE
YOU'RE "SCARED"? C'MON! THIS ISN'T GRADE SCHOOL! YOU CAN'T...AHHH, YOU KNOW WHAT? I GUESS YOU CAN.
HUH?
RICKETY
LOOK... I DON'T WANT TO CAUSE SENSEI TROUBLE, SO KEEP QUIET ABOUT THIS, OKAY? PLEASE?
OK, OK. GOT IT!
AH HA HA
I'M ROOTING FOR YOU, SO DO YOUR BEST, MIYAZAKI!
SO THAT WRAPS UP THAT INVESTIGATION.
CLICK
JJJZZZ
OH, GOOD GRIEF. AT THIS RATE I WON'T BECOME A REPORTER.
HUMPH, MY CLASS IS TOO PEACEFUL.
BIG SCOOPS THAT STIR INTEREST DON'T JUST FALL FROM THE SKY.
HM. IF EVERYBODY KNOWS ABOUT NODOKA, THERE'LL BE A BIG WHOOP-DEE-DOO. BEST TO JUST SPIKE THIS ONE.
WHO KNOWS? IF THIS "LOVE" MOVES SLOWLY ENOUGH, THE WHOLE AGE THING WON'T MATTER IN THE LONG RUN.
WHICH WON'T PLEASE CLASS REP, BUT...
CLICK
OH, THERE'S NEGI-SENSEI!
THE STORY'S DEAD, BUT... SHOULD I TALK TO HIM ANYWAY?
TREMBLE

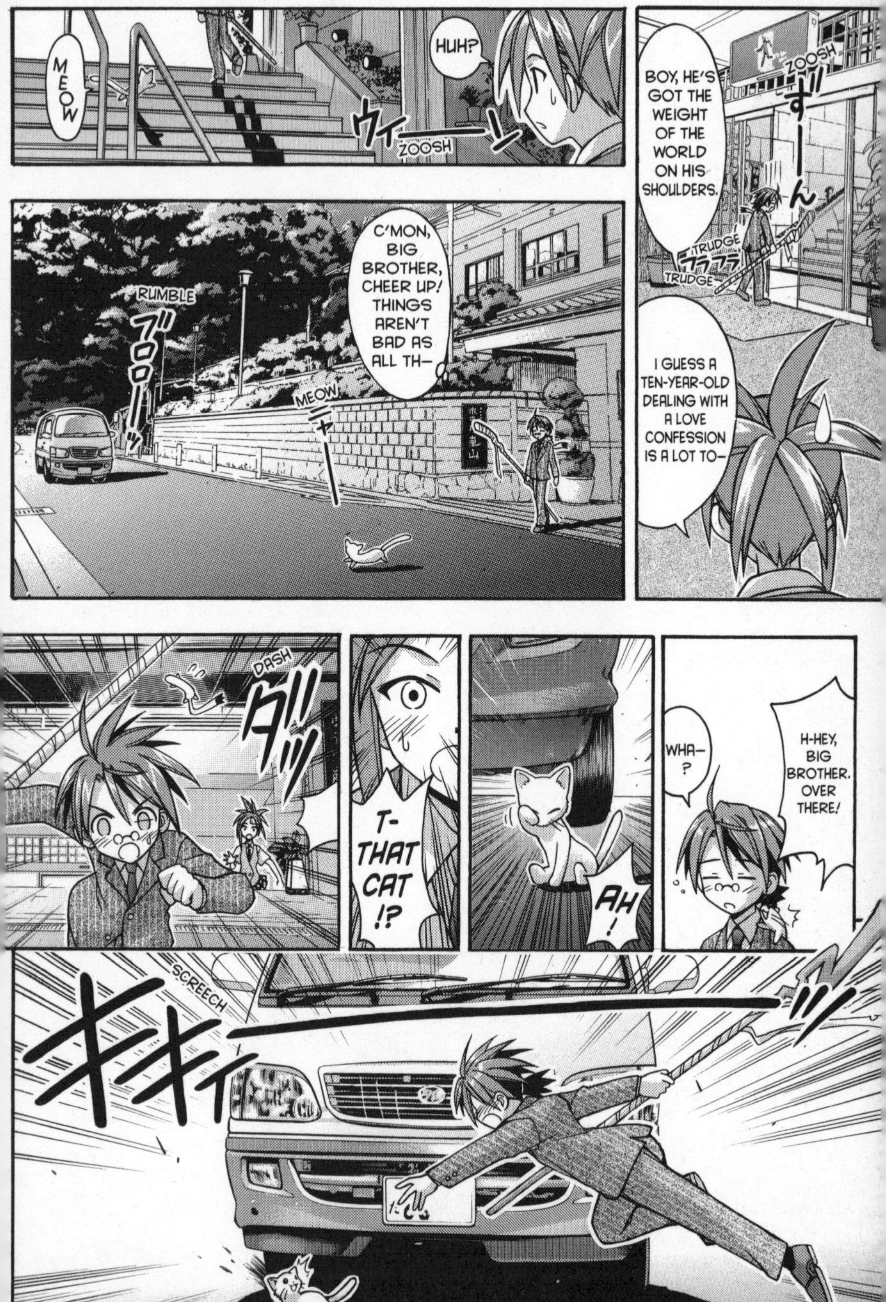
ZOOSH
BOY, HE'S GOT THE WEIGHT OF THE WORLD ON HIS SHOULDERS.
TRUDGE
TRUDGE
I GUESS A TEN-YEAR-OLD DEALING WITH A LOVE CONFESSION IS A LOT TO—
HUH?
ZOOSH
MEOW
C'MON, BIG BROTHER, CHEER UP! THINGS AREN'T BAD AS ALL TH—
RUMBLE
MEOW
H-HEY, BIG BROTHER. OVER THERE!
WHA—?
AH!
T-THAT CAT!?
DASH
SCREECH

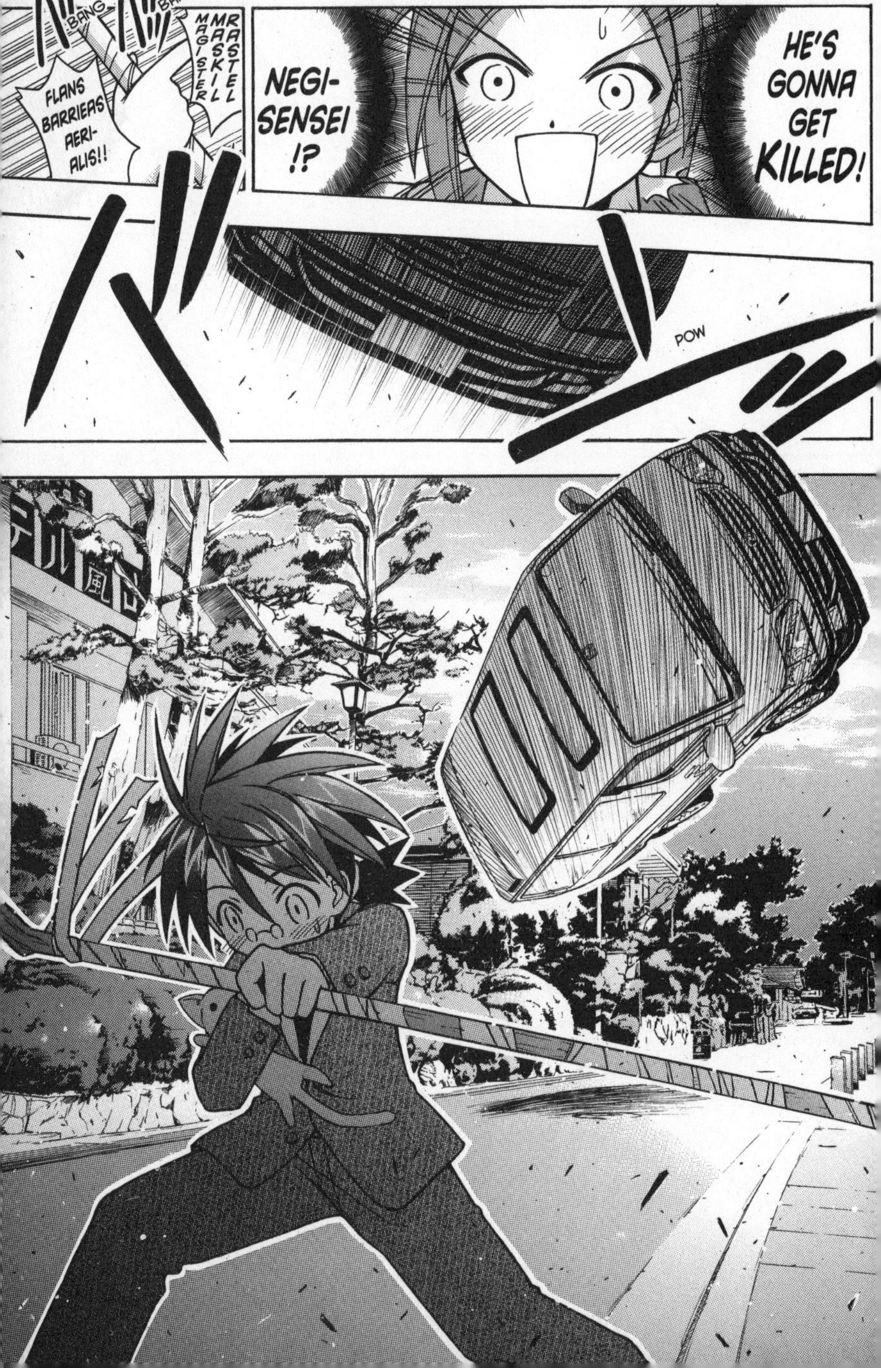
HE'S GONNA GET KILLED!
NEGI-SENSEI !?
RASTEL MASKIL MAGISTER
BANG
BANG
FLANS BARRIERAS AERIALIS!!
POW

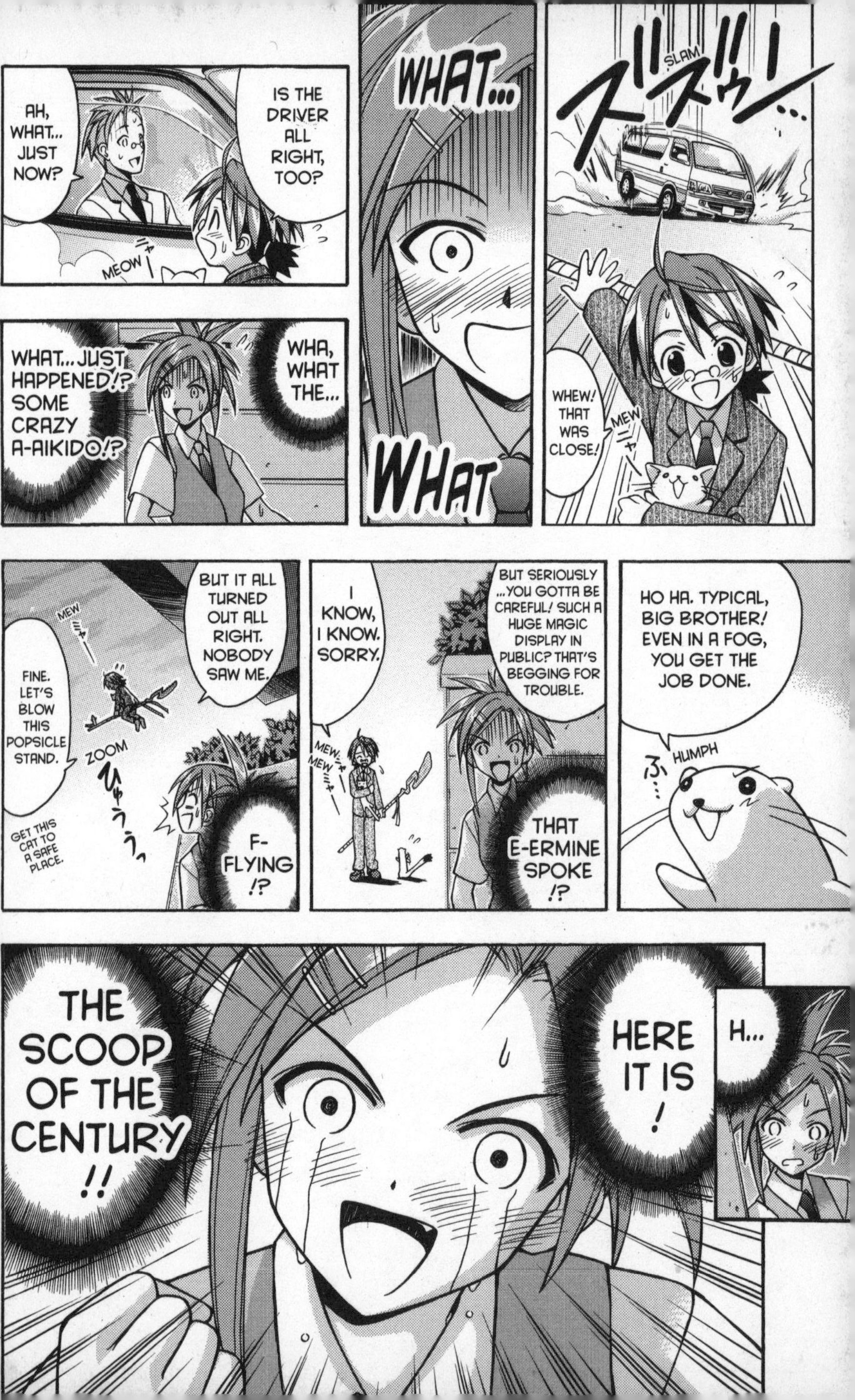
SLAM
WHEW! THAT WAS CLOSE!
MEW
WHAT...
WHAT
IS THE DRIVER ALL RIGHT, TOO?
AH, WHAT... JUST NOW?
MEOW
WHA, WHAT THE...
WHAT... JUST HAPPENED!? SOME CRAZY A-AIKIDO!?
HO HA. TYPICAL, BIG BROTHER! EVEN IN A FOG, YOU GET THE JOB DONE.
HUMPH
BUT SERIOUSLY ...YOU GOTTA BE CAREFUL! SUCH A HUGE MAGIC DISPLAY IN PUBLIC? THAT'S BEGGING FOR TROUBLE.
THAT E-ERMINE SPOKE !?
I KNOW, I KNOW. SORRY.
MEW MEW
BUT IT ALL TURNED OUT ALL RIGHT. NOBODY SAW ME.
MEW
FINE. LET'S BLOW THIS POPSICLE STAND.
ZOOM
GET THIS CAT TO A SAFE PLACE.
F-FLYING !?
H...
HERE IT IS !
THE SCOOP OF THE CENTURY !!

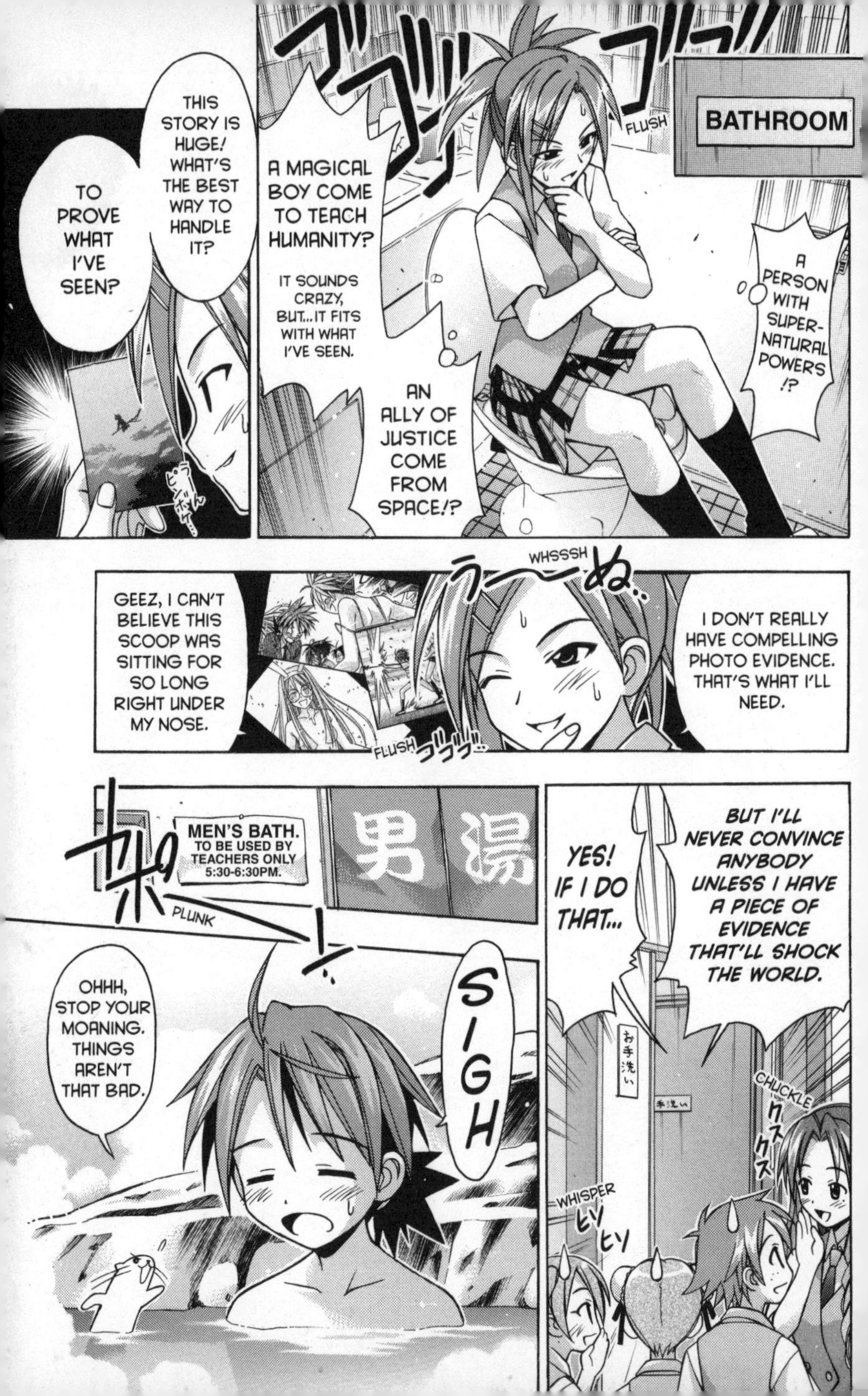
BATHROOM
FLUSH
A PERSON WITH SUPER-NATURAL POWERS!?
A MAGICAL BOY COME TO TEACH HUMANITY?
IT SOUNDS CRAZY, BUT...IT FITS WITH WHAT I'VE SEEN.
AN ALLY OF JUSTICE COME FROM SPACE!?
THIS STORY IS HUGE! WHAT'S THE BEST WAY TO HANDLE IT?
TO PROVE WHAT I'VE SEEN?
WHSSSH
I DON'T REALLY HAVE COMPELLING PHOTO EVIDENCE. THAT'S WHAT I'LL NEED.
GEEZ, I CAN'T BELIEVE THIS SCOOP WAS SITTING FOR SO LONG RIGHT UNDER MY NOSE.
FLUSH
BUT I'LL NEVER CONVINCE ANYBODY UNLESS I HAVE A PIECE OF EVIDENCE THAT'LL SHOCK THE WORLD.
YES! IF I DO THAT...
お手洗い
CHUCKLE
WHISPER
MEN'S BATH. TO BE USED BY TEACHERS ONLY 5:30-6:30PM.
男湯
PLUNK
SIGH
OHHH, STOP YOUR MOANING. THINGS AREN'T THAT BAD.

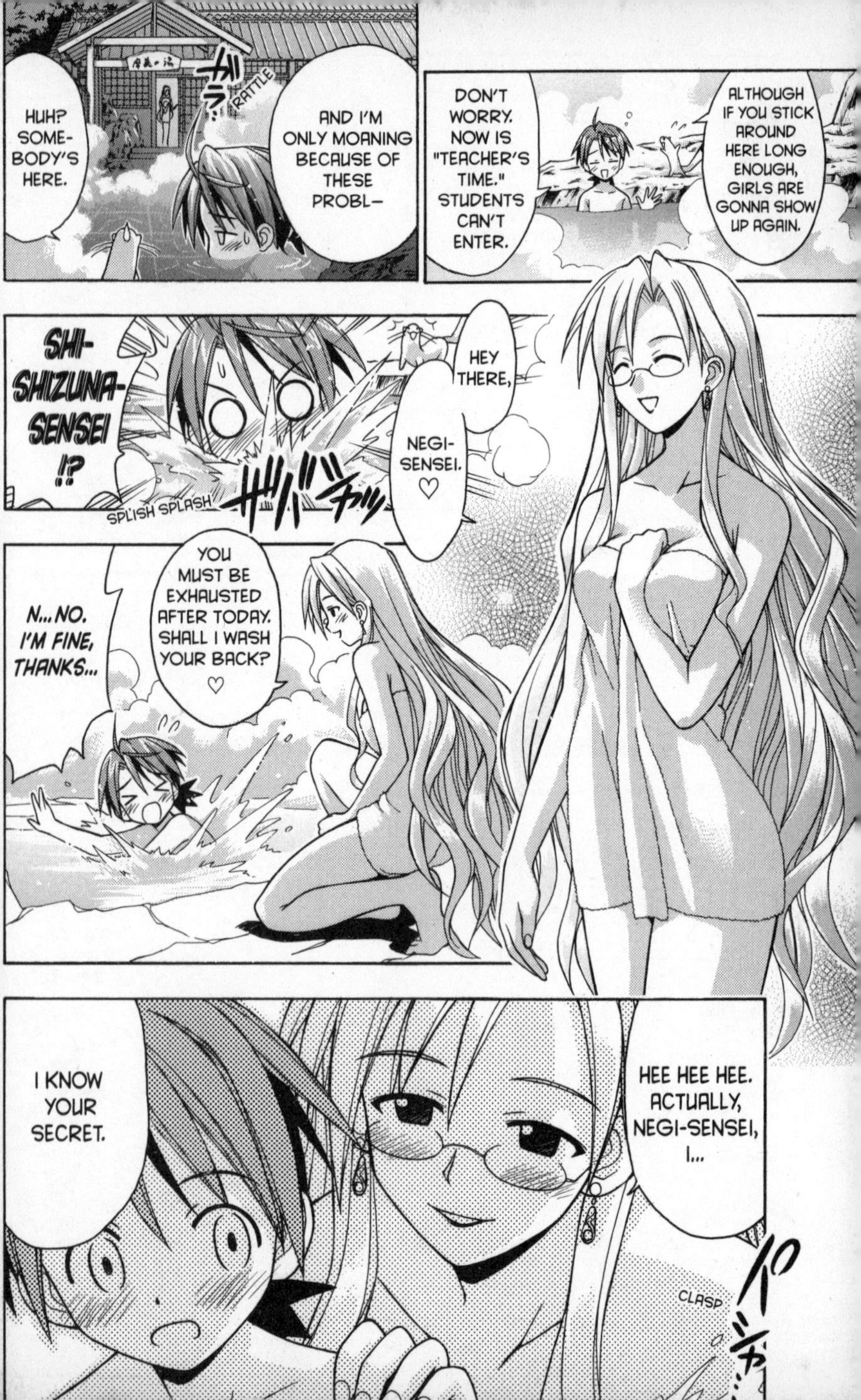
ALTHOUGH IF YOU STICK AROUND HERE LONG ENOUGH, GIRLS ARE GONNA SHOW UP AGAIN.
DON'T WORRY. NOW IS "TEACHER'S TIME." STUDENTS CAN'T ENTER.
AND I'M ONLY MOANING BECAUSE OF THESE PROBL—
RATTLE
HUH? SOME-BODY'S HERE.
HEY THERE,
NEGI-SENSEI. ♡
SHI-SHIZUNA-SENSEI !?
SPLISH SPLASH
YOU MUST BE EXHAUSTED AFTER TODAY. SHALL I WASH YOUR BACK? ♡
N...NO. I'M FINE, THANKS...
HEE HEE HEE. ACTUALLY, NEGI-SENSEI, I...
CLASP
I KNOW YOUR SECRET.

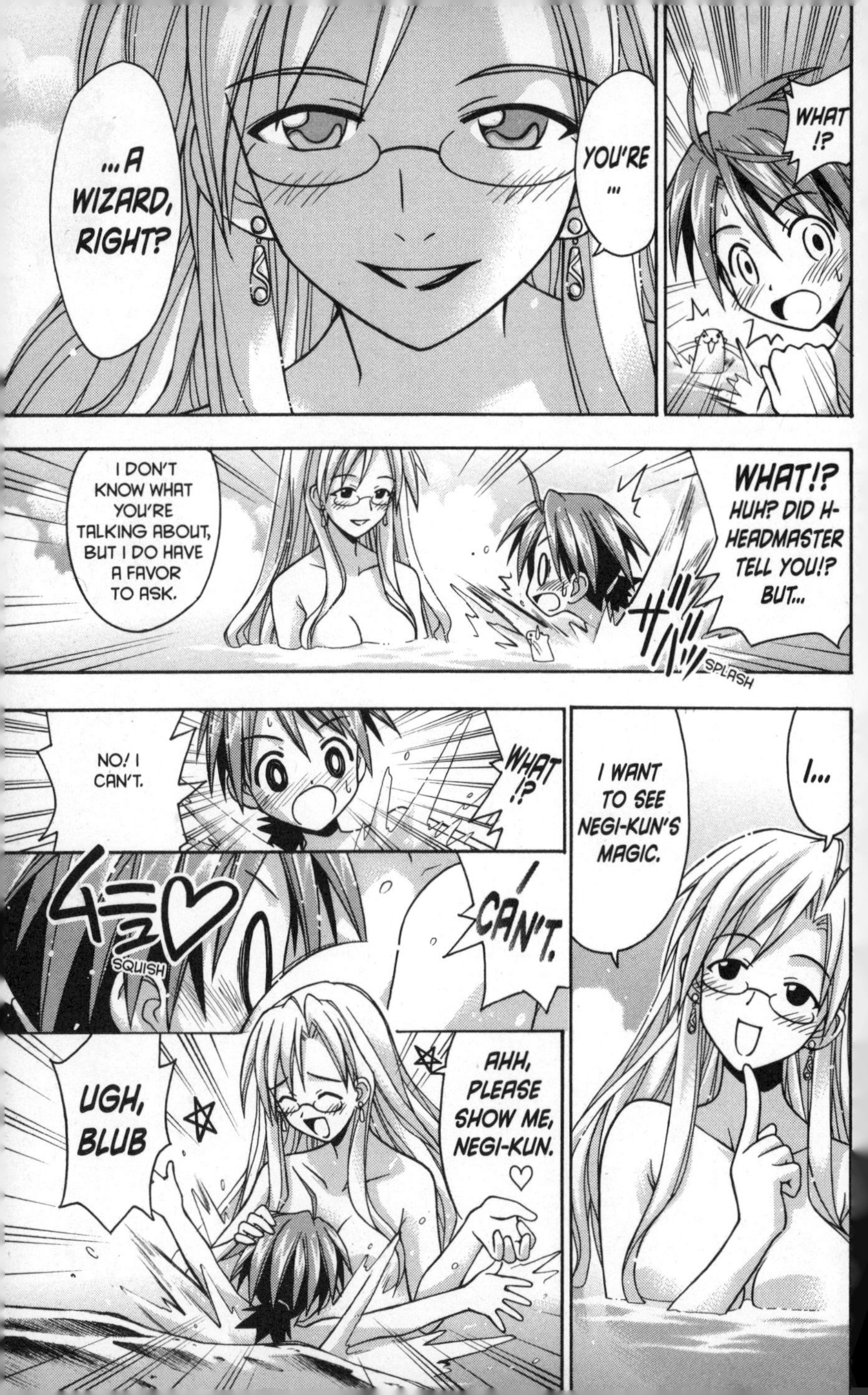

YOU'RE ...
...A WIZARD, RIGHT?
WHAT !?
WHAT!? HUH? DID H-HEADMASTER TELL YOU!? BUT...
SPLASH
I DON'T KNOW WHAT YOU'RE TALKING ABOUT, BUT I DO HAVE A FAVOR TO ASK.
I...
I WANT TO SEE NEGI-KUN'S MAGIC.
WHAT !?
NO! I CAN'T.
I CAN'T.
SQUISH
AHH, PLEASE SHOW ME, NEGI-KUN.
UGH, BLUB

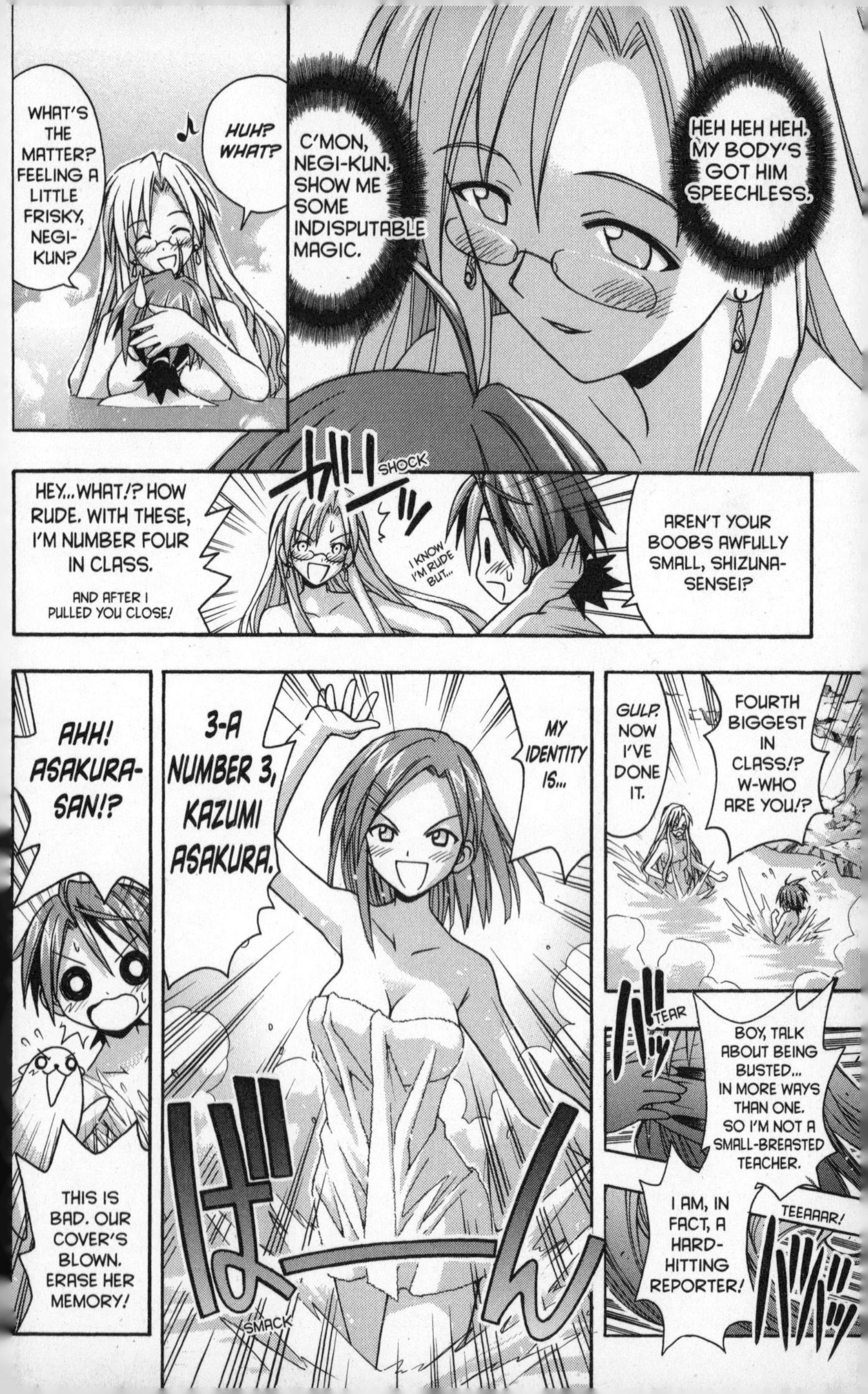
HEH HEH HEH. MY BODY'S GOT HIM SPEECHLESS.
C'MON, NEGI-KUN. SHOW ME SOME INDISPUTABLE MAGIC.
HUH? WHAT?
WHAT'S THE MATTER? FEELING A LITTLE FRISKY, NEGI-KUN?
SHOCK
AREN'T YOUR BOOBS AWFULLY SMALL, SHIZUNA-SENSEI?
I KNOW I'M RUDE BUT...
HEY...WHAT!? HOW RUDE. WITH THESE, I'M NUMBER FOUR IN CLASS.
AND AFTER I PULLED YOU CLOSE!
FOURTH BIGGEST IN CLASS!? W-WHO ARE YOU!?
GULP. NOW I'VE DONE IT.
TEAR
BOY, TALK ABOUT BEING BUSTED... IN MORE WAYS THAN ONE. SO I'M NOT A SMALL-BREASTED TEACHER.
I AM, IN FACT, A HARD-HITTING REPORTER!
TEEAAAR!
MY IDENTITY IS...
3-A NUMBER 3, KAZUMI ASAKURA.
SMACK
AHH! ASAKURA-SAN!?
THIS IS BAD. OUR COVER'S BLOWN. ERASE HER MEMORY!

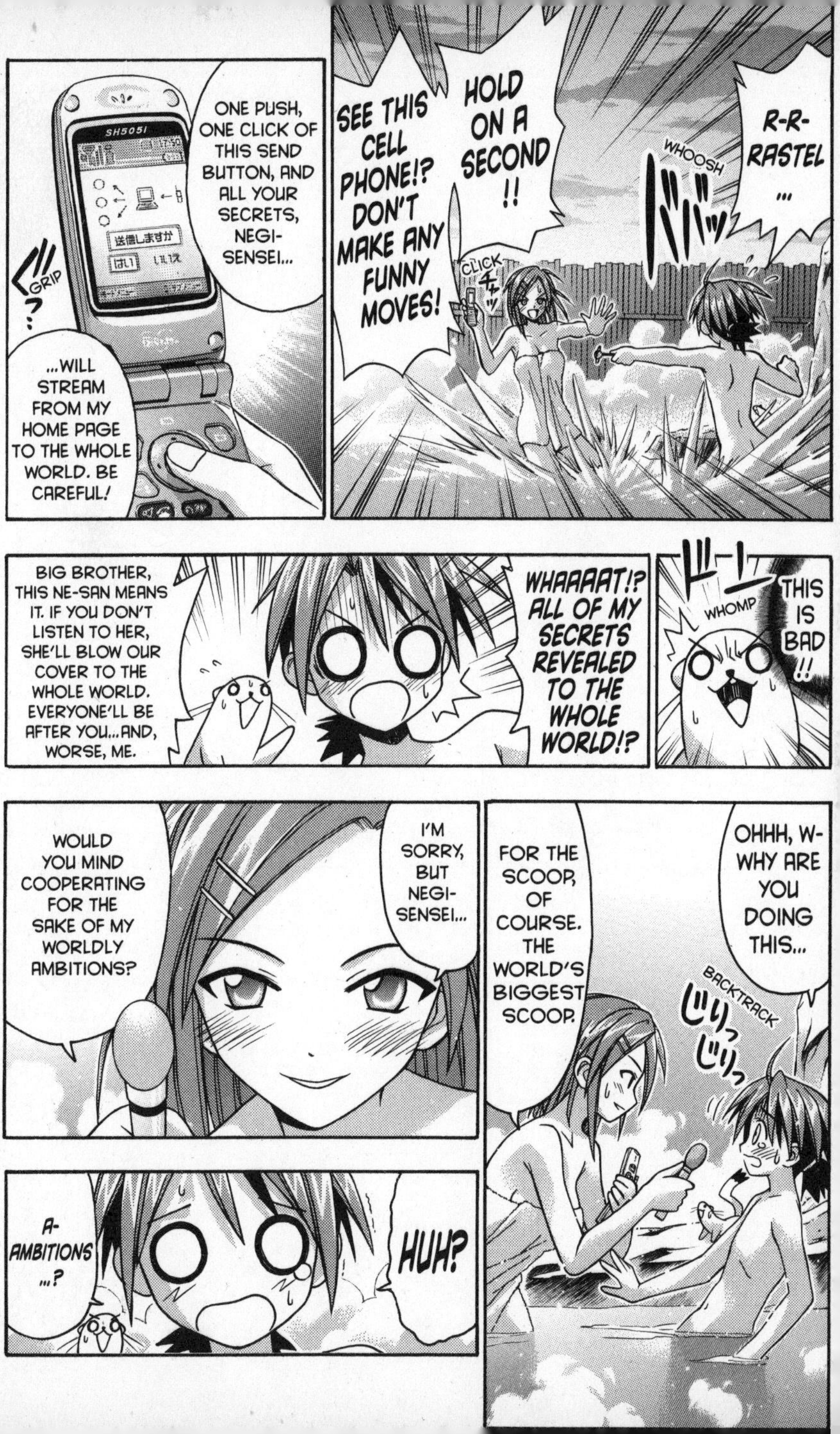
R-R-RASTEL...
WHOOSH
HOLD ON A SECOND!!
SEE THIS CELL PHONE!? DON'T MAKE ANY FUNNY MOVES!
CLICK
SH505i
送信しますか
はい いいえ
ONE PUSH, ONE CLICK OF THIS SEND BUTTON, AND ALL YOUR SECRETS, NEGI-SENSEI...
GRIP
...WILL STREAM FROM MY HOME PAGE TO THE WHOLE WORLD. BE CAREFUL!
WHOMP
THIS IS BAD!!
WHAAAAT!? ALL OF MY SECRETS REVEALED TO THE WHOLE WORLD!?
BIG BROTHER, THIS NE-SAN MEANS IT. IF YOU DON'T LISTEN TO HER, SHE'LL BLOW OUR COVER TO THE WHOLE WORLD. EVERYONE'LL BE AFTER YOU...AND, WORSE, ME.
OHHH, W-WHY ARE YOU DOING THIS...
BACKTRACK
FOR THE SCOOP, OF COURSE. THE WORLD'S BIGGEST SCOOP.
I'M SORRY, BUT NEGI-SENSEI...
WOULD YOU MIND COOPERATING FOR THE SAKE OF MY WORLDLY AMBITIONS?
HUH?
A-AMBITIONS...?

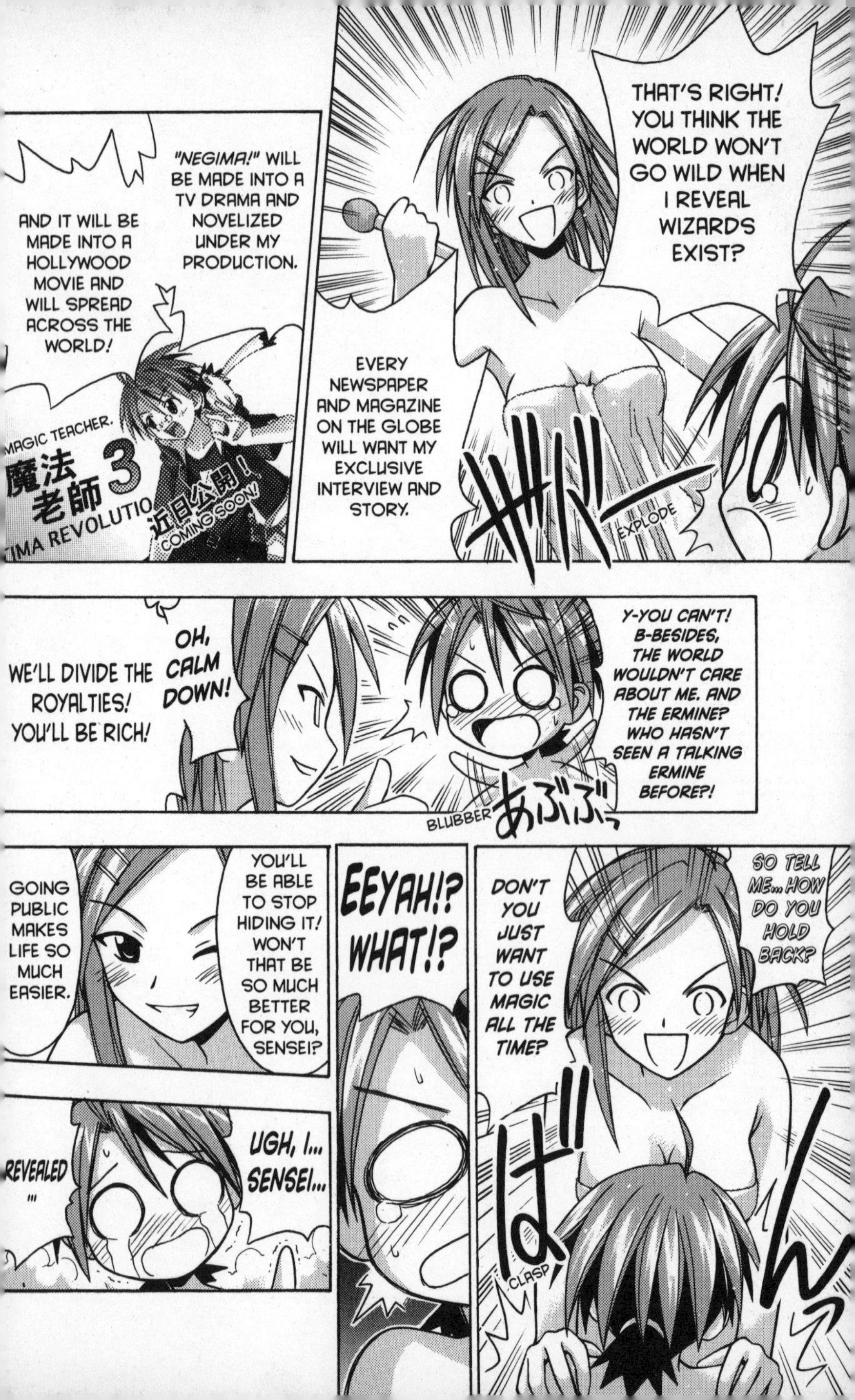
THAT'S RIGHT! YOU THINK THE WORLD WON'T GO WILD WHEN I REVEAL WIZARDS EXIST?
EVERY NEWSPAPER AND MAGAZINE ON THE GLOBE WILL WANT MY EXCLUSIVE INTERVIEW AND STORY.
EXPLODE
"NEGIMA!" WILL BE MADE INTO A TV DRAMA AND NOVELIZED UNDER MY PRODUCTION.
AND IT WILL BE MADE INTO A HOLLYWOOD MOVIE AND WILL SPREAD ACROSS THE WORLD!
MAGIC TEACHER.
魔法老師3
TIMA REVOLUTIO
近日公開！
COMING SOON!
Y-YOU CAN'T! B-BESIDES, THE WORLD WOULDN'T CARE ABOUT ME. AND THE ERMINE? WHO HASN'T SEEN A TALKING ERMINE BEFORE?!
BLUBBER
OH, CALM DOWN!
WE'LL DIVIDE THE ROYALTIES! YOU'LL BE RICH!
SO TELL ME... HOW DO YOU HOLD BACK?
DON'T YOU JUST WANT TO USE MAGIC ALL THE TIME?
CLASP
EEYAH!? WHAT!?
YOU'LL BE ABLE TO STOP HIDING IT! WON'T THAT BE SO MUCH BETTER FOR YOU, SENSEI?
GOING PUBLIC MAKES LIFE SO MUCH EASIER.
UGH, I... SENSEI...
REVEALED!!!

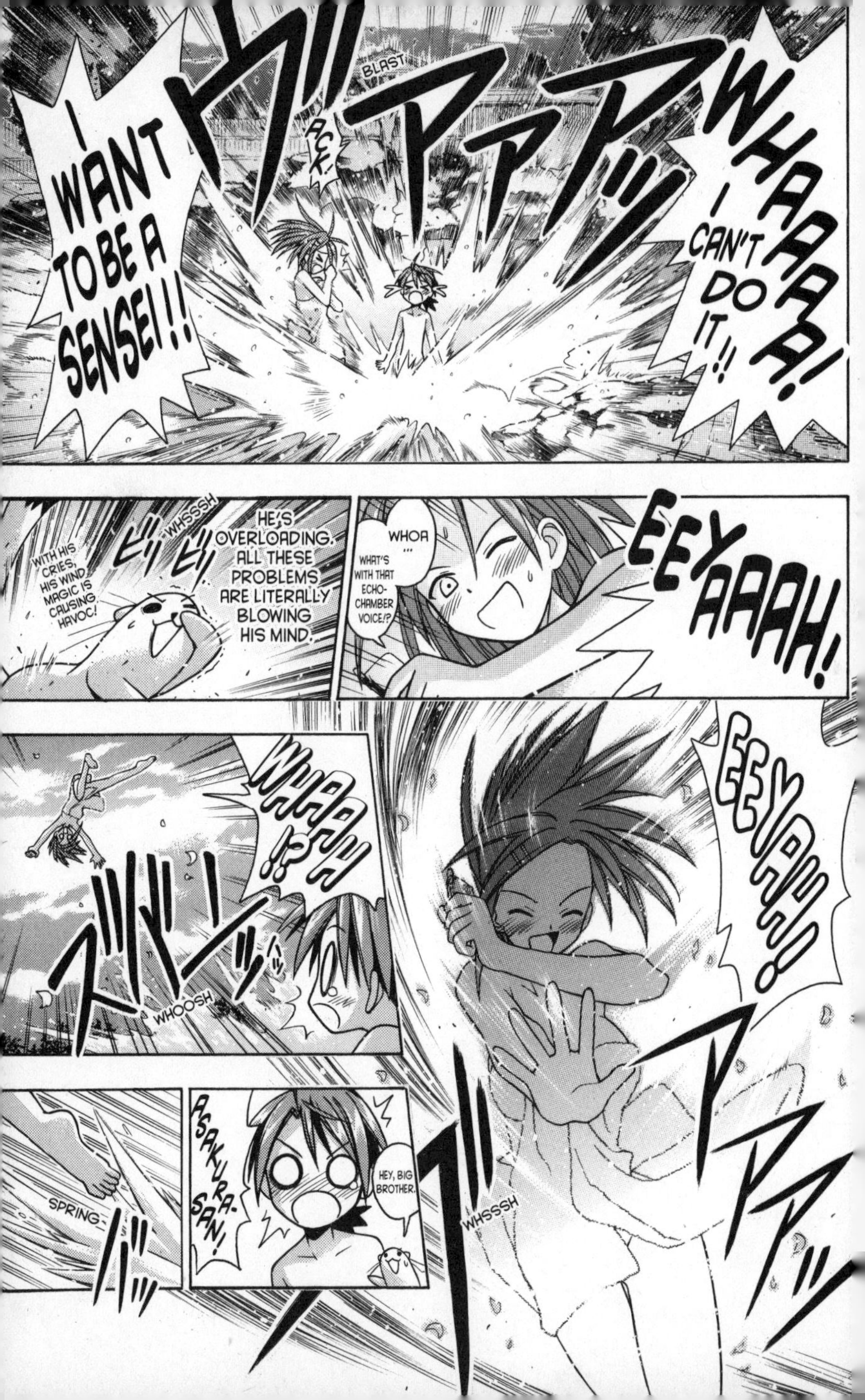
WHAAAA!
I CAN'T DO IT!!
BLAST
ACK!
I WANT TO BE A SENSEI!!
EEYAAAH!
WHOA...
WHAT'S WITH THAT ECHO-CHAMBER VOICE!?
WHSSSH
HE'S OVERLOADING. ALL THESE PROBLEMS ARE LITERALLY BLOWING HIS MIND.
WITH HIS CRIES, HIS WIND MAGIC IS CAUSING HAVOC!
WHOOSH
WHSSSH
HEY, BIG BROTHER.
ASAKURA-SAN!
SPRING

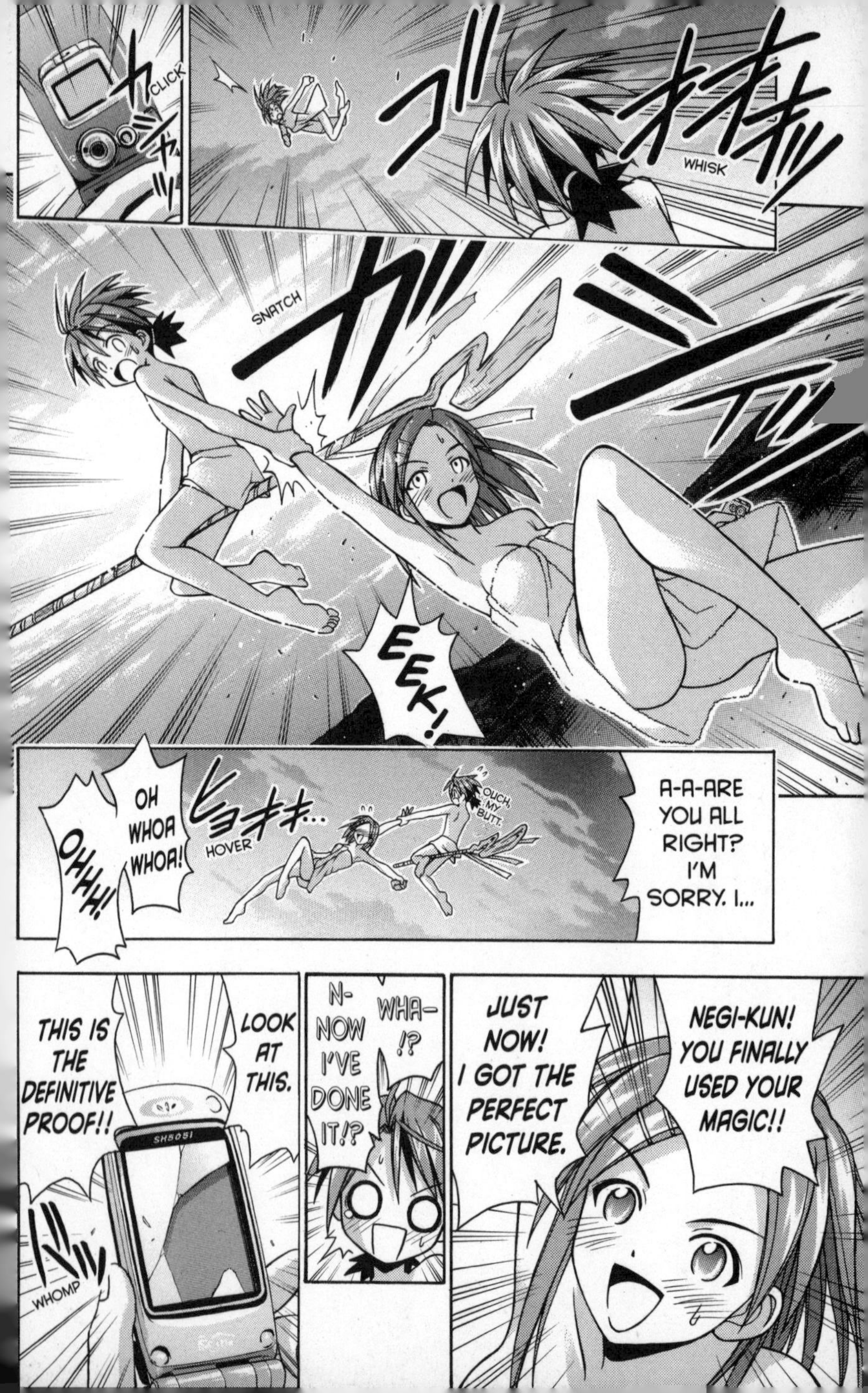
WHISK
CLICK
SNATCH
EEK!
A-A-ARE YOU ALL RIGHT? I'M SORRY. I...
OUCH, MY BUTT.
HOVER
OH WHOA WHOA!
OHHH!
NEGI-KUN! YOU FINALLY USED YOUR MAGIC!!
JUST NOW! I GOT THE PERFECT PICTURE.
WHA- !?
N-NOW I'VE DONE IT!?
LOOK AT THIS.
THIS IS THE DEFINITIVE PROOF!!
SH505I
WHOMP

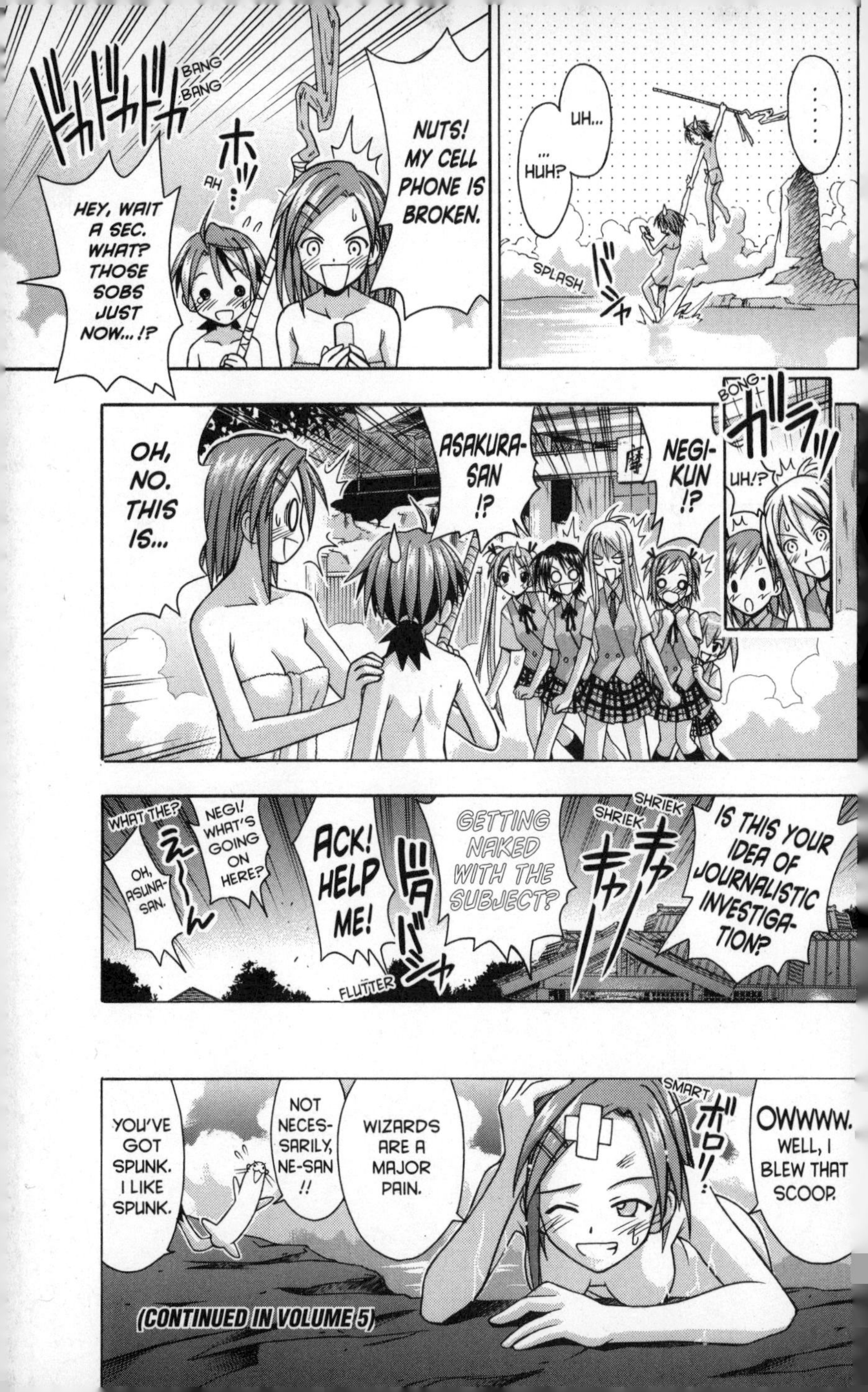

......
UH...
... HUH?
SPLASH
NUTS! MY CELL PHONE IS BROKEN.
AH
HEY, WAIT A SEC. WHAT? THOSE SOBS JUST NOW...!?
BANG BANG
BONG-
UH!?
NEGI-KUN !?
ASAKURA-SAN !?
OH, NO. THIS IS...
IS THIS YOUR IDEA OF JOURNALISTIC INVESTIGA-TION?
SHRIEK SHRIEK
GETTING NAKED WITH THE SUBJECT?
ACK! HELP ME!
FLUTTER
NEGI! WHAT'S GOING ON HERE?
WHAT THE?
OH, ASUNA-SAN.
SMART
OWWWW. WELL, I BLEW THAT SCOOP.
WIZARDS ARE A MAJOR PAIN.
NOT NECES-SARILY, NE-SAN !!
YOU'VE GOT SPUNK. I LIKE SPUNK.
(CONTINUED IN VOLUME 5)

– STAFF –

Ken Akamatsu
Takashi Takemoto
Kenichi Nakamura
Masaki Ohyama
Keiichi Yamashita
Chigusa Amagasaki
Takaaki Miyahara

Thanks To

Ran Ayanaga

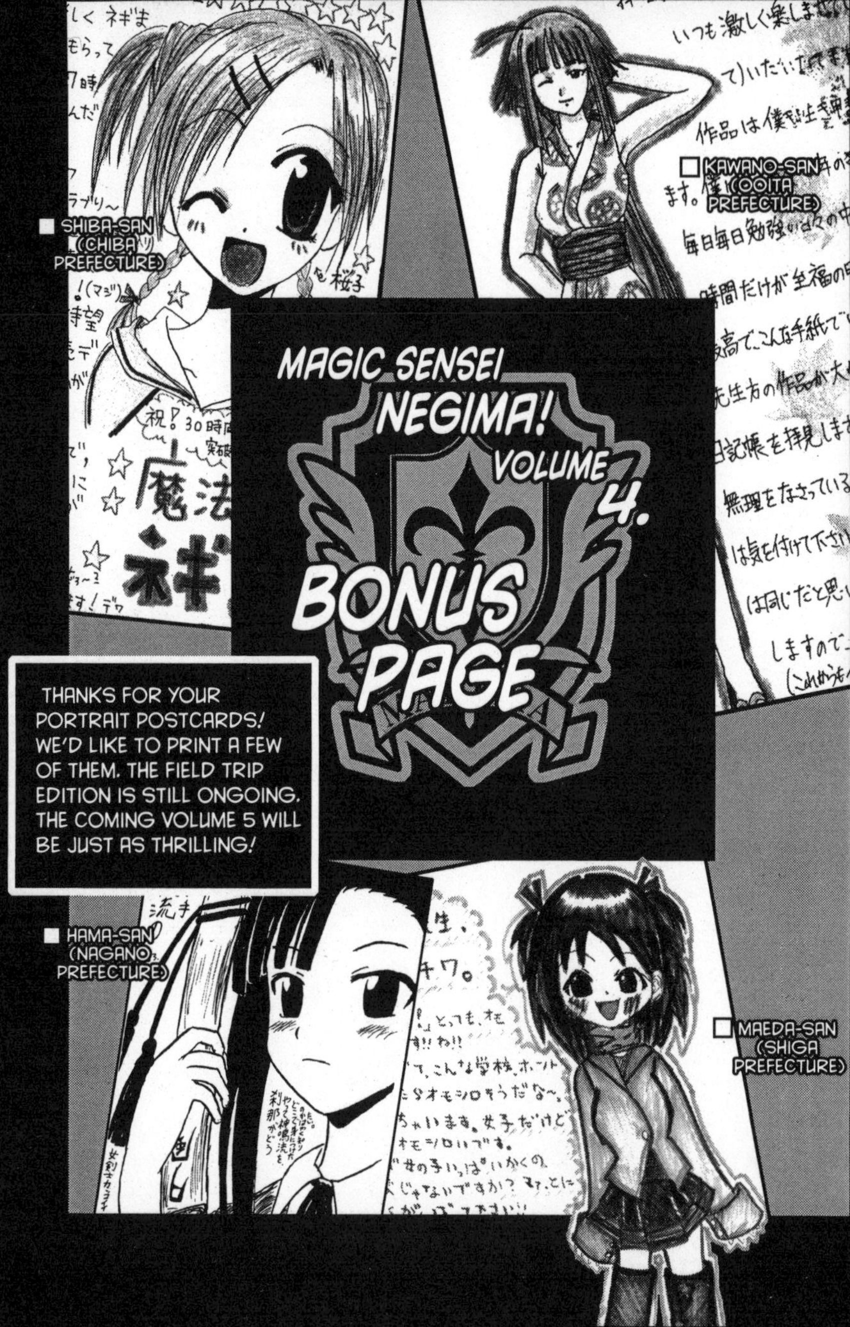
MAGIC SENSEI NEGIMA! VOLUME 4.
BONUS PAGE
THANKS FOR YOUR PORTRAIT POSTCARDS! WE'D LIKE TO PRINT A FEW OF THEM. THE FIELD TRIP EDITION IS STILL ONGOING. THE COMING VOLUME 5 WILL BE JUST AS THRILLING!
SHIBA-SAN (CHIBA PREFECTURE)
KAWANO-SAN (OOITA PREFECTURE)
HAMA-SAN (NAGANO PREFECTURE)
MAEDA-SAN (SHIGA PREFECTURE)

COMPILATION OF MATERIAL FOR THE BEGINNING SETTINGS OF *NEGIMA!*

THE ORIGINAL CHARACTER SKETCHES

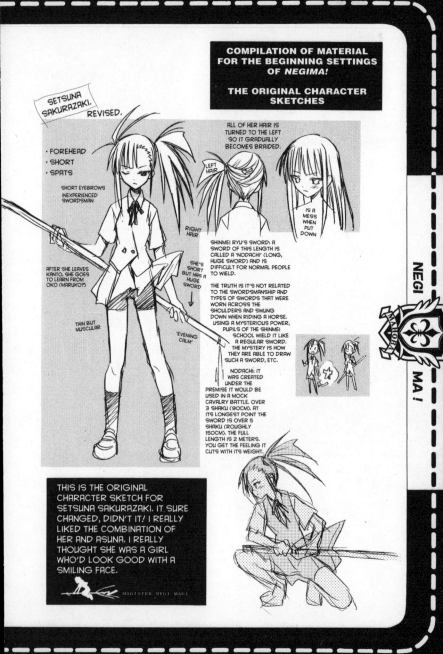

SETSUNA SAKURAZAKI.
REVISED.
ALL OF HER HAIR IS TURNED TO THE LEFT SO IT GRADUALLY BECOMES BRAIDED.
• FOREHEAD
• SHORT
• SPATS
SHORT EYEBROWS
INEXPERIENCED SWORDSMAN
LEFT HAIR
IS A MESS WHEN PUT DOWN
RIGHT HAIR
AFTER SHE LEAVES KANTO, SHE GOES TO LEARN FROM OKO (MARUKO?)
SHE'S SHORT BUT HAS A HUGE SWORD
THIN BUT MUSCULAR
'EVENING CALM'

SHINMEI RYU'S SWORD: A SWORD OF THIS LENGTH IS CALLED A 'NODACHI' (LONG, HUGE SWORD) AND IS DIFFICULT FOR NORMAL PEOPLE TO WIELD.

THE TRUTH IS IT'S NOT RELATED TO THE SWORDSMANSHIP AND TYPES OF SWORDS THAT WERE WORN ACROSS THE SHOULDERS AND SWUNG DOWN WHEN RIDING A HORSE. USING A MYSTERIOUS POWER, PUPILS OF THE SHINMEI SCHOOL WIELD IT LIKE A REGULAR SWORD. THE MYSTERY IS HOW THEY ARE ABLE TO DRAW SUCH A SWORD, ETC.

NODACHI: IT WAS CREATED UNDER THE PREMISE IT WOULD BE USED IN A MOCK CAVALRY BATTLE. OVER 3 SHAKU (90CM). AT ITS LONGEST POINT THE SWORD IS OVER 5 SHAKU (ROUGHLY 150CM). THE FULL LENGTH IS 2 METERS. YOU GET THE FEELING IT CUTS WITH ITS WEIGHT.

THIS IS THE ORIGINAL CHARACTER SKETCH FOR SETSUNA SAKURAZAKI. IT SURE CHANGED, DIDN'T IT! I REALLY LIKED THE COMBINATION OF HER AND ASUNA. I REALLY THOUGHT SHE WAS A GIRL WHO'D LOOK GOOD WITH A SMILING FACE.

MAGISTER NEGI MAGI

NEGI MA!

THIS IS SOME SORTA WEIRD SKETCH. →
WITHOUT A DOUBT THAT THIS IS A FIRST SKETCH (HA HA).
THERE'S A GOOD FEELING WITH THE COMBINATION OF ASAKURA AND CHAMO.

-AKAMATSU

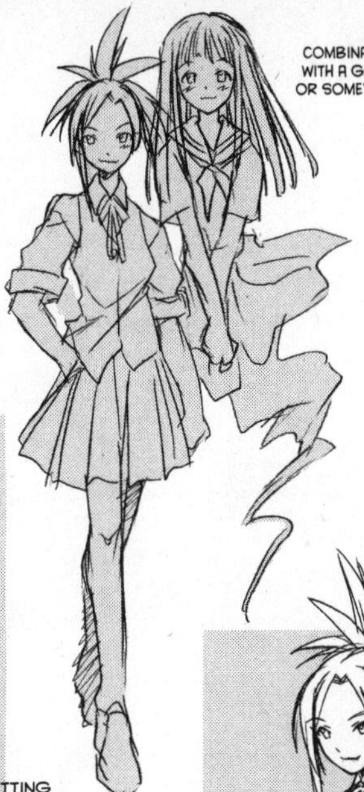
COMBINATION WITH A GHOST OR SOMETHING.

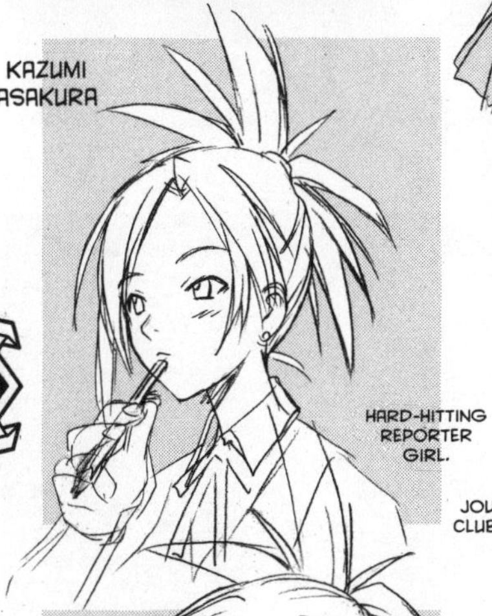
KAZUMI ASAKURA
HARD-HITTING REPORTER GIRL.
JOURNALISM CLUB MEMBER

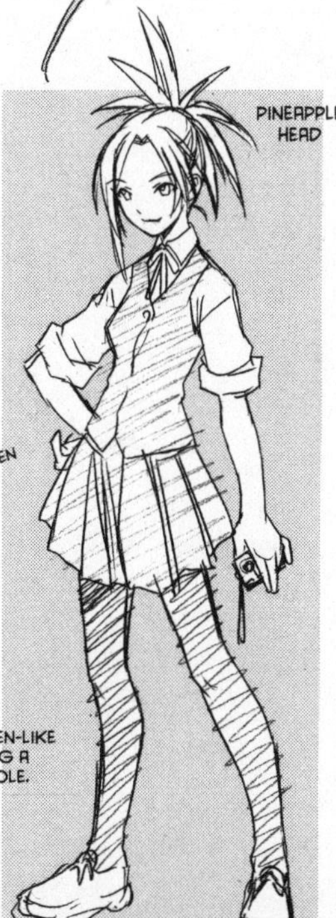
PINEAPPLE HEAD
AN ACTIVE VIXEN
A VILLAIN
KANSAI DIALECT?
LOVE PRINCESS, VIXEN-LIKE CHAIRMAN PLAYING A PROGRESSIVE ROLE.

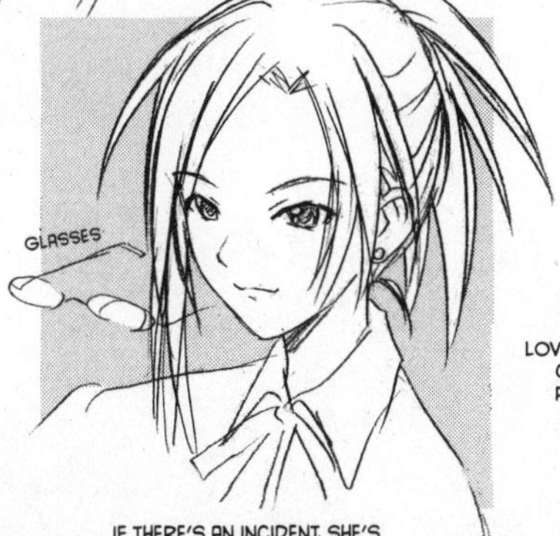
GLASSES
IF THERE'S AN INCIDENT, SHE'S ALWAYS INVOLVED.

NEGIMA! FASHION CONCEPTS

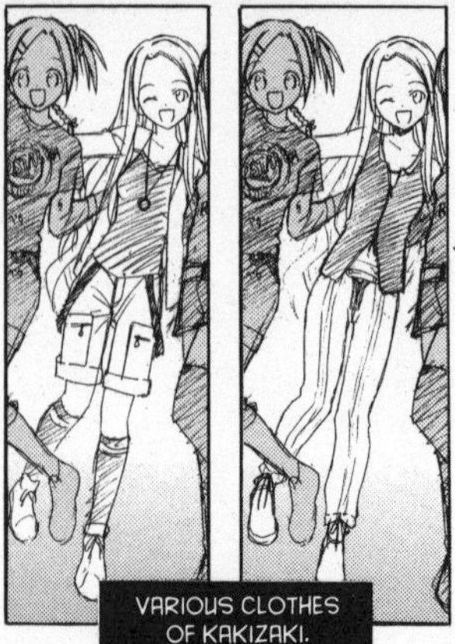

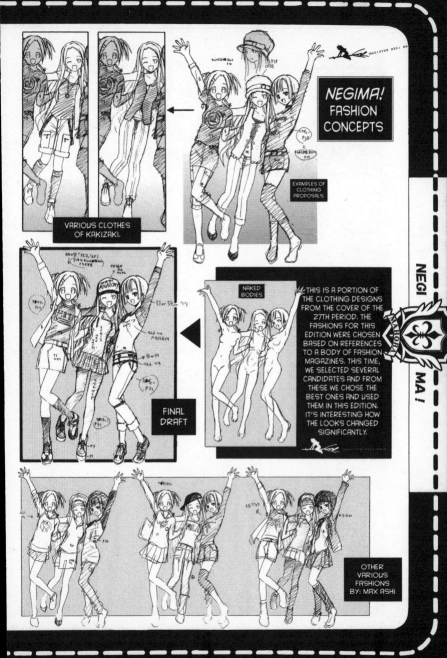

VARIOUS CLOTHES OF KAKIZAKI.

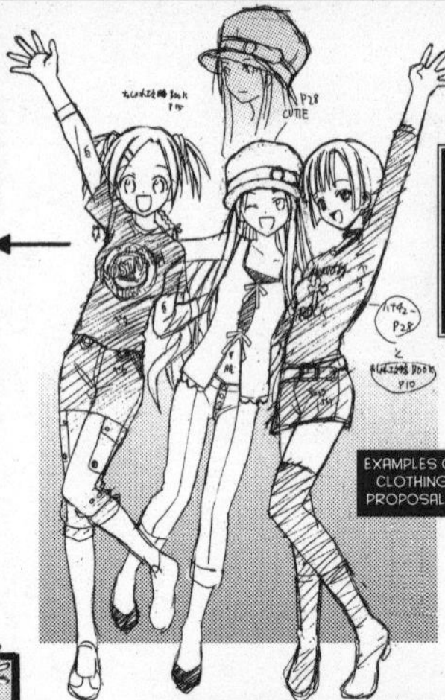

EXAMPLES OF CLOTHING PROPOSALS.

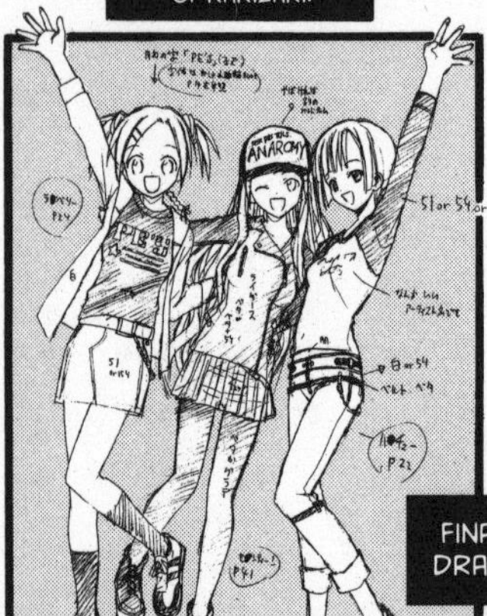
ANARCHY

FINAL DRAFT

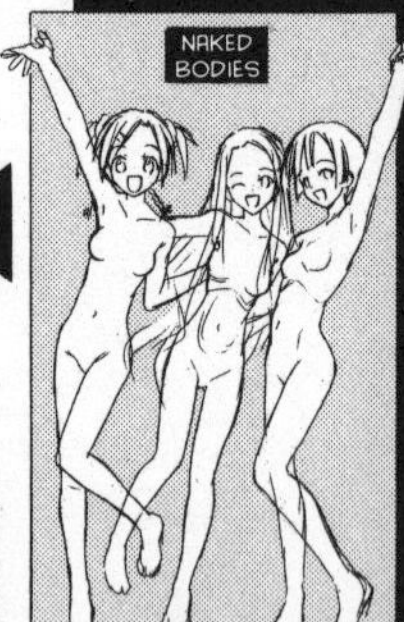

NAKED BODIES

THIS IS A PORTION OF THE CLOTHING DESIGNS FROM THE COVER OF THE 27TH PERIOD. THE FASHIONS FOR THIS EDITION WERE CHOSEN BASED ON REFERENCES TO A BODY OF FASHION MAGAZINES. THIS TIME, WE SELECTED SEVERAL CANDIDATES AND FROM THESE WE CHOSE THE BEST ONES AND USED THEM IN THIS EDITION. IT'S INTERESTING HOW THE LOOKS CHANGED SIGNIFICANTLY.

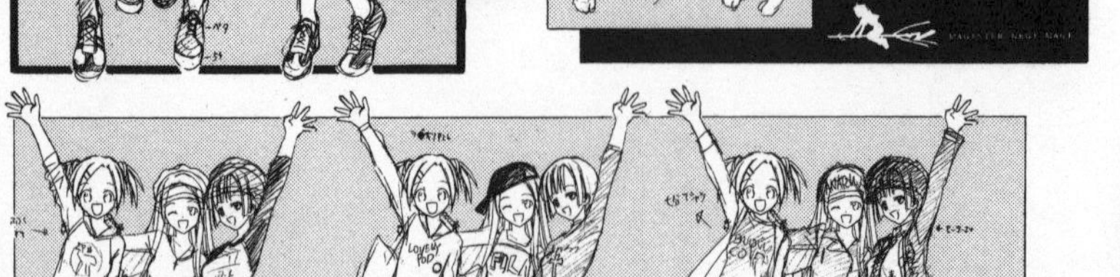

OTHER VARIOUS FASHIONS BY: MAX ASHI

LEXICON
NEGIMARIUM DE CANTU
Negima! Glossary Of Spells

Thirty-first and Thirty-second Periods

Telepathia. (Telepathic Communication.) Telepathia comes from the Greek and means here "a remotely distant sensitivity." Wizards and their partners are able to use their card's power to communicate. However, Negi and Asuna couldn't communicate with each other both ways. It appears that two-way communication needs to have some sort of additional requirement filled.

Flet, une vente. Flans saltatio pulverea. (Blow! Gust of Wind! Wind Flower! Wind And Dirt, Dance Wildly!) Magic that causes a powerful wind. "Dance of wind blown dirt."

Exerceas potentiam Cagurazaca Asuna.(Abilities Activate, Asuna Kagurazaka.) With the establishment of a contract, the wizard's partner gains strength in both body and mind. Depending on each one's unique destiny, they receive different benefits and powers. *Potentia* indicates the powers (related to that, the overt powers are referred to as "*vis*"). The folding fan that Asuna was given is one of those powers.

Ensis exorcizans.(Evil Destroying Sword.) As per the contract, this is the exclusive tool given to Negi's partner, Asuna Kagurazaka. *Exorcizans* means "exorcise magic" and *ensis* is a long sword. In short, "Evil Destroying Sword" can also be called a "Magic Destroying Sword." However, for some reason, Asuna's tool is a folding fan. Additionally, Negi refers to this exclusive item as an artifact, which comes from the Latin, *artifactum,* something made by a skilled craftsman.

Thirty-fourth Period

Flans paries aerialis.(Wind Flower! Wall of Wind!) It's common for wizards to protect themselves from physical harm by surrounding the area around themselves with a magic barrier (refer to the Evangeline story in the Twenty-fourth and Twenty-fifth Periods in *Negima!* Volume 3). In the First Period, Negi also did this when he made the blackboard eraser that was going to fall on his head float in the air. However, it is necessary for Negi (who learned an important lesson when Asuna found out about his magic this way) to recite the spell over again in order to disperse it and not surround himself with the barrier in everyday life.

GRANDAUGHTER OF SCHOOL DEAN

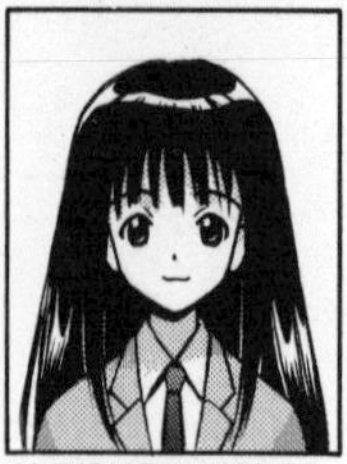

13. KONOKA KONOE

SECRETARY
FORTUNE-TELLING CLUB
LIBRARY CLUB

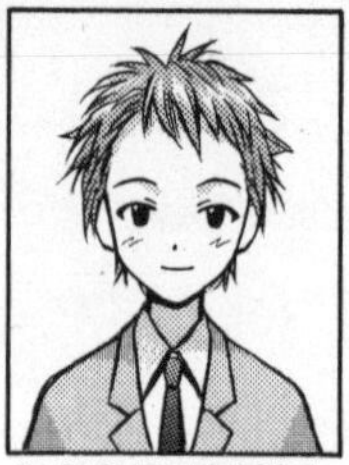

9. KASUGA MISORA

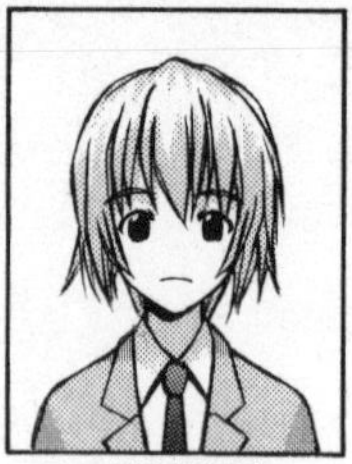

5. AKO IZUMI

NURSE'S OFFICE
SOCCER TEAM
(NON-SCHOOL ACTIVITY)

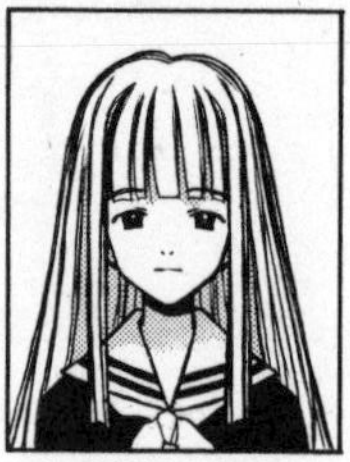

1. SAYO AIZAKA

1940~
DON'T CHANGE HER SEATING

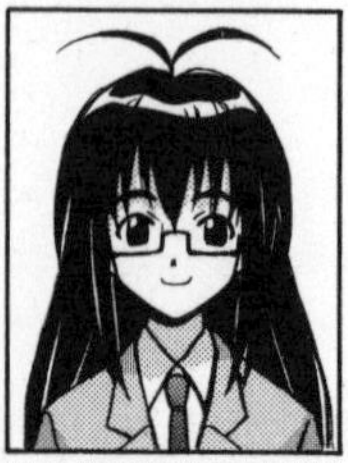

14. HARUNA SAOTOME

MANGA CLUB
LIBRARY CLUB

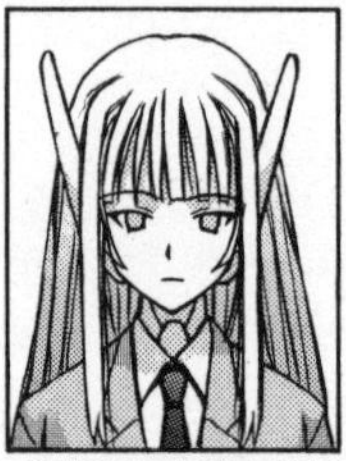

10. CHACHAMARU RAKUSO

TEA CEREMONY CLUB
GO CLUB

CALL ENGINEERING (ext. A08-7796) IN CASE OF EMERGENCY

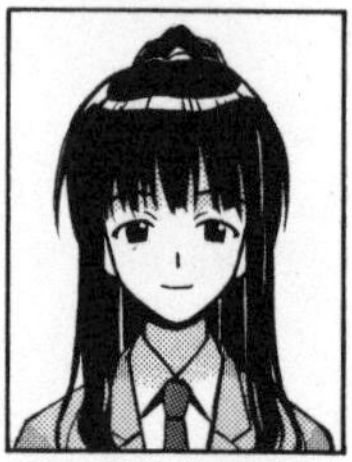

6. AKIRA OKOCHI

SWIM TEAM

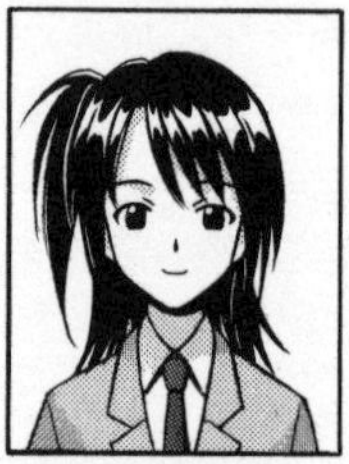

2. YUNA AKASHI

BASKETBALL TEAM

PROFESSOR AKASHI'S DAUGHTER

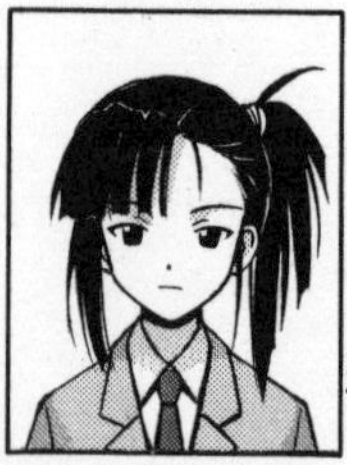

SETSUNA SAKURAZAKI

15 SETSUNA SAKURAZAKI

JAPANESE FENCING

KYOTO SHINMEI STYLE

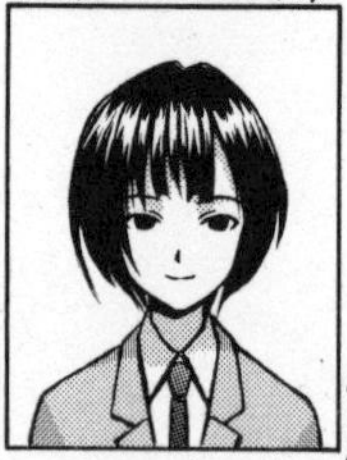

MADOKA

11. MADOKA KUGIMIYA

CHEERLEADER

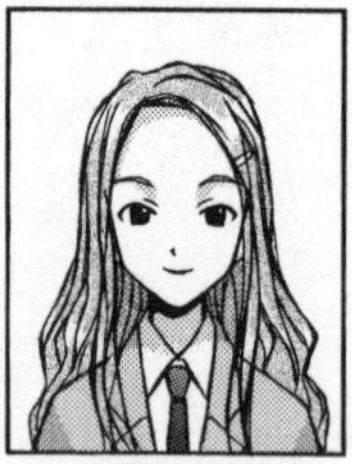

7. KAKIZAKI MISA

CHEERLEADER
CHORUS

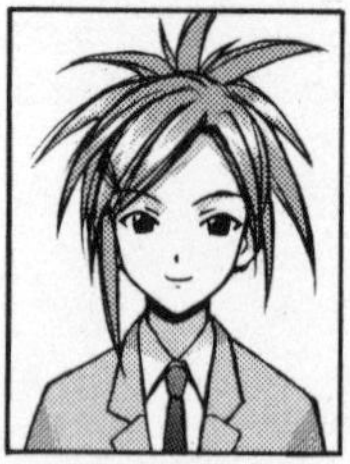

3. KAZUMI ASAKURA

SCHOOL NEWSPAPER

MAHORA NEWS (ext. 809-3780)

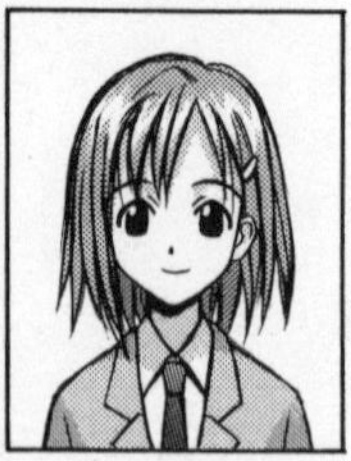

16. MAKIE SASAKI

GYMNASTICS

FEI KU

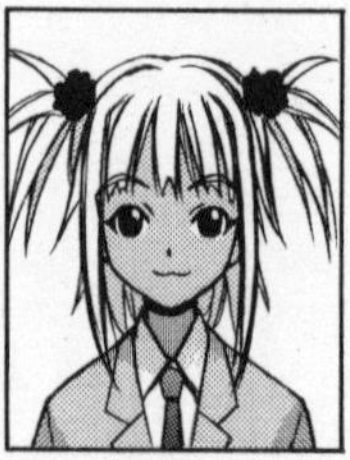

12. FEI KU

CHINESE MARTIAL ARTS
GROUP

A GOOD PERSON JUST AS I THOUGHT

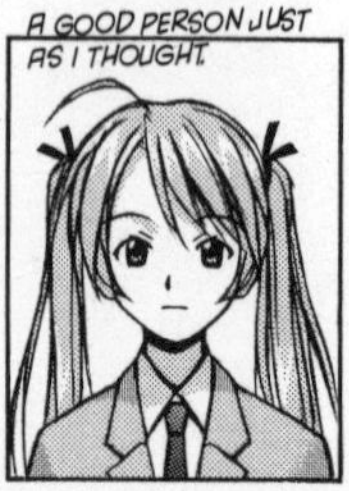

8. ASUNA KAGURAZAKA

ART CLUB

HAS A TERRIBLE KICK

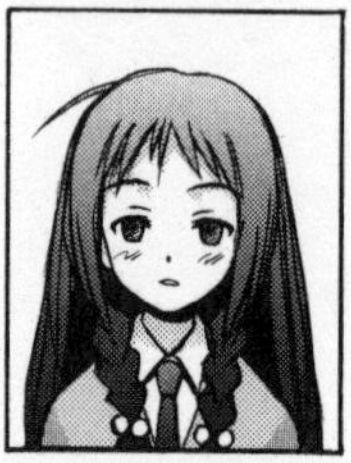

4. YUE AYASE

KID'S LIT CLUB
PHILOSOPHY CLUB
LIBRARY CLUB

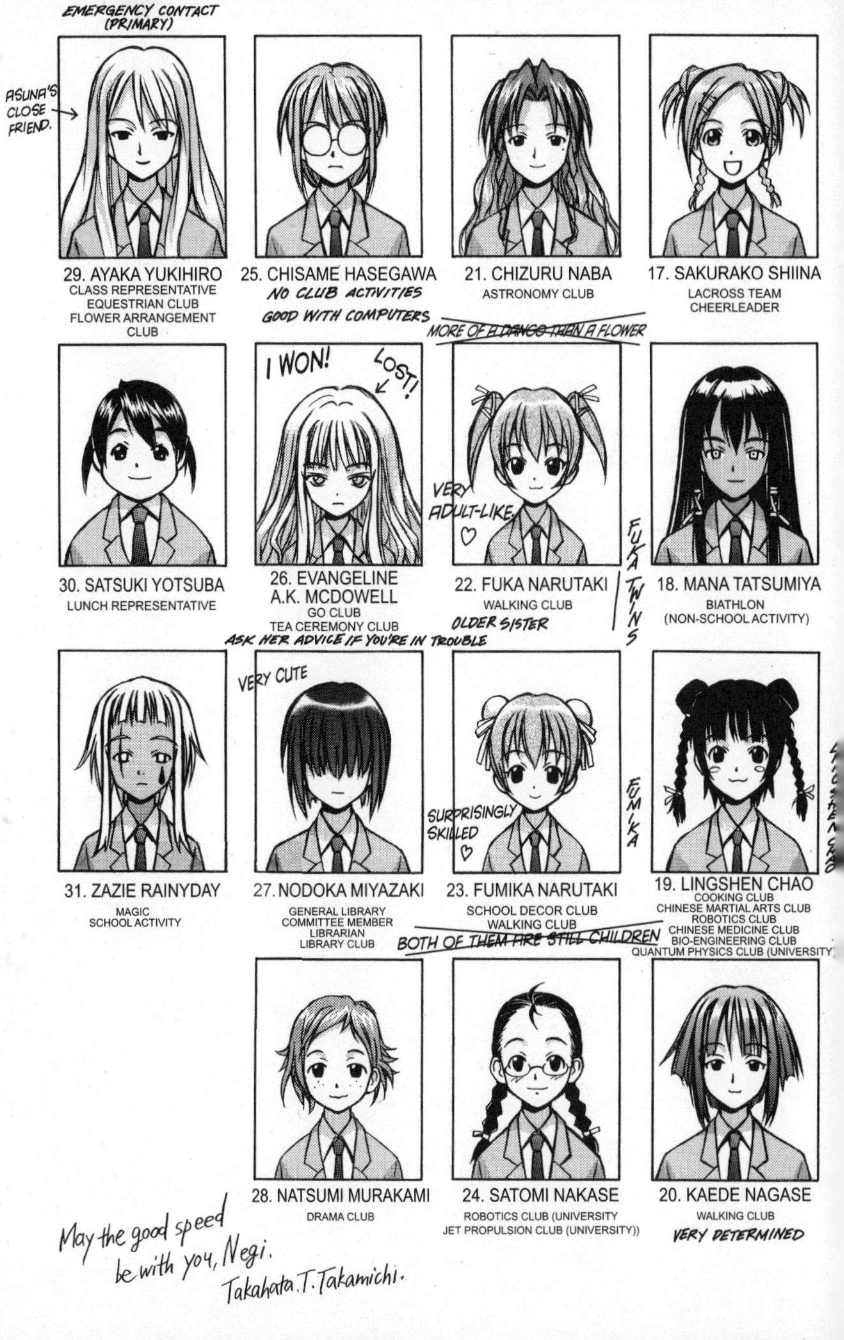
EMERGENCY CONTACT (PRIMARY)
ASUNA'S CLOSE FRIEND.
29. AYAKA YUKIHIRO
CLASS REPRESENTATIVE
EQUESTRIAN CLUB
FLOWER ARRANGEMENT CLUB
25. CHISAME HASEGAWA
NO CLUB ACTIVITIES
GOOD WITH COMPUTERS
21. CHIZURU NABA
ASTRONOMY CLUB
MORE OF A DANGO THAN A FLOWER
17. SAKURAKO SHIINA
LACROSS TEAM
CHEERLEADER
30. SATSUKI YOTSUBA
LUNCH REPRESENTATIVE
I WON!
LOST!
26. EVANGELINE A.K. MCDOWELL
GO CLUB
TEA CEREMONY CLUB
ASK HER ADVICE IF YOU'RE IN TROUBLE
VERY ADULT-LIKE ♡
22. FUKA NARUTAKI
WALKING CLUB
OLDER SISTER
FUKA TWINS
18. MANA TATSUMIYA
BIATHLON
(NON-SCHOOL ACTIVITY)
31. ZAZIE RAINYDAY
MAGIC
SCHOOL ACTIVITY
VERY CUTE
27. NODOKA MIYAZAKI
GENERAL LIBRARY
COMMITTEE MEMBER
LIBRARIAN
LIBRARY CLUB
SURPRISINGLY SKILLED ♡
FUMIKA
23. FUMIKA NARUTAKI
SCHOOL DECOR CLUB
WALKING CLUB
BOTH OF THEM ARE STILL CHILDREN
19. LINGSHEN CHAO
COOKING CLUB
CHINESE MARTIAL ARTS CLUB
ROBOTICS CLUB
CHINESE MEDICINE CLUB
BIO-ENGINEERING CLUB
QUANTUM PHYSICS CLUB (UNIVERSITY)
28. NATSUMI MURAKAMI
DRAMA CLUB
24. SATOMI NAKASE
ROBOTICS CLUB (UNIVERSITY
JET PROPULSION CLUB (UNIVERSITY))
20. KAEDE NAGASE
WALKING CLUB
VERY DETERMINED
May the good speed be with you, Negi.
Takahata.T.Takamichi.

About the Creator

Negima! is only Ken Akamatsu's third manga, although he started working in the field in 1994 with *AI Ga Tomaranai*. Like all of Akamatsu's work to date, it was published in Kodansha's *Shonen Magazine*. *AI Ga Tomaranai* ran for five years before concluding in 1999. In 1998, however, Akamatsu began the work that would make him one of the most popular manga artists in Japan: *Love Hina*. *Love Hina* ran for four years, and before its conclusion in 2002, it would cause Akamatsu to be granted the prestigious Manga of the Year award from Kodansha, as well as going on to become one of the best-selling manga in the United Kingdom.

Translation Notes

Japanese is a tricky language for most Westerners, and translation is often more art than science. For your edification and reading pleasure, here are notes on some of the places where we could have gone in a different direction in our translation of the work, or where a Japanese cultural reference is used.

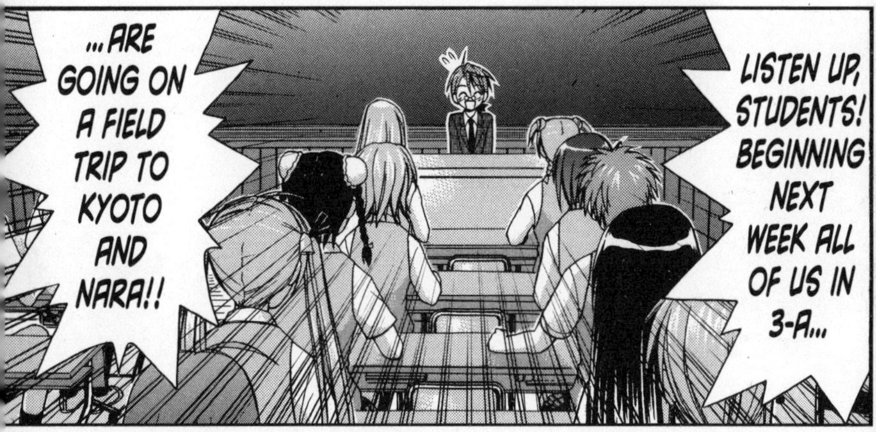
LISTEN UP, STUDENTS! BEGINNING NEXT WEEK ALL OF US IN 3-A...
...ARE GOING ON A FIELD TRIP TO KYOTO AND NARA!!

Kyoto and Nara, page 9

Kyoto was Japan's capital and the emperor's home from 794 until 1868. It is rich in historical sites and buildings – so much so that the city was specifically avoided by American air raids during World War II. Like Kyoto, Nara has historical significance to the Japanese. It was the location of the country's first permanent capital in the year 710. It features some of Japan's oldest Buddhist temples and is about an hour from Kyoto.

Kansai, page 11

Kansai is the area of Japan that encompasses Osaka, Kobe, and the surrounding area. Japan is officially divided into the following eight regions: Hokkaido, Tohoku, Kanto, Chubu, Kansai (also known as Kinki), Chugoku, Shikoku, and Kyushu.

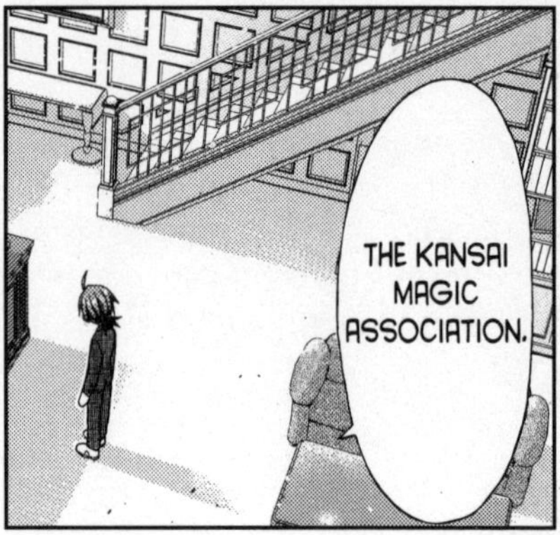
THE KANSAI MAGIC ASSOCIATION.

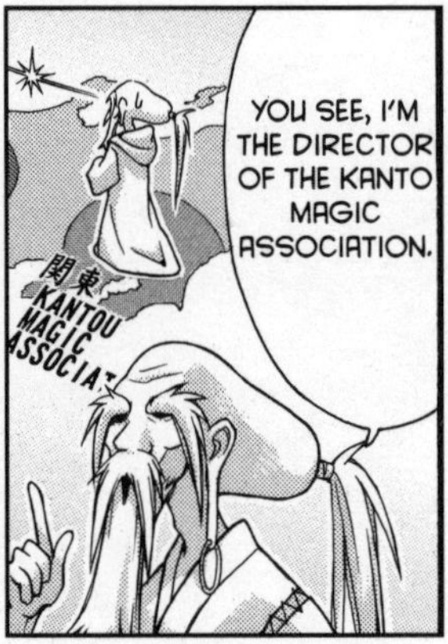
YOU SEE, I'M THE DIRECTOR OF THE KANTO MAGIC ASSOCIATION.
関東
KANTOU MAGIC ASSOCIAT

Kanto, page 11

The Kanto region encompasses Tokyo and the surrounding area.

Matsuya, page 22

Matsuya is a fast-food beef bowl restaurant, very similar to Yoshinoya, which has franchises across Japan and California.

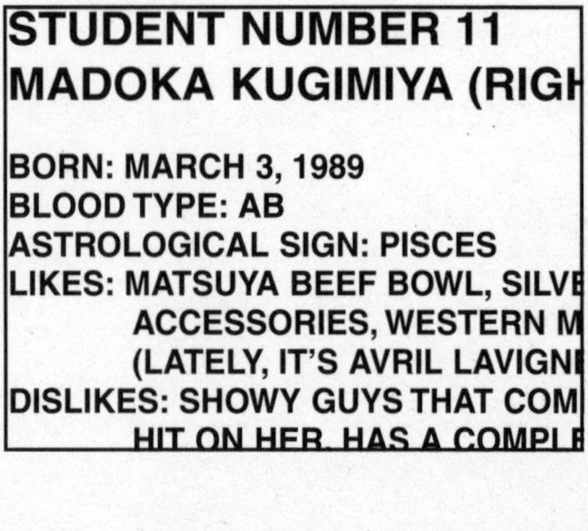
STUDENT NUMBER 11
MADOKA KUGIMIYA (RIGH

BORN: MARCH 3, 1989
BLOOD TYPE: AB
ASTROLOGICAL SIGN: PISCES
LIKES: MATSUYA BEEF BOWL, SILVE
ACCESSORIES, WESTERN M
(LATELY, IT'S AVRIL LAVIGNE
DISLIKES: SHOWY GUYS THAT COM
HIT ON HER. HAS A COMPLE

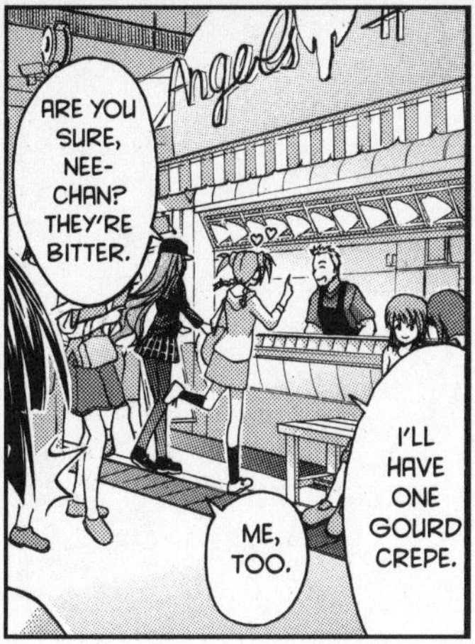
I'LL HAVE ONE GOURD CREPE.
ME, TOO.
ARE YOU SURE, NEE-CHAN? THEY'RE BITTER.

Gouya, page 25

Crepe stands are popular and very common across Japan. When you order a crepe, it is folded and placed in a cardboard cone, making it look a lot like an ice cream cone. Often, the crepe is filled with ice cream, fruit, or some other sweet concoction. In the Japanese text, Sakurako is asking for a *gouya* crepe. *Gouya* is a type of bitter-tasting gourd.

Harajuku, page 27

Harajuku is a part of Tokyo where the trendiest shops are and many young people come to hang out.

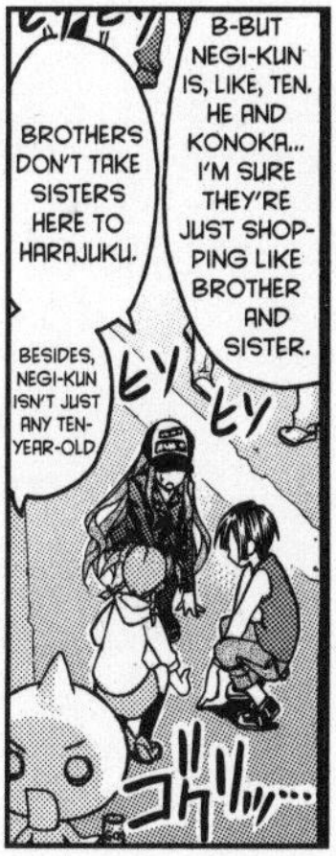
B-BUT NEGI-KUN IS, LIKE, TEN. HE AND KONOKA... I'M SURE THEY'RE JUST SHOP-PING LIKE BROTHER AND SISTER.
BROTHERS DON'T TAKE SISTERS HERE TO HARAJUKU.
BESIDES, NEGI-KUN ISN'T JUST ANY TEN-YEAR-OLD.

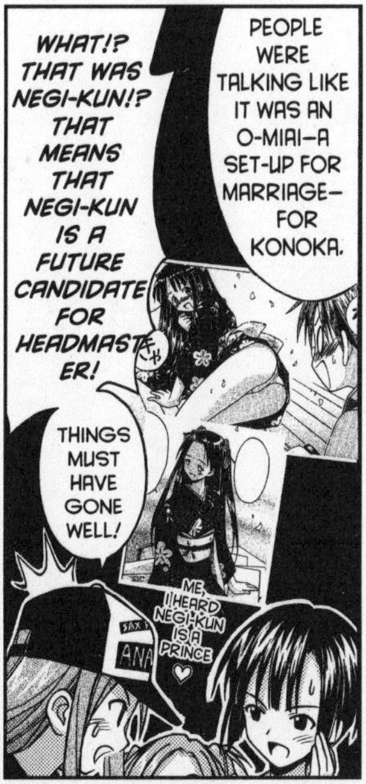
PEOPLE WERE TALKING LIKE IT WAS AN O-MIAI—A SET-UP FOR MARRIAGE—FOR KONOKA.
WHAT!? THAT WAS NEGI-KUN!? THAT MEANS THAT NEGI-KUN IS A FUTURE CANDIDATE FOR HEADMAST-ER!
THINGS MUST HAVE GONE WELL!
ME, I HEARD NEGI-KUN IS A PRINCE

O-miai, page 31

An *O-miai* is a date set up usually by one's parents, where information about each person is exchanged. Somewhat like a blind date, it leads ideally to marriage. *O-miai* are becoming less popular in Japan as people seek to find their own partners. However, they are still used for people who for one reason or another have trouble finding a mate.

Ryokan, page 46

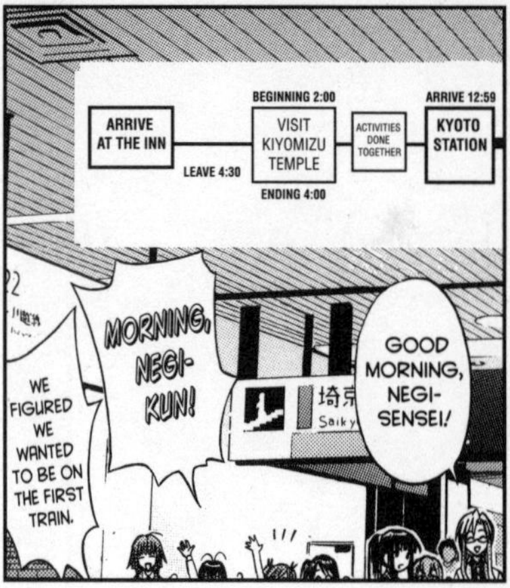
ARRIVE 12:59
KYOTO STATION
ACTIVITIES DONE TOGETHER
BEGINNING 2:00
VISIT KIYOMIZU TEMPLE
ENDING 4:00
LEAVE 4:30
ARRIVE AT THE INN
GOOD MORNING, NEGI-SENSEI!
MORNING, NEGI-KUN!
WE FIGURED WE WANTED TO BE ON THE FIRST TRAIN.

The Japanese text says that the students are going to visit a *ryokan*, but we decided to just call it an inn. A *ryokan* is a traditional family inn. Guests stay in traditional Japanese-style rooms with tatami floor and a *kutatsu* (low table), and sleep on futons.

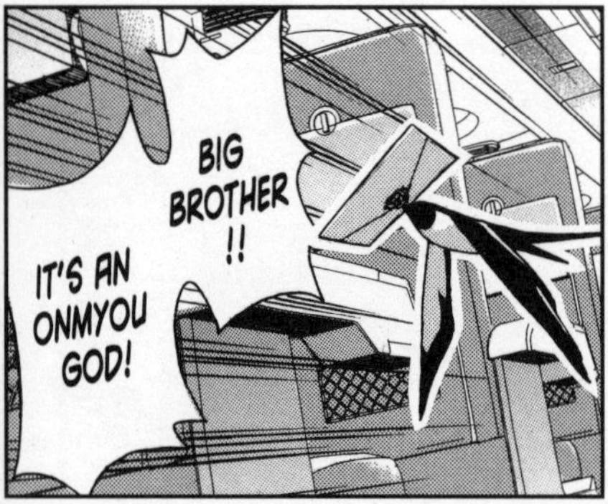
BIG BROTHER !!
IT'S AN ONMYOU GOD!

Onmyou, page 58

Onmyou or *Onyou* is the way of yin and yang, an occult divination system based on the Taoist theory of the five elements. Shinmei Ryu appears to be a mythical character that was an expert in the way of *Onyou*. *Onmyouji* were sorcerers who served as mediators between humans and gods in ancient Japan. For a superficial look, check out the 2001 movie *Onmyouji*.

Gokiburi, page 97

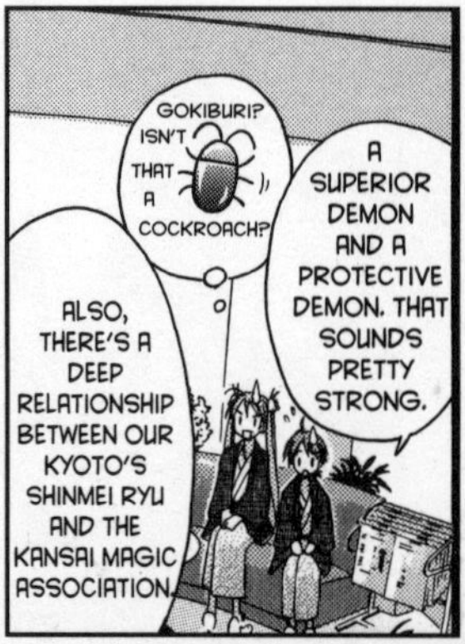
A SUPERIOR DEMON AND A PROTECTIVE DEMON. THAT SOUNDS PRETTY STRONG.
GOKIBURI? ISN'T THAT A COCKROACH?
ALSO, THERE'S A DEEP RELATIONSHIP BETWEEN OUR KYOTO'S SHINMEI RYU AND THE KANSAI MAGIC ASSOCIATION.

While a *goki* is a protective demon, a *gokiburi* is a cockroach. It's a play on words that loses its effect when it's not in Japanese. If we were to try the same thing in English, we'd have to call the demon a . . . um . . . forget we said anything.

Preview of Volume 5

Here is an excerpt from Volume 5, on sale in English now.

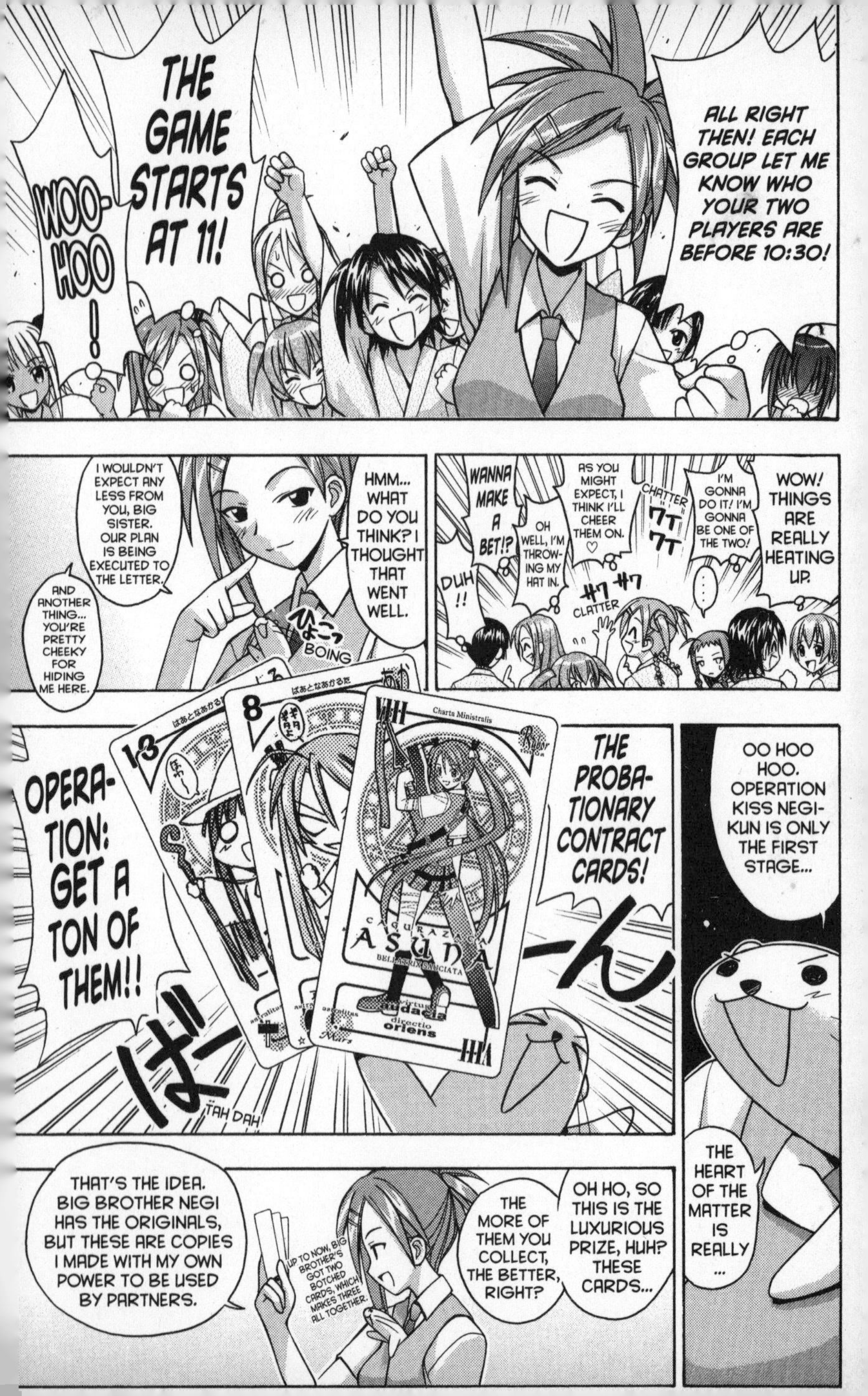

ALL RIGHT THEN! EACH GROUP LET ME KNOW WHO YOUR TWO PLAYERS ARE BEFORE 10:30!
THE GAME STARTS AT 11!
WOO-HOO!
WOW! THINGS ARE REALLY HEATING UP.
I'M GONNA DO IT! I'M GONNA BE ONE OF THE TWO!
CHATTER
...
AS YOU MIGHT EXPECT, I THINK I'LL CHEER THEM ON. ♡
OH WELL, I'M THROWING MY HAT IN.
WANNA MAKE A BET!?
DUH!!
CLATTER
HMM... WHAT DO YOU THINK? I THOUGHT THAT WENT WELL.
I WOULDN'T EXPECT ANY LESS FROM YOU, BIG SISTER. OUR PLAN IS BEING EXECUTED TO THE LETTER.
AND ANOTHER THING... YOU'RE PRETTY CHEEKY FOR HIDING ME HERE.
BOING
OO HOO HOO. OPERATION KISS NEGI-KUN IS ONLY THE FIRST STAGE...
THE PROBATIONARY CONTRACT CARDS!
Charta Ministralis
ASUNA
BELLATRIX SAUCIATA
audacia
directio oriens
OPERATION: GET A TON OF THEM!!
TAH DAH
THE HEART OF THE MATTER IS REALLY ...
OH HO, SO THIS IS THE LUXURIOUS PRIZE, HUH? THESE CARDS...
THE MORE OF THEM YOU COLLECT, THE BETTER, RIGHT?
THAT'S THE IDEA. BIG BROTHER NEGI HAS THE ORIGINALS, BUT THESE ARE COPIES I MADE WITH MY OWN POWER TO BE USED BY PARTNERS.
UP TO NOW, BIG BROTHER'S GOT TWO BOTCHED CARDS, WHICH MAKES THREE ALL TOGETHER.

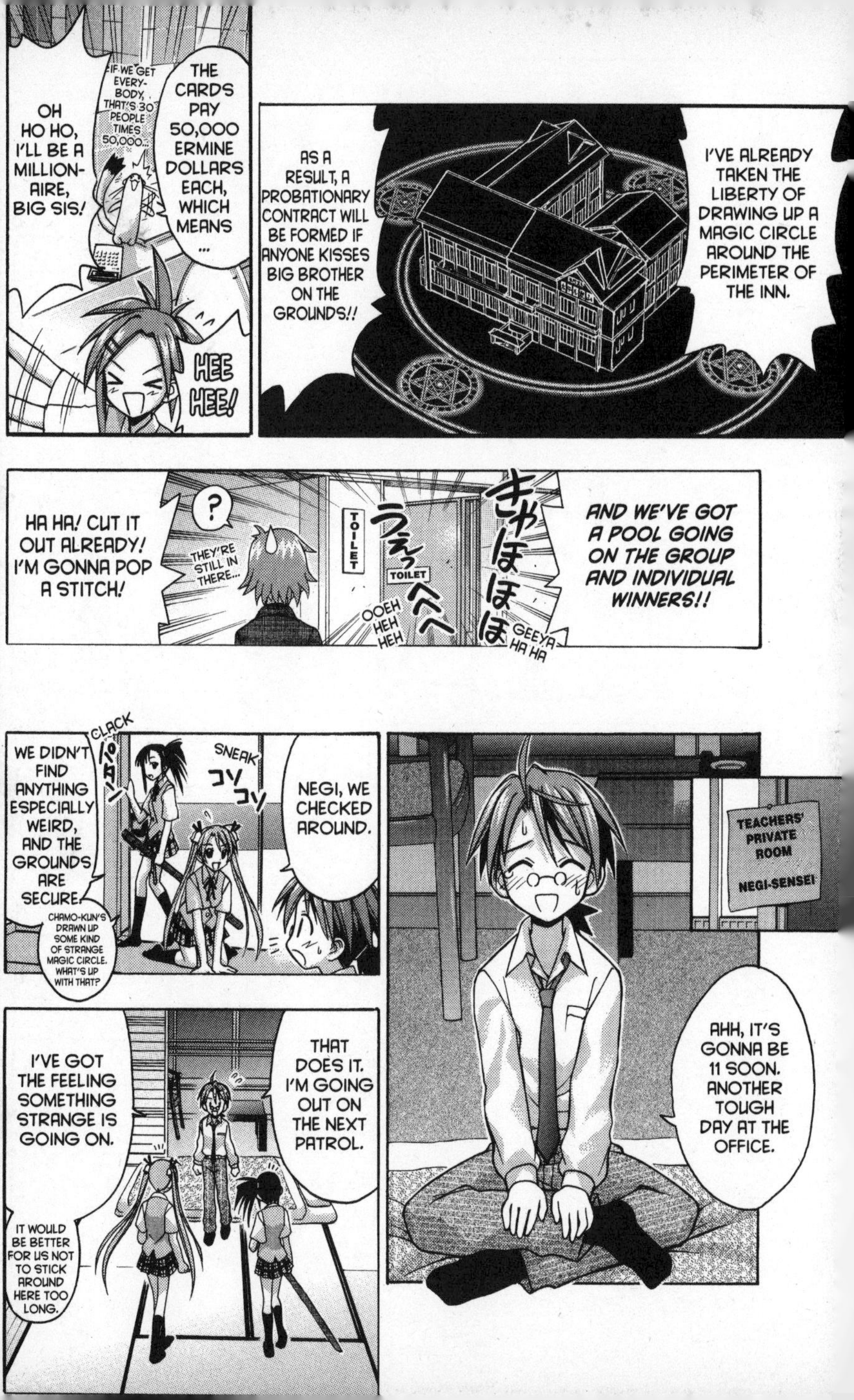
I'VE ALREADY TAKEN THE LIBERTY OF DRAWING UP A MAGIC CIRCLE AROUND THE PERIMETER OF THE INN.
AS A RESULT, A PROBATIONARY CONTRACT WILL BE FORMED IF ANYONE KISSES BIG BROTHER ON THE GROUNDS!!
THE CARDS PAY 50,000 ERMINE DOLLARS EACH, WHICH MEANS ...
IF WE GET EVERY-BODY, THAT'S 30 PEOPLE TIMES 50,000...
OH HO HO, I'LL BE A MILLION-AIRE, BIG SIS!
HEE HEE!
AND WE'VE GOT A POOL GOING ON THE GROUP AND INDIVIDUAL WINNERS!!
きゃほほほ
GEEYA HA HA
うえっへへへ
OOEH HEH HEH
TOILET
TOILET
THEY'RE STILL IN THERE...
?
HA HA! CUT IT OUT ALREADY! I'M GONNA POP A STITCH!
TEACHERS' PRIVATE ROOM NEGI-SENSEI
AHH, IT'S GONNA BE 11 SOON. ANOTHER TOUGH DAY AT THE OFFICE.
CLACK
パタン
SNEAK
コソコソ
NEGI, WE CHECKED AROUND.
WE DIDN'T FIND ANYTHING ESPECIALLY WEIRD, AND THE GROUNDS ARE SECURE.
CHAMO-KUN'S DRAWN UP SOME KIND OF STRANGE MAGIC CIRCLE. WHAT'S UP WITH THAT?
THAT DOES IT. I'M GOING OUT ON THE NEXT PATROL.
I'VE GOT THE FEELING SOMETHING STRANGE IS GOING ON.
IT WOULD BE BETTER FOR US NOT TO STICK AROUND HERE TOO LONG.

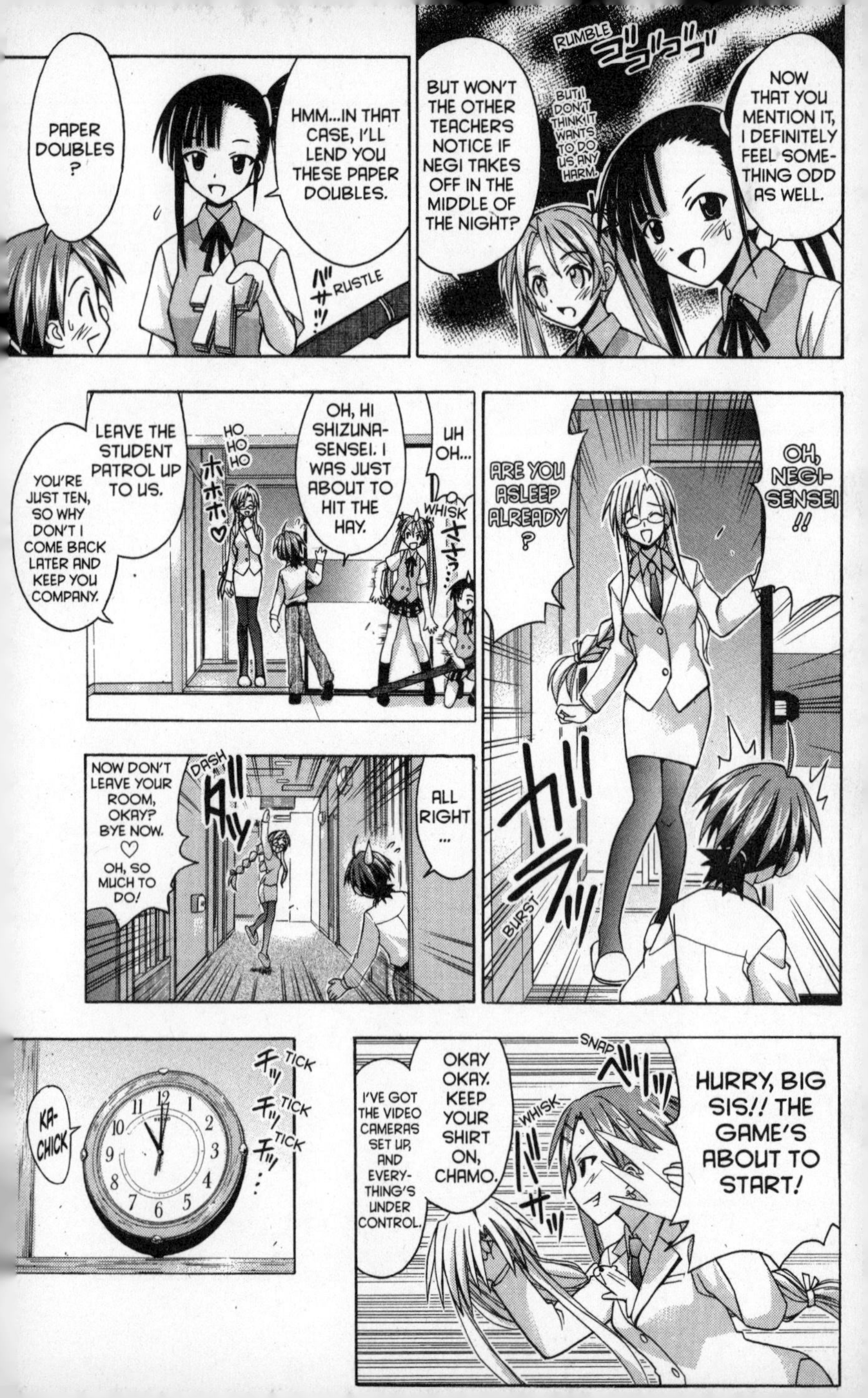

RUMBLE
NOW THAT YOU MENTION IT, I DEFINITELY FEEL SOME-THING ODD AS WELL.
BUT I DON'T THINK IT WANTS TO DO US ANY HARM.
BUT WON'T THE OTHER TEACHERS NOTICE IF NEGI TAKES OFF IN THE MIDDLE OF THE NIGHT?
HMM...IN THAT CASE, I'LL LEND YOU THESE PAPER DOUBLES.
RUSTLE
PAPER DOUBLES ?
OH, NEGI-SENSEI !!
ARE YOU ASLEEP ALREADY ?
BURST
UH OH...
WHISK
OH, HI SHIZUNA-SENSEI. I WAS JUST ABOUT TO HIT THE HAY.
HO HO HO
LEAVE THE STUDENT PATROL UP TO US.
YOU'RE JUST TEN, SO WHY DON'T I COME BACK LATER AND KEEP YOU COMPANY.
ALL RIGHT ...
DASH
NOW DON'T LEAVE YOUR ROOM, OKAY? BYE NOW. ♡
OH, SO MUCH TO DO!
SNAP
HURRY, BIG SIS!! THE GAME'S ABOUT TO START!
WHISK
OKAY OKAY. KEEP YOUR SHIRT ON, CHAMO.
I'VE GOT THE VIDEO CAMERAS SET UP, AND EVERY-THING'S UNDER CONTROL.
TICK
TICK
TICK
KA-CHICK

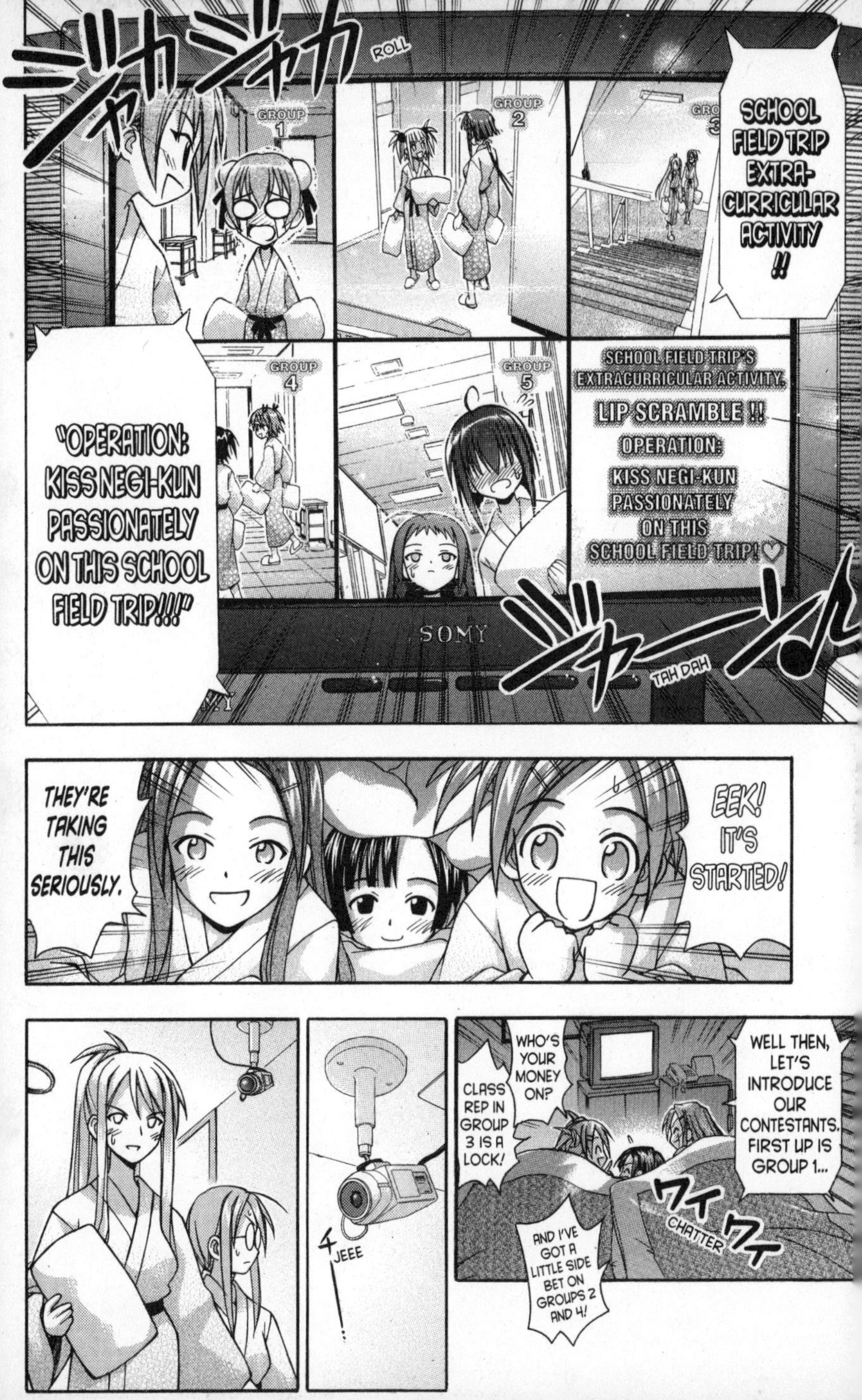
SCHOOL FIELD TRIP EXTRA-CURRICULAR ACTIVITY !!
ジャカジャカ
ROLL
GROUP 3
GROUP 2
GROUP 1
SCHOOL FIELD TRIP'S EXTRACURRICULAR ACTIVITY.
LIP SCRAMBLE !!
OPERATION: KISS NEGI-KUN PASSIONATELY ON THIS SCHOOL FIELD TRIP! ♡
GROUP 5
GROUP 4
"OPERATION: KISS NEGI-KUN PASSIONATELY ON THIS SCHOOL FIELD TRIP!!!"
SOMY
ジャーン♪
TAH DAH
EEK! IT'S STARTED!
THEY'RE TAKING THIS SERIOUSLY.
WELL THEN, LET'S INTRODUCE OUR CONTESTANTS. FIRST UP IS GROUP 1...
WHO'S YOUR MONEY ON?
CLASS REP IN GROUP 3 IS A LOCK!
AND I'VE GOT A LITTLE SIDE BET ON GROUPS 2 AND 4!
ワイワイ
CHATTER
JEEE

School Rumble

BY JIN KOBAYASHI

SUBTLETY IS FOR WIMPS!

She . . . is a second-year high school student with a single all-consuming question: Will the boy she likes ever really notice her?

He . . . is the school's most notorious juvenile delinquent, and he's suddenly come to a shocking realization: He's got a huge crush, and now he must tell her how he feels.

Life-changing obsessions, colossal foul-ups, grand schemes, deep-seated anxieties, and raging hormones—School Rumble portrays high school as it really is: over-the-top comedy!

School Rumble
Jin Kobayashi
Vol. 1

Ages: 16+

Coming soon in January 2007!

Special extras in each volume! Read them all!

tanoshimi

BY OH!GREAT

Itsuki Minami needs no introduction—everybody's heard of the "Babyface" of the Eastside. He's the strongest kid at Higashi Junior High School, easy on the eyes but dangerously tough when he needs to be. Plus, Itsuki lives with the mysterious and sexy Noyamano sisters. Life's never dull, but it becomes downright dangerous when Itsuki leads his school to victory over vindictive Westside punks with gangster connections. Now he stands to lose his school, his friends, and everything he cares about. But in his darkest hour, the Noyamano girls give him an amazing gift, one that just might help him save his school: a pair of Air Trecks. These high-tech skates are more than just supercool. They'll enable Itsuki to execute the wildest, most aggressive moves ever seen—and introduce him to a thrilling and terrifying new world.

Ages: 16 +

Coming in October 2006!
Special extras in each volume! Read them all!

Basilisk

ORIGINAL STORY BY FŪTARO YAMADA
MANGA BY MASAKI SEGAWA

THE BATTLE BEGINS

Basilisk
1
THE KOUGA NINJA SCROLLS
ORIGINAL STORY BY FŪTARO YAMADA
MANGA BY MASAKI SEGAWA

Mature: Ages 18+

The Iga clan and the Kouga clan have been sworn enemies for more than four hundred years. Only the Hanzo Hattori truce has kept the two families from all-out war. Now, under the order of Shogun Ieyasu Tokugawa, the truce has been dissolved. Ten ninja from each clan must fight to the death in order to determine who will be the next Tokugawa Shogun. The surviving clan will rule for the next thousand years.

But not all the clan members are in agreement. Oboro of the Iga clan and Gennosuke of the Kouga clan have fallen deeply in love. Now these star-crossed lovers have been pitted against each other. Can their romance conquer a centuries-old rivalry? Or is their love destined to end in death?

Special extras in each volume! Read them all!

tanoshimi

xxxHOLiC™

BY CLAMP

Watanuki Kimihiro is haunted by visions. When he finds himself irresistibly drawn into a shop owned by Yûko, a mysterious witch, he is offered the chance to rid himself of the spirits that plague him. He accepts, but soon realizes that he's just been tricked into working for the shop to pay off the cost of Yûko's services! But this isn't any ordinary kind of shop . . . In this shop, Yûko grants wishes to those in need. But they must have the strength of will not only to truly understand their need, but to give up something incredibly precious in return.

CLAMP
CREATORS OF CHOBITS!
1
xxxHOLiC

Ages: 13+

Special extras in each volume! Read them all!

tanoshimi

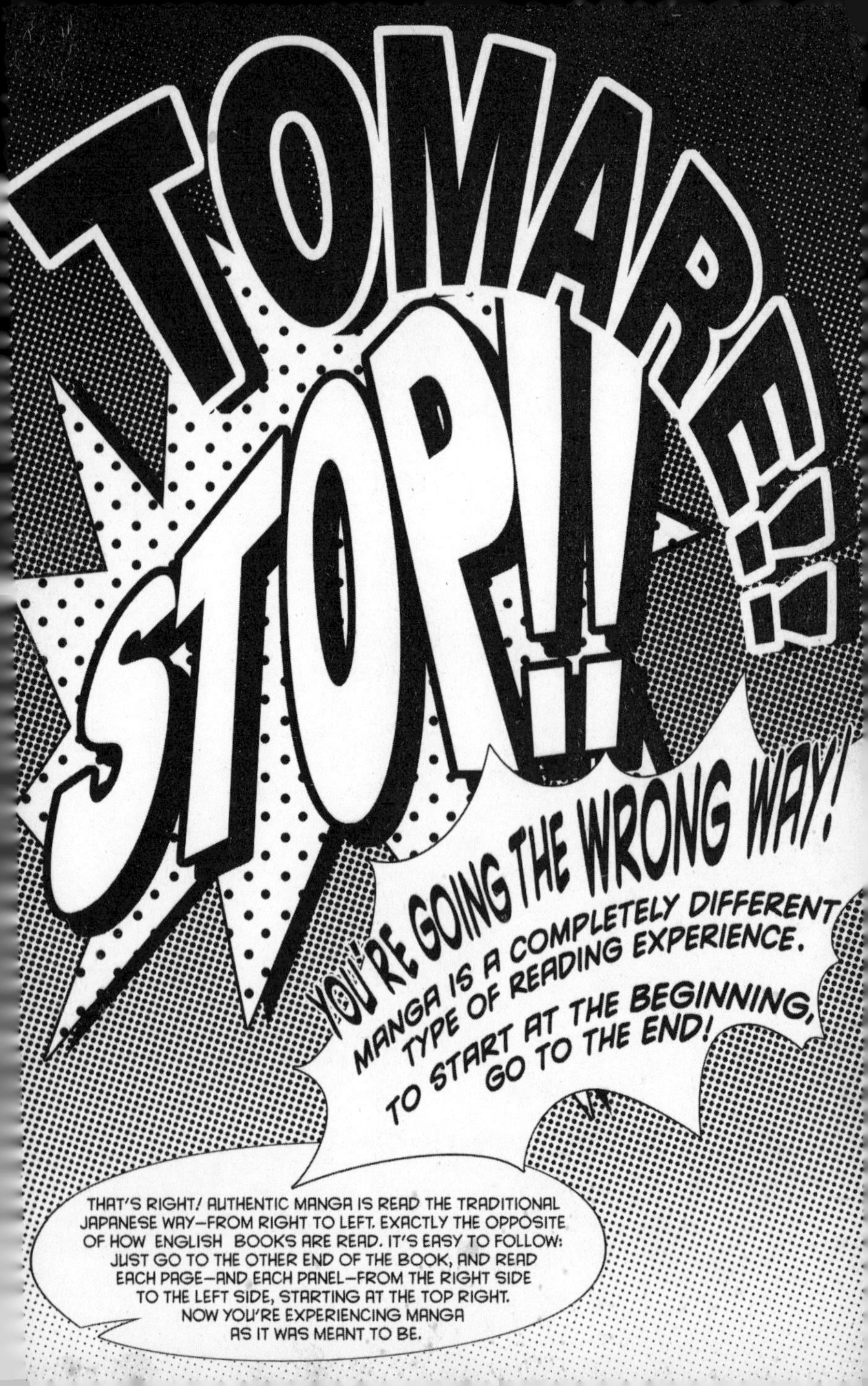
TOMARE!!
STOP!!
YOU'RE GOING THE WRONG WAY!
MANGA IS A COMPLETELY DIFFERENT TYPE OF READING EXPERIENCE.
TO START AT THE BEGINNING, GO TO THE END!
THAT'S RIGHT! AUTHENTIC MANGA IS READ THE TRADITIONAL JAPANESE WAY—FROM RIGHT TO LEFT. EXACTLY THE OPPOSITE OF HOW ENGLISH BOOKS ARE READ. IT'S EASY TO FOLLOW: JUST GO TO THE OTHER END OF THE BOOK, AND READ EACH PAGE—AND EACH PANEL—FROM THE RIGHT SIDE TO THE LEFT SIDE, STARTING AT THE TOP RIGHT. NOW YOU'RE EXPERIENCING MANGA AS IT WAS MEANT TO BE.